Death and
Eternal Life

Also by John Hick
Published by Westminster/John Knox Press

The Metaphor of God Incarnate
God Has Many Names

DEATH
AND
ETERNAL
LIFE

John Hick

With a New Preface by the Author

Westminster/John Knox Press
Louisville, Kentucky

Cover design by Drew Stevens

This book is printed on acid-free paper that meets the American National Standards Institute Z39.48 standard. ∞

Published by Westminster/John Knox Press
Louisville, Kentucky

PRINTED IN THE UNITED STATES OF AMERICA
9 8 7 6 5 4 3 2

Library of Congress Cataloging-in-Publication Data

Hick, John
    Death and eternal life / John Hick ; with a new pref.
         p.   cm.
    Includes bibliographical references and index.
    Originally published: London : Collins, 1976.
    ISBN 0-664-25509-4 (alk. paper)

    1. Future life   2. Death—Religious aspects.   I. Title
BL535.H52   1994
291.2'3—dc20   93-32903

TO HAZEL

*without whose constant support the
book could not have been written*

Contents

Contents

Contents

Contents

Contents

Preface to the Westminster/John Knox Edition

Whilst books on death come and go, death itself is a constant fact. But it is a fact the consciousness of which we normally set aside or repress. It has been said that the human species is the only one that knows that it is mortal and that refuses to believe it! But the beginning of wisdom is the acceptance of our mortality. Thus in an ancient Buddhist story a mother whose small son has just died comes to the Buddha begging him miraculously to bring the boy back to life. He tells her to go round the village collecting mustard seeds, but only from houses in which there has not been a death. She eventually comes back to him, with no mustard seeds, but with a new realization and acceptance of the universality of death.

The story is particularly poignant because it concerns the death of a child, and youth is usually a time when it is not yet necessary to be aware of mortality. The normal healthy state of the young is to be subjectively immortal: the young cannot imagine what it is like to be middle-aged, or old, or to be approaching the end of life. The prevalence today of deaths on the television screen—several every day watched by many viewers—does little to affect this situation, for TV deaths generally serve to make death unreal rather than real. However, it may well be that TV pictures of war and starvation, and the alarming number of violent deaths of young males (particularly young black males) in inner-city shootings, as well as in automobile crashes, and a realization of the threat of impending environmental disaster are today making death more of a reality to the young in the West than it has been since the time a century ago, and prior to that, when it was common for young children to die, so that death was a familiar event within the family.

Insofar as the subjective immortality of the young is intact, there is no harm in it, in spite of the fact that it is illusory. But the time, often around the age of forty, when we become consciously mortal begins a phase in which a fundamental consolidation may occur in our understanding of the nature of life and our engagement in it. This consolidation does not usually come about consciously and at a given moment, but unconsciously and over a period of time. In recognizing our mortality, do we accept the reality of time and our own existence as temporal creatures who are part of a universe of ceaseless change? Or do we try to protect ourselves from change and mortality by walls of possessions and wealth, of power, domination, fame? Such protective walls are built on shifting sands. At some stage, if only the final stage of impending death, they all dissolve.

The religions of the world would liberate us from these false securities, enabling us to accept the fleeting character of what western theology calls the contingency of the world, and eastern thought, the realm of *maya*. The redeemed or liberated or awakened person can then live fully in the present moment, including its bad as well as its good moments, aware that the ultimate meaning of the ceaseless process of life is good: in the words of Julian of Norwich, "All shall be well, and all shall be well, and all manner of things shall be well."

This ultimate goodness of the total project of human life is spelled out in very different ways by the different religions, and involves in each case their conceptions of the goals of the creative and liberative process. In this book those different conceptions are described and compared.

When we listen to what the great religious traditions say about our future beyond the grave, it becomes important to distinguish between eschatologies, or pictures of the ultimate state (which may well transcend individual existence as we know it), and pareschatologies, or pictures of what happens between death and that ultimate state. Many of the apparently conflicting doctrines concerning an after-life are reconcilable in the light of this distinction. It is even possible, as I shall suggest, to see the major religions as pointing convergingly toward a common, very general conception of the eschaton, the final and eternal state—very general because beyond our present conceptual resources, although with different expectations concerning the pareschaton—the sphere or spheres, life or lives through which humankind moves toward that end.

But of course set over against all religious understanding of life, here and hereafter, is the naturalistic, or purely secular, conviction that we are only enormously complex forms of complex life who, like the grass and the insects, live and die and are then no more: "When you're dead you're dead!" This view is also examined in this book. In contrast to it, it seems to me that the claim of the religions that this life is part of a much larger existence that transcends our lifespan as animal organisms, whether through the continuation of individual consciousness or through participation in a greater transpersonal life, is very likely to be true. I shall argue that this is not ruled out by established scientific findings or by any agreed philosophical arguments. Both the survival of the mind, without a body, and also the reconstitution or "resurrection" of the psycho-physical person in another spatial environment are—I shall argue—realistically conceivable, as also are some forms of rebirth on this earth. Human survival is thus not impossible; and I shall further demonstrate that any religious understanding of human existence—not merely of one's own existence but of the life of humanity as a whole—positively requires some kind of immortality belief and would be radically incoherent without it.

My main basis, then, for thinking it likely that our total existence is larger than our present life on this earth is an acceptance of a religious, as distinguished from a naturalistic, interpretation of the universe and of human life as part of it. I have spelled out this connection in chapter 8. It is possible that I am mistaken in seeing such a connection; nevertheless, my view at present is that if, after I have died, I find that I still consciously exist, I shall not be in the least surprised!

Whilst this is a religiously based belief, it is assisted by some of the phenomena studied by parapsychology. Since this book was first published, even more such phenomena have come into prominence. These consist in the reports of people who have been "clinically dead" (i.e., assumed from all the clinical signs to have died) for periods ranging from a few seconds to as much as twenty minutes, and then resuscitated. A flood of such reports were published in the late 1970s in, for example, Raymond Moody's *Life After Life*, Karl Otis and Erlandur Haraldsson's *At the Hour of Death*, and Maurice Rawlings' *Beyond Death's Door*; a considerable literature discussing their significance exists.

Sometimes these "near-death experiences" are preceded by out-of-body episodes in which one finds oneself looking down on one's own body lying unconscious on the ground or on a bed or an operating table. Among these many such accounts are some in which the patient's "floating" consciousness observed and later reported things or people or events about which it could not have had any normal body-based awareness.

In the near-death experiences themselves a number of elements regularly recur, though often not all on the same occasion. These include hearing a loud noise, the sensation of being drawn through a dark tunnel, emergence into a place of light and beauty, meeting with deceased relatives and friends, the encounter with a shining "being of light" in whose presence they are conscious of an immense love and acceptance, a rapid but vivid review of one's own life, approaching a border beyond which there is felt to be no return and then being sent or drawn back, sometimes reluctantly, into the body. In a small minority of cases, the experience is not perceived as positive in these ways but, on the contrary, horrific and terrifying. But what is perhaps most striking in the majority of cases is the effect of the experience in the subsequent lives of the persons concerned. To many who have been resuscitated, their experience while clinically dead was the most impressive religious experience that they have undergone, profoundly affecting their outlook ever after. The encounter with the loving and accepting "being of light" gives them an experiential assurance of the divine love; whereas the experience as a whole removes the natural fear of death, which they now see as a gateway to another and enhanced form of life.

How are we to interpret these phenomena? Since the patients have proven capable of being resuscitated, we know that they were not completely dead. Was their experience, then, a vivid dream produced by a brain that is losing oxygen; or was it a psychological act of self-assurance in the face of impending extinction; or was it the first authentic glimpse of a post-mortem mode of consciousness, or at least of the interface between this life and another? I believe that more research and more thought is necessary before we can confidently categorize these experiences. It remains at present another intriguing mystery within the larger cluster of mysteries surrounding the fact of death.

Finally, this book was written before most of us had begun to replace the traditional male language in which one spoke of *man, mankind,* and *he* when referring to human beings generally, without using inclusive language. Unfortunately, considerations of cost have made it impossible to purge the text of the old language, and I can only apologize to those, including myself, whom it now offends.

But perhaps the main feature of the book that has encouraged me to make it available again is that it treats the subject of death on a global basis, seeking insights from both east and west, and from psychology, parapsychology, sociology, and philosophy, as well as from religion. For truth-seeking requires not only accurate reasoning but also an openness to ideas and information from any and every relevant source.

In the original preface to this book I thanked by name a number of people in India and Sri Lanka who helped me, during visits amounting to almost a year, to understand better the Hindu and Theravada Buddhist conceptions of reincarnation or rebirth. At the university founded by Rabindranath Tagore at Santiniketan, and at Benaras Hindu University, and Punjabi University, and the Sri Aurobindo Ashram at Pondicherry and at Peradeniya near Kandy in Sri Lanka, as well as at several other places, I had invaluable learning experiences that added greatly to my reading of the Hindu, Sikh, and Buddhist texts and commentaries. I came away from both India and Sri Lanka feeling that I had been privileged to have had at least some slight encounter with two great living faiths other than that by which I had been formed; and having also, with my wife—who joined me for part of each visit—experienced the unforgettable openhanded and open-spirited hospitality of these lands and cultures.

JOHN HICK

March 1993

Part I

INTRODUCTORY

CHAPTER I

On Method

1. A TANTALIZING MYSTERY

What is the appropriate method for investigating death and eternal life? Indeed, can *any* method be appropriate to so impossibly vast and tantalizingly mysterious a subject? It is impossibly vast because death is a central concern of all the religions of the world, and has been reflected upon by nearly all the great religious, and also non-religious, thinkers; so that much of the literature of the faiths and philosophies of all ages, written in many ancient and modern languages, is relevant to it. And yet despite this immense literature the subject remains impenetrably obscure. We still do not know what happens to a man when he dies. In the time of the Buddha, some two and a half thousand years ago, there was as great a multiplicity of rival views as today.[1] Is the death of the body the extinction of the person? or does he survive as a continuing consciousness? or as a resurrected person? with a spiritual body? in perpetuity or for a limited period? Will he be born again to live another earthly life? Is there time or timelessness beyond death? Is the individual absorbed back into some great spiritual reality, like a drop returning to the ocean? We do not know the answers to any of these questions, and it remains true that to know what happens we must each wait and see – or, it may be, wait and not see!

Why then, one might wonder, should anyone attempt to think and to write about so immense a mystery? Would it not be more prudent, not to say more modest, to refrain from so properly daunting an undertaking? The answer of course, which is witnessed to by the vast literature to which I have referred, is that we shall not be able to refrain from speculating about death until we can refrain from speculating about life; for the one is inseparable from the other. This is the justification for the endeavours embodied in the innumerable writings on this subject, including the present one – that death is as much and as mysterious a fact as life and that the two mysteries are inextricably bound together. If we wish to think realistically about life we cannot avoid also thinking about death.

2. THE METHOD OF SPELLING OUT POSSIBILITIES

Because of the profound obscurity of the subject our first principle of method must be to spell out possibilities rather than to deal in alleged certainties. We must look seriously at all the main theories and speculations and consider, so far as we can, their respective strengths and weaknesses – even, in a very broad sense of the term, their relative probabilities. But we must not in the end delude ourselves that we have achieved knowledge where before we were in ignorance. Nevertheless there may be degrees of obscurity. For example, if there is life after death there may be a better possibility of picturing its more proximate than its more ultimate phases. It will therefore be useful to distinguish between pareschatologies and eschatologies. Whereas eschatology is the doctrine of the *eschata* or last things, and thus of the ultimate state of man, pareschatology[2] is, by analogy, the doctrine of the *para-eschata*, or next-to-last things, and thus of the human future between the present life and man's ultimate state. And it may well be possible to speculate more profitably about pareschatology than about eschatology. For if there is continued human existence after bodily death it is possible that its more immediate phases may bear sufficient analogy to our present state for some of our speculations about it to be not wholly misleading. Indeed, the very fact of the continued existence of a conscious personality would seem to carry with it certain minimal implications: certain basic continuities must hold if we are to speak of individual identity and life. It may therefore be possible to make some limited discriminations between rival pareschatologies – theories concerning a next stage of human existence. But there are reasons (to be formulated in chapter 20) to suppose that no mode of existence analogous to our present life could continue for ever, through unlimited time. And when we try to think beyond this to an eternal, transtemporal destiny we are trying to conceive of something beyond the reach even of our most ambitious imaginings. The best that could be hoped is that in some of its more ultimate speculations the human mind is looking in what is in the most general sense a right direction, or at any rate that it is not looking in a totally wrong direction. But if we use this directional image it must be in terms of astronomical distances. To be looking in the direction of some unimaginably remote constellation, altogether beyond the range of our vision, may merely mean that I am, say, facing north rather than south! The hope that our thoughts might in this very general sense be oriented in the right direction – without however any assurance that they *are* – must be sufficient incentive for the kind of constructive exercise attempted in chapter 22.

Because the subject-matter of pareschatologies is less remote and may be less incommensurate with our present existence than that of eschatologies, the greater part of the enquiry will be concerned with the former. And here the basic method will be to spell out possible human futures beyond death. We shall be asking such questions as: What might it be to survive as a disembodied mind? What might the resurrection of the body, or of the flesh, mean? What might a spiritual body be? What could be meant by heaven, hell, purgatory? How can the idea of reincarnation be understood? . . .

However, it might seem that the policy of spelling out, elaborating, giving more detailed content to, such ideas as these runs counter to the basic common sense in this area of sticking to deliberately vague and general conceptions. For the more detailed we make our mental pictures of the life to come, the less likelihood there must be of their conforming to reality. Since we are shooting in the dark, is not a blunderbuss more apt to hit the target than a high-precision rifle? Should we not then do better to avoid any spelling out and be content with some very general doctrine, such as (for theists) that although we do not know what to expect after death we can have faith that whatever may happen will be an expression of the divine goodness and love? There is an attraction in such a policy of deliberate vagueness. Nevertheless I do not think that it is in the end helpful. Consider further the statement that man's destiny will express the divine goodness and love, this being taken as a proposition which is not to be further explicated. It sounds, at first, a welcome and reassuring doctrine. But, we must ask, are we speaking of what is good and loving from the divine or from the human point of view? Surely we must set the unknown divine point of view above the known human one and be content to wait and see what is ordained for us by a wisdom beyond our comprehension. We must not abandon our professed agnosticism by assuming that what *we* should regard as loving coincides with God's unknown will,

> For my thoughts are not your thoughts,
> neither are your ways my ways, says the Lord.
> For as the heavens are higher than the earth,
> so are my ways higher than your ways,
> and my thoughts than your thoughts.[3]

We cannot assume, for example, that it would violate the divine love to allow us at death to cease to exist; or to put the life of which we have been formed back into the lump, like the potter with his clay; or to have us survive only as insubstantial shades in sheol, as was believed by the ancient Hebrews throughout much of their history; or to predestine us from birth, some to eternal bliss and others to eternal torment, as Augustine and Calvin taught. If all these possible expressions of an unknown divine providence are included, along with such other destinies as we should ourselves desire, then our doctrine loses its comfortable character. So far as we can profess to know, it might mean anything, whether welcome or highly unwelcome from our present 'fallen', egoistic, sin-bound point of view. But a doctrine which can mean anything means nothing. So long, then, as we refrain from spelling out our faith it must remain empty. It is only reassuring if we have covertly imported some very large assumptions – for example, that the divine love will in some fashion hold us individually in existence beyond death; and that the destiny which God appoints will eventually, if not immediately, be one of positive fulfilment and joy, rather than of perpetual grief and agony in some sphere in which the creator's love is known as wrath and his goodness as unbending justice. Further, the initial assumption that we shall be held in existence by the divine love after death immediately involves us in questions concerning continued consciousness and memory, embodiment or bodilessness, recognition and communication, and all the other difficult and complex issues which arise as soon as we venture beyond comforting generalities.

Thus if we are to think deliberately and responsibly about human destiny it does not seem that we can after all avoid the task of spelling out conceptions of it. This is not merely a possible method – it is the only possible method. The proposal to be content with deliberate vagueness is an unhelpful proposal; for to choose vagueness here is either to opt for an empty form of words or to be making a disguised affirmation of major but unexamined assumptions.

However, will not the spelling out which I am recommending merely produce a medley of pictures between which we have no grounds for discrimination? The answer, I think, is that the process of spelling out also functions to some extent as a test of viability. It can reveal, first, whether the theory, as a set of propositions, has a consistent meaning or is merely a heap of incompatible fragments. Second, it can reveal whether the 'picture' being proposed is sufficiently extensive and coherent to constitute a possible account of that which it is seeking hypothetically to describe. And it can reveal, third, to what extent a theory succeeds in making sense of such data as have been accepted, whether from revelation, from the findings of anthropology, psychology, genetics, parapsychology, or other sources. Thus 'spelling out' results in a preliminary winnowing of theories, some appearing increasingly incoherent and implausible as they are expanded whilst others come progressively to present a more solid and believable possibility. The next stage in the consideration of those theories which have been able to expand into coherent pictures is to draw out their larger religious and metaphysical implications; and these in turn may, from a given standpoint, provide reasons for preferring one picture to another. For example, I shall argue that the concept of the survival of the mind, as developed in a classic paper by H. H. Price, is conceptually viable but carries with it unwelcome theological implications.[4] Thus by making use of considerations drawn from wider systems of belief it may be possible to take some steps at least in the critical assessment of pareschatological theories – though, as I have already stressed, this process cannot lead to a stronger

conclusion than that some theories seem slightly more acceptable than others.

There are many, of course, who would reject such a pluralistic approach, feeling entitled either definitively to affirm
some specific conception of a life to come, or to reject
absolutely the idea of personal survival in any form. Against
this negative dogma I shall try to show that life after death is
not impossible, although to accept it as a possibility depends
upon a different understanding of man's nature than that
which underlies the negative dogma; and against those who
profess positive knowledge of man's destiny beyond the grave
I shall try to show that a number of very different conceptions
of the after-life are theoretically viable and that we have at
present no decisive means of choosing between them.

3. THE PRINCIPLE OF OPENNESS TO ALL DATA

A second principle of method must be that in a subject of such
obscurity and yet such importance, in which questions receive
so many different answers, we must not exclude any potential
source of light merely because it is not a part of our own
cultural or sub-cultural heritage. More specifically, we must
take account of the teachings of all the main religious traditions
and philosophies, and also of work in the still fairly new para-
science of psychical research, as well as of the relevant findings
of such orthodox sciences as anthropology, sociology, psychology and genetics.

As regards parapsychology, or psychical research, which is
still a controversial field, seen by some as a morass of credulity
and superstition, I can only repeat what has often been said –
namely, that it is invariably those who have not yet examined
the scientific literature of the subject who dismiss it in this
way. I do not think that anyone who reads the highly critical
and judicious reports by such distinguished researchers as
Mrs Henry Sidgwick, Richard Hodgson, R. H. Thouless,
S. G. Soal, J. B. Rhine and Ian Stevenson, or the analytical
discussions by William James, C. D. Broad, H. H. Price and
Anthony Flew – to name only a few – can seriously doubt that
parapsychology is concerned with phenomena which demand
a careful scientific attention and that they have for nearly a
century been receiving such attention in the work published,

for example, by the british and the american Societies for Psychical Research.

The argument for taking account of what the religions and philosophies of the world say about human destiny is less controversial. Any writer on death and immortality is likely to start from within a particular religious tradition, which he either affirms or opposes, and within a particular historical culture. But if he restricts himself to the resources of his own religio-cultural milieu he will be interpreting the phenomenon of death from a restricted standpoint which is not warranted by the universality of the phenomenon itself. The experiences and reflections of all human faiths and cultures are relevant to the understanding of our mortality. This is *par excellence* a topic to which a trans-confessional and trans-cultural approach is appropriate. To say this is not to question the value of the more restricted studies which comprise most of the existing literature of the subject. These are exercises in christian, or islamic, or buddhist, or hindu, etc., exegesis and doctrinal construction. Such exercises have their own validity and importance, not only in the service of their own traditions but also as providing essential material for attempts at a more global philosophy or theology of death. The present enquiry is undertaken from a christian standpoint. It is not however offered primarily as a contribution to christian theology, but rather as a christian contribution to global or human theology – a notion which will be defined further in the next section. Culturally, it is undertaken from within our relatively affluent western technological society – although parts of it have been written in the 'third world', where teeming populations oppressed by desperate poverty and threatened by starvation cast a somewhat different light upon many of the issues of human life and destiny.

Taking seriously the variety of human views concerning man's destiny does not necessarily require an encyclopedic treatment of after-life beliefs throughout the world and throughout the ages. Indeed, we shall not be concerned here, except for occasional samplings, with the details of the innumerable overlapping religious and philosophical thought-worlds, but only with the three major options for man's understanding of death into which the many traditions group themselves. These are: (1) the materialist and humanist rejection of belief in any form of personal survival; (2) the western and semitic belief in the preservation of the individual personality beyond death, whether as disembodied mind or reconstituted psychophysical being, in an ultimate heavenly state in which some or all are eternally to dwell; and (3) the eastern belief in the continual rebirth of what we can for the moment call the soul, until (according to hindu thought) it attains to a realization of its identity with the one infinite and eternal Spirit, or (according to Buddhism) until it attains to nirvana by obliterating within itself the needs and drives which have kept the illusion-bound and pain-bearing ego going through life after life. Instead, however, of regarding the two religious options as mutually exclusive alternatives I shall suggest that they point beyond themselves, and that their pointings converge along lines which I shall try to trace in part V.

In examining each of these major possibilities I have tried not to be blinded by my own particular starting-point to insights and suggestions coming from beyond the christian and western traditions. I have tried to see christian beliefs concerning human destiny not only as a Christian sees them, but also in the significantly different ways in which western materialists and men of the eastern faiths are liable to see them; and likewise to understand the humanist conception of human nature sympathetically, even though I also criticize it; and again to see the great strengths and attractions of the hindu and buddhist doctrines. This latter requires of most Christians a deliberate effort both of the reason and of the imagination; and I invite christian readers to make this effort with me, resolutely setting aside the all-too-natural prejudice that ideas, such as karma and rebirth, which are strange to us are therefore in some objective sense odd, improbable or unbelievable. The selection of that which is seen by different people as bizarre, and accordingly not to be taken seriously, is notoriously culture-relative. And I would likewise invite readers in the hindu and buddhist worlds to make a similar effort towards those christian and western beliefs which initially seem strange and implausible to them.

But can a person really transcend the culture which forms

the intellectual air that he breathes; or the religion or philosophy through which he looks out upon the world? Ultimately the answer can only be No. The westerner may 'transcend' his western cultural outlook; but the result is still (to easterners) recognizably a sympathetic christian appreciation of, say, Buddhism or Hinduism rather than a buddhist or hindu appreciation of them; and the same is true when the roles are reversed. We can only live satisfactorily within the circumstances and thought-forms of a particular culture and we can only worship satisfactorily in the modes of a particular religious tradition. To renounce all concrete human patterns would be to exist in a vacuum. There can thus be only a relative transcending of one's *Sitz im Leben*, a standing partly in and partly out of one's cultural milieu. But this is I think sufficient to open up the possibility of a 'global' approach to the question of our human destiny.

4. THE IDEA OF A GLOBAL THEOLOGY OF DEATH

We must distinguish between two aspects of a religion: on the one hand, its central affirmations concerning the nature of reality, including its affirmations about human destiny – these affirmations being, ultimately, true or false; and on the other hand, the mythology, with its often rich poetic elaborations and its concrete cultic expressions, which has grown up alongside the central affirmations in the same cultural soil but which is not in the same sense true or false. It is because affirmations about the nature of reality are true or false or, more probably, partly true and partly false, that the theologies of the different religions can be compared with one another, that agreements and disagreements can be registered, and that the possibility of syntheses and even of a comprehensive global theology[5] cannot be excluded in advance. On the other hand, it is because religious myth and the practice of piety are phenomena of human culture that a global religion will never come about so long as there is – as let us hope there will always be – a wide variety of different styles of human existence. For the mythic and cultic substances of a religion are aspects of a civilization; and civilizations, as comprehensive forms of human life, cannot be compared in respect of truth and falsity. We are not concerned here, then, with the possibility of a global religion but with the possibility of a global theology. If this proves feasible it will be developed out of a comparison of the theological affirmations of the different world faiths. The various confessional theologies may turn out to be in final opposition to one another; or it may become possible to see them as partial accounts, from different angles, of a more complex ultimate reality or process. The project of global theology will then be the attempt to use these different affirmations, and the modes of religious experience on which they are based, as data for the construction of comprehensive religious theories. Such a theology would consist in a body of hypotheses about the nature of reality, expressing the basic common ground of the world religions, and receiving mythic expression and devotional content in different ways within different historical traditions.

Clearly, the hope for any such common core of ultimate beliefs presupposes a certain view of man's religious life – a 'copernican' in distinction from a 'ptolemaic' view.[6] By a 'ptolemaic' standpoint I mean the conviction that one's own religion is at the centre of the religious universe and provides a touchstone for the truth of all other faith-worlds. Thus for example a 'ptolemaic' christian theology sees Christianity as the only gateway to salvation, through which all must in the end come, and either dismisses the other religions as positively harmful or, at best, as having only partial and interim value and to be graded by their approximation to or their divergence from the christian norm. A 'ptolemaic' faith can have the triumphant invulnerability of what R. M. Hare has called a *blik* – a comprehensive interpretation which no evidence is allowed to threaten because it interprets all the evidence from its own standpoint. The 'ptolemaic' believer is thus in a position analogous to that of the solipsist. The latter remains unshaken in his solipsist faith by any new experiences that may come to him, for all experiences are automatically categorized as private phenomena of his own mind. And the 'ptolemaic' believer remains unshaken by any evidences of deep piety and saintly life within other religions because he is convinced that he already possesses the truth, the whole truth, and nothing but the truth. However, if the 'ptolemaic' vision falters, perhaps through contact with people of other faiths, the disturbing fact will appear that there are a number of possible 'ptolemaic' centres, and that the one which an individual occupies is, in at least 99% of cases, determined by the accident of his birth. A person born in Egypt or Pakistan is very likely to be a Muslim; one born in Burma or Tibet is very likely to be a Buddhist; one born in most parts of India is very likely to be a Hindu; one born in Britain or the USA is very likely to be a Christian – allowing in each case for a majority of merely nominal as well as a minority of true believers. From a firmly 'ptolemaic' standpoint this geographical distribution of faith, if it is noticed at all, has to be accepted as a puzzling fact; and if the 'ptolemaist' allows himself to dwell upon it, it will only bring home to him his extreme good fortune in having been born in a part of the earth which offers a privileged likelihood of knowing the truth and finding salvation. If however, as a theologian, he tries to rationalize this situation and to develop a 'ptolemaic' interpretation of the wider religious life of mankind, he is likely sooner or later to find that the increasingly complicated epicycles of theory to which he has to resort become decreasingly plausible; and he may well become ready for a copernican revolution in his theology of religions.

The copernican revolution in astronomy consisted in the realization that the sun is at the centre of the solar system and that our earth is one of a number of planets revolving around it. The analogous copernican revolution in theology is a shift from the picture of the religious life of mankind as centring upon and culminating in one's own religion, to a view of the religions as different responses to variously overlapping aspects of the same Ultimate Reality. I am assuming here a distinction between the primitive forms of natural religion and the great traditions of revelation which originated in the world-wide spiritual awakening which Karl Jaspers has called the axial period, which he dates from about 800 BC to 200 BC.[7] It was in this axial period that the great world faiths arose out of the religious experience of the hebrew prophets, the brahminical writers of the Upanishads, Zoroaster, the Buddha, Confucius, the writer of the Bhagavad Gita, Socrates and Plato, followed after a gap by Jesus and the rise of Christianity and after another gap by Mohammed and the rise of Islam –

both rooted in the work of the hebrew prophets during the axial period. In all of these streams of religious life there is a conception of the transcendent Eternal, conceived of as personal or as non-personal or as both. As the Jahweh of Judaism, the triune God of Christianity, the Allah of Islam, the Krishna, the Shiva and the Vishnu of theistic Hinduism, the Eternal has been experienced and conceptualized in personal terms. In the Brahman of advaita Vedanta, the Dharma Body of the Buddha in mahayana Buddhism, and the Nibbana of the Theravada, the Eternal has been experienced and conceptualized in non-personal terms. But surely, the inevitable objection will come, the transcendent Eternal, the Ultimate Reality, must be either personal or not personal. This would be true if we conceived of Ultimate Reality as a finite object. In a finite entity, personality and impersonality are mutually incompatible. But why should they be incompatible in the Infinite? The Eternal may be – and has in fact been experienced as being – personal, encountered as the divine Thou of the Bible, the Bhagavad Gita, the Koran, the Granth, without this genuinely personal character exhausting its infinity, so that the same Reality may also be – and has in fact been experienced as being – the Ground of Being, the Depth of Being, Being-Itself, the Abyss, the Void, the *Ungrund*, the Absolute of advaita Vedanta and also of certain strands of western mysticism.

These apprehensions of the Eternal, then, having arisen with the force of revelation in the minds of certain supremely enlightened spirits, have become mixed with different streams of human culture, conceptualized in terms of different philosophical traditions, and subject to different historical influences, to constitute the vast religio-cultural complexes which we know today as the great world faiths. Starting in or expanding into different parts of the world, they have now existed for centuries as separate cultural realities, becoming more distinctive, variegated and many-branched as they have developed. There have of course been important episodes of interaction between, for example, Hinduism and Buddhism, Islam and Christianity, and Islam and Hinduism; but these were primarily hostile encounters rather than occasions of constructive mutual influence. The outcome of nearly three thousand years of mankind's religious history is thus some half-dozen major faiths each influential in the life of a different section of humanity. These religio-cultural blocks have for a long time proved rather stable, with only marginal penetrations of one faith into a culture dominated by another; for the more successful missionary thrusts have not been 'sideways', but 'downwards' into the remaining areas of primal religion. However, during approximately the last hundred years the picture has been changing. Serious scholarly work has been done in the history and comparative study of religions, replacing caricatures with responsible portraits. The great faiths have begun to interact with one another. Hinduism and Buddhism have both undergone renaissances which, paradoxically, they owe in part to the impact upon them of christian missions. In the course of its nineteenth-century revival Hinduism, for example, adopted into parts of its pluriform life a social concern derived from Christianity; and the towering figure of Gandhi shows christian as well as hindu influences. And in the other direction there has, particularly since the second world war, been a growing popular western interest in the eastern faiths and particularly in their methods of meditation and spiritual training. Young people from Europe and the United States go to India to sit at the feet of a guru, hoping to find values, meanings and illuminations with which the affluent and materialistic west has been unable to provide them. We may expect that the great religions will continue to interact and influence one another and that in their future developments each will absorb more from the others. In time they will probably come to see each other somewhat as the different christian denominations have progressively come to see one another after several generations of the ecumenical movement – that is, as distinct, as appealing on the whole to different types and groups, and as friendly rivals who were once, but are no longer, enemies.

If one sees man's religious life in this 'copernican' fashion, a global theology is at least a possible project. It must of course be a co-operative work spanning several generations and involving the contributions of numerous scholars and thinkers in the different traditions. The present book is in part an attempt to see whether, in the particular area of the theology of death, a global approach is possible. My tentative conclusion is that in their central witness the great faiths of east and west permit, and by their convergent permission even point towards, a common conception of human destiny. To suggest that they 'point to' a common view is not however to say that their different teachings, formed and expressed in the different categories of different cultures, are identical. Clearly, they are not. What I shall try to show is that each points beyond its own official dogmas and that these pointings converge upon an hypothesis which can to some extent be formulated. In chapter 22 an attempt will be made to do this.

NOTES

1. 'Brahma-Gala Suttanta', *Digha-Nikaya* (*Dialogues of the Buddha*, part I, pp. 26–55).
2. The rather rare greek word *pareschatos* means 'penultimate', or 'next to last', and enables us to coin 'pareschatology' as the study of the next-to-last things, on analogy with 'eschatology', the study of the last things. I am grateful to my colleague Michael Goulder for this useful word.
3. Isaiah 55: 8–9.
4. See chapter 14.
5. It will be evident that I am here, and throughout this book, using 'theology' in a deliberately wide sense to include the study of systems of religious thought (such as Buddhism) which recognize no *theos*.
6. This distinction is developed and its implications examined in my *God and the Universe of Faiths*.
7. Karl Jaspers, *The Origin and Goal of History*, ch. 1.

CHAPTER 2

What Is Man?

I. THE SELF

Our language divides human nature into various aspects or parts, the primary division being between the physical and the non-physical. The concept of the body, as the physical aspect, is reasonably clear, for the body can be seen and felt, weighed and measured. But the language of the non-physical uses a bewildering variety of terms – mind, soul, self, I, person, spirit, ego, consciousness, psyche, the subconscious, the unconscious, the id, the superego, mentality, transcendental unity of apperception, etc.; and eastern thought adds many more, the two most important being *jiva* (or *jivatman*) and *atman* – which latter I shall treat hereafter as an adopted english word. It is impossible to fit this plethora of terms into a single system, and we therefore have to decide carefully which to use and with what meanings.

Let us begin with the thinking, feeling, willing, remembering consciousness which is now composing these sentences, and let us call this a self. Each one who reads these sentences is likewise a self, aware of himself in a direct way in which he is not aware of anyone else. Further, the self that each of us knows as himself or herself is an embodied self, cognizing the world from a unique perspective within it. Modern psychology enables us to add that the self has subconscious and unconscious depths as well as a conscious surface; so that we may expand the notion of the self to include such unconscious mental life as is able directly to influence consciousness.

How has this embodied self been formed? The answer seems to be that a package of genetic information has programmed the growth of a living organism in continuous interaction with its environment – the developing self exercising throughout a measure of free creativity within the narrow limits of an inherited nature and of a given world.

Perhaps the most striking feature of the initial formation of an individual is the enormous number of possible genetic codes out of which the one that is actualized has been apparently randomly selected. Behind each of us there lies an astronomical number of other possible arrangements of the same genetic material. If we confine attention for the moment to the father's contribution, there are some three to six hundred million sperm which he has launched on their race to reach and fertilize the ovum. These, say, four hundred million sperm are not however completely alike, as identical copies of each other. On the contrary, each one is unique. In each case of the millions of formations of sperm cells, through the complex process of meiotic division, a partial reshuffling of the parental genes takes place, producing unpredictable results. For a slightly different course is taken each time in the selection and arrangement of the twenty-three out of the father's forty-six chromosomes that are to constitute his sperm's contribution to the full genetic complement of a member of the next generation. The ordering of the chromosomes in the sperm cell is itself partly a matter of chance, depending upon which out of each pair of chromosomes happens to be on one side and which on the other when the two sets separate to form new cells. But the degree of randomness thus introduced (calculated as at least eight million potentially different arrangements) is multiplied by scattered breaks and re-formations in many of the chromosomes in the 'crossing over' stage of meiosis. So it is that each of the four hundred or so million sperm cells carries, in its details, a different genetic code. But only one out of these four hundred million can win the race to the ovum. Nevertheless this vast number is apparently needed. A single sperm, unsupported by its millions of companions, would not be able to make its way across the mucus area at the entry to the uterus, up the fallopian tube, and through the membrane protecting the egg. For each sperm produces only a minute quantity of the enzyme which digests the material to be penetrated, and it is only by the combined action of many that a way is made through to the target. Thus hundreds of millions of sperm perish in enabling one of their number to continue in the life of a new organism.

Approximately half of the four hundred million or so sperm

carry the Y sex chromosome which will result in a male embryo whilst the other half carry the X chromosome which will produce a female. And each of these two hundred or so million possible or notional males, and likewise each of the two hundred or so million possible females, is unique, differing from its potential brothers and sisters in a number of ways, mostly very slight but some, arising from major mutations, far from slight.

But this family of some four hundred million potential children, only one of whom will actually be conceived and born, is really only a family of four hundred million half-children! For the sperm carries only half the total complement of human chromosomes. Meanwhile the mother has been producing egg cells, though not nearly as many as the father produces sperm cells, and usually only one at a time. Each of these eggs contains its own unique arrangement of chromosomes, and the vast range of possibilities which lies behind the formation of a particular sperm cell likewise lies behind the formation of a particular egg cell. Thus there is a further enormous multiplication in the possibilities out of which a particular genetic code is selected when it is actualized by the union of a particular sperm with a particular egg. And it is out of this astronomical number of different potential individuals, exhibiting the kinds of differences that can occur between children of the same parents, that a single individual comes into being.

Thus the process whereby a particular code begins to be actualized includes, according to the geneticists, crucial elements of randomness. This is not however randomness in the sense in which the term is used in quantum physics. The units with which the geneticist is dealing are not the sub-atomic particles to which indeterminacy is ascribed, but complex molecular structures; and presumably their individual behaviour is not unpredictable in principle, as is apparently the case with electrons, but only unpredictable in fact. The 'shuffling' of the chromosomes in the formation of sperm cells, and again the selection of one sperm out of some four hundred million different ones to fertilize the ovum, are random processes, then, only in the sense that they are beyond human prediction. Presumably the continuity of cause and effect, and hence of predictability in principle, is not suspended; but the processes involved are so complex that their outcome is unpredictable in practice, and in that sense random from the human point of view. I accordingly use the term 'random' here in this weaker sense.

What, then, are the implications for the nature and status of the human being of this area of randomness in the selection of a genetic code for actualization?

From a religious point of view the randomness out of which we have come is an aspect of the radical contingency of our existence. We are not 'self-made men', but products of forces at work outside and prior to ourselves. Our dependent status is ultimately traced by religious thought back to the dependence of the entire natural order upon the creative will of God. Thus far our emergence out of the bewildering complexity of the genetic process is not in tension with the basic theological conception of man's utter contingency as a created being. But we must also ask how well this agrees with the traditional religious conception of the human being as an immortal soul.

2. THE SOUL IN CHRISTIAN THOUGHT

Indeed, do we need the word 'soul' as well as 'self'? We are using 'self' as the name for that from which our thought necessarily starts, namely the consciousness which is now composing these sentences, or which is now reading them, and which is a source of volitions and a subject of perceptions and emotions. The christian concept of soul undoubtedly includes this conscious self, which earns rewards and deserves penalties, which becomes or fails to become aware of God by faith, and which is to enjoy hereafter the blissful life of heaven or to suffer eternal loss of heaven. For it is clear from Jesus' parables that the self which faces judgement after death is the same self that has lived on earth in the body. Dives and Lazarus remember their former lives and are aware of the moral appropriateness of the consequences which they encounter after death.[1] In the parable of the sheep and the goats those who stand before the King for judgement are conscious of being the same persons who had served or who had rejected 'the least of his brethren' in their earthly need.[2] In short, the self that is to be judged hereafter, and rewarded or punished in respect of choices made in this life, is the conscious, responsible personal mind and will who has made those fateful choices. But is the soul more than this conscious self, plus its pre- and un-conscious depths? We have seen, in broad terms, how the self is formed: how is the soul said to have been formed?

The question was much discussed in the fourth and fifth centuries, and at the height of the debate three rival answers were in the field. One was the theory of Origen and his followers that the soul existed in the heavenly realms before descending into this world, and that its present imprisonment in a material body is the result of a primeval fall from grace. This origenist doctrine of pre-existence, bordering as it does upon the eastern family of soul-concepts, was never widely accepted and was formally condemned by the church at the Council of Constantinople in AD 540. The more prevalent early view, especially among the latin Fathers, was traducianism, the theory that the soul-substance which God breathed into Adam has been passed down through generation after generation of his descendants by continual division.[3] Thus the soul of the newly born baby derives, with its body, from the parents, and is ultimately of the same substance as the soul of Adam. As Neander expressed it, 'The soul of the first man was the fountain-head of all human souls: all the varieties of individual human nature are but modifications of that one spiritual substance.'[4] To some extent it is possible to translate this doctrine into the language of genetic science. For we can think of the transmission of characteristics in terms of a common human gene pool which flows down the generations. Thus the genetic basis of each new human self, or soul, comes from the human gene pool via the parents. It does not of course go back, as the traducianists supposed, to a single first man. But nevertheless traducianism can be seen as a mythological version of what actually happens as described by the science of genetics. Traducianism also agreed well with the dominant augustinian understanding of original sin as an inherited flaw. In spite of this, however, it was gradually abandoned, and the official teaching of the catholic church became increasingly committed to creationism – the idea that each soul is a new divine creation which God attaches to the growing foetus at some point between conception and birth: accordingly 'God is daily making souls'.[5] This view was later enshrined in the declaration of the first Vatican Council that 'God creates a new soul and infuses it into each man'.[6]

How far does this creationist doctrine agree with the findings of modern science? The answer, I suggest, is that the idea of the special divine creation of souls and their infusion into growing embryos has been rendered otiose by our knowledge of the genetic process. It has become metaphysical in the pejorative sense of being a pseudo-hypothesis whose truth or falsity makes no observable difference. For if the creationist doctrine is to have any substance, so as to be worth either affirming or denying, it must entail that there are characteristics of the self which are derived neither from genetic inheritance nor from interaction with the environment. If the divinely infused soul is to have a function in the economy of human existence it must form the inner core of individuality, the unique personal essence of a human being, providing the ultimate ground of human individuation. There would be no value in postulating a soul without content, as a mere quality-less psychic atom. Souls would not then differ from one another except numerically. Such a conception of the soul as feature-less would deny all point to the notion that God has specifically created each individual human soul. For it would then be the body rather than the soul that acts as the principle of individuation, constituting one person as different from another. Everything that is distinctive of the individual would be a product of heredity and environment, and the soul would be a needless concept. It would refer at most to a metaphysical substratum – in Locke's disparaging phrase a 'something, I know not what' – underlying our mental life, but not to an essential self carrying the unique characteristics of the individual.

If then there is to be any point to the traditional claim that souls are special divine creations they must be the bearers of some at least of the distinctive characteristics of the individual. And these characteristics must be ones which do not arise from the inherited genetic code. For the picture of God creating souls and infusing them into bodies involves a distinction between those characteristics that are carried by the soul and those that are already built genetically into the developing structure of the body. Thus to speak of the divinely inserted soul as any kind of real entity, playing a real part in the make-up of the human being, is to commit oneself to the claim that there are innate personal qualities which have not been inherited from one's parents but which have been implanted by the Creator.

However, this idea of innate but not inherited qualities is, to say the least, highly problematic. It has long been clear, even without benefit of special scientific knowledge, that children are almost as often like a parent in basic personality traits as in purely physical characteristics. Thus it is evident that some aspects at least of one's innate character are inherited, even if there should be still other aspects which represent a special divine creation. And the restriction of the boundaries of the soul thus called for by common observation is carried much further by modern genetics. For many characteristics which might have been supposed to be attributes of the soul are now believed to be part of our genetic inheritance. C. D. Darlington lists as follows those characteristics of the human individual to which there is an important genetic contribution:

> Our hormone systems and hence our temperaments, whether sanguine, melancholy or choleric; timid or courageous; observant, reflective, or impulsive. Hence our social habits, whether solitary or gregarious; affectionate or morose; settled or nomadic; useful, deranged, or criminal; hence also the company we keep, and our capacities and directions of love and hatred. Our perception and appreciation of taste, touch and smell, sound and colour, harmony and pattern. Our capacities and qualities for memory, whether for sound, sight, number or form. Our kinds and degrees of imagination, visualization and reason. Hence our understanding of truth and beauty. Hence also our educability in all these respects, or lack of it, and our capacity and choice in work and leisure.[7]

Eysenck adds that 'we have considerable evidence that there is a strong hereditary basis for extraversion/introversion and also for emotionality or neuroticism'.[8] And it is maintained by many geneticists that various special aptitudes, such as those for mathematics and for music, are inherited. But if our temperamental type and character structure, our intelligence, imaginative range and special aptitudes, all develop in directions and within limits that are genetically prescribed, it seems that this pre-established framework of possibility must be distinct from the divinely infused soul, as part of its earthly environment. The body to which the soul is said to be attached already contains genetic information selecting the personal characteristics that can and cannot be developed; and this information is part of the range of environmental factors amid which the soul is placed when it is inserted into the body. In other words we must (on this view) bracket inheritance and environment together as jointly constituting the world into which the soul comes. Inheritance provides the more immediate and individual setting of the soul's life, whilst the external world provides its less immediate and more public environment – the two being of course in continual interaction and jointly constituting the concrete situation within which the soul carries on its own life of spiritual progress or regress.[9]

The task facing such a view is to indicate an adequate content and function for the soul after genetics has pared so much away.

It might be suggested, for instance, that the soul is the locus of our personal and moral freedom. I shall argue that we have to presume our own freedom, as minds and wills, because any claim to have rational grounds for believing that we are totally determined is necessarily self-refuting.[10] Assuming then the (limited) freedom of the will, might we not identify the soul with this freedom? The answer, I think, is that freedom as a purely formal condition would not be sufficient to constitute the soul as the principle of individuation. We must add to it at least the basic personal nature in virtue of which the individual exercises his freedom in one way rather than in another. We should then identify the soul with certain fundamental dispositional characteristics – presumably our basic moral and religious attitudes. We should be postulating a central core of character which lies behind and expresses itself in the specific features of the ego, something which influences the pattern of development of our inherited potentialities. Such a soul behind the ego would fit the specifications of the reincarnating *linga sharira* of vedantic teaching and will be discussed more fully under that heading in chapter 17. But at this point let us ask to what extent such an idea is compatible with the account of man given today by the biological sciences.

The answer seems to be that whilst it cannot be proved that the two factors of heredity and environment between them account for the entire range of the individual's character traits, it certainly seems that they do and that there is no need to postulate in addition the influence of a soul or of a *linga sharira* carrying basic dispositional characteristics either supplied directly by God or developed in previous earthly lives. We have already noted the genetic basis of personality. Building upon this, there is a good deal of established co-relation between experiences in early childhood and later moral attitudes; and without spelling this out in detail it can be said to give rise to a reasonable and fairly strong presumption that a man's moral character is formed during this life, through learning in response to environmental events. There is thus so much evidence of the formation of moral character through the individual's interaction with environmental circumstances, on the basis of his inherited physical make-up, that there is no need to postulate ethical dispositions carried in a specially created soul or in a *linga sharira*.[11] From this point of view such an hypothesis is redundant. At the same time, so long as we assume the reality of human freedom it must be impossible decisively to rule out such a conception. For the basic moral and spiritual dispositions which are said to inhere in the soul presumably actualize themselves in our fundamental choices as free beings. And so long as one man freely differs from another in his moral and spiritual attitudes it will be impossible to disprove the claim that this difference is due to basic dispositions which were either implanted by God at conception or formed in previous lives.

3. 'SOUL' AS A VALUE WORD

What however – let us ask – hangs upon the traditional christian insistence on the special divine creation of each human soul? What has been the significance of this idea within the western understanding of man? This understanding, as it has developed through the centuries and as it has worked itself out in western theology and philosophy, social theory and the arts, and as it has been expressed in the organization of human life, sees the human being as a unique individual who is valued and sustained by his Creator and who in virtue of his relationship to the Eternal may enjoy an eternal life.

How does this agree with the random character of the process of meiosis in the formation of the individual sperm cell, and again with the randomness of the process by which one out of some four hundred million sperm, carrying their variant genetic codes, is selected to fertilize an ovum?

We have seen the difficulty of basing the traditional christian valuation of man upon a doctrine of the special divine creation of the soul, defined as a metaphysical entity which God inserts or infuses into the body. Are we then to justify the high value of the human individual by saying that the hand of God has been secretly at work guiding the details of the meiotic division of cells, or in aiding one particular divinely favoured sperm in its race to the ovum? To suppose this would be to invoke the 'God of the gaps' in a way which recent christian thought has for the most part renounced. God, we have been saying, is the lord of the natural order, not merely of the gaps in the natural order. To be sure, such miraculous divine interventions cannot be disproved. But are there positive grounds for insisting upon the special divine determination of the initial genetic make-up of each human person? Is there not on the contrary a strong theological motive for disclaiming this? For do we really want to claim that God has specifically bestowed upon each individual the basic good and bad tendencies of character with which he is born? Would not this make God the direct author of evil as well as good? Is it not therefore theologically preferable, as well as being in accordance with the picture indicated by the human sciences, to say that the genetic process includes a genuine element of unpredictable contingency?

As well as setting aside, as I think we must, the temptation to locate God's activity in the still unmapped intricacies of the genetic process, we have also seen reasons to abandon the notion of the soul as a divinely created and infused entity.

This does not however necessarily mean that the term 'soul' can no longer have any proper use, but only that it should not be used as the name of a spiritual substance or entity. But we also commonly use the word as an indicator of value. 'Save Our Souls', for example, the time-honoured distress signal at sea, is not only a call for help but at the same time a reminder of the value of those in danger, as fellow human beings and children of God. 'You have no soul', said to an uncultured philistine, means that he lacks the capacity to appreciate value. When something is 'soul-destroying' it is values that are in danger of destruction. 'Soul food' and 'soul music' are symbols of the values of the black community in its search for justice and civil rights. And indeed I think it will be found that the word normally has a valuational connotation. It could well be that this feature of our modern use of the term points to its primary meaning within our processes of communication and that the metaphysical theories of the soul have become mythological ways of affirming the unique value of the individual human person. If we accept this suggestion we shall not be opposed to the continued use of soul-language, or even to speaking of human beings as souls, or as having souls, in distinction perhaps from the lower animals; for such language will express that sense of the sacredness of human personality and of the inalienable rights of the human individual which we have already seen to be the moral and political content of the western idea of the soul. Nor need the church cease to strive to save souls; but the souls to be saved are simply people and not some mysterious religious entity concealed within them. To speak of man as a soul is to speak mythologically, but in a way which is bound up with important practical attitudes and practices. The myth of the soul expresses a faith in the intrinsic value of the human individual as an end in himself.

'Soul', then, is a valuing name for the self. The self has been gradually formed by the interaction of a partly random selection of genetic information with a particular historical environment; and in the course of this interaction an element of individual freedom, or creativity, is exercised. Accordingly, soul exists only as a potentiality in the unborn embryo and even in the newly born baby. 'Soul' connotes the moral and

spiritual personality which the child becomes in interaction
with its human environment; and it is impossible to say in
general terms at what age the growing human organism
becomes a soul. As a practical implication of this understanding
of soul-language it would seem to follow that, whatever other
considerations may weigh for and against the permissibility of
abortion, there is no objection to it on the ground that the
foetus is or has a soul. This is ultimately because – as will be
developed later – personality is essentially interpersonal: a
human being is a person in virtue of his or her relationship to
other persons within the human community.[12] The embryo is
a *potential* soul – that is to say, a potential moral/spiritual self;
but the selection by the human community of the point at
which a potential self is accounted an actual self involves an
unavoidable element of arbitrariness. In some societies a baby
has not been counted as having been born until many months
after parturition.[13] The idea, embodied in the laws governing
abortion in a number of western societies, that an embryo in
the first three or four months of its growth is not yet an actual
person, but that in the last three months it is much nearer to
being a person, and is definitively categorized as a person at
birth, is conservative in an area in which a conservative bias
seems much more appropriate than the contrary bias.

4. MAN IN THE MAKING

This emphasis upon human potentiality completes an important shift of emphasis in theological anthropology from the
question of origins to the question of ends. It is not what man
has come from but what he is going to that is important. We
must assume that the picture being built up by the natural
sciences of the origin of man, both individually and as a
species, is basically correct and is progressively becoming more
adequate and accurate as research continues. According to this
picture, life on this planet began with natural chemical
reactions occurring under the influence of radiations falling
upon the earth's surface. Thus began the long, slow evolution
of the forms of life, a process which has eventually produced
man. And each human individual comes about through the
partially random selection of a specific genetic code out of the
virtually infinite range of possibilities contained even in the

portion of genetic material lodged in his parents. This is, in broadest outline, the picture of man's beginning as it emerges from the physicists', chemists' and biologists' researches. And Christianity does not offer a different or rival account of our human origins. It says, in its hebraic myth of man's genesis, that he has been created out of the dust of the earth; but the details of the creative process, from dust to the immensely complex religious and valuing human animal, are for the relevant sciences to trace.

If soul-language expresses a valuation of mankind, so that the soul is the human person seen and valued in this special way, then we must renounce the idea that whereas the body has been produced by natural processes the soul has been produced by a special act of divine creation. We have to say that the soul is a divine creation in the same sense as the body – namely through the instrumentality of the entire evolution of the universe and within this of the development of life on our planet. Distinctively human mentality and spirituality emerges, in accordance with the divine purpose, in complex bodily organisms. But once it has emerged it is the vehicle, according to christian faith, of a continuing creative activity only the beginnings of which have so far taken place.

The biblical myth of Adam and Eve and their fall from grace, as it came to be interpreted in the mainstream of christian tradition, cannot readily accommodate this conception. If we insist upon continuing to use the language of that tradition we have to qualify the meanings of our key terms until we no longer mean what other people hear us say. We find ourselves speaking of a fall which did not take place at any point in time, from a paradisal condition which did not exist at any place. But on the other hand the alternative strand of christian theology, which began as early as the second century AD in the work of some of the hellenistic fathers, such as Irenaeus and Clement of Alexandria, can readily absorb the new empirical knowledge.[14] Irenaeus distinguished between what he called the image of God and the likeness of God, and suggested a two-stage conception of the divine creation of man. The *imago dei* is man's nature as a rational, personal and moral animal. Thus man in society, man the ethical being, man the creator of culture, exists in the image of God. It has taken many hundreds of millions of years of biological evolution to produce him, and yet even so he is only the raw material for the second stage of the creative process, which is the bringing of man, thus fashioned as person in the divine image, into the finite likeness of God. This latter state represents the fulfilment of the potentialities of our human nature, the completed humanization of man in a society of mutual love. Whereas the first stage of creation is an exercise of divine power, the second stage is of a different kind; for the creatures who have been brought into existence in God's image are endowed with a real though limited freedom, and their further growth into the finite divine 'likeness' has to take place through their own free responses within the world in which they find themselves. Human life as we know it is the sphere in which this second stage of creation is taking place; though it seems clear that if the process is to be completed it must continue in each individual life far beyond our earthly threescore years and ten.

Such a religious interpretation of human existence is teleologically and indeed eschatologically oriented. The final meaning of man's life lies in the future state to which, in God's purpose, he is moving. And from this point of view man's lowly beginnings are not in contradiction with his high destiny. The origin of life out of the dust of the earth – or rather, in the scientifically preferred metaphor, out of the primeval soup; the emergence of the human species from lower forms of life to form the apex of the evolutionary process; the programming of the individual genetic code through an unpredictable rearranging of the chromosomes; and again the unpredictable selection of one out of hundreds of millions of sperm to fertilize an ovum, are the ways in which man has been brought upon the stage. They do not in themselves tell us what he is here for or what his future is to be. The religions, however, do profess to tell us this. The christian faith, in the irenaean version of its theology, suggests that this complex process whereby man has been created as a personal being in God's image makes possible his cognitive freedom in relation to his Maker. Finding himself as part of an autonomous natural order, whose functioning can at all points be described without reference to a creator, man is not compelled to be conscious of God. He has an innate tendency to interpret his experience religiously, and if he gives rein to this tendency his resulting awareness of the divine is the kind of partially free awareness that we call faith. Thus man's existence as part of the natural order ensures his status as a relatively free being over against the infinite Creator. The finite creature is able to come as a (relatively) free person to know and worship God because his embeddedness in nature has initially set him at an epistemic distance from the divine Being. Thus the processes by which men and women are formed may be understood, theologically, as an aspect of the self-governing natural order on which depends man's cognitive freedom in relation to his Creator. God wills to exist an autonomous physical universe, structured towards the production of rational and personal life – an organization of matter which may well be developing not only on this earth but on millions of planets of millions of stars in millions of galaxies. The virtually infinite complexity of the cosmic process makes it to us, as finite minds existing within it, a law-governed realm which however includes randomness and unpredictability in its details; and as such it constitutes an environment within which we may grow as free beings towards that fullness of personal life, in conscious relationship to God, which represents the divine purpose for us.

5. FROM EGO TO ATMAN

We now have before us the concept of self, and the fact that we are embodied selves; and we have also the word 'soul' which refers to the self but at the same time claims for it a unique value. (In some of the following chapters, discussing different religious and philosophical positions, I shall however have to use 'soul' in other ways than this; for the term is ubiquitous and unavoidable and yet occurs in many different contexts and with almost as many meanings.) And we have noted that the 'I' is the self-conscious self but that the self in its entirety includes also the individual subconscious and unconscious.

I propose in addition to use the two further groups of terms 'ego, egoity, egoism' and 'person, personality, personal' to indicate two polar aspects of the self. As ego the self is an enclosed entity, constituted and protected by its boundaries. As such it is essentially finite, an atomic entity excluding and excluded by other such entities. Its basic concern, as a unit of conscious existence, is its own preservation. The self as ego protects itself and its autonomy not only in maintaining its embodied life as an animal organism – by seeking nourishment, avoiding danger, fleeing from or fighting enemies – but also by subtle cognitive choices in its awareness of the environment. At the physical level there is comparatively little scope for moulding the world through our perception of it. We are of course always aware of the world from a particular perspective in space, constituting a horizoning circle with the percipient at the centre; but within this perspective the material world compels us to cognize it substantially as it is or to suffer pain and even extinction. But on the social level, at which we operate in terms of values as well as physics, our egocentric perspective inevitably produces a distortion of values and a false awareness of the social reality of which we are part. Ethically, we live in *maya*, illusion; or we are 'fallen' creatures whose moral self is corrupted by sin. Whereas physically the percipient is at the centre of his perceived world in a purely spatial and non-valuational sense, socially he experiences himself as the centre of value, the most important person in his world; and he has a strong tendency to interpret and experience social situations so as to preserve his egocentric poise. In this aspect, the self is inherently self-centred, and exists in permanent *Angst* or (in buddhist terminology) *dukkha*, being perpetually threatened by the rival egoisms of its neighbours as well as by the contingencies of the surrounding world.

But there is another aspect of the self, in tension with its egoity. This is our personal nature. For personality is essentially interpersonal and consists in our relationships with other persons. As one of the leading personalist thinkers of the last generation wrote, 'Personality is mutual in its very being. The self is one term in a relation between two selves. It cannot be prior to that relation and equally, of course, the relation cannot be prior to it. "I" exist only as one member of the "*you and I*". The self only exists in the communion of selves.'[15] Or as a contemporary sociologist puts it, 'As soon as one observes phenomena that are specifically human, one enters the realm of the social.'[16] Thus, whilst the self as ego is essentially finite because bounded, the self as personal is in principle infinite, or virtually infinite, as a part of the totality of interpersonal life. This interpersonal potentiality of selfhood seeks its full realization in a society of selves each wholly open to the others in a perfect mutuality in which egoity has been transcended. For whereas the self as ego is solitary and protective, the self as personal is open to others and lives in interaction with them. Further, it is inherently self-giving, for mutual self-giving is the life-blood of community; and inherently loving, for it is the valuing of one another, which we call love, that creates and sustains community.

In addition to these two polar aspects of the self, its self-enclosed egoity and its self-giving interpersonality, there is a further important dimension of depth. For we must include in the self the subconscious and unconscious mental life which interacts with consciousness. This includes both the memories and other mental contents of which the individual is not at present aware but which are accessible to his consciousness, and also material which has been repressed in the course of building up the autonomous ego-self. But it is an illuminating hypothesis that 'beneath' this individual unconscious there lies the common or collective unconscious of mankind. Such an hypothesis was invoked by C. G. Jung to account for certain basic images or archetypes which appear in mythology and dreams throughout the world.[17] It has also been invoked to account for the phenomenon of telepathy; for if individual minds go down through their subliminal life to a common unconscious of humanity, this might provide the connection through which telepathy works.[18] The central hindu notion of the atman, the universal self which all the separate human consciousnesses unitedly are in the depth of their being, is also the concept of a collective unconscious. There is however an important difference between the jungian collective unconscious and the atman. The former is a product of man's semi-animal past, before the full development of human individuality. As a contemporary jungian psychologist says,

We may hazard a guess that the primordial images, or archetypes, formed themselves during the thousands of years when the human brain and human consciousness were

emerging from an animal state . . . The archetypes are the
result of the many recurring experiences of life: like the
rising and setting of the sun, the coming of spring and
autumn in temperate climates and of the rains in more
torrid zones, birth and death, the finding of a mate, or of
food, or escape from danger . . . They typify the triumphs
and disasters, hopes and fears, joys and sorrows of our
remote ancestors; the men who had not discovered speech
and who lived even before the Paleolithic hunters (who had
at least potentially our own qualities of mind) appeared upon
the earth.[19]

In contrast, 'atman' refers to the ideal state of human
consciousness which waits to be realized through the negating
of individual egoity. Thus, whilst the collective unconscious is
an explanatory concept, used to account for certain phenomena
of mythology, dreams and extra-sensory perception, the atman
is an eschatological concept, used in the formation of a religious
picture of the universe. I shall later be using the word 'atman'
(adopted as an english word) in this sense,[20] a sense which
leaves open the issue between the (*advaitist*) view that the
atman is an undifferentiated unity and the (*vishishtadvaitist*)
view of it as a many-in-one and one-in-many. This use of the
term likewise leaves open the more ultimate theological
question of the relation between the atman, as eschatological
humanity, and God, Ultimate Reality, Brahman. It thus leaves
open the debate between the (*advaitist*) view that atman *is*
Brahman and the (*vishishtadvaitist*) view of a complex creature-
Creator relationship.
   The broad picture which begins to form, as an hypothesis
in global theology, is one in which mental life emerges in the
increasing complexification of the evolutionary process, and
develops through semi-individuality within a collective consciousness such as we glimpse in the close-knit communal life
of primitive tribes, into the plurality of fully differentiated
selves which we now experience. This latter is the phase of
individual freedom and responsibility, protected by boundaries
drawn by the ego aspect of the self. In this phase, coterminous
with human history, we have the opportunity voluntarily to
transcend egoity; and precisely this is the challenge addressed

to us by all the great religions. The task of moving from the multiplicity of ego-selves to the higher unity of interpersonal life is however far too great to be accomplished within this present earthly existence. The goal is a return to unity at a higher level, a movement from pre-individualized unity through separate egoity to a supra-individual unity. Again, it is a movement from the collective unconscious, through the self-negating of the ego which has created the unconscious, to the fully realized collective consciousness of the atman. But here we are beginning to look across a wide range of investigations to the constructive discussion of part V.

NOTES

1. Luke 16: 19–31.
2. Matthew 25: 31–46.
3. This was taught, for example, by Tertullian (*A Treatise on the Soul*, ch. 27), who thought of the soul as some kind of subtle material entity.
4. Quoted by W. R. Alger, *A Critical History of the Doctrine of the Future Life*, p. 11.
5. Jerome, *Epistle* 37, 9 (J. P. Migne, *Patrologia Latina*, vol. 30, col. 265).
6. *Schema of the Dogmatic Constitution on the Principal Mysteries of the Faith*, ch. 2. More recently the papal encyclical *Humani generis* (1950) reaffirmed that 'souls are immediately created by God' (para. 36). The doctrine was taught by St Thomas in the *Summa Theologica*, part I, q. 118, art. 3. There is a similar (although not quite identical) teaching in the jewish Talmud: 'All souls were made during the six days of creation; and therefore generation is not by traduction, but by infusion of a soul into body' (quoted by Alger, op. cit., p. 9).
7. C. D. Darlington, *Genetics and Man*, p. 241.
8. H. J. Eysenck, *Crime and Personality*, p. 102.
9. Something rather like this was suggested as a possibility by the zoologist H. S. Jennings in *The Biological Basis of Human Nature*, pp. 297–8.
10. See chapter 6, section 3.
11. See further, chapter 19, section 5.
12. Chapter 2, section 5, and chapter 22, section 3.
13. For example, in the Meru tribe in Kenya 'the baby was made into a human, after the first tooth appeared, through the ceremony by which an ancestor's name was conferred upon it' (John V. Taylor, *The Primal Vision*, p. 93).

14. I have discussed the irenaean view of man in *Evil and the God of Love*, ch. 9.

15. John Macmurray, *Interpreting the Universe*, p. 137.

16. Peter Berger and Thomas Luckmann, *The Social Construction of Reality*, p. 69.

17. The notion of the collective unconscious is presented by Jung in a number of writings, including 'The Personal and the Collective (or Transpersonal) Unconscious', in *Collected Works*, vol. 7, and 'The Archetypes and the Collective Unconscious', in *Collected Works*, vol. 9.

18. This theory is presented, e.g., by Whately Carington in *Telepathy*.

19. Frieda Fordham, *An Introduction to Jung's Psychology*, pp. 24–5.

20. In chapter 22.

CHAPTER 3

The Origins of After-Life and Immortality Beliefs

I. PRIMITIVE MAN

In his relation to death man is unique among the animal species, and indeed doubly unique. For alone among the animals he knows that he is going to die; and further, he not only knows it but – in an important sense – does not believe it! As far back as we are able to find traces of distinctively human life we find that man has done something which no other species does: he has buried the corpses of his own kind, or otherwise deliberately disposed of them, thus revealing a sense of the special significance of death. Further, these earliest evidences show that he did not think of death as the cessation of existence. We are told of 'unmistakable indications of a conception of the continuance of life after death' as long as half a million years ago, found in caves near Peking.[1] Neanderthal man, living on earth from about 100,000 to about 25,000 years ago, placed food and flint implements in the graves which he dug. Old Stone Age men, the Cro-Magnons, who roamed through southern Europe and Africa from about 25,000 to about 10,000 years ago, hunting bison, horses, and other large beasts, likewise buried weapons, ornaments and food with their dead and daubed red ochre (the colour of blood) on corpses or in graves. In the New Stone Age, from about 10,000 to about 5,000 years ago, neolithic men adopted even more complex funeral practices. Often the body was placed in the contracted or foetal posture. Sometimes wives and slaves were sacrificed and buried with a chieftain; and immense labour was put into the creation of stone burial chambers.

All this shows that our prehistoric ancestors assumed that in some sense and in some form humans continue to exist after their deaths, so as to have a use for the precious objects which were buried with them. However, the archaeological evidence does not take us beyond this. For further light on the attitudes to death and the after-life beliefs of early man we have to turn to the studies made of surviving primitive peoples in Australia, Polynesia, Africa and South America, particularly in the nineteenth century and up to about the first world war. These studies show that some kind of after-life belief was universal, and took a number of forms. The common theme was the notion of a 'soul' in the sense of 'an ethereal surviving being',[2] a double or shade or image of the bodily individual. That which survives death was not at this stage thought of as mind in distinction from body but rather as a shadowy and insubstantial counterpart of the body. The shade was assumed to continue after death, generally in a dim underworld beneath the level of the graves, which were sometimes thought of as entrances to the nether world. The dead were often thought of as potentially dangerous to the living and as needing to be either placated or tricked into quiescence. Sometimes however a chief or leader was imagined to go to a distant part of the earth, or up into the sky, and was venerated and perhaps in due course worshipped as a god. Some tribes have believed in happier hunting grounds beyond the grave; for example, 'In the Kimbunda country of South-West Africa, souls live on in "Kalunga", the world where it is day when it is night here; and with plenty of food and drink, and women to serve them, and hunting and dancing for pastime, they lead a life which seems a corrected edition of this.'[3] But the much more general belief was in a descent into the lower world in which the shade carried on a gradually fading life until eventually it passed out of memory and existence. This was not a conception of eternal life, or immortality, but of ghostly survival. A man could not be supposed to cease to exist at death; but on the other hand there was no thought of positive immortality. The idea of reincarnation, or transmigration, is also found among many primitive peoples, and Frazer conjectured that it may well have been even more widespread than the direct evidence now shows.[4] Indeed, Paul Radin speaks of the belief in some form of reincarnation as 'universally present in all the simple food-gathering and fishing-hunting civilizations'.[5]

We must not assume, however, that acceptance of the momentous premiss that all men are mortal as an item of public knowledge is as old as the fact which it expresses. In the earliest stages of man's cultural development death was not seen as the natural and inevitable end of every life. The primitive mind (perhaps like the mind of the young child[6]) seems to have been unaware of human beings as having a limited life-span and as subject to inevitable death from the wearing out of the body if not from disease, accident or violence. Lévy-Brühl[7] has assembled evidence that among nineteenth-century savages in Australia death, however it came, was thought of as being due to the magical action of an enemy;[8] and he adds that 'this attitude of mind is not peculiar to Australian tribes only. It is to be found occurring almost uniformly among uncivilized peoples who are widely removed from each other.'[9] Thus the primitive mind was not conscious of a general liability to death such as is expressed by the proposition that all men are mortal. Death was thought of as being due to particular and contingent causes; people did not just die but were killed. Such a view of death in primitive society is not however at all astonishing, since it must so largely have corresponded with the facts; for it has been estimated that prehistoric man's average life-span was only about eighteen years, death being usually due to violent causes.[10] And as the universality of death came to be recognized myths developed to explain how man, usually thought of as originally immortal, had become subject to death – whether through the jealousy or niggardliness of the gods[11] or the carelessness of their agents[12] or the fault of man himself.[13]

That when men did die they continued in existence in some form seems to have been for primitive man a matter-of-fact belief which did not significantly contribute to his ethico-religious system. With the exceptions of ancient Egypt and India, where the idea of an after-life appropriate to men's deserts emerged earlier than elsewhere, there seems to have been no thought of a judgement of the dead with contrasting fates awaiting the good and the wicked or the pious and the impious. With few exceptions there was no sense of the departed as being in a heavenly state, better off than they had been on earth; or on the other hand in a hell receiving just retribution for their sins. Indeed, the early belief in an after-life does not seem to have reflected human hopes or fears but rather to have been the product of an inability to think of vividly remembered persons as non-existent, perhaps re-inforced by dreams of the departed,[14] together with a vague association of their state with the grave and hence with a dark region beneath the earth. As John Baillie emphasizes, 'The fact of survival essentially belongs . . . not to the savage's religion but to his lay philosophy of things – as we should say, to his natural science.'[15] The matter-of-factness of the primitive's after-life belief is stressed by J. G. Frazer in his monumental three-volume work, *The Belief in Immortality*, when he says that 'it is impossible not to be struck by the strength, and perhaps we may say the universality, of the natural belief in immortality among the savage races of mankind. With them a life after death is not a matter of speculation and conjecture, of hope and fear; it is a practical certainty which the individual as little dreams of doubting as he doubts the reality of his conscious existence. He assumes it without enquiry and acts upon it without hesitation, as if it were one of the best-ascertained truths within the limits of human experience.'[16]

2. SHEOL AND HADES

To what extent the earliest written accounts of the state of the dead, in ancient greek and hebrew literature, reflect the older Stone Age conception or represent some degree of development beyond it is uncertain; but if there was a development it does not appear to have been very considerable. The early greek conception of the after-life, expressed in the *Iliad* and the *Odyssey*, centred upon the *psyche* or soul, which Erwin Rohde described as 'the body's shadow-image' or 'a feebler double of the man'.[17] At death this descends into erebus or hades where, whilst still recognizable and still bearing its earthly name, it persists as a depleted, joyless entity, a mere bloodless shadow of its former embodied self: 'There remaineth then even in the house of Hades a spirit and phantom of the dead, albeit the life be not anywise therein.'[18] To quote Rohde, 'Down in the murky underworld they now float unconscious, or, at most, with a twilight half-consciousness, wailing in a shrill diminutive voice, helpless, indifferent.'[19] And in an often cited passage the shade of the great Achilles, briefly reenergized by the blood of a goat, says, 'Nay, speak not comfortably to me of death, oh great Odysseus. Rather would I live upon the earth as the hireling of another, with a landless man who had no great livelihood, than bear sway among all the dead that be departed.'[20]

As has often been pointed out, the ancient hebrew sheol is similar in conception to the greek hades. Sheol was thought of as a vast underground cavern or pit – probably the tribal burial place magnified into a dark subterranean world – where the dead exist or persist. The prospect was wholly uninviting, so that Job could cry:

> Let me alone, that I may find a little comfort
> before I go whence I shall not return,
> to the land of gloom and deep darkness,
> the land of gloom and chaos,
> where light is as darkness.[21]

Further, the descent into sheol was irreversible: 'He who goes down to sheol does not come up',[22] although there are also texts which suggest God's power over death and sheol and which thus provide the starting-point for the development in the post-exilic period of the idea of the resurrection of the dead. The general Old Testament view however was that to go down to sheol was to pass for ever out of the land of the living and out of the on-going life of the nation in its covenant relationship with Yahweh. The dead were not in active communion with God. So the psalmist says, 'The dead do not praise the Lord, nor do any that go down into silence.'[23] Again,

> For my soul is full of troubles,
> and my life draws near to Sheol.
> I am reckoned among those who go down to the Pit;
> I am a man who has no strength,
> like one forsaken among the dead,
> like the slain that lie in the grave,
> like those whom thou dost remember no more,
> for they are cut off from thy hand . . .
> Dost thou work wonders for the dead?
> Do the shades rise up to praise thee?

Is thy steadfast love declared in the grave,
    or thy faithfulness in Abaddon?
Are thy wonders known in the darkness,
    or thy saving help in the land of forgetfulness?[24]

– all rhetorical questions which expect the answer No.

3. THE SIGNIFICANCE OF THE PRIMITIVE BELIEFS

We have now glanced at the earliest phase of human thought
in which there was, either universally or with only small local
exceptions, the belief in an undesired because pointless
survival, but as yet no thought of a valuable immortality. This
first phase extends back as far into man's prehistory as any life
that can be described as human; and it continues down to the
savages who have been observed as recently as the nineteenth
and twentieth centuries in parts of the world remote from the
influences of civilization. The early literatures of Greece and
Israel reflect a state of belief continuous with this, and in the
next section we shall trace within them the transition from the
thought of an undesired survival to that of a desired immortality. We shall also note that other even earlier civilizations in
Egypt and India had already moved into the next stage of
thought about human destiny. But let us pause at this point
to consider the significance of this earliest phase for our
enquiry as a whole. Its significance is that it altogether fails to
substantiate what is today perhaps the most widespread theory
of the origin of the belief in a life after death. This is the theory
that men came to believe in survival for the simple reason that
they wished to survive and to experience a better life beyond
the grave. In reaction against the hardships of their present
existence our earliest ancestors – according to this theory –
projected the compensatory idea of heaven. A poem of Rupert
Brooke's beautifully expresses this conception:

> Fish (fly-replete, in depth of June,
> Dawdling away their wat'ry noon)
> Ponder deep wisdom, dark or clear,
> Each secret fishy hope or fear.
> Fish say, they have their Stream and Pond;
> But is there anything Beyond?

This life cannot be All, they swear,
For how unpleasant, if it were!
One may not doubt that, somehow, Good
Shall come of Water and of Mud;
And, sure, the reverent eye must see
A Purpose in Liquidity.
We darkly know, by Faith we cry,
The future is not Wholly Dry.
Mud unto mud! – Death eddies near –
Not here the appointed End, not here!
But somewhere, beyond Space and Time,
Is wetter water, slimier slime!
And there (they trust) there swimmeth One
Who swam ere rivers were begun,
Immense, of fishy form and mind,
Squamous, omnipotent, and kind;
And under that Almighty Fin,
The littlest fish may enter in.
Oh! never fly conceals a hook,
Fish say, in the Eternal Brook,
But more than mundane weeds are there,
And mud, celestially fair;
Fat caterpillars drift around,
And Paradisal grubs are found;
Unfading moths, immortal flies,
And the worm that never dies.
And in that Heaven of all their wish,
There shall be no more land, say fish![25]

Such a theory is attractive to an age schooled in the exposure
of motives by modern psychology. But nevertheless we have
already seen that it does not accord with our indications of
early man's thoughts. For the most general primitive attitude
to the dead of which we have evidence was not one of envy,
but more of fear or pity. The dead were not usually thought of
as having passed on to a higher and happier life but rather as
having lapsed into an altogether less desirable state of mere
half-existence. The life of the spirit world is, says E. O. James,
'generally regarded as a mutilated existence [in which] the
complete personality is seldom if ever thought to be reassembled

after death'.[26] Again, Erwin Rohde, writing about the ancient Greeks, says, 'Hope would never have beguiled itself with the anticipation of a state of things which neither afforded men the chance of further activity after death, nor, on the other hand, gave them rest from the toil of life; one which promised them only a restless, purposeless fluttering to and fro, an existence, indeed, but without any of the content that might have made it worthy of the name of life.'[27] Or again, Durkheim remarks that 'even among the most advanced peoples, it was only a pale and sad existence that shades led in Sheol or Erebus, and could hardly attenuate the regrets occasioned by the memories of the life lost!'[28]

Nor does the notion of the origin of after-life beliefs as an instrument of political control have any historical plausibility. It was not a matter of the masses being reconciled to their present harsh lot by the thought that the social roles would be reversed and the last be first and the first last. For the privileged few who were sometimes thought of as going to a better world were the kings and heroes who had already enjoyed all the privileges of the present world. Instead of death being the occasion of a great social revolution, the inequalities of this life were assumed to continue in the next. Tylor says that 'mere transfer from one life to another makes chiefs and slaves here chiefs and slaves hereafter', and gives a number of examples from different parts of the world.[29]

Thus the 'pie in the sky when you die' view of the origin of man's conviction of an after-life is not supported by the evidences of anthropology. On the contrary, 'for the vast majority of mankind, the idea that the soul gains by passing out of this world is very rare indeed'.[30] Whilst the desire for a better existence, or for future compensation for present privations, may have reinforced after-life beliefs in the period since heaven established its reputation as a place of bliss, such wishful thinking can hardly lie at the origin of early men's belief in their survival; for the post-mortem states in which they believed were not such as to hold any attraction, or to offer any worthwhile compensation, for the vast majority of people.

But having excluded this popular but improbable theory we have to say that the origin of the belief in an after-life remains a matter of conjecture. Recent speculations see the belief as derived from the rituals associated with death.[31] But such a theory seems to 'put the cart before the horse'; for do not the rituals presuppose some belief, however inarticulate? Probably the idea of an after-life had both positive and negative sources, the positive source being that indicated by Frazer when he said that the savage

> finds a very strong argument for immortality in the phenom-ena of dreams, which are strictly a part of his inner life, though in his ignorance he commonly fails to discriminate them from what we popularly call waking realities. Hence when the images of persons whom he knows to be dead appear to him in a dream, he naturally infers that these persons still exist somewhere and somehow apart from their bodies, of the decay or destruction of which he may have had ocular demonstration. How could he see dead people, he asks, if they did not exist?[32]

And the negative source is perhaps the basic difficulty of thinking of oneself as non-existent. For the primitive mind it was doubtless much easier to assume some kind of continuation after death than to suppose that the individual – who after all was still present in memory and in dreams – had ceased to be. There is however also yet another possibility, brought to light by the psychoanalysts, who believe the unconscious to be convinced of its own immortality.[33] This may merely reflect the surface fact of the conscious individual's inability to think of himself as non-existent. Or it may reflect a deeper fact – an immortality of the true self, in indian terms the *atman* which lies behind the transitory ego and which is said to be ultimately one with the eternal Self, *Paramatman.* This is a possibility to be considered further in chapter 22.

4. THE EMERGENCE OF BELIEF IN A DESIRABLE IMMORTALITY

We have seen that the primitive outlook assumed an existence beyond the grave but that this existence was generally thought of as colourless and pointless, the mere persistence of an insubstantial wraith. The belief in a desirable immortality depends, logically and historically, upon the notion of *value* both in the human individual and in a higher reality which is superior even to the power of death. This higher value-bearing reality is God or the gods or the eternal Good; and man's answering value consists in either moral goodness or in an awareness of inner union with the divine. The logic of the matter is that only the thought of man as having value, together with a religious conviction about the sovereignty of value in the universe, can give rise to hopes and fears sufficient to disturb purely natural assumptions about death – in the case of early man the assumption of an attenuated prolongation and decline beyond the grave. This is borne out historically in the earliest beliefs in a desirable immortality – in ancient Egypt, where the idea of the judgement of the dead and the consequent notions of heaven and hell first appeared; to some extent in the vedic religion of ancient India; in classical Greece, where the mystery cults offered men a blessed immortality by mystical union with the divine; and at the end of the prophetic period of Judaism, when the notions of the resurrection of the dead, judgement, and heaven and hell became established. What is primarily of interest for our present enquiry is that in each case though in different ways the thought of a good after-life arose in connection with a wider vision of man's situation in which value, embodied in divine powers, determines man's destiny.

But the bringing to bear of moral and religious ideas upon the fate of the individual presupposed a yet more fundamental development which was taking place at the same time – the emergence of the idea of the autonomous individual person.

We have already noted that in the case of outstanding individuals, but only of these, peoples in transition from the primitive state to the early civilizations already entertained the thought of a better life beyond the grave. In the *Odyssey*, for example, the sea god tells King Menelaus that 'the deathless gods will convey thee to the Elysian plain and the world's end, where is Rhadamanthus of the fair hair, where life is easiest for men. No snow is there, nor yet great storm, nor any rain; but always ocean sendeth forth the breeze of the shrill West to blow cool on men: yea, for thou hast Helen to wife, and thereby they deem thee to be son of Zeus.'[34] The elysian plain was not a heaven, in the sense of a blissful spiritual state; rather, those whom the gods favoured (not on account of special virtues but because they had divine blood in their veins or had married into the family of the immortals) were exempt from death and were translated to a wondrous region of the earth. Again, in the faith of the ancient Hebrews certain great souls – Enoch[35] and Elijah[36] – were taken up into heaven without having died. There was also, as we have seen, the belief among some primitive peoples that kings and heroes may go to a better place whilst the mass of ordinary mortals lapse into the grey world beneath the earth.

The first emergence of the idea of a blessed hereafter as a privilege of kings and other outstanding leaders may well reflect the fact that they were, in our modern sense of the word, the first individuals. They were singled out as representative persons; or, in ancient Greece, as descendants or favourites of the gods; or again, in Israel, as great servants of Yahweh. But the generality of men and women saw themselves as parts of a collective social organism whose life continued on earth out of an indefinite past and into an indefinite future: as individuals perished and went down to the underworld others were born and the life of the tribe went on. What we can call soul was originally vaguely thought of as a larger life embodied in the successive members of the group. Durkheim expressed this by saying that 'the soul is nothing other than the totemic principle incarnate in each individual';[37] and at death this individualized life returned to the tribal collective. There was thus personal immortality only for the chiefs and leaders whose role invested them with representative individuality; and what Cornford has called 'the democratic extension of immortality to all human beings'[38] was a later development. He describes the earlier stage as follows:

> The soul has been held to be immortal, primarily because it was at first impersonal and superindividual – the soul of a group, which outlives every generation of its members. Beginning as the collective and impersonal life of the group, it becomes confounded . . . with the individual personality of the chief; and there was, probably, a stage in which only chiefs or heroes had immortal souls. The tradition of such a phrase seems to survive in Hesiod's Age of Bronze – a class

of immortals which consists of the heroes who fought at Ilion and Thebes, but does not include the undistinguished mass of their followers.[39]

This notion of corporate personality is clearly expressed in the literature of the ancient, pre-exilic Hebrews. As J. N. Schofield puts it,

> The individual as a self-conscious unit had not emerged. Every man was part of a blood-group, a family, clan, or tribe bound together by the fact that the same blood flowed through the veins of all the members. For some purposes he appears to have been treated as part of the family of which he was chief, and, for others, as part of the larger group of which he was a son, so that for some offences the sins of the fathers were visited upon the children, and for others the fathers suffered for their children's sins. The group provided each member with food and clothing; it gave him social security and justice; it protected him against his foes, and the individual's life was so bound up with his group that he would never question the value of community life. Apart from it, he had no rights, freedom, or property; within it, all these were guaranteed.[40]

Thus Yahweh was the god, not primarily of individual Israelites, but of Israel as a people. The collective responsibility of the tribe is well illustrated by the killing of certain Gibeonites by Saul, king of Israel. This crime gave rise to a blood-guilt which was punished by a prolonged famine. So the new king, David, asked the Gibeonites what could be done to expiate the offence. They demanded the death of seven of Saul's sons (i.e. descendants), 'and he gave them into the hands of the Gibeonites, and they hanged them on the mountain before the Lord'.[41] Wheeler Robinson comments, 'There was no thought of any injustice to the individual men who were killed. They perished as an act of social justice, which was demanded by the contemporary religion of Israel.'[42]

In this stage of hebrew history, before the individual had achieved individual self-consciousness over against his surrounding group, the idea of personal immortality had yet to develop. 'The Israelite felt that he went on living in his

children to a degree that really made their life his own . . .
Hence the importance attached by the Hebrew to a numerous
posterity; it is not said to the good man that he shall be
rewarded in some future life, but

> Thou shalt know also that thy seed shall be great,
> And thine offspring as the grass of the earth.'[43]

It is commonly supposed that it was in Jaspers' 'axial period',
between about 800 and about 200 BC, that the idea of the
autonomous, responsible human individual was born[44] – and
hence, in due course, the question of his personal destiny after
death. There seems however to be an exception to this otherwise valid generalization in the very early egyptian belief in a
desirable personal immortality – though it is not clear how
soon this was applied to circles beyond the Pharaoh and his
nobles; and a partial exception also in the early vedic religion
of India.

In ancient Egypt, as long ago as the middle of the third
millennium BC, there was belief in a judgement of the dead on
moral as well as ritual grounds: 'The belief was already
current', says S. G. F. Brandon, 'that one's behaviour here
could decisively affect one's condition after death.'[45] There is
a remarkable instance of this in an inscription in the Sixth-
Dynasty (*c.* 2350–2200 BC) tomb of a nobleman called Herkhuf
in which he sets forth the basis of his hope for a good immortality. As well as claiming to have been a good son and
brother and a loyal subject of the king, Herkhuf says, 'I gave
bread to the hungry, clothing to the naked, I ferried him who
had no boat . . . Never did I say aught evil, to a powerful one
against any people, (for) I desired that it might be well with
me in the Great God's presence. Never did I [judge two
brothers] in such a way that a son was deprived of his paternal
possession . . . '[46] Brandon comments that this inscription
'constitutes one of the most significant documents both in the
history of ethics and in the evolution of the idea of a *post-
mortem* judgment'.[47] In the *Instruction for King Meri-ka-re*
(Tenth Dynasty, *c.* 2150–2060 BC) the old king warns his son
about the future judgement: 'Do not trust in length of years,
for they regard a lifetime as (but) an hour. A man remains
after death, and his deeds are placed beside him in heaps.

However, existence yonder is for eternity, and he who complains of it is a fool. (But) as for him who reaches it without wrongdoing, he shall exist yonder like a god, stepping out freely like the lords of eternity.'[48] And in the later texts collected in the *Book of the Dead* there are vivid pictures of the judgement of Osiris before whom a man's heart is weighed against a feather, symbolizing Ma-a-t, the moral principle.[49] In one text the deceased declares his innocence, saying to the gods who act as Osiris' assessors, 'I have not robbed; I have not killed men; I have not plundered the property of God; I have not lied; I have not defiled any man's wife; I have not defiled myself; I have not cursed the king; I have not acted deceitfully; I have not committed wickedness; I have not turned a deaf ear to the words of the Law.'[50]

All this represents, in a period perhaps a thousand years before the time of Moses, a developed moral consciousness being applied to the already existing belief in an after-life. In the earlier stage of human prehistory the concept of individual moral responsibility had (if we may judge from the thought-ways of surviving primitives) not yet emerged, and the idea that all – except perhaps for occasional great leaders – descended into a common underworld beneath the earth was not yet disturbed by distinctions of moral worth. But in the religion of ancient Egypt we see ethical considerations prompting the thought of a blessed future for the righteous and a contrasting punishment for the wicked.

In ancient India, among the aryan invaders of the mid-second millennium BC whose faith is reflected in the earliest sections of the Vedas, there is also a conception, though considerably less central and less developed, of life in this world as leading the individual to bliss or destruction. Thus in a hymn to the great god Vishnu the worshipper says, 'May I attain to that his dear place, where men devoted to the Gods are exulting';[51] and in the following hymn to Yama, god of the realm of the departed, we read:

Meet Yama, meet the fathers, meet the merit of free or
    ordered acts, in highest heaven.
Leave sin and evil, seek anew thy dwelling, and bright
    with glory wear another body.[52]

The Aryans were a world- and life-affirming people and their conception of heaven seems to have been one of the enjoyment, in an embodied state, of the fulfilment of earthly wishes:

O Pavamana, place me in that deathless, undecaying world
Wherein the light of heaven is set, and everlasting lustre
    shines.
    Flow, Indu, flow for Indra's sake.

Make me immortal in that realm where dwells the king,
    Vivasvan's son,
Where is the secret shrine of heaven, where are those waters
    young and fresh.
    Flow, Indu, flow for Indra's sake.

Make me immortal in that realm where they move even
    as they list,
In the third sphere of inmost heaven, where lucid worlds
    are full of light.
    Flow, Indu, flow for Indra's sake.

Make me immortal in that realm of eager wish and strong
    desire,
The region of the radiant Moon, where food and full
    delight are found.
    Flow, Indu, flow for Indra's sake.

Make me immortal in that realm where happiness and
    transports, where
Joys and felicities combine, and longing wishes are
    fulfilled.
    Flow, Indu, flow for Indra's sake.[53]

There was however also a darker side. Evil-doers were perhaps at first thought of as being annihilated by death; but later there is the notion of a black underground for the wicked, and talk of the gods Indra and Soma hurling sinners down to hell.[54]

This vedic conception of the after-life, somewhat similar to the norsemen's dreams of Valhalla, perhaps comes closer than any other early eschatology to being compatible with the wish-fulfilment theory. And yet it still does not fit the specifications of a compensatory projection, for in the Vedas heaven was only for the few, being 'regarded as the reward of those who practice rigorous penance, of heroes who risk their lives in battle, and above all of those who bestow liberal sacrificial gifts'.[55]

Coming down to the axial age, the ancient Hebrews' grasp of the notion of the autonomous responsible individual seems to have been prompted by convergent religious and social developments. The religious influence was the new understanding of Yahweh taught by the great prophets of the seventh and sixth centuries. (There was also a parallel development in Iran, at about the same time, in the teachings of Zoroaster.) It was Jeremiah who first explicitly formulated the idea of individual as distinguished from corporate moral responsibility. Rejecting the thought that 'the fathers have eaten sour grapes, and the children's teeth are set on edge', he proclaimed, 'But every one shall die for his own sin; each man who eats sour grapes, *his* teeth shall be set on edge.'[56] And Ezekiel strengthened the thought of the personal relationship between Yahweh and the individual Israelite when he declared as God's message: 'Behold, all souls are mine; the soul of the father as well as the soul of the son is mine: the soul that sins shall die.'[57] This new religious insight was related to a new historical situation. So long as the stream of national life continued in full spate the individual was carried along in it, and the immortality of the nation did not require an individual immortality for its separate members. But with the crushing babylonian conquest of Judah in the sixth century and the exile of so many of Jerusalem's leading citizens, faith in continuing national existence was shaken and the individual became more conscious of his own personal status and destiny. 'With the disappearance of the nation, as such,' says Oesterley, 'the individual came to his own.'[58] And with this dawning individual self-consciousness there came the agonizing question of God's justice to the individual, so powerfully and poignantly expressed in the book of Job. Possibly the question of the fate of the martyrs in the Maccabean period made the issue especially urgent. In this situation belief in the resurrection of the dead (probably received from Zoroastrianism) spread among the Hebrews during the last two or three centuries before Christ. The thought that God's love for his children cannot be terminated by death but will hold the individual in being beyond the grave required belief in some form of after-life; and the form which the belief took conformed to the hebraic understanding of man as, in Wheeler Robinson's well-known phrase, 'an animated body, and not an incarnated soul'[59] – or as we more naturally say today, a psycho-physical unity and not a 'ghost in the machine'. Accordingly we read in Daniel, 'And many of those who sleep in the dust of the earth shall awake, some to everlasting life, and some to shame and everlasting contempt.'[60] The doctrine of the resurrection was mainly developed in the apocalyptic writings of the time between the Old Testament prophets and the life of Jesus, and consisted of no one single fixed conception. 'Sometimes the righteous are to be resurrected to a kingdom established on this present earth; sometimes it is to be on a "purified" or renewed earth; sometimes it is limited in duration and precedes the dawning of the age to come; sometimes it is a purely heavenly and "spiritual" conception in which the idea of resurrection may or may not play a part.'[61] It was this variety of ideas that was to form the background of New Testament eschatology.

Among the Greeks the idea of a blessed after-life came through the mystery cults – the earlier eleusinian and the later dionysian and orphic mysteries. These faiths and practices focused and deepened a gradually forming concern for personal immortality. The pure, who had been initiated into the secret ritual of the worship of Demeter, were promised a privileged fate after death: 'Blessed is the man who has beheld these holy acts; but he that is uninitiated and has no share in the holy ceremonies shall not enjoy a like fate after his death, in the gloomy darkness of Hades.'[62] Originally the festival of Demeter, with its promise of far-reaching benefits, seems to have been confined to a small circle of the noble families of Eleusis; but it was gradually opened to the Athenians and eventually became a major festival for the whole of Greece. 'It was these promises', says Rohde, 'of a blessed immortality that for centuries drew so many worshippers to the Eleusinian festival.'[63] For later generations of Greeks the worship of Dionysus, originating in Thrace but becoming widespread by the sixth century, involved frenzied dancing on hilltops by the light of flickering pine torches, to the sound of cymbals, flutes and kettledrums and under the influence of intoxicating drinks, until the devotee entered a state of ecstasy – a 'stepping out- side' of himself in a sacred madness in which he experienced an expanded consciousness which was a foretaste of eternal life and in which he felt himself to have become one with the deity. It was here, says Jaeger, that 'we find for the first time the belief in the soul of man as something different and separable from the body'.[64] And there seems to be general agreement 'that just in this wild "enthusiasm" or possession by the god, this "ecstasy" in which the individual seems to pass out of himself and feel himself one with the god whose rites he is celebrating, lay the germ of a new conception of the soul and its destiny'.[65]

The dionysian cult spread, developed, and became fused with other strands of greek religion, flowing eventually into the orphic mystery movement, whose great theologian was Pythagoras and whose myths were to exert a deep influence on Socrates and Plato. The sense of being purified from an original taint was an important aspect of the ecstatic experience in these movements. In the developed theology of Orphism the divine soul had fallen into the realm of matter and become fragmented into individual human souls; and their salvation meant their rescue from this fallen state and ultimately their reunification in the divine life.[66] The many sparks of divinity had to progress through successive incarnations to the point at which they became aware of their identity with the universal self. The similarity of this philosophy with that which had been developing among the upanishadic writers of India is evident, though whether indian thought exerted any historical influence in Greece remains quite uncertain.

In the dialogues of Plato we see the end of the transition from primitive ideas of the survival of depleted shades or ghosts to the ardent desire for and belief in an immortality in which the highest possibilities glimpsed in this life may be fulfilled. And we see in the thought of Socrates and Plato the essential dependence of any such positive conception of immortality upon faith in an eternal realm or being, infinite in reality and value, through relationship to which men can enjoy a shared eternity. In the Dialogues the soul (*psyche*) which survives death is no longer thought of as an ethereal body but as the mind or inner self; it is no longer a quasi-physical 'thing' but the centre of consciousness and of morally responsible choice. Accordingly the most important concern in life is to attend to 'the perfecting of your soul'.[67] The soul is inherently immortal (and Plato has his – logically inconclusive – philosophical arguments for this), but its attainment of a *good* immortality depends upon its moral quality. The message of the originally orphic myths of judgement, rebirth, and the ascent of the purified soul to the eternal realm with which Plato ends the *Phaedo*, *Phaedrus*, *Gorgias* and *Republic* is a profound moral challenge. Some kind of after-life awaits everyone; but only those who have achieved an affinity with the eternal reality, which is absolute Goodness, will be able to find everlasting joy. Thus human survival, which was in the earlier periods a mere valueless circumstance without moral or religious meaning, became in the thought of Socrates and Plato a fact of urgent existential significance:

> 'But there is a further point, gentlemen,' said Socrates, 'which deserves your attention. If the soul is immortal, it demands our care not only for that part of time which we call life, but for all time; and indeed it would seem now that it will be extremely dangerous to neglect it. If death were a release from everything, it would be a boon for the wicked, because by dying they would be released not only from the body but also from their own wickedness together with the soul; but as it is, since the soul is clearly immortal, it can have no escape or security from evil except by becoming as good and wise as it possibly can. For it takes nothing with it to the next world except its education and training . . . '[68]

This has been only the barest outline of a history which contains many fascinating variations and complexities which are not however important for our very broad picture. What is important is the fact that the idea of a desirable immortality, as distinguished from that of an undesired because pointless and joyless survival, arose with the emergence of individual self-consciousness and as a correlate of faith in a higher reality which was the source of value.

NOTES

1. E. O. James in *Historia Religionum*, ed. C. J. Bleeker and Geo Widengren, vol. I, p. 24.
2. E. B. Tylor, *Primitive Culture*, vol. II, p. 24. On the idea of the 'astral body', see p. 422, n. 12.
3. ibid., p. 77. Cf. J. G. Frazer, *The Belief in Immortality and the Worship of the Dead*, vol. I, pp. 138–9.
4. *The Belief in Immortality*, vol. I, p. 29.
5. *Primitive Religion*, p. 270.
6. Cf. Jean Piaget, *The Language and Thought of the Child*, p. 178. For a critique of Piaget's analysis, see Sylvia Anthony, *The Discovery of Death in Childhood and After*, ch. 10. On the child's awareness of death, see further Marjorie Editha Mitchell, *The Child's Attitude to Death*; and Kastenbaum and Aisenberg, *The Psychology of Death*, pp. 9–37.
7. Lucien Levy-Brühl, *Primitive Mentality*, ch. 1.
8. For example, 'All ailments of every kind, from the simplest to the most serious, are without exception attributed to the malign influence of an enemy in either human or spirit shape' (Spencer and Gillen, *The Native Tribes of Central Australia*, 1899, p. 530, quoted by Lévy-Brühl, p. 39). Again, 'When any black, whether old or young, dies, an enemy is supposed, during the night, to have made an incision in his side and removed his kidney fat. Even the most intelligent natives cannot be convinced that any death proceeds from natural causes' (Hugh Jamieson, *Letters from Victorian Pioneers*, p. 247, quoted by Lévy-Brühl, p. 38). And, 'If a man is killed in battle, or dies in consequence of a wound, he is supposed to have been "charmed" ' (A. Meyer, *The Native Races of South Australia*, 1879, p. 199, quoted by Lévy-Brühl, p. 40).
9. *Primitive Mentality*, p. 40.
10. Louis I. Dublin, *Factbook on Man – From Birth to Death*, p. 394.
11. As in the babylonian Gilgamesh Epic (about 2000 BC), in which it is said that 'when the gods created mankind, they allotted death to mankind, [but] life they retained in their keeping' (Alexander Heidel, *The Gilgamesh Epic and Old Testament Parallels*, p. 138). See also Jacques Choron, *Death and Western Thought*, p. 14.
12. As among the Nama Hottentots: cf. G. Murdock, *Our Primitive Contemporaries*, p. 501.
13. Genesis 2: 17; 3: 19. Also, E. E. Evans-Pritchard, *Nuer Religion*, pp. 20–1.
14. See below, p. 63.
15. *And the Life Everlasting*, p. 64.

16. J. G. Frazer, *The Belief in Immortality and the Worship of the Dead*, vol. I, p. 468.

17. Erwin Rohde, *Psyche: The Cult of Souls and Belief in Immortality among the Greeks*, p. 6. There are later corrections to Rohde's interpretation of the homeric *psyche* in Werner Jaeger's *The Theology of the Early Greek Philosophers*, ch. 5; but these do not affect the present discussion.

18. *Iliad*, 23, 103.

19. *Psyche*, p. 9.

20. *Odyssey*, book XI, 488–91. Cf. the Yoruba saying, 'A corner in this world is better than a corner in the world of spirits', quoted by Tylor, *Primitive Culture*, vol. II, p. 80.

21. Job 10: 20–2.

22. ibid., 7: 9. The ancient Sumerians, Babylonians and Assyrians likewise thought of death as descent into a dark under-realm from which there is no return (Helmer Ringgren, *Religions of the Ancient Near East*, pp. 46–8, 121–3).

23. Psalm 115: 17–18.

24. Psalm 88: 3–5, 10–12. On the idea of sheol and its development, see for example, Helmer Ringgren, *Israelite Religion*, ch. 2, sect. 11.

25. 'Heaven', in *The Poetical Works of Rupert Brooke*.

26. E. O. James, *The Beginnings of Religion*, p. 129.

27. *Psyche*, p. 55.

28. Emile Durkheim, *The Elementary Forms of the Religious Life*, p. 267.

29. Tylor, *Primitive Culture*, vol. II, pp. 85–6, 68. In much later history, it is true, our common mortality may well have served as a democratizing thought. John S. Dunne, in his interesting study of the relation between mythologies of death and the stages of human society, has pointed out that 'death had begun to appear as the nemesis of the hierarchical organization of mankind already in the fifteenth century [AD] with the dance of death, the double tombs, and suchlike images of death as the great equalizer, the irresistible force which knows no distinctions of rank' (*The City of the Gods: A Study in Myth and Mortality*, p. 192; cf. pp. 172–3). Indeed, during the two or three previous centuries the parable of Dives and Lazarus had figured in popular preaching as a sign of the coming reversal of the positions of rich and poor. For example, the fourteenth-century *Summa Predecantium* of John Bromyard speaks with relish of the future agonies of the rich and powerful: 'In place of scented baths, their body shall have a narrow pit in the earth, and there they shall have a bath more foul than any bath of pitch and sulphur. In place of a soft couch, they shall have a bed more grievious and hard than all the nails and spikes in the world . . . instead of laughter, weeping; instead of gluttony and drunkenness, hunger and thirst without end; instead of gaming with dice and the like, grief; and in place of the torment which for a time

they inflicted on others, they shall have eternal torment.' This and other examples are quoted by Boase, *Death in the Middle Ages*, pp. 44–5, who adds that 'this could be dangerous, revolutionary stuff, and it is not surprising that itinerant preachers were often associated with peasant risings; but more generally it may have had an opiate effect, redeeming present misery by hopes of future bliss'.

30. E. O. James, *The Beginnings of Religion*, p. 129.

31. E. O. James in Bleeker and Widengren, op. cit., p. 36.

32. *The Belief in Immortality*, vol. I, p. 27. Cf. pp. 139–40.

33. Sigmund Freud, *Collected Papers*, vol. IV, pp. 305, 313; Lloyd C. Elam, 'A Psychiatric Perspective on Death', in *Perspectives on Death*, ed. Liston O. Mills, p. 198; Elisabeth Kübler-Ross, *On Death and Dying*, pp. 2, 37.

34. *Odyssey*, book IV, ll. 560f. For an account of the widespread notion of the islands of the blessed, see Tylor, *Primitive Culture*, vol. II, pp. 61f.

35. Genesis 5: 24.

36. 2 Kings 2: 11.

37. Emile Durkheim, *The Elementary Forms of the Religious Life*, p. 248.

38. F. M. Cornford, *From Religion to Philosophy*, p. 109.

39. ibid., pp. 108–9.

40. J. N. Schofield, *The Religious Background of the Bible*, pp. 267–8.

41. 2 Samuel 21: 9.

42. H. Wheeler Robinson, *The Religious Ideas of the Old Testament*, p. 88.

43. ibid., p. 91, quoting Job 5: 25.

44. Karl Jaspers, *The Origin and Goal of History*, ch. 1.

45. S. G. F. Brandon, *The Judgment of the Dead*, p. 9.

46. Quoted ibid., p. 15.

47. ibid.

48. Quoted ibid., p. 20.

49. *The Book of the Dead*, p. 26.

50. ibid., pp. 23–4.

51. Rig-Veda, I, 154, 5 (S. Radhakrishnan and C. A. Moore, *A Sourcebook in Indian Philosophy*, p. 33).

52. ibid., X, 14, 8 (J. B. Alphonso-Karkala, *An Anthology of Indian Literature*, p. 32).

53. ibid., IX, 113, 7–11 (Radhakrishnan and Moore, p. 34).

54. A. A. Macdonell, 'Immortality in Indian Thought', in *Immortality*, ed. James Marchant, pp. 44–5. Cf. Louis Renou, *Religions of Ancient India*, p. 28.

55. A. A. Macdonell, op. cit., pp. 43–4. Cf. H. W. Wallis, *The Cosmology of the Rigveda*, p. 66.

56. Jeremiah 31: 30.

57. Ezekiel 18: 4.

58. W. O. E. Oesterley, *Immortality and the Unseen World: A Study in Old Testament Religion*, p. 206.

59. 'Hebrew Psychology', in *The People and the Book*, ed. A. S. Peake, p. 362.

60. Daniel 12: 2. This is 'our earliest dateable intertestamental reference to a resurrection from the dead' (George W. E. Nickelsburg, Jr, *Resurrection, Immortality and Eternal Life in Intertestamental Judaism*, p. 11).

61. D. S. Russell, *The Method and Message of Jewish Apocalyptic*, p. 369.

62. Quoted by Rohde, *Psyche*, p. 219.

63. ibid., p. 223.

64. Werner Jaeger, 'The Greek Ideas of Immortality', in *Immortality and Resurrection*, ed. Krister Stendahl, p. 103.

65. A. S. Pringle-Pattison, *The Idea of Immortality*, p. 23.

66. In the orphic myth of the fall, Dionysus in the form of a bull was killed by the Titans and his body torn to pieces and eaten. Zeus then destroyed the Titans with a thunderbolt and the human race emerged from their ashes. Thus each man contains both a divine element, the soul, and a titanic element, the body.

67. *Apology*, 30A.

68. *Phaedo*, 107C (*The Last Days of Socrates*, p. 170).

Part II

THE
CONTEMPORARY
SITUATION

CHAPTER 4

The Changing Sociology of Death

I. CHANGING ATTITUDES TO DEATH

It has frequently been remarked that whereas death was openly talked about in western countries a century ago, but sex was taboo, the roles are now reversed. In the permissive society of today sex is a topic of unrestricted conversation but death has for some time been almost unmentionable in polite society. There are signs that we may now be near the end of this period of taboo; but if so the change is not yet sufficiently advanced to be adequately described and analysed. It is however possible to trace the previous change from the situation in which death was a ready topic of discourse to one in which it has become the great embarrassment. It is not of course possible to put a precise date upon such a transition. But we can say broadly that the experience of death in western societies in the twentieth century stands in contrast to that of the nineteenth and earlier centuries.

At first sight this may seem a paradoxical statement. For the basic circumstance, namely the death rate (in the crude sense of the proportion of each generation who die), has remained constant throughout human history at one hundred per cent! Nevertheless despite this fact our normal awareness of death is significantly different from the normal awareness of it a century ago and earlier. This difference is a result of social changes stemming from the immense scientific and technological advances of the last hundred years. Asepsis and immunization, a vast range of new or greatly improved diagnostic, therapeutic and surgical techniques, better medicines, hospitals, sanitation and diet have between them considerably lengthened the human life-span in developed societies. It has been estimated that prehistoric man lived on average only about 18 years.[1] In ancient Greece the average span may have been about 20 years, and perhaps 22 years in ancient Rome.[2] In England during the Middle Ages it is estimated at about 33, and in eighteenth-century Europe at about 36. In 1841 the average expectation of life in Britain for a man was 40 and for a woman 42; today it is between 69 and 70 for men and 75 for women – an increase of nearly three-quarters. And in the 'developed' world as a whole the average span of life seems, after a period of rapid rise, to have reached a plateau at or a little above the biblical norm of three score years and ten.

These figures reveal a considerable change in the temporal shape of human life as compared with a century ago and earlier, carrying with it a significant postponement of the intrusion of the inevitable personal awareness of death. It is another aspect of the same change that today it is happily very rare for children to die, whereas a hundred and more years ago it was quite common for a third or more of a family of children to die at birth or in childhood. This was the age of large families of ten or twelve or fifteen children, of whom five or six or more might well perish before reaching adolescence. Indeed in 1870 (in this respect a typical nineteenth-century year) the number of people who died in Britain before reaching the age of 20 was equal to approximately 32% of all the children born in the country in that year. (In 1970 the equivalent figure was approximately 3.6%.[3]) One consequence of this was that children were familiar with death, the deaths of their own young brothers and sisters. And it is of course the death of our contemporaries that most powerfully brings home to us the fact of our own mortality. This must normally have happened to children in victorian England, whereas today it is often only in late middle age that one's contemporaries start to die. Thus our experience of death tends to occur much later in life, and indeed much later in a much longer life, than it did for our great-grandparents and their forebears.

The dramatic modern decrease in infant mortality must have produced a different attitude to the deaths of children. In the days when this was so common that when a baby was born it had only a two-thirds likelihood of attaining to adult life, this fact must have affected the ways in which parents felt about the loss of a child. We naturally grieve much more for a death that is unexpected than for one that is to be anticipated in the ordinary course of nature. And there seems in the past to have been a somewhat philosophic attitude to the deaths of children. Thus Rousseau could write, 'Although we know approximately the limits of human life and our chance of attaining those limits, nothing is more uncertain than the length of the life of any of us. Very few reach old age. The chief risks occur at the beginning of life; the shorter our past life, the less we must hope to live. Of all the children who are born scarcely one half reach adolescence, and it is very likely your pupil will not live to be a man.'[4] Indeed, Philippe Ariès, in his historical study of childhood, argues that our modern concept of childhood had not developed in medieval Europe because of the very high infant mortality rate.[5] Infants were too likely to die to be individually important; and by the time a child had survived the period of total dependence upon his mother or nurse he was accounted an adult. Accordingly the early portraits show children as small adults. Reflecting this era when the child's hold upon life was so very insecure, Montaigne in the sixteenth century could write, 'I have lost two or three children in their infancy, not without regret, but without great sorrow.'[6] Today if one loses a child in infancy the experience is likely to be far more traumatic and harrowing; and this presumably because the deaths of infants are now so relatively rare.

Indeed, in the simpler and less fragmented societies in which most people have lived in the past death seems to have been accepted with relatively little fuss. As recently as a quarter of a century ago in a Northumberland village, where I served as a presbyterian minister, there was a more realistic and matter-of-fact attitude to death than is usual among the mutually anonymous masses of a great city. And Solzhenitsyn has one of his characters, in a russian cancer hospital in the 1960s, remember 'how the old folks used to die back home on the Kama – Russians, Tartars, Votyaks or whatever they were. They didn't puff themselves up or fight against it or brag that they weren't going to die – they took death calmly. They didn't shirk squaring things up, they prepared themselves quietly and in good time, deciding who should have the mare, who the foal, who the coat and who the boots. And they departed easily, as if they were just moving into a new house.'[7]

In a stable, closed community the individual felt himself to be a part of a social organism, and death was of social as well as of personal significance. Throughout the Middle Ages and down towards the end of the nineteenth century death was a public event. Pictures of death-bed scenes are invariably crowded, not only with the priest and doctor but also with friends and neighbours and even perhaps passers-by. Instead of dying alone or in the presence of only one or two of those who were closest to him, a man died within the community, supported by the common beliefs and expectations of the group of which he was a part. In the medieval world there was indeed, at any rate among the elite, a ritual of dying, involving the setting in order of one's worldly affairs, forgiving one's enemies, receiving absolution, blessing one's children, and commending oneself to God – and then it would seem that death, accepted and expected, soon quietly came. In the France of Charlemagne, for example, the knight, performing the ceremony of death, would lie on his back with his face to heaven. He would remember his life and his friends; then express pardon towards any who had wronged him and commend the living to God. Finally, turning from this world to the next, he confessed his sins and recommended his soul to God, receiving priestly absolution with the burning of incense and the sprinkling of holy water. As Ariès says, 'death was a ritual organized by the dying person himself, who presided over it and knew its protocol. Should he forget or cheat, it was up to those present, the doctor or the priest, to recall him to a routine which was both Christian and customary.'[8]

2. THE CONTEMPORARY TABOO

All this is very different from death in our own society today. Geoffrey Gorer has described the way in which from being a socially recognized inevitability death has become an embarrassing private trauma in which almost any outside solace, except from intimates, has become an intrusion.[9] One important change affecting our modern experience of death is that death is, in Dr Michael Wilson's words, 'sanitated out of society into institutions'.[10] In 1956 a little over half the deaths in Britain occurred in hospitals, nursing homes and other medical and geriatric institutions;[11] and today the proportion is undoubtedly higher. In the United States the proportion is

higher still: in 1958, 60.9% of all deaths occurred in institutions,[12] and it is estimated that today this proportion has risen
to over two-thirds or even as much as 80%.[13] This means that
people very often die out of sight of their relatives, causing as
little emotional disturbance to the family's course of life as
possible. The household does not feel the presence upstairs of
the dying person; and the members of the family do not have
the pain or the satisfaction of ministering to him or her. In
contrast to this, nineteenth-century novels contain numerous
death-bed scenes and in this they must reflect, though no
doubt often in a dramatically heightened form, the actual
experience of families at that time. Indeed, Ariès says that
'until the eighteenth century no portrayal of a deathbed scene
failed to include children'.[14] Not only are there pathetic
descriptions of the deaths of children (as in Dickens' *Old
Curiosity Shop*, Mrs Henry Wood's *East Lynne* or Mrs Craik's
John Halifax, Gentleman) but also, because adults generally
died at an earlier age than today, children are shown as
attending their parents on their death-beds. Today however
the sons and daughters are generally grown up and with
homes and families of their own. This fact contributed to the
need for the hospitalization of terminal patients. Further, today
the dying person who is under medical care, and who is often
in hospital, is probably, towards the end, under heavy
sedation.[15] His approach to death is no longer an experience
in which his family participates with him, or indeed in which
he himself consciously participates. And, in general, death
instead of being perforce everybody's business has been taken
over by specialists – the physician, the funeral director, and
the clergyman.[16] This institutionalization of death, whilst it
brings the resources of medical science to bear in aid of the
dying, must also have the effect of reinforcing our cultural
taboo upon death. An event that takes place under sedation in
the privacy of a curtained hospital bed can the more easily be
kept behind psychological curtains as something that is not
talked about.

This cultural taboo extends even into the hospitals themselves. Glaser and Strauss, discussing their research into
awareness of dying in american hospitals, say, 'The social and
psychological problems involved in terminality are perhaps

most acute when the dying person knows that he is dying. For this reason, among others, American physicians are quite reluctant to disclose impending death to their patients, and nurses are expected not to disclose it without the consent of the responsible physicians.'[17] The same is true in Britain.[18] 'It is a common remark', says Dr Wilson, 'that *death* is a forbidden word in hospital: but in this matter hospitals reflect the attitude of society.'[19] And he cites examples, one of which is taken from a 1970 meeting of medical students:

> A case was described in which a patient was operated on and found to have an inoperable carcinoma. Whereupon her abdomen was sewn up, and later the patient was told (at her husband's request) that she had had her gall bladder removed and would be alright. The patient was not however reassured. Whereupon the ward sister went down the ward and returned with a bottle containing gall stones (not the patient's own) which was shown to the patient with a 'Now are you satisfied?'
>
> The nurse in question is not irresponsible or unusual. She is efficient and cares for her patients. What is it that causes a good person to behave so deviously? I suggest that people who work in hospital, quite apart from their own feelings about death, are at the receiving end of the feelings of a society which asks of its hospitals that death shall be averted and concealed . . .
>
> In the face of death fabrication is common in hospital. It is a difficulty of the chaplain's ministry in hospital that he is expected to be a party to keeping up a fantasy which makes truth-in-relationship impossible.[20]

There is however a form in which we are all today extremely familiar with the phenomenon of death – indeed, familiar almost to the point of boredom – namely on the television screen. Children as well as adults see men being shot and otherwise deprived of life very frequently on films and TV. It was reported from a meeting of the American Academy of Pediatrics in 1971 that by the time a child in the United States is fourteen years old he can be expected to have seen, on average, 18,000 people killed on television![21] This does not however constitute a facing of our mortality, but is on the contrary another defence against it, another device for *not* facing it. For those 18,000 deaths on the screen simply trivialize death and make it unreal to the viewer. They turn the fact of death into part of the magic world of the screen which is unconsciously bracketed as unreal.[22] Of course the TV screen also sometimes shows us real corpses, slain in war or killed in some natural disaster. This makes death visible; and yet only death in exceptional forms, for this is not the end which the ordinary person may expect.

But of course the most extreme refusal, within our contemporary culture, to accept the fact of death occurs in the development of the new technology of cryonics. To quote one of the prophets of cryonic hope, 'We don't have long to wait before we shall know how to freeze the human organism without injuring it. When that happens, we shall have to replace cemeteries by dormitories, so that each of us may have the chance for immortality that the present state of knowledge seems to promise.'[23] Accordingly another cryonics enthusiast can make the truly promethean remark that 'death is an imposition on the human race, and no longer acceptable'.[24] And in 1973 it was reported that there is not only a Cryonics Society of New York, Inc., but also at least five other such societies in the United States and one in France, 'to encourage and promote freezing of the newly-dead rather than burying or incinerating them, in order that these individuals (still regarded as such) may be revived at some time in the future when technological means have been developed'.[25]

3. A NEW AWARENESS OF DEATH

Underlying both the earlier frank acceptance of death and our contemporary taboo upon it, probably the basic continuing human attitude to our mortality is an acceptance which is demanded by death's inevitability and universality. Death comes impartially to everyone; there are no privileged or underprivileged in this matter; we are all in the end in the same boat, together not only with all our contemporaries but also with all our ancestors and all our descendants. It is presumably this that makes possible a general human acceptance of our common mortality. We acknowledge that there is 'a time to be born, and a time to die'.[26] Within this tacit framework it has, I suspect, always been normal for the young, having survived the perils of childhood – as they were until comparatively recently – to think little about death until middle age. The young are thus subjectively immortal, whereas the middle-aged are subjectively mortal; and this is presumably one of the factors constituting the generation gap between them. Even in time of war, when the statistical expectation of life is dramatically reduced, the young soldier habitually assumes that although many others will be killed, he personally will live. But somewhere around the age of forty most people begin to become consciously mortal; and according to C. G. Jung it is important that they should then come to terms with their mortality. 'From the middle of life onward', he says, 'only he remains vitally alive who is ready to *die with life*. For in the secret hour of life's midday the parabola is reversed, death is born. The second half of life does not signify ascent, unfolding, increase, exuberance, but death, since the end is its goal. The negation of life's fulfilment is synonymous with the refusal to accept its ending. Both mean not wanting to live, and not wanting to live is identical with not wanting to die. Waxing and waning make one curve.'[27]

Has the arrival of the nuclear age, heralded by the two atomic bombs exploded upon the cities of Hiroshima and Nagasaki in August 1945, affected our consciousness of death? Has it undermined the subjective immortality of those who have been born under the sign of the nuclear mushroom? The possibility of a massive thermonuclear exchange in which hundreds of millions would be killed has perhaps more recently been overlaid in the minds of many young people by the prospect of the suicide of our civilization within their own lifetime by a deadly combination of population explosion, mounting environmental pollution, and the rapid depletion of our basic resources. Do those growing up in such a world discount the future and see death closing in upon the human race, voiding long-term hopes and plans? Despite these more recent anxieties, the *Psychology Today* 1971 survey of attitudes to death concluded, 'The largest single factor relating to death in the 1970s may well be the threat of atomic bombs, and in a chain reaction, it might be that this heightened concern with atomic deaths accounts in part for our outwardly disdainful attitude toward life itself: excessive risk-taking, burning-out with drugs, daring authority, flaunting tradition, and the many other destructive and self-destructive behaviors toward ourselves and toward our institutions and traditions. One young college woman wrote: "I can't say that I think this or do such and such because we all may die tomorrow, but I'm convinced that in all our minds there's an underlying nagging fear that the world could blow up, a fear which today is more silent than in the bomb-shelter era of a few years ago but perhaps even more strongly felt and exhibited in minute, imperceptible ways." '[28]

Hans Morgenthau, in an interesting essay on 'Death in the Nuclear Age',[29] points out how radically the possibility of nuclear war threatens the secular conception of immortality as an immortality in this world through our own contribution to its continuing life: 'The man endowed with a creative mind knows himself to be a member in an unbroken chain emerging from the past and reaching into the future, which is made of the same stuff his mind is made of and, hence, is capable of participating in, and perpetuating, his mind's creation. He may be mortal, but humanity is not, and so he will be immortal in his works.'[30] But it is precisely this hope of immortality within the human future that is undermined by the possibility of a massive thermonuclear exchange:

> Man gives his life and death meaning by his ability to make himself and his works remembered after his death. Patroclus dies to be avenged by Achilles. Hector dies to be mourned by Priam. Yet if Patroclus, Hector, and all those who could remember them were killed simultaneously, what would become of the meaning of Patroclus's and Hector's death? Their lives and deaths would lose their meaning. They would die, not like men but like beasts, killed in the mass . . . Of their deeds, nothing would remain but the faint hope of remembrance in distant places. The very concept of fame would disappear, and the historians, the professional immortalizers, would have nothing to report. What has been preserved and created through the mind, will, and hands of man would be dissolved like man himself. Civilization itself would perish. Perhaps in some faraway place some evidence would be preserved of the perished civilization and of the

men who created it. Nothing more than that would be left of the immortality man had once been able to achieve through the persistence of his fame and the permanence of his works.[31]

Morgenthau believes that the significance of the nuclear age has, fortunately, not yet sunk into the human consciousness. But 'a secular age, which has lost faith in individual immortality in another world and is aware of the impending doom of the world through which it tries to perpetuate itself here and now, is left without a remedy. Once it has become aware of its condition, it must despair. It is the saving grace of our age that it has not yet become aware of its condition.'[32]

There are however signs that the twentieth-century cultural taboo upon death may be coming to an end. I began this chapter with the commonplace that death has replaced sex as the great unmentionable. It is a commonplace because we are increasingly conscious of the taboo; and this in turn suggests that its power is waning. For when such an inhibition ceases to hold unnoticed sway, but is the subject of critical and satirical comment (as in Nancy Mitford's *The American Way of Death* (1963) or, earlier, Evelyn Waugh's *The Loved One* (1948)), its days are probably numbered. Again, the 1971 *Psychology Today* survey reported that 'readers of *Psychology Today* apparently feel that [death] is more important than sex; the single biggest surprise in the results of the *P.T.* death questionnaire was the sheer volume of response. More than 30,000 readers returned the research questionnaires, and more than 2,000 of them sent substantial letters with their replies. This broke the record set by the *P.T.* sex questionnaire, which fetched somewhat over 20,000 replies. It was almost as though thousands of persons had been waiting for a legitimate occasion to unburden themselves about death and then felt somehow cleansed after writing their unspoken thoughts. Several letters said as much, indicating how grateful the respondents were and how meaningful the exercise had been to them.'[33]

Further, there has recently been an increase in the number of philosophical and theological books being published on death, some of which will be discussed in later chapters. Again, there is the explosion of publication on the psychology of dying, particularly in the United States, on which I commented in the preface. And it is certainly the case that medico-ethical problems relating to death are increasingly receiving attention: Is it the physician's duty to keep a terminal patient alive as long as possible and at all costs; or to enable him to die with dignity before reaching the last extremities of pain, debilitation, helplessness and the undermining of personality? Should a dying patient be told that he is dying? May a dead patient's organs be transplanted into the living? To what extent should medical and nursing resources be devoted to the care of the dying instead of to the cure of the curable? And related and overlapping issues in the legal realm concern abortion, euthanasia, suicide and capital punishment. All this suggests, although it does not prove, that a change is taking place in the focusing of public attention and that the cultural taboo upon death may be in process of being discarded.

As a possible explanation of such a change the hypothesis has been floated that a preoccupation with death appears in literature and the arts whenever men are conscious of living at the end of an era. Thus the renaissance writers were largely concerned with mortality. In Europe, north of the Alps, the fourteenth, fifteenth and sixteenth centuries saw a 'cult of the charnel house',[34] when many tombs of the great consisted of two tiers, with an effigy on the top of the prince or bishop in his finery, and beneath it another effigy of his skeleton or decaying corpse; and it was this same period that marked the end of the Middle Ages and the birth of the modern world.[35] (On the other hand, as a quite independent factor, the fourteenth century had experienced in the Black Death a terrible reminder of man's mortality.) Again, in the last decades of the nineteenth century a *fin de siècle* spirit was abroad, accompanied by a great interest in death expressed both in the arts and in the rise of the spiritualist movement. To the art historian Carla Gottlieb 'this poses the question as to whether the coincidence between the preoccupation with death and the end of an era is accidental'.[36] If it is not accidental – and I do not feel entitled to go beyond this 'if' – it will not be difficult to correlate a renewed interest today in our mortality with the 'underlying nagging fear that the world could blow up' referred to above in connection with the possibility of thermonuclear warfare.

Hans Morgenthau, in his discussion already quoted of the impact of nuclear power on our attitudes to death, speaks of ours as 'a secular age, which has lost faith in individual immortality in another world'. He is here endorsing the accepted self-image of urban, industrialized western man, a self-image the validity of which has been confirmed by various surveys. In Britain a BBC report of 1955 indicated that about 43% of its public (which is virtually coterminous with the population as a whole) professes to believe in a life after death. This nation-wide state of mind on the subject has undoubtedly affected opinion within the Churches, drawing it down towards this half-hearted (or to be more precise 43%-hearted) level. For example, the Mass Observation document *Puzzled People*, published in 1947, reported that 'two out of five of those who say they believe in God are by no means sure that there is any life after death, half of these being fairly convinced that there isn't'.[37] And the Gallup Poll's *Television and Religion* survey, published in 1964, reported that some 74% of Roman Catholics in this country believe in an after-life, some 56% of Freechurchmen, and some 49% of Anglicans. These figures are for the official or nominal memberships. The figures for regular church-attenders are higher and are grouped closer together, namely Roman Catholics 88%, Freechurchmen 86%, and Anglicans 85%.[38] That there are 12–15% of regular committed worshippers who say that they do not believe in a life after death indicates a fairly marked move away from traditional christian teaching on this matter, a movement which is no doubt also expressed in quite large variations of strength of conviction within the still-believing majority.

This considerable decline within society as a whole, accompanied by a lesser decline within the churches, of the belief in personal immortality clearly reflects the assumption within our culture that we should only believe in what we experience, plus what the accredited sciences certify to us. The after-life falls outside this sphere and is accordingly dismissed as a fantasy of wishful thinking. In face of this contemporary cultural rejection, christian theology since the second world war presents a spectrum of disarray. The more strongly traditional theologians have simply reaffirmed the biblical images of resurrection, judgement, heaven and hell. More moderately traditional theologians have reaffirmed the general conception of an after-life, but have importantly modified it by abandoning the idea of hell in favour of a belief in universal salvation. However, neither group has made any serious attempt to 'spell out' the content of its eschatology in face of the challenge of contemporary secular thought. This part of the christian tradition has not revealed, in the work of recent theologians, any hitherto untapped resources for developing a coherent and credible picture of man's wider situation as a creature made by God for eternal life. But if the conservative and liberal theologians have helped to confirm the contemporary secular mind in its rejection of Christianity, through their inability to do more than parade the mythology of former ages before the modern world, radical theologians have also contributed to the same result in opposite ways. They have been so embarrassed by the traditional christian hope that they have tried either to suppress the eschatological element within Christianity altogether or else to present it without the scandalous affirmation of personal life after death. Thus we have become familiar with passages such as this: 'It is still possible to produce massive rationalizations in an effort to devise a world-picture with room for either the immortality of the soul or the resurrection of the body, but such efforts always remain only rationalizations or endeavours to accommodate the picture of the past to the present. Christians should not try to force themselves to conceive what is inconceivable in their world.'[39] Or again: 'Men of other ages and cultures, subscribing to different psychologies, could develop doctrines of the "immortality of the soul" according to which man's true essence is divine and survives . death; to modern psychology and medicine, man appears as a psychosomatic unity whose spiritual life is inseparably bound to its physical base. The end of the body, therefore, is the end of man, except to the degree his ideas and attitudes and actions continue to affect the communities and cultures within which he has lived and worked.'[40] We shall meet further examples in chapter 11.

NOTES

1. Louis I. Dublin, *Factbook on Man*, p. 394.
2. Monroe Lerner, 'When, Why, and Where People Die', in *The Dying Patient*, ed. Orville G. Brim, Jr, Howard E. Freeman, Sol Levine and Norman A. Scotch, p. 8.
3. *Annual Abstract of Statistics*, no. 108, 1971, tables 22, 29.
4. Jean Jacques Rousseau, *Emile*, p. 42.
5. Philippe Ariès, *Centuries of Childhood*, ch. 2.
6. Quoted by Ariès, p. 39.
7. Alexander Solzhenitsyn, *Cancer Ward*, pp. 110–11. Compare with this Tolstoy's earlier picture, in *The Death of Ivan Ilych* (1886), of the approach to death of an upper-middle-class city lawyer.
8. Philippe Ariès, *Western Attitudes toward Death*, pp. 11–12.
9. Geoffrey Gorer, *Death, Grief, and Mourning*. See also Philippe Ariès, *Western Attitudes toward Death*, ch. 4.
10. Michael Wilson, *The Hospital – A Place of Truth: A Study of the Role of the Hospital Chaplain*, p. 116. See also Johann Hofmeier, 'The Present-Day Experience of Death', in *Concilium*, vol. 4, no. 10 (April 1974).
11. *Peace at the Last: A Survey of Terminal Care in the United Kingdom*, p. 15.
12. Monroe Lerner, 'When, Why, and Where People Die', in *The Dying Patient*, p. 21.
13. ibid., p. 7; and Bayliss Manning, 'Legal and Policy Issues in the Allocation of Death', in *The Dying Patient*, p. 255.
14. Philippe Ariès, *Western Attitudes toward Death*, p. 12. It has been argued that the death-bed scenes in victorian novels were often used by their authors to combat the rising religious doubt of the time. Thus Walter E. Houghton says, 'The death scenes which fill the Victorian novels are clearly connected with the religious crisis. They are intended to help the reader sustain his faith by dissolving religious doubt in a solution of warm sentiment. When the heart is so strongly moved, the skeptical intellect is silenced; and when feelings of profound love and pity are centered on a beautiful soul who is gone forever, the least religious affirmation, the slightest reference to heaven or angels, or to reunion with those who have gone before (and no decent death-bed in any novel was without them) was sufficient to invoke a powerful sense of reassurance' (*The Victorian Frame of Mind, 1830–1870*, p. 277). Houghton also draws attention to the way in which in his last moments the dying character often sees his loved ones who are waiting for him or hears the sound of heavenly music – for example in George Eliot's *Scenes of Clerical Life*, 'The Sad Fortunes of the Rev.

Amos Barton', ch. 8; and Charlotte Yonge's *The Daisy Chain*, part II, ch. 25.

15. Dr John Hinton reports a survey conclusion that 'in hospital, a third of the patients knew nothing of their last day of existence and only 6 per cent were conscious shortly before they died' (*Dying*, p. 77).

16. On these specialist roles, see Kastenbaum and Aisenberg, *The Psychology of Death*, pp. 208f.

17. Barney G. Glaser and Anselm L. Strauss, *Awareness of Dying*, p. 5.

18. Cartwright and Anderson report from their survey that 'only one in 20 of the people who died (excluding those dying unexpectedly) were said to have been told they were going to die by a doctor. Almost a third were thought to have realised this without being told so by anyone. Just over two fifths of the relatives felt the person did not know and the remaining fifth were uncertain. Relatives were more likely to feel it was better when the person did not know than when he did. Doctors appeared to share this view. The main way they coped with dying patients was by not telling them they were dying. This was not because they felt this should be someone else's responsibility. On the contrary, most of the doctors we asked thought that if a person *was* to be told he was dying, his GP should be the one to do this' (Ann Cartwright and John L. Anderson, 'Help for the Dying', in *New Society*, 21 June 1973, p. 680). See also Geoffrey Gorer, *Death, Grief, and Mourning in Contemporary Britain*, p. 17.

19. *The Hospital – A Place of Truth*, p. 116.

20. ibid., p. 117. Cf. Kastenbaum and Aisenberg, *The Psychology of Death*, pp. 206–7.

21. *The Times*, 19 October 1971.

22. Cf. Robert E. Kavanaugh, *Facing Death*, p. 13.

23. Jean Rostand, quoted by Alan Harrington, *The Immortalist: An Approach to the Engineering of Man's Divinity*, p. 214.

24. Harrington, op. cit., p. 11.

25. ibid., p. 215.

26. Ecclesiastes 3: 2.

27. C. G. Jung, 'The Soul and Death', in *Collected Works*, vol. 8, p. 407.

28. *Psychology Today*, June 1971, p. 80. The report is reprinted as an appendix to Shneidman's *Deaths of Man*.

29. In *The Modern Vision of Death*, ed. Nathan A. Scott, Jr. See also Gil Elliot, *Twentieth-Century Book of the Dead*.

30. ibid., p. 73.

31. ibid., pp. 75–6. Cf. Robert Jay Lifton and Eric Olson, *Living and Dying*, ch. 5.

32. ibid., p. 76.

33. *Psychology Today*, June 1971, p. 48.

34. T. S. R. Boase, *Death in the Middle Ages*, p. 102. This book is an

illustrated study of the themes of death, judgement and remembrance in art during the flowering of the Middle Ages. On the limitation to Europe north of the Alps, in distinction from renaissance Italy, of this morbid fascination with the physical aspects of death, see pp. 106–9. See also J. Huizinga, *The Waning of the Middle Ages*, ch. 11.

35. For an alternative analysis of the tremendous interest in death in northern Europe from the mid-fourteenth centuty to the mid-sixteenth, see Theodore Spencer, *Death and Elizabethan Tragedy*, chs. 1, 2.

36. Carla Gottlieb, 'Modern Art and Death', in *The Meaning of Death*, ed. Herman Feifel, p. 158.

37. *Puzzled People*, p. 27.

38. *Television and Religion*, pp. 50–1.

39. Milton C. McGatch, *Death: Meaning and Mortality in Christian Thought and Contemporary Culture*, p. 184.

40. Gordon D. Kaufman, *Systematic Theology: A Historicist Perspective*, p. 464.

CHAPTER 5

Death in Contemporary Philosophy

I. MARTIN HEIDEGGER

Although there has been embarrassed silence about death in our popular culture, and equally embarrassed speech from many of the theologians, some of the secular philosophers have treated the subject with intense seriousness. Apart from the neo-wittgensteinian development to be discussed later in this chapter, british-american linguistic philosophy has indeed had little to say about our mortality; but on the other hand death has been a central theme of the leading continental existentialists. So far from disregarding it, they have seen man's conscious or suppressed awareness of death as a central feature of our human situation. For *Homo sapiens* alone among the animals knows that he is going to die and lives in awareness of that final horizon; and the existentialists have explored the implications of this for man's self-understanding and for his attitude to life. Martin Heidegger and Jean-Paul Sartre in particular have done this in interestingly different ways.

Heidegger uses a highly abstract terminology, and if we are to take account of his thought we have to follow him into his own rarified world of metaphysical abstractions. Man, he says, is radically distinct from everything non-human; and he expresses this distinction by saying that whilst other things *are*, only men *exist*. 'The being that exists is man. Man alone exists. Rocks are, but they do not exist. Trees are, but they do not exist. Horses are, but they do not exist.'[1] And angels and God, if they are, do not exist. Man's way of existing, his existential character, is Dasein, 'being-there', i.e. being-there in and in inescapable relationship with the world. Existence is potentiality-for-Being, and hence a Dasein, a human being, is essentially temporal. Further, as potentiality, Dasein is inherently incomplete. For 'if existence is definitive for Dasein's Being and if its essence is constituted in part by potentiality-for-Being, then, as long as Dasein exists, it must in each case, as such a potentiality, *not yet be* something'.[2] Hence 'it is essential to the basic constitution of Dasein that there is *constantly something still to be settled*'.[3] Further, Dasein's inherent incompleteness moves, not towards completeness, but towards death. 'The "end" of Being-in-the-world is death. This end, which belongs to the potentiality-for-Being – that is to say, to existence – limits and determines in every case whatever totality is possible for Dasein.'[4] To be alive is to be incomplete, and for my life to have been completed would be for me to be dead. 'As long as Dasein *is* as an entity, it has never reached its "wholeness". But if it gains such "wholeness", this gain becomes the utter loss of Being-in-the-world.'[5] Hence Dasein's possibility of Being-a-whole must at the same time be a Being-towards-death. Meaning is to be found within human life not by ignoring our mortality but by taking the inevitability of death fully and frankly into account. Further, we must not assume that death necessarily means fulfilment: 'So little is it the case that Dasein comes to its ripeness only with death, that Dasein may well have passed its ripeness before the end. For the most part, Dasein ends in unfulfilment, or else by having disintegrated and been used up.'[6]

In seeking an existentialist analysis of death, Heidegger continues, we must avoid the mistake of focusing attention upon the deaths of others. For death as anticipated and met for oneself is a different phenomenon from the death of another, however closely or sympathetically observed. '*No one can take the Other's dying away from him.* Of course someone can "go to his death for another" . . . Such "dying for" can never signify that the Other has thus had his death taken away in even the slightest degree. Dying is something that every Dasein itself must take upon itself at the time. By its very essence, death is in every case mine, in so far as it "is" at all.'[7]

Because death lies before us all, our existence is a movement towards it. Dasein is thus a 'Being-towards-the-end'.[8] In one of Heidegger's most famous phrases, it is *Sein-zum-Tode*, Being-towards-death.[9] As Being-towards-death Dasein exists in face of 'the possibility of the absolute impossibility of Dasein'.[10] Further, that our possibility of being is thus bracketed by an impossibility of being is not a situation chosen by us but one into which we are 'thrown' and which creates within us a fundamental anxiety which 'amounts to the disclosedness of the fact that Dasein exists as thrown Being *towards* its end'.[11] For '*the state-of-mind which can hold open the utter and constant threat to itself arising from Dasein's ownmost individualized Being, is anxiety.* In this state-of-mind, Dasein finds itself *face to face* with the "nothing" of the possible impossibility of its existence . . . Being-towards-death is essentially anxiety.'[12]

Heidegger has much that is perceptive to say concerning the false ways in which we try to cope with this anxiety about the end which is drawing ever closer. For example, 'This evasive concealment in the face of death dominates everydayness so stubbornly that, in Being with one another, the "neighbours" often still keep talking the "dying person" into the belief that he will escape death and soon return to the tranquillized everydayness of the world of his concern. Such "solicitude" is meant to "console" him . . . At bottom, however, this is a tranquillization not only for him who is "dying" but just as much for those who "console" him . . . Indeed the dying of Others is seen often enough as a social inconvenience, if not even a downright tactlessness, against which the public is to be guarded.'[13] All this 'everyday falling evasion *in the face of* death is an *inauthentic* Being-*towards*-death'.[14] There can however be an authentic way of Being-towards-death: by deliberately accepting death a Dasein can exist authentically in face of it.

Heidegger has defined death, in his own terminology, as follows: '*Death, as the end of Dasein, is Dasein's ownmost possibility – non-relational, certain and as such indefinite, not to be outstripped.*'[15] As Dasein's 'ownmost possibility' death is that in face of which the person is most fully and distinctively himself. Each person dies for himself and by himself. Thus 'the non-relational character of death, as understood in anticipation, individualizes Dasein down to itself . . . The entity which anticipates its non-relational possibility, is thus forced by that very anticipation into the possibility of taking over from itself its ownmost Being, and doing so of its own accord.'[16] Thus it is the fact that we die, or rather the fact that we know that we are going to die, that makes us unique personal individuals. In the fact of death we are able to experience our own individuality. Hence, mortality is of the essence of distinctively human existence.

Death, as Dasein's 'ownmost possibility', is also 'not to be outstripped'. *Überholen* means to overhaul, overtake, outstrip; but presumably in this context the basic sense is that death cannot be escaped or evaded but has to be accepted as inevitable. Heidegger appears to be making the same or a very closely related point when he emphasizes that death is certain but indefinite as regards the time when it will come. But in accepting death as inescapable one can become free in relation to it. 'Anticipation discloses to existence that its uttermost possibility lies in giving itself up, and thus it shatters all one's tenaciousness to whatever existence one has reached.'[17] The anticipation of death reveals to Dasein the possibility of being authentically itself in 'an *impassioned freedom towards death*'[18] in which anxiety remains but is used for the achieving of authenticity. Thus 'the possibility of Dasein's having an authentic potentiality-for-Being-a-whole emerges'.[19] If we fully confront, accept and affirm our own mortality we thereby conquer it, so that it can no longer lead us into inauthentic existence. There is something here of Nietzsche's conception of 'free death': 'My death I commend to you, the free death which comes to me because I *will*.'[20]

It is I think possible to see that behind Heidegger's existentialist categories of thought and his tortuous abstract terminology there is a straightforward, and within its limits a penetrating and convincing, psychological understanding of the (or at any rate of a) human attitude to death. This understanding is that death constitutes a fundamental threat to us, engendering anxiety at the realization of our own finitude, surrounded as we are by limitless nothingness; but that if we can deliberately confront and accept our own coming death we shall preserve our personal integrity in face of it. Sartre has well summarized Heidegger's teaching: 'It is by projecting itself freely towards its final possibility that the *Dasein* will attain authentic existence and wrench itself away from everyday banality in order to attain the irreplaceable uniqueness of the person.'[21]

It is, incidentally, to be noted that Heidegger presents this psychological analysis independently of the question whether men in fact have a further existence beyond the frontier of death. As he says, 'If "death" is defined as the "end" of Dasein – that is to say, of Being-in-the-world – this does not imply any ontical decision whether "after death" still another Being is possible, either higher or lower, or whether Dasein "lives on" or even "outlasts" itself and is "immortal".'[22]

2. JEAN-PAUL SARTRE

Jean-Paul Sartre shares with Heidegger his repudiation of the modern cultural concealment of death and his realistic aware-ness of mortality as a central aspect of distinctively human existence. But Sartre differs from Heidegger – whose *Sein und Zeit* he had studied closely – in also repudiating the optimistic idea that acceptance of one's own coming end makes possible a meaningful form of Being-towards-death. On the contrary, Sartre maintains that death deprives life of the only kind of meaning that it might conceivably have had.

If the length of a human life was known, because all men died at the end of a natural span, then death, in giving a clearly defined shape to life would thereby endow it with coherence and meaning. A death that predictably completes life could give it retrospective significance, like the resolved chord of a piece of music; and the whole of life could be lived meaning-fully within that framework. But in fact death is not the com-pletion of a known span. It may come unexpectedly at any moment. And even when, in the event, it comes at the natural end of a long life, this cannot be known in advance and there-fore cannot be lived towards as something anticipated. 'If only deaths from old age existed (or deaths by explicit condemna-tion), then I could *wait for* my death. But the unique quality of death is the fact that it can always before the end surprise those who wait for it at such and such a date . . . This means that one can *wait for* a death from old age only blindly or in bad faith.'[23]

Sartre expresses in another way what he regards as the destructive character of mortality when he says that the meaning of our present experiences waits upon their further development in our future experiences. For example, speaking of adolescent love, he says, 'The adolescent is perfectly conscious of the mystic sense of his conduct, and at the same time he must entrust himself to all his future in order to determine whether he is in process of "passing through a crisis of puberty" or of engaging himself in earnest in the way of devotion.'[24] And in general the significance of our choices is determined by the larger pattern of our life as this reveals itself over the years. It is of the nature of a being who lives through time that the final context of each moment, determining the meaning of that moment, is his life as a whole; and until that context is revealed each moment has a provisional character, awaiting its meaning:

> Thus it is necessary to consider our life as being made up not only of waitings but of waitings which themselves wait for waitings. There we have the very structure of selfness: to be oneself is to come to oneself. These waitings evidently all include a reference to a final term which would be *waited for* without waiting for anything more. A repose which would be *being* and no longer a waiting for being. The whole series is suspended from this final term which on principle is never *given* and which is the value of our being – that is, evidently, a plenitude of the type 'in-itself-for-itself'. By means of this final term the recovery of our past would be made once and for all. We should know for always whether a particular youthful experience had been fruitful or ill-starred, whether a particular crisis of puberty was a caprice or a real pre-formation of my later engagements; the curve of our life would be fixed forever.[25]

Thus Sartre relates the idea of the meaningfulness of a man's life to a pattern that it can display or a goal that it can attain. For him the question 'Does history have a meaning?' is the question 'Is history completed or *only terminated?*'[26] And the same question applies to an individual life. Only a completed life has achieved a meaning.

> For example, this young man has lived for thirty years in the expectation of becoming a great writer, but this waiting itself is not enough; it becomes a vain and senseless obstinacy or a profound comprehension of his value according to the

books which he writes. His first book has appeared, but by
itself what does it mean? It is the book of a beginner. Let
us admit that it is good; still it gets its meaning through
the future. If it is unique, it is at once inauguration and
testament. He had only one book to write; he is limited and
cut off by his work; he will not be 'a great writer'. If the
novel is one in a mediocre series, it is an 'accident'. If it is
followed by other better books, it can classify its author in
the first rank . . . [27]

And Sartre holds that even if death does not *in fact* intervene
to terminate an incomplete life, the knowledge that it may at
any moment do so blights our lives with final meaninglessness.
For 'if it is only *chance* which decides the character of our death
and therefore of our life, then even the death which most
resembles the end of a melody can not be waited for as such;
luck by determining it for me removes from it any character
as an harmonious end. An end of a melody in order to confer
its meaning on the melody must emanate from the melody
itself. A death like that of Sophocles [*sic*] will therefore
resemble a resolved chord but will not *be* one, just as the group
of letters formed by the falling of alphabet blocks will perhaps
resemble a word but will not be one. Thus this perpetual
appearance of chance at the heart of my projects can not be
apprehended as *my* possibility but, on the contrary, as the
nihilation of all my possibilities, a nihilation which *itself is no
longer a part of my possibilities*.'[28] Death then, for Sartre,
deprives life of meaning by making it a matter of chance
whether or not a pattern ever emerges. Instead of being a
completion which gives retrospective meaning to the whole of
a life, death cuts arbitrarily and unpredictably across the line
of life, denying it any meaning. 'If I am a waiting for waitings
for waiting and if suddenly the object of my final waiting and
the one who awaits it are suppressed, the waiting takes on
retrospectively the character of *absurdity*.'[29] Thus, Sartre
concludes that 'death is never that which gives life its meanings;
it is, on the contrary, that which on principle removes all
meaning from life. If we must die, then our life has no meaning
because its problems receive no solution and because the very
meaning of the problems remains undetermined.'[30]

Sartre's thought on the subject of death provides a helpful beginning to a clarification of the relation between death and the meaning of life. I shall pursue this theme further and on a broader front in chapter 8 and shall argue in disagreement with Sartre but in agreement with many secular humanists that a man's life can, if he is fortunate, achieve a rounded completion and satisfactoriness despite his mortality. But I shall go on to argue that this in fact happens only to the fortunate few, and that life can only have positive meaning for mankind in general if there is further life after bodily death in which a meaning-bestowing end is achieved.

3. D. Z. PHILLIPS

The other contemporary philosophical development, in addition to existentialism, in which attention has been given to the fact of death and the idea of immortality is the neo-wittgensteinian movement. Wittgenstein had written some interesting sentences about death in the 'mystical' final pages of the *Tractatus Logico-Philosophicus* – for example:

> If we take eternity to mean not infinite temporal duration but timelessness, then eternal life belongs to those who live in the present. Our life has no end in just the way in which our visual field has no limits.[31]

This and other sayings of Wittgenstein's provide the starting-point for D. Z. Phillips' recent interpretation of the language of immortality, in its context of the religious 'language-game', in terms of the quality of our present earthly life. Phillips begins by connecting soul-talk with morality. For example if we say of someone, 'He'd sell his soul for money', this remark 'is a moral observation about a person, one which expresses the degraded state that person is in. A man's soul, in this context, refers to his integrity, to the complex set of practices and beliefs which acting with integrity would cover for that person. Might not talk about the immortality of the soul play a similar role?'[32] In short, the idea of immortality belongs to the moral realm; the 'eternal' character of a life – of a mortal, earthly life – is its timeless quality of moral excellence. Accordingly 'it would be foolish to speak of eternal life as some kind of appendage to human existence, something which happens *after* human life on earth is over. Eternal life is the reality of goodness, that in terms of which human life is to be assessed . . . Eternity is not *more* life, but this life seen under certain moral and religious modes of thought.'[33]

This, according to Phillips, is the moral content of the idea of immortality. But he says that it also has a further religious content. 'The religious notions of eternity and immortality I have in mind', he says, 'are closely connected with the idea of overcoming death.'[34] And by this Phillips means that 'in turning away from the temporal to the eternal, the believer is said to attain immortality and to overcome death'.[35] Such turning is a dying to the self, an acceptance of one's contingent finitude and mortality. 'Death's lesson for the believer is to force him to recognise what all his natural instincts want to resist, namely, that he has no claims on the way things go. Most of all, he is forced to realise that his own life is not a necessity.'[36] And he then quotes this striking passage from Simone Weil:

> The principal claim which we think we have on the universe is that our personality should continue. This claim implies all the others. The instinct of self-preservation makes us feel this continuation to be a necessity, and we believe that a necessity is a right. We are like the beggar who said to Talleyrand: 'Sir, I must live', and to whom Talleyrand replied, 'I do not see the necessity for that.' Our personality is entirely dependent on external circumstances which have unlimited power to crush it. But we would rather die than admit this. From our point of view the equilibrium of the world is a combination of circumstances so ordered that our personality remains intact and seems to belong to us. All the circumstances of the past which have wounded our personality appear to us to be disturbances of balance which should infallibly be made up for one day or another by phenomena having a contrary effect. We live on the expectation of these compensations. The near approach of death is horrible chiefly because it forces the knowledge upon us that these compensations will never come.[37]

This, says Phillips, 'is the contrast between the temporal (that is, the concern with the self), and the eternal (that is, the concern with self-renunciation) . . . The soul which is rooted in the mortal is the soul where the ego is dominant in the way which Simone Weil describes in such penetrating detail in her works. The immortality of the soul by contrast refers to a person's relation to the self-effacement and love of others involved in dying to the self. Death is overcome in that dying to the self is the meaning of the believer's life.'[38] Thus, paradoxically, 'true immortality' is to be found in renunciation of the hope of immortality and in acceptance of our mortal finitude. 'I am suggesting then', says Phillips, 'that eternal life for the believer is participation in the life of God, and that this life has to do with dying to the self, seeing that all things are a gift from God, that nothing is ours by right or necessity.'[39]

Such participation in the life of God must occur during our present earthly life since this is the only time in which we do or shall exist. And so Phillips, not unnaturally, supposes someone to raise at this point the objection that 'all this tells us something only about the relation of an individual to God during this present life. It says nothing of the destiny of the soul after death.'[40] In reply to such an objection he invokes the idea of the 'eternal predicates' that can be ascribed to the dead. Predicates apply to people at a time and for a time, since to be alive is to be undergoing change. But the dead do not change. 'The will of the dead cannot be changed; it is fixed and unchanging. Here, the predicates are eternal predicates. When a man dies, what he is, the state of his soul, is fixed forever.'[41] Thus the eternal destiny of the soul after death consists in the fact that the individual's character can no longer alter or be altered: he can only be thought of as unchangeable and in that sense eternal. I shall pass over the very fanciful sense in which, according to Phillips, the living can pray for the dead, and the even more fanciful sense in which the dead can be said to pray for the living,[42] and consider this idea of immortality through the attribution of 'eternal predicates'. Although at first the concept may, by analogy with the eternal truths of logic and mathematics, seem clear it is in fact almost limitlessly vague. For we are not dealing with mathematical or logical but with moral and personal predicates. These attributes of the soul embody value judgements, and must be predicated of someone *by* someone – whether by himself, by other human beings, or by God. Not however, in this case, by himself. For at death he has ceased to exist as a living centre of consciousness and accordingly he is not 'there' at points in time subsequent to his death to make moral judgements about himself. Nor can these judgements be made by God, for God does not, according to Phillips, exist as an independent centre of consciousness additional to all the living human consciousnesses. This is the clear implication of the conception of God expounded in his writings. For example, he says in *Death and Immortality* that 'in learning by contemplation, attention, renunciation, what forgiving, thanking, loving, etc., mean in these contexts, the believer is participating in the reality of God; *this is what we mean by God's reality*'.[43] The existence of God, we could therefore say, is the existence of man's religious life. Accordingly, the activity of attributing moral predicates to those who have died cannot take place in the mind of God. The only people who can make moral – or indeed any other – judgements are the living. Thus the attributing of 'eternal predicates' to the dead has to be done by those who have survived them and who knew them or who know about them. For there is, in Phillips' philosophy, no other possible locus for the activity of attributing value predicates to deceased persons. That the dead are thus at the mercy of the living, in whose memories and interpretations they exist, is a point powerfully made by Jean-Paul Sartre. 'To be dead', he says, 'is to be a prey for the living.'[44] For 'to die is to exist only through the Other, and to owe to him one's meaning . . . '[45] Further, any dead person about whom the living make their judgements was in continuous change throughout his life – as indeed Phillips himself emphasizes – and must have been characterized at different times by many different and, not infrequently, incompatible predicates. People's characters normally develop through the years, and sometimes also undergo changes of direction as a result of the impact of some important experience, whether favourable or adverse. At one time a man may be young, thoughtless and selfish and twenty years later he may be wiser and more socially responsible. At one time someone may be a useless drunkard and at a later time a sober solid citizen. At one time he may be kindly and affectionate, but at a later time, having been betrayed and swindled, he may have become suspicious and grasping. And so on. Are his 'eternal predicates', then, those which characterized him at birth, or at the age of majority, or at some point in middle life, or in old age, or at the moment of death? One is perhaps inclined to select the time of death as the great 'moment of truth' at which a man's character becomes eternally fixed. And this might well be appropriate in terms of the catholic doctrine of the final decision, according to which although the soul has a real existence after death it can no longer undergo further moral and spiritual growth.[46] But we have noted that for Phillips the eternal predicates of the dead can only mean those moral qualities that are attributed to them by the living on the basis of their memories of the deceased. And it is by no means clear that these memories either generally are, or should be, focused upon the hour of death. The friends and relatives of one who has died may well remember him as he was in full vigour, and may attribute to him the moral qualities which he displayed at that time. For he will usually have been at his most distinctive and memorable during his main period of achievement rather than in his declining years or in his last hours: indeed, he may have died in a coma or under sedation, and he may have been senile for several years before death. Again, very different predicates may be attributed to the same individual by different people. This is most strikingly the case with those whose lives have a public and therefore often a controversial character. Historians utter very different moral judgements about, for example, Mary Queen of Scots, Oliver Cromwell, Lenin, President Roosevelt, and Marshal Pétain. Which writers, or which readers, determine the 'eternal predicates' of these figures? Who establishes their status 'in God'? And what happens to a great man's 'eternal predicates' when the prevailing historical judgement changes with the discovery of new data? At a lower level, when Mr Alderman X, former mayor of the town, dies many members of the community may think of him as wise, honest and public-spirited; but on the other hand his political associates may think that he was cunning, devious and self-seeking. Are these strongly incompatible characteristics all 'eternal predicates' of the late Alderman X? Or does a majority opinion settle a man's 'eternal predicates'? And if so, how large a majority? But it is not only historical and public figures who are thus thought of in different ways. Anyone is liable to be assessed somewhat variously, sometimes very variously, by spouse, children, employers, employees, friends, enemies and casual acquaintances.

In view of all these inbuilt ambiguities the concept of the 'eternal predicates' of the dead seems to me so amorphous as to be virtually meaningless.

As we shall see in chapter 8, the 'language game' views of religion represented by Phillips, on the one hand, and scientific humanism on the other hand, differ only in their preferences for different kinds of language. The one opts for religious and the other for scientific language to describe our human situation. But both agree that a man's consciousness ends absolutely at bodily death and that talk of his immortality or eternal life or his overcoming of death can have meaning only as the elliptical expression of a judgement concerning the quality of his present earthly life.

NOTES

1. 'The Way Back into the Ground of Metaphysics', in *Existentialism from Dostoevsky to Sartre*, ed. Walter Kaufmann, p. 214.
2. Martin Heidegger, *Being and Time*, p. 276.
3. ibid., p. 279.
4. ibid., pp. 276–7.
5. ibid., p. 280.
6. ibid., p. 288.
7. ibid., p. 284.
8. ibid., p. 289.
9. ibid., p. 294.
10. ibid.
11. ibid., p. 295.
12. ibid., p. 310.
13. ibid., pp. 297–8.
14. ibid., p. 303.
15. ibid.
16. ibid., p. 308.
17. ibid.
18. ibid., p. 311.

19. ibid.

20. Friedrich Nietzsche, *Thus Spake Zarathustra*, part I, 'Of Free Death'.

21. Jean-Paul Sartre, *Being and Nothingness*, p. 534.

22. *Being and Time*, p. 292.

23. Sartre, *Being and Nothingness*, p. 536.

24. ibid., p. 537.

25. ibid., p. 538.

26. ibid., p. 544.

27. ibid., p. 539.

28. ibid., pp. 536–7.

29. ibid., p. 539.

30. ibid., pp. 539–40.

31. Ludwig Wittgenstein, *Tractatus Logico-Philosophicus*, 6.4311, p. 147.

32. D. Z. Phillips, *Death and Immortality*, p. 43.

33. ibid., pp. 48–9. A somewhat similar view is expressed by Stewart Sutherland in 'What Happens after Death?', in *Scottish Journal of Theology*, vol. 22, no. 4 (December 1969).

34. *Death and Immortality*, p. 50.

35. ibid.

36. ibid., pp. 52–3.

37. Simone Weil, *Waiting on God*, p. 151.

38. *Death and Immortality*, pp. 53–4.

39. ibid., pp. 54–5.

40. ibid., p. 55.

41. ibid., p. 57.

42. On prayers for the dead Phillips says, 'To begin with, prayers for the dead may change the status of the dead *in God*, which is the only way the status of the dead can change. By the living praying for the souls of the departed, the relationship between the living and the dead in God is changed. Since God's activity in this context is to be understood in terms of his spirit at work in the prayers of believers, it makes sense to speak of the prayers of the living changing the status of the dead in God's eyes . . . Here, what is important to note is that what it makes sense to say about the dead in petitionary prayers is determined, to a large extent, by the relation of the dead to God when they were alive' (ibid., pp. 57–8). And on the prayers of the dead for the living he says, 'Surely, one might think, if the dead are said to pray for the living, this must imply some kind of duration after death, another existence in which certain activities are carried on, namely, prayers for the living . . . [However] if the dead pray for us, we cannot equate such prayers with the prayers of the living. The prayers of the dead are prayers *from or in eternity*. We cannot ask of them questions which are appropriate to ask of the prayers of the living: Were they verbal prayers or silent prayers? How long did they last? Were they

said with difficulty or easily? and so on. The activity of the dead is the activity of the eternal in them' (ibid., p. 58).

43. ibid., p. 55 (Phillips' italics).
44. Jean-Paul Sartre, *Being and Nothingness*, p. 543.
45. ibid., p. 544. See Sartre's whole discussion on pp. 541–5.
46. This doctrine is discussed in chapter 12, section 2.

CHAPTER 6

Mind and Body

I. THE OPTIONS

We have the two concepts of body and mind, and various rival views of the relation between them. According to the currently much discussed mind/brain identity theory the two concepts refer to the same entity. This is the monistic option; all the others are dualist, regarding body and mind as distinct entities, and indeed entities of basically different kinds, but offering varying accounts of the relation between them. One such account is that the mind is unilaterally dependent upon the body and has no independent efficacy – this being the epiphenomenalist thesis. Another dualist view is that although mind and body are entities of different kinds, and the mind influences the body as much as the body influences the mind, yet the latter cannot function apart from the body: the conjunction of the two is required for the occurrence of consciousness. And the remaining view is that body and mind are entities of different kinds, mysteriously locked together in our present existence, but that the mind may nevertheless be able to survive the death of the body. I am going to argue that this last view cannot be ruled out. I do not claim that a capacity of the mind to survive the decay of the body can be established by philosophical argument, but I claim that it cannot be excluded either by philosophical argument or by empirical evidence. Inspection of the notions of mind and body and evidence of mind/brain correlation, I shall argue, leave the door open, or at least unlocked, to a belief in the survival of the conscious self.

2. MIND/BRAIN IDENTITY

Let us begin with the mind/brain identity theory. According to this, whilst the names 'mind' and 'brain' have different meanings, they nevertheless in fact refer to the same object. As examples of such contingent identity, 'morning star' and 'evening star',[1] or 'cloud' and 'mass of particles in suspension',[2] or 'lightning' and 'motion of electrical charges',[3] or volume of water and collection of molecules each containing two atoms of hydrogen and one of oxygen,[4] or heat and molecular motion, are names or descriptions which pick out different characteristics of the same object or process. Just as that which we call the morning star is, as a matter of contingent fact, the same thing as that which we call the evening star, so as a matter of contingent fact what the physiologist calls a certain kind of brain activity is what in ordinary language we call thought. And just as it is an empirical hypothesis, confirmable or disconfirmable by observation and experiment, that a cloud is the same thing as a mass of particles in suspension, or that the morning star is the same heavenly body as the evening star, so too – according to the mind/brain identity theory – it is an empirical hypothesis, confirmable or disconfirmable by empirical evidence, that thoughts are identically the same as brain processes. Thus U. T. Place says, ' "Consciousness is a process in the brain" in my view is neither self-contradictory nor self-evident; it is a reasonable scientific hypothesis, in the way that the statement "Lightning is a motion of electric charges" is a reasonable scientific hypothesis.'[5] On this view thoughts are not effects or by-products or epiphenomena of cerebral events, but thoughts and brain processes are the same things. Thus, as Herbert Feigl says, 'instead of conceiving of two realms or two concomitant types of events, we have only one reality which is represented in two different conceptual systems – on the one hand, that of physics and on the other hand, where applicable . . . that of phenomenological psychology'.[6]

All other contingent identities – such as that of a cloud with particles in suspension – are established on the evidence of observation and, very often, experiment. What kind of evidence is there, then, for mind/brain identity? There is considerable evidence of mind/brain correlation – that is, for supposing that for every mental event there is a corresponding brain event. But to point to brain-mapping, and the exploration of the functions of the different areas of the cortex, and the progressive identification of the specific brain activity related to a particular mental activity, is to offer evidence for mind/brain correlation, not for mind/brain identity. It seems a reasonable hope that we may in due course be able to trace a complete correlation, so that for every mental event there will be known to be an appropriate brain event. Such a conclusion will be compatible with mind/ brain identity; but it will be equally compatible with the other main theories in the philosophy of mind, namely epiphenomenalism and dualistic interaction.

Amongst these rival theories mind/brain identity has, surely, the least initial plausibility. For, prima facie, thoughts on the one hand, and electro-chemical events in the physical brain on the other, seem to be realities of quite different kinds. My consciousness of, for example, the night sky, as a visual field consisting of millions of points of light against a dark blue background does not seem in the least like a bit of grey matter, and still less like electro-chemical change in a bit of grey matter. The theory that my consciousness of the night sky is, identically, a set of physical changes in grey matter is thus paradoxical in the extreme. It will be said by the mind/brain identity theorist that although the experience of seeing the night sky is, phenomenally, admittedly very different from an episode of cerebral activity, yet the two may nevertheless be one and the same: what is subjectively the experience of seeing the night sky may be, objectively, a brain state or states. It must I think be granted that this is a conceptual possibility. To this extent the mind/brain identity theorists may be said to have made out their case. But they normally claim to have provided reasons for believing that this theoretical possibility is in fact realized. Against this it must be insisted that evidence of mind/brain correlation is not evidence of mind/brain identity. It is of course compatible with identity; but it is positive evidence of no more than correlation. Further, the prima facie state of affairs remains one of distinction, and indeed radical distinction, rather than of identity. For there is the inescapable difference that our own mental states are known by us directly whilst our brain states are known to us indirectly, on evidence. Thus whilst it is entirely plausible that something going on in my brain *causes* my consciousness of the night sky, sustains it, and is indispensable to it, the claim that my consciousness of the night sky literally *is* – exclusively and without remainder – my grey matter functioning in a certain way is a claim that two things which are apparently different *in kind* are really one and the same; and this surely requires positive arguments beyond its bare conceptual possibility.

There is, as I have acknowledged, ample evidence of mind/ brain correlation. But what sort of evidence could there possibly be that this correlation is a case of identity? To show that two things or processes, A and B, which are prima facie distinct, are really one and the same thing, and that that thing is a physical object, it must be shown that A and B exist or occur at the same place (and also the same time). For if they exist or occur at different places they cannot be identically the same physical object. We can begin to apply this test, for we can locate a brain process in space, namely in a part of the cerebrum. But how could we possibly locate a mental event in space, other than by simply begging the question at issue and assuming that in locating the brain event we have thereby located the mental event? We can have evidence that we are pointing to the brain correlate of a certain thought; but we need further evidence for the identity of the thought with its brain correlate. And not only is there no such evidence, but it seems impossible to conceive what such evidence might consist of. As Norman Malcolm asks, 'How do we make the further test of whether my *thought* occurred inside my skull? For it would have to be a *further* test: it would have to be logically independent of the test for the presence of the brain process, because [the mind/ brain identity] thesis is that the identity is *contingent*. But no one has any notion of what it would mean to test for the occurrence of the thought inside my skull *independently* of testing for a brain process. The idea of such a test is not intelligible.'[7]

That there is and could be no empirical evidence for mind/ brain identity (in distinction from mind/brain correlation) has perhaps been concealed by the analogies used by the mind/ brain identity·theorists to explain the general notion of contingent identity. They have assumed, as in the quotation above from U. T. Place, that mind/brain identity is a hypothesis of the same kind, confirmable or disconfirmable in basically the same kind of way, as the hypothesis that lightning is a motion of electrical charges. But this assumption merely begs the question at issue. All the examples used are, inevitably, examples of a physical entity or process being identified by two different names, each of which is the name of a physical entity or process. The morning star and the evening star are both stars; the cloud and the particles in suspension are both physical objects; the flashing lightning and the electrical discharge are both processes in space; the water and the molecules of H_2O are alike physical things. These analogies make clear how, within the domain of the physical, one and the same entity or process may be observed in different circumstances and be given different names, and also how it may be an empirical discovery that the two apparently different things are really one and the same. But to assume that such cases offer a valid analogy for the identity of a physical event with a mental event is simply to beg the question at issue, which is precisely whether physical and mental events can be identical.[8]

It would therefore be extremely rash to regard the mind/ brain identity theory as being entitled to forbid the idea of the mind's surviving the death of the body. And it is not in any way a qualification of this conclusion that even if the mind/ brain identity thesis were regarded as established, it would still not touch the idea (to be discussed in chapter 15) of immortality by resurrection, in the sense of the divine reconstitution of the bodily person.

3. EPIPHENOMENALISM

Let us now turn to epiphenomenalism – the view that whilst consciousness is different from the physical activity of the brain it is nevertheless generated by that activity and has no independent existence or causality. According to this theory consciousness is a mere epiphenomenon, mirroring in a mysteriously different medium what goes on in the brain. Accordingly the states of the brain determine the states of the mind, and never vice versa.

The Achilles heel of this theory is, I think, its entailment of determinism. For if the mind is an epiphenomenon it is wholly determined by the physical brain; and this in turn is an integral part of the wider causal system of the material world. We assume of the physical system of nature that every constituent event is caused; that given the causal nexus which has produced it, an event that has occurred could not have failed to occur; and that the universe, as a causal system, constitutes a temporal continuum of which the earlier states determine the later, so that an observer knowing the entire state of the system at one point in time could, in principle, calculate its state at any later point in time. We may call this thesis total determinism. And if it should prove to suffer from some fundamental philosophical malady, epiphenomenalism will catch the same disease by logical contagion. I believe that total determinism does in fact suffer from the crippling circumstance that any argument (whether offered as probative or as probable) for the conclusion that it is rational to believe the total determinist thesis must be logically suicidal, or self-refuting.

The nerve of this claim is that the concept of rational belief presupposes intellectual freedom; so that a mind whose history is determined cannot be said rationally to believe anything or therefore rationally to believe that total determinism is true. Thus any attempt rationally to establish total determinism involves the contradiction that in arguing for it the mind must presume itself not to be completely determined, but to be freely judging, recognizing logical relations, assessing relevance and considering reasons; whereas if the determinist conclusion is true the mind is, and always has been, completely determined and has never been freely judging, etc. Thus if the mind has the intellectual freedom to come to rational conclusions, it cannot rationally conclude that it is not free rationally to conclude. That would be absurd because self-refuting, in the same way that it would be self-refuting and therefore absurd for someone to profess to prove that he himself does not exist. There would be a logical incompatibility between his conclusions (that he does not exist) and – not his arguments for this conclusion, but – the fact that he is there producing the arguments. And there is, I am suggesting, a similar incompatibility between a man's conclusion that he (as well as everything and everyone else) is totally determined and – not his arguments for this conclusion, but – his implied claim that he is a rational mind who has seen the validity of certain reasonings and who is offering these reasons to convince other rational minds.[9]

But, it might be said at this point, if the brain, of which the mind is an epiphenomenon, is an immensely complex fleshly computer, why should not this computer be programmed to reason logically and to come to correct conclusions? And why, specifically, should it not be programmed to prove, or rationally to conclude, that the determinist thesis is true? In reply we must distinguish between the sense in which a brain which is a wholly determined system could, and the sense in which it could not, properly be said to come to the *reasoned* conclusion that it is itself wholly determined. There is, I think, no doubt that a mechanical computer, or a human brain, could be programmed or determined to print out or to utter aloud or to itself a series of propositions constituting an argument for total determinism or even (if there is one) a proof of total determinism, and at the end of this process to present the conclusion that the total determinist thesis is true. Thus far the picture of a determined system being determined to produce a proof or argument that it is itself determined raises no problem. But a problem emerges when we universalize the picture in accordance with the total determinist thesis. Imagine a totally determined world, inhabited only by wholly determined 'people'. And imagine a group of them programmed to discuss philosophy and to consider the question of freedom versus determinism. Half of them are programmed to come to the conclusion that the world, including themselves as parts of it, and including their present processes of reasoning as parts of themselves, are determined, whilst the other half are programmed to come with equal confidence to the opposite conclusion. For as well as having the concept of being determined we also have the concept of being not determined, or not wholly determined. And so let us imagine a non-determined observer watching the proceedings of this group of programmed individuals from outside the determined world. He listens to their arguments, which are based upon the character of their world, and judges the argument for determinism to be sound. He is accordingly convinced that the individuals in that world are indeed wholly determined. The argument for this seems to him irrefutable and its conclusion inescapable. But surely, we must now add, he (the observer) believes that they (the inhabitants of the totally determined world) are determined in a different sense of 'believe' from that in which those of them who are programmed to believe that they are determined believe it. For their belief that they are determined does not arise from the soundness of their arguments but from the fact that they are causally determined to think those arguments sound, just as the other half of the group are causally determined to think those same arguments unsound.

And so we have the distinction between a wholly determined individual concluding that he is himself wholly determined, and an intellectually free individual concluding that the other is wholly determined. And clearly if the total determinist thesis is true, and universally true, only the first sort of concluding can ever occur. The only sort of belief in total determinism that can exist (if total determinism is in fact true) is a programmed belief which does not arise from reasoning and judgement but from physical causes which go back in an unbroken chain coterminous with the history of the physical universe.

Now since we do in fact make this distinction, our concept of rational belief is linked with our concept of intellectual freedom. Accordingly a world in which there was (or is) no intellectual freedom would be (or is) a world in which there is no rational belief. Therefore the belief that the world is totally determined cannot rationally claim to be a rational belief. Hence an argument for total determinism is necessarily self-refuting, or logically suicidal. Rational argumentation cannot conclude that there is no such thing as rational argumentation.

What follows from this is, not that total determinism may not be true, nor that there may not be sound arguments or even proofs of its truth, but that if it is true we can never rationally believe that it is true. Therefore in discussing the matter we can only assume that we are not wholly determined; and hence that our thought processes are not mere epiphenomena of the physical brain.

It should be added that this argument against epiphenomenalism, via its entailment of determinism, also applies to the mind/brain identity thesis. For that, too, entails that our thought processes are, as brain processes, part of the unitary system of physical nature.

In rejecting mind/brain identity, then, we accept mind/brain dualism. We accept, that is to say, that mind is a reality of a different kind from matter. And in rejecting epiphenomenalism we reject a unilateral relationship between brain and mind. We allow for the fact that states of the mind may act causally upon the brain as well as vice versa. We allow for the fact that, for example, in composing these sentences I am doing mental work, which is presumably causing the state of my brain to undergo certain modifications from moment to moment. And whenever the human being acts as a conscious agent, deliberately performing any action, including speaking, we must presume – having rejected mind/brain identity and epiphenomenalism – that mind is initiating brain events. Indeed, this will be equally true, assuming complete mind/brain correlation, of purely 'inner' mental activity which is not expressed in outward action: for example, going through a process of reasoning, or trying to remember something that one has for the moment forgotten. But causality in the other direction, from body to mind, is equally evident a fact. As we perceive the world around us from moment to moment in ordinary waking consciousness, sensory input is affecting the brain and through the brain is providing the content of our awareness. Further, when the brain is tired the mind flags; when the brain is anaesthetized or concussed, consciousness is suspended; all sorts of drugs affect the quality of consciousness; the senility of the brain is senility of the personality; various mental illnesses are treated by drugs and by electric shocks to the brain; the operation of prefrontal lobotomy affects the personality as a whole; and indeed, 'there is hardly any behavioural, mental, or moral activity of which human beings are capable which cannot be eliminated or distorted to a greater or lesser extent by cerebral accidents'.[10] It thus seems that mind and brain are independent but interacting realities, each of which can causally affect the other. Such a relationship between two entities of the same basic kind is common enough; but the interaction of body and mind, as entities of basically different kinds, is unique and utterly mysterious. And yet the evidence for this mysterious reciprocal causality is overwhelming – for in every moment of waking life the mind is either acting in the world through its initiation of brain activity, or being affected by the world through modifications of the state of the brain; or indeed both at once. Given this ever growing body of evidence, we can only avoid the conclusion of continuous interaction by adopting either the mind/brain identity theory or epiphenomenalism; and we have seen reasons for accepting neither.

4. ESP AND THE MIND/BODY PROBLEM

Herbert Feigl, in the course of an exposition of the mind/brain identity theory, remarks that 'it is conceivable that some of the . . . still extremely problematic and controversial "facts" of parapsychology will require emergentist or even interactionistic explanations'[11] of the relation between the mind and the body. It seems to me that he is here considerably understating the challenge which parapsychology offers to materialist views of the mind. For there are not many today who would deny that extra-sensory perception is an established though very mysterious fact. More specifically, the occasional influence of mind upon mind, without any normal means of communication between them, which is labelled telepathy, and the occasional awareness of physical states of affairs at a distance, in the absence of sense perception of them, which is labelled clairvoyance, can reasonably be claimed as established facts; and it seems likely, difficult though this is to accept, that clairvoyance is also sometimes precognitive. The experimental evidence for ESP in these forms is now very strong, and is probably well enough known for detailed description no longer to be necessary: references to some of the main experimental work are listed in a note.[12]

Most of this experimental work has been quantitative. For example, packs of cards marked in equal numbers with five different symbols (named Zener cards, after the experimenter who devised them) are thoroughly shuffled and are then turned up one at a time by the sender. The percipient, who is placed where he cannot see the cards or the sender, 'guesses' them. Since he has each time one chance in five of guessing correctly, if only 'chance' is operating his score should approximate to 20%, and the longer the run the closer should be the approximation. But very good ESP subjects have exceeded chance expectation in their scores by margins which give 'odds against chance' of millions or even billions to one.[13] However, for the ordinary, non-mathematically minded person 'spontaneous' cases are generally more impressive than statistical probabilities. There are, for example, numerous well-attested cases of 'crisis apparitions', in which A and B (who are usually relatives or close friends) are at a distance when A undergoes some crisis, often a fatal accident, and B, who had no reason to expect this, has within the next twelve or so hours a vivid hallucination of A, sometimes in a form which indicates the nature of the crisis. I shall cite, almost at random, a single case out of the many that have been recorded, and give a list of references to the main published collections:

> The percipient's half-brother, an airman, had been shot down in France on the 19th March, 1917, early in the morning. She herself was in India. 'My brother', she says, 'appeared to me on the 19th March, 1917. At the time I was either sewing or talking to my baby, I cannot remember quite what I was doing at that moment. The baby was on the bed. I had a very strong feeling I must turn round; on doing so, I saw my brother Eldred W. Bowyer-Bower. Thinking he was alive and had been sent out to India, I was simply delighted to see him, and turned round quickly to put baby in a safe place on the bed, so that I could go on talking to my brother; then turned again and put my hand out to him, when I found he was not there. I thought, he is only joking, so I called him and looked everywhere I could think of looking. It was only when I could not find him I became very frightened and the awful fear that he might be dead. I felt very sick and giddy . . . Two weeks later I saw in the paper he was missing.'[14]

The most economic explanation of such an incident is that the one who experiences the hallucination has, at some level of his unconscious mind, been affected telepathically by the mind of the one undergoing the crisis, and that the 'information' received in this way presents itself to consciousness in the form of an hallucination – often at night when the mind is relatively detached from the world. (In the fully attested cases the percipient tells others of the apparition before news of the crisis has arrived by normal means. This necessarily happens less often in these days of radio communication than when news from abroad came by ship.)

It is not credible that the hundreds of recorded and attested cases of crisis apparitions represent pure coincidences – it just happening to be the case that what is often the only vivid hallucination the percipient has ever had takes the form of seeing a relative or friend at or shortly after the moment when the latter, who is at a distance, has undergone some significant crisis. We have to postulate some connection between the two individuals in virtue of which the one reacts in this way to what is happening to the other. 'Telepathy' is simply the accepted label for this mysterious connection. The difficult question is not whether it occurs but as to its nature.

The importance of this question is shown by the claim that telepathy disproves any theory of the relation between mind and body which would rule out the possibility of the mind's surviving the death of the body.[15] For theories which regard consciousness as merely an epiphenomenon of the brain, or the mind as identical with (and therefore in no circumstances separable from) the brain, exclude any possibility of our mentality outliving our body. According to such theories the mind is totally dependent upon the brain, with no independent status or efficacy, and adds only the reflexive fact of awareness to the functioning of the brain as a physical system. It is therefore impossible, on these theories, for one mind to influence another except through some chain of physical cause and effect – for example, by brain A causing the vocal chords of body A to emit sounds which impinge upon the ears of body B and thus affect brain B, this cerebral activity being reflected in consciousness B. But if, on the contrary, mind A can produce effects in mind B directly, without any such physical causation being initiated in the one body and terminating in the other, then the epiphenomenalist and mind/brain identity theories are disproved; and one importance of telepathy is that it seems to constitute precisely such direct influence of mind upon mind without physical mediation.

But can a physical account of telepathy in fact be ruled out? A physical basis for telepathy would presumably have to consist in some kind of radiation emanating from the sender and being picked up by the percipient in a way analogous to that in which radio waves are transmitted and received. The main systematic research into this possibility has been that undertaken by russian scientists at the Leningrad Institute for Brain Research and the Physiological Institute of the Faculty of Biology at the University of Leningrad and reported by Professor L. L. Vasiliev in his *Experiments in Mental Suggestion* in 1962. As one would expect of marxist scientists, Vasiliev and his colleagues assumed that telepathy must be a physical phenomenon, and considered that it is an effect of the electrical activity generated in the cerebral cortex when mental activity is occurring. One of the main forms of telepathic causation used by Vasiliev and his colleagues consisted in hypnotic suggestion at a distance. The subject was induced to go into a hypnotic trance, and then to awaken out of it, by someone at a distance who was making the hypnogenic suggestions only in his own mind. This proved a successful method of demonstrating the phenomenon of telepathy, and Vasiliev then proceeded to test the electromagnetic theory by placing the sender in a chamber made of sheet lead 3 mm. in thickness. Similar experiments were made with iron instead of lead, and with iron as well as lead. Vasiliev's conclusion was that 'screening by iron or lead in the manner in which screening was effected by us does not prevent the diffusion of the supposed waves and radiations that transmit mental suggestion'.[16] Further, not only did the screening of the sender in these ways not prevent telepathic hypnotic suggestion, but neither did it weaken or delay it. Thus the russian experiments tell strongly against an electromagnetic explanation of telepathy.

Vasiliev also tried to determine whether differences in the distance between the sender and the recipient affect telepathic mental suggestion. For all known forms of radiation take time to travel and are attenuated by distance. It proved extremely difficult to make an accurate measurement of the time taken by the process of telepathic suggestion, but it was possible to test its relative efficacy over short distances of a few metres as compared with long distances, such as the 1700 kilometres between Sebastopol and Leningrad, and no evidence emerged of diminuation or attenuation over the longer distances.[17]

One further type of experimental evidence which points

strongly away from any kind of physical theory is the pre-cognitive ESP which has been demonstrated, for example, by Soal and Goldney, in which the percipient was found to be correctly guessing, not the card that the sender was currently looking at, but the next card in the pack, yet to be exposed.[18] In such cases a physical explanation would require the effect to occur – paradoxically, to say the least – before its cause.

The alternative to a physical account of ESP is a psycho-logical one according to which A's psychological state 'echoes' itself in B's psychological state. The kind of theory that has been suggested to account for this postulates a common unconscious through which different consciousnesses are connected. That is to say, whilst individual minds constitute separate and distinct streams of consciousness and of sub-conscious mental life, at the deepest level of the unconscious they merge; and it is in virtue of this basic unity of psychic life that the phenomenon which we call telepathy is able to occur.[19] This notion of the ultimate unity of all human minds is one which we shall have to explore more fully in another context;[20] but it must be counted to its credit that it might provide the basis for an understanding of ESP.

It should be added, however, that an explanation of telepathy in terms of a postulated common unconscious cannot also serve to explain the other main form of ESP, namely clair-voyance. However, this limitation, and the further questions to which it points, do not directly concern us here.

It should be stressed that a psychological, as distinguished from a physical, theory of ESP does not run counter to the assumption, for which there is as we have seen considerable evidence, that the mind and brain function together, so that for every state of the mind there is a corresponding state of the brain. A total mind/brain correspondence is compatible with a psychological as well as with a physical account of ESP. Sometimes the mind/brain correspondence is produced by physical input into the brain via the nervous system of the body – as when information from the retina passes along the optic nerve to produce an effect in a part of the brain, the mental correlate of which is the conscious experience of seeing. And sometimes the mind/brain correspondence is initiated within consciousness, as when we exercise our will, the brain correlate of this mental activity then affecting our nervous system and producing bodily movements in the form, for exarhple, of speech. Thus states of the mind/brain correspondence can be produced either from outside, by physical causes, or from within, being initiated by the mind. On a psychological theory of ESP it is the latter kind of causation that produces the mind/brain correspondence in a telepathic percipient. That is to say, when a certain thought or image occurs in B's consciousness and brain, echoing a thought or image in the mind and brain of A, it is B's mind that causes his brain to be in that state, and not vice versa. But the mind/brain correspondence, which we are supposing always to obtain, is not violated.

The proper conclusion would seem to be that it is extremely probable that telepathy is psychologically rather than physically based, and involves a direct connection of some kind between mind and mind. If so, it is incompatible with those theories which regard the mind as epiphenomenal to the functioning of the brain; and to that extent the existence of telepathy considerably decreases the *a priori* improbability of the survival of the mind after the death of the body.

The independent reality of mind and brain, as mutually interacting entities or processes, is of course compatible both with the simultaneous perishing of both and with the mind surviving the death of the body. Neither possibility can thus far be said to be in any objective sense more probable than the other. Intuitively, it seems odd that of two realities whose careers have been carried on in continuous interaction, one should be mortal and the other immortal. But it also seems, intuitively, odd to deny that of two independent realities of basically different kinds, one might be capable of surviving the other. A naturalistic or humanist thinker will tend to be more impressed by the first oddness, and a religious thinker by the second; but the conclusions which each reaches will reflect his philosophy as a whole rather than being a logical implicate of the evidence of mind/brain interaction.

NOTES

1. J. J. C. Smart, in *The Mind-Brain Identity Theory*, ed. C. V. Borst, p. 57.

2. U. T. Place, in Borst, p. 46.

3. ibid., p. 44.

4. Thomas Nagel, in Borst, p. 214.

5. Borst, p. 44.

6. ibid., p. 41.

7. ibid., p. 175. See also Malcolm's *Problems of Mind*, pp. 67–70.

8. Saul Kripke, in the course of his important discussions of the concept of identity, brings out in his own way the failure of any analogy between contingent identities in the physical world and mind/brain identity (Saul A. Kripke, 'Naming and Necessity', in *Semantics of Natural Language*, ed. G. Harman and D. Davidson, pp. 340–1). There are, however, critiques of Kripke's arguments in Fred Feldman, 'Kripke on the Identity Theory', and William G. Lycan, 'Kripke and the Materialists', in *The Journal of Philosophy*, vol. 71, no. 18 (24 October 1974).

9. This argument has been used by a number of twentieth-century philosophers, including John Lucas, *The Freedom of the Will*, ch. 21, who also lists other uses and discussions.

10. W. H. Thorpe, *Animal Nature and Human Nature*, p. 324. In spite of this Thorpe rejects the mind/brain identity theory.

11. Borst, op. cit., pp. 35–6. Other mind/brain identity theorists have also noted the threat to their position from parapsychology. Thus D. M. Armstrong speaks of parapsychology as 'the small black cloud on the horizon of a materialist theory of mind' (*A Materialist Theory of Mind*, p. 365); and Keith Campbell acknowledges that 'if even a single example of para-normal phenomena is genuine, Central State Materialism is false' (*Body and Mind*, p. 91).

12. Robert H. Thouless, *From Anecdote to Experiment in Psychical Research*, provides a general up-to-date summary. Other important publications are: J. B. Rhine, *Extrasensory Perception* and *New Frontiers of the Mind*; Whately Carington, *Telepathy*; S. G. Soal, *The Experimental Situation in Psychical Research*; S. G. Soal and F. Bateman, *Modern Experiments in Telepathy*; and L. L. Vasiliev, *Experiments in Mental Suggestion*. (On the controversy concerning one of Soal's reports, see 'The Soal-Goldney Experiments with Basil Shackleton: A Discussion', in *Proc. SPR*, vol. 56, part 209 (October 1974).) There is a useful 'Guide to the Experimental Evidence for ESP' by John Beloff, in *Science and ESP*, ed. J. R. Smythies.

13. Details are given by, for example, Robert Thouless in *From Anecdote to Experiment in Psychical Research*, pp. 87–92.

14. *Proc. SPR*, vol. 33 (1923), pp. 170–1. G. N. M. Tyrrell, *Apparitions*, is a valuable analytical study of the subject. Important collections are E. Gurney, F. W. H. Myers and F. Podmore, *Phantasms of the Living*; Mrs Henry Sidgwick and Alice Johnson, 'Report on the Census of Hallucinations', in *Proc. SPR*, vol. 10 (1894); F. W. H. Myers, *Human Personality and Its Survival of Bodily Death*.

15. This claim is made, for example, by H. H. Price, 'Psychical Research and Human Personality', in *Hibbert Journal*, January 1949, reprinted in *Science and ESP*, ed. J. R. Smythies.

16. L. L. Vasiliev, *Experiments in Mental Suggestion*, p. 100.

17. ibid., ch. 8 and p. 133. Despite his abandonment of the electromagnetic theory, and the powerful objections which he cites to all other known physical theories of ESP, Vasiliev ends his book in the faith that a physical basis for telepathy will one day be found. But it is fair to emphasize that this is a faith that is demanded by Vasiliev's materialist philosophy. The hope for a physical explanation of ESP is kept alive in this country by Adrian Dobbs in 'The Feasibility of a Physical Theory of ESP', in *Science and ESP*, ed. J. R. Smythies; and C. J. Ducasse, without referring to Vasiliev's work, has important criticisms of J. B. Rhine's partly similar argument against a physical explanation (*A Critical Examination of the Belief in a Life after Death*, pp. 134–5).

18. S. G. Soal and F. Bateman, *Modern Experiments in Telepathy*.

19. Cf. Whately Carington, *Telepathy*.

20. Chapter 22.

CHAPTER 7

The Contribution of Parapsychology

I. TRANCE MEDIUMSHIP

One significance of extra-sensory perception has been discussed in the previous chapter; we turn now to the other main concern of parapsychology, or psychical research, namely the question of man's survival of bodily death, approached through the investigation of ostensible mediumistic communications with the dead. I shall not discuss at all the physical phenomena of mediumship – materializations, levitations, etc. – because the possibility of deliberate fraud, which can I believe for all practical purposes be excluded in the best cases of trance mediumship, always haunts the reports of these events. And I shall discuss trance mediumship largely on the basis of the classic period of psychical research, in the last decades of the nineteenth and the early decades of the twentieth centuries, when the best mediums yet known were being investigated by very able and distinguished persons in the british and american Societies for Psychical Research. During this period there were a small number of exceptional mediums – above all Mrs Piper, Mrs Leonard, and the lady (Mrs Coombe-Tennant) who was known as Mrs Willett – whom we may confidently believe not to have been consciously fraudulent, who were telepathically sensitive to a remarkable degree, and through whom there came apparent communications from the 'dead' which have impressed many as being veridical.

In trance mediumship the medium sits down and goes into a sleep-like state in which his or her own consciousness is apparently suspended and replaced by the consciousness of someone who has died and who is in this way communicating with those still on earth. Let us for the moment use the spiritualist terminology and refer to the supposed communicators as spirits, and to the living persons who attend the mediumistic seance as sitters. Usually, the same spirit (called the medium's control) apparently uses the medium's speech organs at a number of different seances and relays messages from other spirits, whom he often speaks of as standing around him and with whom he apparently converses as well as with the sitters.[1] Quite often sitters are convinced that they are indeed in this way in communication with deceased relatives and friends whom they can identify both by the content and by the manner of their utterances. Sometimes the spirits have been able to give information which was not known to the medium, and sometimes even information which was not at the time known to the sitters, but which was subsequently verified. (A good example of all these features – a communicator, entirely unknown to the medium, being accurately described by the control and conveying numerous messages which were in character, including a large amount of correct information which could not have been known to the medium and some that was not at the time known to the sitters – is that of the 'A.V.B.' communications through Mrs Lenoard.[2]) The most readily available interpretation of all this, and the one that is asserted in the communications themselves, is that deceased persons, still alive as conscious individuals, are communicating with those still 'in the body'. If we accept this interpretation, we are in possession both of good evidence for the fact of human survival after bodily death and also of a number of statements describing the actual conditions of life beyond the grave.

However, even on the hypothesis that communication between the living and the dead does take place in this way, it is impossible to believe that *all* ostensible communications from the departed are what they profess to be. There is undoubtedly a vast amount of conscious and unconscious fraud on the part of mediums and of wishful thinking, self-deception, and misremembering on the part of sitters; and responsible advocates of the spiritualist interpretation of mediumship would only wish to claim that a small part of the total mass of material does in fact constitute genuine spirit communication. Amidst a vast depressing fog of commonplace, vague or puerile material there are rare flashes of information or of characterization which seem to come straight from a distinctive discarnate personality. However, even here fraud, though not in the legal sense, is an important possibility. For as well as conscious dishonesty and cheating there may well be unconscious simulation and the use of information acquired unconsciously from the living in the form of telepathic impressions. Indeed, discussion in this field has largely centred upon the very difficult question whether there is any evidence that would enable us definitively to choose between the spiritualistic and the telepathy-from-the-living theories of mediumship.

2. THE UNCONSCIOUS FRAUD HYPOTHESIS

Let us spell out more fully the 'unconscious fraud' hypothesis. This has two aspects: first, that the trance personae (to use the term adopted by C. D. Broad and others in speaking of the ostensible spirit personalities who manifest themselves in the mediumistic trance) are each some kind of fragment or secondary personality of the medium; and second, that the source of their supernormally acquired information is telepathy between the medium and living persons, usually the sitters but sometimes others as well. The secondary-personality aspect of the theory was developed by a number of the early psychical researchers, as important a contribution as any being that of Mrs Henry Sidgwick (Principal of Newnham College, Cambridge) in her classic 1915 report, 'A Contribution to the Study of the Psychology of Mrs Piper's Trance Phenomena'.[3] The telepathy aspect of the theory was also canvassed by the early researchers, and has been discussed by a number of writers since.[4]

An important part is played in the 'unconscious fraud' theory by the role-playing power of the human mind which shows itself, under hypnosis, even in persons who do not normally display any acting ability or interest. Anyone who has witnessed a hypnotist's stage performance will have seen ordinary people, under hypnosis, in a state of temporary hallucination as to their own present situation and even, in a sense, their own identity. In this state they are able to enter wholeheartedly into all sorts of often strange roles – imagining that they are riding bicycles, or talking to men from Mars, or even that they are themselves from Mars, etc. The 'information' which they are acting out has in this case been suggested to them by the hypnotist, and the hallucinated individual then devotes his own dramatic powers to sustaining the role (for example, that of a visitor from outer space) and uses his intelligence and inventiveness in responding to tests and challenges. (Sometimes, however, another level of his mind remains outside the role and monitors what is going on without being able to intervene.) The first part of the 'unconscious fraud' theory sees mediumship as continuous in character with these recognized, if unusual, phenomena. According to this hypothesis the mediumistic trance is or is closely analogous to a state of self-induced hypnosis. The entranced state is a dreamy condition of consciousness in which role-playing is natural; and the type of role played depends very largely upon suggestions received from the circle in which the 'sensitive' lives. Thus we find that in different cultures essentially the same phenomenon has taken different forms. E. R. Dodds, writing in his own field of classical studies, has reminded parapsychologists that there was considerable activity in neoplatonist circles (described by such writers as Iamblichus and Michael Psellus) of a kind which we should today classify as mediumistic. 'On the whole', he says, 'the resemblances between the phenomena described by the Neoplatonists and those recorded as occurring in the *séance*-room to-day appear sufficiently numerous and striking to afford *prima facie* ground for the assumption that the facts underlying the two sets of records are of the same order and referable to similar agencies . . . [And yet] with all the parallelisms I have enumerated there is associated one fundamental difference, viz. that what the spiritualists attribute to the activity of a discarnate human mind the Neoplatonists attribute to gods or daemons.'[5] Again, the witches of the seventeenth and eighteenth centuries, many of whom seem to have been the equivalents of present-day mediums, attributed their paranormal information not to the spirits of the dead but to demons. Thus it looks as though in the *katokoi* of the late graeco-roman world, in sixteenth- and seventeenth-century witchcraft, and in the spiritualist medium-ship which began in the mid-nineteenth century, we see essentially the same paranormal phenomena exhibited, but interpreted and reported in widely different terms in accord-ance with the ideas prevailing in these different cultures. It could be that in the ancient world the belief that the spirits of the dead were confined underground in hades, and in christian Europe that they were distributed to heaven, hell and purgatory, required some non-spiritualist way of understanding the trance phenomena, but that the crisis of christian belief in the nineteenth century opened the way to a spiritualist theory and made it seem a more natural interpretation than one in terms of gods or demons. At any rate the theory and practice of spiritualist mediumship, which developed and spread very rapidly in the United States and then Europe from about 1850 onwards,[6] provided an environment in which the capacity for self-hypnosis was cultivated and in which it most readily took the form of a role-playing in which spirits of the dead are personated. Somewhat as the cultural milieu in which stage hypnotism takes place today may lead the hypnotist to suggest to his subjects that they are visitors from outer space, a suggestion which they then act out with all the resources at their command, so the spiritualist sub-culture suggests a departed-spirit role to a medium going into a self-induced hypnotic trance. The role is then played out, sometimes with great skill and sometimes, it would seem, with the benefit of telepathically received impressions.

In support of this theory there is positive evidence that some of the control personae are not what they profess to be. I shall take as an example the case of one of Mrs Piper's principal controls, Phinuit, who was the subject of a very careful and thorough analytical report by Richard Hodgson in 1892.[7] The Phinuit-persona claimed that he was the spirit of a french doctor whose full name was Jean Phinuit Scliville and who had lived in the first half of the nineteenth century and had practised in London as well as in France and Belgium. However, he was unable to speak French; he displayed no more knowledge of medicine than an ordinary layman; and there were no records of his having attended the medical schools at which he claimed to have studied and practised. Thus far he seems to have been fraudulent. On the other hand, those who discovered this were entirely convinced both that he was distinct from Mrs Piper's normal waking self and that he had access to information, about both the living and the dead, which was not possessed by the waking Mrs Piper.

Hodgson himself came to two tentative conclusions. His

earlier conclusion was in terms of 'an auto-hypnotic trance in which a secondary personality of Mrs Piper either erroneously believes itself to be, or consciously and falsely pretends to be, the "spirit" of a deceased human being, Phinuit or Scliville, and further fictitiously represents various other personalities according to the latent ideas of some of the sitters'.[8] He later however added the further conclusion that some of the material produced by Mrs Piper in trance seemed to go beyond what might be obtained by thought-transference from the living sitters and thus to suggest some kind of real contact with the departed. But whether or not the telepathic information used by the Phinuit-persona was derived from the dead as well as from the living, there remains a strong case for holding that the persona itself was a phase of the medium's own personality and not the independently existing individual whom it professed to be.

The same conclusion seems to be warranted concerning the various other Piper controls, and likewise concerning the other major mediums' controls, in so far as it has been possible to test their identity. They all seem to be fragments or phases of some kind of the medium's own mind, rather than independent persons. And if this is the case, it inevitably raises the question whether the other spirit personae who enter into the drama may not likewise be other than what they profess to be. If the medium's mind is unconsciously personating the control, may it not be playing all the other roles as well? May it not be that the performance of the control, addressing the living audience in the seance, is a play, and that the performance of the communicators, addressing the control, is a play within a play, a dream-like experience of the control, who is himself some kind of secondary personality of the medium? This seems to have been the view of William James, who also made a careful study of the Piper phenomena and who favoured 'the idea of their [the communicators] all being dream creations of Mrs Piper, probably having no existence except when she is in trance, but consolidated by repetition into personalities consistent enough to play their several roles'.[9]

According to the 'unconscious fraud' theory, then, the personae who take part in the trance situation are not the independent persons whom they profess to be and apparently believe themselves to be. A conversation between, for example, Phinuit and various living people was not an episode in the continuous existence of a person known as Phinuit who was busy doing other things when he was not conversing on earth through Mrs Piper. On the contrary, Phinuit only existed within the trance situation. He came into existence when Mrs Piper went into trance in circumstances which suggested the Phinuit role to her, and he ceased to exist when she woke up. He thus *existed* in a sense very like that in which the visitor from Mars exists whom a hypnotized subject temporarily believes himself to be.

It seems to me significant, and a point which is not always given sufficient weight, that the trance personae give no convincing impression of carrying on an existence of their own between seances. Their life seems to be lived in their conversations with those on earth, and they do not speak, except in the most slight and general way, about a coherent existence within which these conversations are only brief episodes.[10] This feature of the communications does not of course decisively rule out the possibility that the spirit personae are what they claim to be; for it might be said (and has been said) that in limiting themselves to what can be expressed through the medium's brain and mind they have to leave behind their consciousness of the next world and of their life within it and are only able to speak about earthly affairs. But such an explanation begins a decisive move away from the idea that a spirit communicator is, in any full and straightforward sense, a still-living person with all his characteristics and powers. The situation, it would seem, must at least be more complex than that; and the question now centres upon the extent of this complexity and whether it still permits us to speak of named individuals surviving death.

The second part of the 'unconscious fraud' theory has already been brought into the discussion. This is the suggestion that people who are able, more or less at will, to enter the auto-hypnotic state are often also good ESP subjects, liable to receive telepathic impressions from their sitters' minds and indeed sometimes also from the minds of others who are not present but with whom there is some point of contact.

As supporting evidence for the telepathic origin of much of

the information displayed in the mediumistic trance one may point to cases in which facts about and characterizations of persons unknown to the sensitive have been produced in circumstances which are not capable of a spiritualist interpretation. Eugène Osty describes a number of cases of this kind.[11] Even more striking is the well-known Gordon Davis case, in which a medium was able to produce a convincing personation of someone, including even a direct voice imitation of his speech, the voice presenting itself as that of a departed spirit communicating with earth, although the individual was subsequently discovered to be alive and well and to have been at the time of the seance carrying on his business as an estate agent. In such a case we see the medium using telepathically acquired information in an unconscious role-playing which has an impressive dramatic quality and exhibits numerous features that would have counted as evidence of spirit communication were it not for the fact that the 'spirit' was still alive on earth.[12]

On the assumption that mediumistic controls represent some kind of part or phase or activity of the medium's own mind, dramatizing on the basis of telepathically acquired impressions, there has been much discussion as to whether they should be classed as full secondary personalities or only as fleeting auto-hypnotic roles. However, it may well be that instead of thinking in terms of such clear-cut alternatives we should envisage a continuum of states shading into one another, with normal dreams and reveries at one extreme and fully-fledged multiple personalities at the other, and with trance personae somewhere in between but often approaching the status of a secondary personality. Spirit 'controls' often exhibit the phenomenon of regression to childhood that is characteristic of nearly all the full secondary personalities that have been studied – for example, Janet's 'Leontine', Morton Prince's 'Sally' and Walter Franklin Prince's 'Margaret'. Likewise, many controls have been children (for example, Mrs Leonard's 'Feda') or are Red Indians or others to whom a limited english vocabulary is appropriate. On the other hand, a mediumistic control is not entirely like the standard secondary personality. In the classic cases of the latter, two or more personalities, each with its own characteristics and memory, alternate in the same body, each being apparently a fully-fledged individual capable of carrying on a normal social life. But the mediumistic control only operates within the trance situation and plays, and is probably only capable of playing, a very limited role. Morton Prince, in his study *The Dissociation of a Personality*, saw the trance persona as a relatively undeveloped form of secondary personality. Referring to the mediumistic trance he says:

> In such cases the second personality does not obtain a completely independent existence, but comes out of its shell, so to speak, only under special conditions when the subject goes into a 'trance'. The external life of personalities of this sort, so far as it is carried on independently of the principal consciousness, is extremely restricted, being confined to the experiences of the so-called 'seance'. Although such a personality is complete in having possession of the faculties of an ordinary human being, there is very little independence in the sense of a person who spontaneously and voluntarily moves about in a social world, and works, acts, and plays like any human being. It is questionable how far such a personality would be capable of carrying on all the functions of a social life, and of adapting itself to its environment. Hypnotic states, that is, artificially induced types of disintegration, are rarely, if ever, sufficiently complete, and possessed of adequate spontaneous adaptability to the environment to constitute veritable personalities.[13]

In the 1930s Whately Carington carried out a series of word-association tests to try to establish identity or lack of identity between the waking personality of the medium and her trance control. The method had been devised by C. G. Jung to locate emotional complexes. A series of words are called out and the patient is asked to respond with the first word that comes into his head. His reaction times for different test words are noted (longer pauses indicating some kind of inhibition), and also whether he produces the same response words on a second run (a change of word being likewise significant). Carington's basic principle was that if the waking medium and her control showed the same pattern of reactions this would be evidence that they shared a common unconscious and thus that the trance persona was not a distinct personality from that of the medium. His experiments were not conclusive, but suggested a relation of counter-similarity between medium and control. That is to say, the two did not display the same pattern of reactions, nor a randomly related one, but complementary patterns. Where one showed a significant reaction the other did not, and vice versa, without overlap. This suggested that a single body of emotional material was divided between them. Thus Carington's experiments tended to support the view that mediumistic controls represent some kind of fragment or phase of the total mental life of the medium.[14]

3. 'PSYCHIC FACTOR' OR SPIRIT COMMUNICATOR?

I think, then, that we must proceed on the assumption that the controls and other spirit personae with whom a sitter finds himself in dialogue are not the independent personalities whom they profess to be, but parts or aspects of the medium's own mind. As such, their conscious existence is confined to their activity within the mediumistic trance, though a spirit who operates on a number of occasions presumably exists between trances as some kind of persisting formation within the medium's unconscious. But it would be a mistake to think that this conclusion rules out the possibility of mediumistic communication between the living and the 'dead'. What it indicates is that if there is such communication it must be a matter of spirits somehow using the machinery of dramatic personation in which, together with ESP sensitivity and a capacity for self-hypnosis, mediumship apparently consists. The 'information' going into the initial creation of a spirit persona would perhaps be largely derived telepathically from the sitters' minds, but the personation would then be further strengthened and its activity to some extent directed by the 'spirit' whose personation it is. Thus the medium's mind would be telepathically affected by the mind of a deceased person, who would thereby operate as a causal factor in the production of a trance persona representing himself. Spirit communication would then be more or less authentic according to the degree of influence being exerted by the spirit being represented, such influence ranging from mere fleeting impulses mingled with other material to fairly long continuous conversations in which a spirit is the dominant causal influence affecting the medium.

A theory of this kind was propounded by Kenneth Richmond in his important analytical study of Mrs Leonard's mediumship:

> I think we can argue, with a minimum of fantasy, the existence of an impulse to dramatise on the part of the medium (a natural and respectable impulse when the mediumship is of a high grade), combined in greater or lesser degree with an impulse to co-operate with and assist the dramatisation on the part of a discarnate person. Essentially, we are in touch, at a sitting, with a subliminal actor in the medium (there is plenty of evidence to be gathered from hypnotic experiments for the existence of a subliminal actor in the human mind), who in turn is in more or less close telepathic touch with the original of the role. But we are not dealing, at any rate in the case of a reliable medium, with an actor depending on a memorised part; the actor is extemporising, and we are assuming a telepathic collaborator to account for the extemporisation effectively reproducing a verifiable character unknown to the medium.[15]

This would seem to be a possible interpretation of the best elements in the enormous mass of material that has been produced through trance utterance and automatic writing. It remains however a major difficulty for most of us in the assessment of this theory that only those who knew the ostensible communicator well in life are in a position to judge whether the proceedings bear the authentic stamp of his presence somewhere behind the scenes of the trance drama. One notes with interest that a number of highly responsible and competent observers who have been in this position have reported their own conviction that they were in touch, though no doubt through a complex and often extremely unreliable psychological machinery, with deceased persons whom they had previously known well. For example we find Richard Hodgson, whose originally sceptical attitude is evident from his earlier report, eventually concluding that he had been in genuine communication with the dead through Mrs Piper. Speaking of the Piper communicators he says, 'Among these are more than half-a-dozen intimate friends of my own, who have produced upon me the impression, through different written communications, that they are the personalities I knew, with characteristic intelligence and emotion, questioning me and answering me under difficulties, but with their peculiar individual and responsive minds in some sense actually there.'[16] It would be quite unwarranted for a reader of this and similar reports to assert that they are mistaken; but equally unjustified for him to be confident that they are not.

In considering the possibility that someone who has died may communicate with the living in this way we are presuming the continued existence of that individual as a persisting consciousness and will, a still living personal being. We are supposing him to be carrying on a career of some kind in the next world, and in the midst of this occasionally to take time to visit his equivalent of a medium – who would presumably be a spirit 'control'. We are assuming, in other words, that the dead have a real life of their own, continuing to develop through time as persons, and that within this life they from time to time indulge in their side of the process of mediumistic communication. But I have already remarked upon the strange absence from the recorded communications as a whole of indications of any such background of a busy next-world life which is being briefly interrupted for the purpose of interaction with this world. The spirits do not seem to speak out of the context of a continuing life; they seem to lack a credible environment of their own, a community of which they are a part, real next-world tasks, interests and purposes. They seem instead to be still very much what they were in this world. And we must, I think, consider the possibility that whilst the spirit of Mr X is indeed, sometimes at least, an ingredient in the trance personation of Mr X, this spirit is nevertheless not a full, still living Mr X but something more like what C. D. Broad called a psychic factor – consisting of mental and emotional formations, including memories and dispositional traits, which persist as a system for a longer or shorter time after death and with a greater or less degree of coherence. To quote Broad:

This psychic factor is not itself a mind, but it may carry modifications due to experiences which happened to John

Jones while he was alive. And it may become temporarily united with the organism of an entranced medium. If so, a little temporary 'mind' (a 'mindkin', if I may use that expression) will be formed. Since this mindkin will contain the same psychic factor as the mind of John Jones it will not be surprising if it displays some traits characteristic of John Jones, and some memories of events in his earthly life.[17]

Such a psychic factor will not be a conscious living person, but a kind of psychic body (comparable in some ways with the *linga sharira* or 'subtle body' of vedantic theory[18]) which becomes temporarily reincarnated in the mediumistic trance. Thus Mr X will not have existed as a conscious living being since his death; but a more or less authentic version of him will come briefly to life in the linkage of a persisting psychic factor with the role-playing activity of the entranced medium. Such a theory would account for the apparently almost total this-world orientation of the communicators. It would however entail a somewhat depressing conception of the state of those who have died, reminiscent of the widespread ancient thought of the departed as thin, insubstantial shades, lacking any real life and consigned to a dim shadowy underworld. Indeed, the psychic factor theory could be described as a modern version of the widespread ancient conception, of which the mesopotamian *kur-nu-gi-a* ('land of no return'[19]), the hebrew sheol,[20] and the greek hades are the principal examples.[21] In hades, for example, the shades of the dead persisted without any real life, indeed without consciousness or memory. They could only be restored to a brief personal existence by a temporary infusion of life from the living.[22] Thus, Odysseus, visiting the underworld, could only communicate with the dead after they had drunk the blood (the life substance) of an animal sacrificed for the purpose.[23] If such a shade, or psychic factor, is all that persists of the empirical self, then any true immortality must presuppose a more complex view of human nature, such as is explored in some strands both of eastern and of western thought, in which the 'true' self is other than the present conscious ego.

It could however be objected that there are exceptions to the general truth that communicating spirits say nothing about the nature of their present existence beyond the grave and give no impression of living a real life in another environment. For it is not uncommon for a communicator to say that he 'has met Uncle Fred, who is happy and well', etc. However, this is never filled out with an account of how Uncle Fred spends his time; and such messages might not implausibly be attributed to the influence of the spiritualist theory which has suggested a departed-spirit role to the trance persona. But in one well-known body of communications, those published by Sir Oliver Lodge as coming from his son Raymond, who had been killed in the first world war, there is a good deal of information about the next world. Raymond reports that those who had been maimed in the war receive new limbs; people at first wear clothes but later graduate to shining robes; houses made of brick, and food and drink, are created to meet people's expectations.[24] In the following much-cited passage Mrs Leonard's Feda is speaking, relaying Raymond's words, 'People here try to provide everything that is wanted. A chap came over the other day, who *would* have a cigar. "That's finished them," he thought. He means he thought they would never be able to provide that. But there are laboratories over here, and they manufacture all sorts of things in them. Not like you do, out of solid matter, but out of essences, and ethers, and gases.'[25] And there is much more of the same general kind. However, Lodge himself added a footnote at one point: 'I confess that I think that Feda may have got a great deal of this, perhaps all of it, from people who have read or written some of the books referred to in my introductory remarks';[26] and in general it seems quite possible to regard these accounts of the next world as deriving from ideas current in spiritualist circles and familiar to both the medium and the sitters. Indeed, it has been remarked that 'the communicators who appear through Mrs Leonard speak as if they were still surrounded by a terrestrial environment, and still engaged in terrestrial occupations, while the communicators through Mrs Willett do not mention these things, and are strangely reticent about their present state'[27] – Mrs Leonard having been a spiritualist and Mrs Willett not. Further, whilst the Raymond material contains numerous statements about there being houses and streets, etc., in the world to come, there are still no specific descriptions of particular houses or streets, and no indication of how Raymond spent the greater part of his time when he was not conversing with his parents through a medium. Thus whilst it is true that there is material describing the next world – the Raymond scripts being a good example – I do not find that they remove the suspicion that the spirit communicators exist only within the trance situation and that their conversation is not related to the solid content of a life being actively lived in its own environment.

An objection of a different kind to the psychic factor theory was put by E. R. Dodds,[28] who pointed out that a spirit communicator sometimes shows knowledge of events which have occurred on earth since his death. But the psychic factor is not a consciousness and therefore could not be observing what is taking place on earth. The information in question must, then, be acquired telepathically by the medium. But in that case, why not attribute the entire phenomenon to the telepathic powers of the medium? Does not the theory of a psychic factor become otiose? The answer, I think, is that the psychic factor, whilst far from being proved, would nevertheless help to explain the vividness of the personation, embodying as it seems to do genuine characteristics and memories of the deceased; but that the trance performance would often also require an admixture of telepathic impressions being received by the medium.

The conclusion to which I am led is a very open and uncertain one. It is extremely probable that the spirits, particularly the controls, who seem to be communicating directly in the mediumistic trance, are some kind of secondary personality of the medium. It is possible that they are built up entirely out of telepathic impressions received by the medium from the living. But when one reads the detailed transcripts of the best sittings with the best mediums – for example, the 'Hodgson' scripts through Mrs Willett – one is at least strongly tempted to think that a distinctive still-living mind was communicating. Again, however, it is possible that instead of such communications being with living personalities the medium is only tapping some kind of persisting psychic traces – mental fragments – left behind by the dead. If so, it could be that this is all that exists of the individual after bodily death, and that the full person has definitively perished; or it could perhaps be that the true self is alive, beyond our ken, and that these psychic traces are no more him than is the physical body which he has left to decay in the grave. But it would be unwise to be dogmatic. It is also possible that there is sometimes telepathic contact between a medium and a surviving human person, the result being presented through the machinery of a secondary personality of the medium. In that case we may have from such sources some general indications of the state of the dead, perhaps in what is known in tibetan Buddhism as the *bardo* world. This possibility will be pursued a little further in chapter 20, section 3.

NOTES

1. This is the most usual procedure. Sometimes a control, or a communicator other than the control, instead of using the medium's normal voice, accent and intonation, uses the medium's vocal cords, and indeed her body as a whole, to speak so far as he can directly in his own voice and with his own accent and mannerisms. (It is also reported that sometimes a communicator's own voice is apparently produced directly, by some supernormal means, out of the air.) Other mediums, however, do not go into trance, or only into very light trance, and their normal waking consciousness remains in control, except for one hand, which produces 'automatic writing'. Indeed some of the best material has come in this way.

2. Miss Radclyffe-Hall and (Una) Lady Troubridge, 'On a Series of Sittings with Mrs Osborne Leonard', in *Proc. SPR*, vol. 30, part 78 (1919). The case is summarized in G. N. M. Tyrrell, *Science and Psychical Phenomena*, ch. 13.

3. *Proc. SPR*, vol. 28, part 71 (1915).

4. Professor E. R. Dodds offers a strongly argued summary and defence of it in his paper 'Why I do not Believe in Survival', in *Proc. SPR*, vol. 42, part 135 (1934). For an important critical discussion, see G. N. M. Tyrrell, *Science and Psychical Phenomena*.

5. E. R. Dodds, 'Supernormal Occurrences in Classical Antiquity', in *Journal of the SPR*, vol. 27 (1931–2), p. 220.

6. For an account of the origins and rapid spread of the modern spiritualist movement, see, e.g., Joseph McCabe, *Spiritualism: A Popular History from 1847*.

7. Richard Hodgson, 'A Record of Observations of Certain Phenomena of Trance', in *Proc. SPR*, vol. 8, part 21 (1892).

8. op. cit., p. 57.

9. 'Report on Mrs Piper's Hodgson-Control', in *Proc. SPR*, vol. 23, part 58 (1909), p. 3. Further support for this view is afforded by the fact that Mrs Piper's 'Hodgson' control professed to have met in the next world not only the novelist George Eliot but also one of her fictional characters, Adam Bede (Mrs Henry Sidgwick, 'A Contribution to the Study of the Psychology of Mrs Piper's Trance Phenomena', in *Proc. SPR*, vol. 28, part 71 (1915), pp. 117, 500); and claimed to pass on messages from a non-existent niece, Bessie Beals, for whom one of the sitters asked: 'She [Bessie Beals] said little at first, but communicated more fully by the third sitting, and connected specific memories with the sitter – mainly, though not entirely, such as might be suggested by his statements and questions' (Mrs Henry Sidgwick, ibid., p. 177).

10. Professor J. H. Hyslop, in the course of a book-length report on the Piper mediumship, confessed that 'there is not one sentence in my record from which I could even pretend to deduce a conception of what the life beyond the grave is' ('A Further Record of Observations of Certain Trance Phenomena', in *Proc. SPR*, vol. 16, part 41 (1901), p. 291).

11. Eugène Osty, *Supernormal Faculties in Man*, ch. 5.

12. S. G. Soal, 'A Report on Some Communications Received through Mrs Blanche Cooper', in *Proc. SPR*, vol. 35, part 96 (1925), pp. 560–89. Other cases of the same kind are described in the *Journal of the American SPR*, vol. 13 (1919), pp. 130–6, 281–3, 492–4; in *Proc. SPR*, vol. 32 (1922), p. 133; and in John F. Thomas, *Beyond Normal Cognition*, pp. 206–7.

13. Morton Prince, *The Dissociation of a Personality*, pp. 4–5.

14. Whately Carington, 'The Quantitative Study of Trance Personalities, I', in *Proc. SPR*, vol. 42, part 136 (1934); 'The Quantitative Study of Trance Personalities, II', in *Proc. SPR*, vol. 43, part 141 (1935); 'The Quantitative Study of Trance Personalities, III', in *Proc. SPR*, vol. 44, part 149 (1936–7); and Robert H. Thouless, 'Review of Mr Whately Carington's Work on Trance Personalities', in *Proc. SPR*, vol. 44, part 150 (1936–7).

15. 'Preliminary Studies of the Recorded Leonard Material', in *Proc. SPR*, vol. 44, part 145 (1936–7), p. 22.

16. Richard Hodgson, 'A Further Record of Observations of Certain Phenomena of Trance', in *Proc. SPR*, vol. 13, part 33 (1897–8), p. 369. Other examples are: J. H. Hyslop, 'A Further Record of Observations of Certain Trance Phenomena', in *Proc SPR*, vol. 16, part 41 (1901), chs. 4, 6; Sir Oliver Lodge, *Raymond or Life and Death*.

17. C. D. Broad, *The Mind and Its Place in Nature*, pp. 540–1.

18. See chapter 17, section 3.

19. S. G. F. Brandon, *The Judgment of the Dead*, p. 51.

20. On the rather different earlier and later conceptions of sheol in the Old Testament period, see R. H. Charles, *Eschatology*, pp. 33–43.

21. A similar view is reported from southern Melanesia, where the underworld has been believed to be inhabited by shadowy, half-real beings. Cf. Brandon, op. cit., p. 136.

22. Cf. W. K. C. Guthrie, *The Greeks and Their Gods*, pp. 277–9.

23. *Odyssey*, book XI, ll. 152–3.

24. Oliver Lodge, *Raymond or Life and Death*, pp. 194ff.

25. ibid., p. 197.

26. ibid., p. 196n.

27. G. N. M. Tyrrell, *Science and Psychical Phenomena*, p. 302. It was also remarked at one time that spirits communicating through french mediums usually taught reincarnation whilst those communicating through english mediums denied reincarnation – a difference corresponding to the state of spiritualist opinion in the two countries.

28. E. R. Dodds, 'Why I do not Believe in Survival', in *Proc. SPR*, vol. 42, part 135 (1934), p. 155.

CHAPTER 8

Humanism and Death

I. THE HUMANIST ACCEPTANCE OF DEATH

There can undoubtedly be a naturalistic or humanist acceptance of death, both as a theoretical understanding of it and as
an emotional attitude towards it.

Amongst humanist thinkers there are of course different
approaches to the interpretation of death, but the biological
approach would probably be regarded by most as being both
legitimate and illuminating. Death is seen from this point of
view as a necessary part of the process of evolution. If new
members of any species, including man, were continually
being born without this recruitment being balanced by a
continual loss by death, the earth would soon have neither
space nor sustenance for them and the species would ex-
terminate itself through overcrowding. It is thus essential that
each generation in its turn be removed to make room for the
next. From the beginning of life there has had to be this
continual succession of new individual members of the
species, for it is through the small random differences occurring in each generation that the species has been able both to
improve its adaptation to and respond to changes in its
environment. As F. A. E. Crew says:

The habitats in which animals and plants have their being
are, and always have been, subject to sudden or gradual
change of considerable magnitude. If a species is to flourish
its characterization must be in harmony with the conditions
of the environment, it must therefore be capable of change
and be able to adjust and adapt to change . . . The capacity
to adjust and to adapt is at its peak in the young and
becomes progressively diminished with advancing age . . .
Natural death can therefore be regarded as the removal from
the population of such as are incapable of adjusting to
changing conditions. Had the conditions on this earth been

completely and permanently stable there would have been no need for the development of the ability to adjust, to learn new tricks in order to be able to cope, but in the external physical world (and also in the social world invented by man) change is everywhere and all the time, and so in order to ensure that a species shall be biologically efficient there came into being a system of replacement. The old, inefficient in respect of the abilities to reproduce and to adapt, are removed by natural death and replaced by the young, efficient in reproduction and adaptability.[1]

Seeing himself, then, as a member of the human species, which he values for the simple but sufficient reason that he is a part of it, a humanist may be able to accept his own future demise with equanimity as a contribution to the on-going life of the race. For 'when the individual has contributed adequately to the stream of life the purpose of being an individual has been served'.[2] Thus Dr Crew, writing at the age of eighty, said:

> Because I am old I can accept the idea that death is the end of me as an individual without any undue disquiet. I have lived a long and a very full life. I have loved and have been loved. I have passed on a genetic endowment to posterity – there are now two great grandchildren – and so have ensured continuance. A few of the results of my activities as a scientist have become embodied in the very texture of the science I tried to serve – this is the immortality that every scientist hopes for. I have enjoyed the privilege, as a university teacher, of being in a position to influence the thought of many hundreds of young people and in them and their lives I shall continue to live on vicariously for a while. All the things I care for will continue for they will be served by those who come after me. I find great pleasure in the thought that those who stand on my shoulders will see much further than I did in my time. What more could any man want?[3]

And, to be content with just one other example of this attitude, out of the many that could be adduced, Arnold Toynbee writing at the age of seventy-nine remarked that as one of the generation of Englishmen who had survived the first world war he felt that he had already enjoyed fifty bonus years of life. He continues:

> The tale of my bonus years of life has now mounted up to more than half a century. This time-bonus has been particularly valuable to me, because I have been an historian, and historians, like philosophers and politicians, need more time than mathematicians, ballet-dancers, or football-players to achieve results in their particular line of work. If I had died . . . in my middle twenties – the age, at death, of my contemporaries who were killed in the First World War – I should have died without leaving any memorial to speak of. The posthumous published work of my scholar contemporaries who were killed in 1915–16 is pathetically small in amount, though some of it is high in quality and great in promise. The loss of their, and their German fellow victims', potential contributions to mankind's cumulative intellectual achievement has been a loss to the world, not just to their personal friends.
>
> 'In the midst of life we are in death.' Having lived with this experience, as I now have, for more than fifty years, I am indeed familiar with death. I shall therefore have no excuse if, when my turn comes to die – and, at my age, death cannot be far off – I fail to face death readily and cheerfully.[4]

It is not necessary to quote further statements of the same kind from other humanist writers. The tradition of a philosophical and non-religious acceptance of human mortality, including one's own mortality, goes back throughout the modern period, with David Hume as its first great representative.[5] And in the ancient world it was abundantly represented among the epicurean and stoic philosophers.[6]

I want now to look at this attitude in its contrast to that taught by the great religions. These claim that as well as being an animal, 'made out of the dust of the earth', man is (according to the theistic faiths) a being created for eternal fellowship with God or (according to the non-theistic faiths) a 'spark of divinity' temporally separated from the Eternal Mind, or a consciousness capable of attaining to the perfect state of nirvana. Against this, humanism asserts that man is simply an animal, destined to perish like all other living species. Man's consciousness and personality depend absolutely upon the functioning of the brain and cease to exist when the brain, and the body as a whole, dies. For consciousness is a temporary by-product of the mammalian nervous system when this has evolved to a certain level of complexity, and there can accordingly be no question of the conscious personality surviving the death of the body.[7]

The broader implications of this humanist hypothesis are very far-reaching and probably no one in modern times has faced them more resolutely than Bertrand Russell. In a famous early essay called 'A Free Man's Worship', whose point of view he reaffirmed in the third volume of his autobiography published the year before his death, Russell wrote:

> That Man is the product of causes which had no prevision of the end they were achieving; that his origin, his growth, his hopes and fears, his loves and his beliefs, are but the outcome of accidental collocations of atoms; that no fire, no heroism, no intensity of thought and feeling, can preserve an individual life beyond the grave; that all the labours of the ages, all the devotion, all the inspiration, all the noonday brightness of human genius, are destined to extinction in the vast death of the solar system, and that the whole temple of Man's achievement must inevitably be buried beneath the débris of a universe in ruins – all these things, if not quite beyond dispute, are yet so nearly certain, that no philosophy which rejects them can hope to stand. Only within the scaffolding of these truths, only on the firm foundation of unyielding despair, can the soul's habitation henceforth be safely built.[8]

The picture which Russell here paints of man's situation is an explicitly pessimistic one. Life on this planet is doomed sooner or later to extinction, and the values which have been developed in the course of it will become extinct with mankind. In some, a like thought has engendered the despairing sense of meaninglessness which is expressed at many points in modern literature. For example, in Somerset Maugham's *Of Human Bondage* there is a powerful passage which presumably reflects its author's own attitude:

> Philip asked himself desperately what was the use of living
> at all. It all seemed inane . . . The effort was so incommen-
> surate with the result . . . Pain and disease and unhappiness
> weighed down the scale so heavily. What did it all mean?
> . . . The rain fell alike upon the just and upon the unjust,
> and for nothing was there a why and a wherefore . . .
> Suddenly the answer occurred to him . . . The answer was
> obvious. Life had no meaning. On the earth, satellite of a
> star speeding through space, living things had arisen under
> the influence of conditions which were part of the planet's
> history; and as there had been a beginning of life upon it so,
> under the influence of other conditions, there would be an
> end: man, no more significant than other forms of life, had
> come not as the climax of creation but as a physical reaction
> to the environment . . . There was no meaning in life, and
> man by living served no end. It was immaterial whether he
> was born or not born, whether he lived or ceased to live.
> Life was insignificant and death without consequence . . . [9]

However, Maugham (or at any rate Philip) eventually came
to terms with his sense òf the meaninglessness of human life,
in the thought that since nothing ultimately matters there can
be nothing to regret:

> Philip exulted, as he had exulted in his boyhood when the
> weight of a belief in God was lifted from his shoulders: it
> seemed to him that the last burden of responsibility was
> taken from him; and for the first time he was utterly free.
> His insignificance was turned to power, and he felt himself
> suddenly equal with the cruel fate which had seemed to
> persecute him; for, if life was meaningless, the world was
> robbed of its cruelty. What he did or left undone did not
> matter. Failure was unimportant and success amounted to
> nothing. He was the most inconsiderate creature in that
> swarming mass of mankind which for a brief space occupied
> the surface of the earth; and he was almighty because he had
> wrenched from chaos the secret of its nothingness . . . He
> felt inclined to leap and sing. He had not been so happy for
> months.[10]

This is a positive if somewhat frenetic acceptance of the implications of a naturalistic view of the universe. Others again have reacted more serenely to the humanist vision, seeing that within this context of cosmic purposelessness the individual's life can nevertheless be purposeful, yielding deep joys and satisfactions, and can thus be acceptable as a whole despite its unavoidable brevity. Man may be but a fleeting and accidental phenomenon in the infinite vastness of space and time; but nonetheless human love, friendship, loyalty and goodness, the endless beauties both of the natural world and of human artistic creation, and the achievements of human thought and science, are all self-justifying and their value is not diminished by the humanist understanding of man's ultimate situation. Further, it is possible that before this planet ceases to be habitable man may succeed in emigrating to another home in the solar system, or even to another solar system, and may indeed go on for ever finding new worlds on which to live as old ones cease to support him. Thus the race may prove to be immortal, successive generations endlessly arising to enjoy the values of human existence. Such vastly enlarged views of man's future, in which the planet earth has long since ceased to play any part, have been made familiar to our imaginations by contemporary science fiction.[11]

2. THE BASIC RELIGIOUS ARGUMENT FOR IMMORTALITY

To this extent humanism can perhaps claim to offer an optimistic view of life. But only, I now want to suggest, as an elitist doctrine for the fortunate few. The comparatively contented humanist writers whom I have quoted – and the same would be equally likely to be true of other humanist authors – have belonged to the small educated and affluent minority of mankind. And it is generally true that for those, including most of the readers and the writer of this book, who inhabit our affluent western societies life can be acceptable and indeed positively good without any reference to the idea of an afterlife. We have always been adequately fed and housed and clothed. We are recipients of an education which opens to us many of the riches of human culture. We live in a relatively stable society in which work can be purposeful and satisfying, in which the family can flourish, and to which we can hope to make our own small contribution. All these things are excellent. But let us not forget that they are all things which the majority of the human race unhappily lacks and has always lacked. Instead of citing statistics to support this statement I shall quote the following passage by Barbara Ward and René Dubos in their report written for the 1972 Stockholm Conference on the Human Environment:

> But the actual life of most of mankind has been cramped with back-breaking labour, exposed to deadly or debilitating disease, prey to wars and famines, haunted by the loss of children, filled with fear and the ignorance that breeds more fear. At the end, for everyone, stands dreaded unknown death. To long for joy, support and comfort, to react violently against fear and anguish is quite simply the human condition.[12]

This is largely because of endemic poverty. According to a 1970 United Nations report, one hundred children are born in developing countries every half-minute. Twenty of these will die within the year. Another sixty will suffer from malnutrition during their early years, and will have no access to medical care during their childhood. And more than half the world's population over ten have never been to school.[13]

If we are to transcend our own personal and atypically fortunate standpoint in order to survey the human situation as a whole we can perhaps best think of the satisfactoriness of man's life in terms of the fulfilling of its potential. The human potential includes love and friendship, co-operation between people in common causes, enjoyment of the natural world and appreciation of all the innumerable aspects of human thought and art. Given a state of society functioning at a technological level at which men's attention is not excessively absorbed in the struggle to survive, and given a human environment which is both adequately stable and adequately stimulating, men and women are capable of creating and enjoying all that has in fact been produced and enjoyed in the realms of philosophy and religion, science and technology, music, painting, poetry, prose, drama, dance, architecture, and all the other dimensions of human culture.

But we have to remember that this potentiality has in fact

been realized to any appreciable extent only in a very small minority of human lives. Most of the earth's inhabitants, in every generation including the present one, have had to live in a condition of chronic malnutrition and under threat of starvation, and very many have always had to dwell in the insecurity of oppression, exploitation and slavery, constantly menaced by the possibility of disasters of both human and natural origin. Even today, to quote from the journal *The Ecologist*, 'while most people receive the bare minimum of calories necessary for survival a large proportion are deprived of the nutrients (especially protein) essential for intellectual development. They are alive, but unable to realize their full potential.'[14] They are suffering from what has come to be called absolute poverty, which has been defined by the President of the World Bank as 'a condition of life so limited as to prevent realisation of the potential of the genes with which one is born. A condition of life so degrading as to insult human dignity – and yet a condition of life so common as to be the lot of some 40% of the peoples of the developing countries.'[15]

What however of the more intimate goods of personal relationship and family life – are not these independent both of poverty and of affluence? The answer, I think, must be both affirmative and negative. The family is indeed the main focus of the deepest personal satisfactions. And it is true that mutual love within a family does not directly depend upon economic welfare. But at the same time it does make a great difference to the happiness of the family if it is starving and without hope; and to the satisfaction involved in bringing up children if it is known that they must live on the starvation line and must lack both education and decent work. We in our minority western situation expect our children to be able to receive more or less as full an education as they are capable of assimilating, to find decent jobs, and to live in a society in which a predominantly satisfying life is possible. But this 'we' includes only a small minority of the human beings now alive, and an even smaller proportion of all the human beings who have lived during the hundred thousand or so years of the period over which it is possible to speak of man.

And when we take account of these sombre facts it is hard

to deny what the Buddha formulated as the first of his Four Noble Truths, namely that all life is permeated by *dukkha*, ill or suffering. As he said in his sermon at Sarnath, 'Birth is ill, decay is ill, sickness is ill, death is ill. To be conjoined with what one dislikes means suffering. To be disjoined from what one likes means suffering. Not to get what one wants, also that means suffering.'[16]

At this point we may profitably continue to listen to the witness of Buddhism and the concurring witness of the other faiths of indian origin. We shall have to attend at a later stage to the conceptions which these religions present of the nature of human fulfilment either as nirvana or as realization of oneness with the Absolute Mind. The insight I want to heed at the moment is that such fulfilment is not to be attained in a single earthly life. Gautama, for example, when he attained to enlightenment at Bodh Gaya and became a Buddha had, so he believed, already lived hundreds of thousands of previous lives, which he remembered in that period of final spiritual attainment. One earthly life is not enough. Likewise in the hindu understanding of the process of human completion, when a man attains to *moksha*, enlightenment, and becomes *jivanmukti*, a vast – perhaps infinite – number of lives lies behind him. Once again, it is believed that a single life is not enough. And this, surely, is realistic. In western and christian terms, if we understand the divine purpose for human beings as their realization of the human potential, their full human-ization, it is clear that this does not usually occur within the space of a single earthly life. Within this one life some men advance a long way towards the fulfilment of the human potential, most advance a little, but many hardly advance at all and some on the contrary regress. The general picture is certainly not one in which the human potential is normally or even often fulfilled in the course of this present life. Erich Fromm has well said that 'living is a process of continuous birth. The tragedy in the life of most of us is that we die before we are fully born.'[17]

We shall examine later the idea of successive reincarnations with which the indian religions match this insight, and likewise its equivalent in western thought in the idea of continued life, with the possibility of further spiritual growth, in other spheres beyond this world. We are not at this stage concerned with the differences between these ideas or with their respective merits but rather with what they have in common. This is a recognition that if the human potential is to be fulfilled in the lives of individual men and women, those lives must be prolonged far beyond the limits of our present bodily existence. The self that is to be perfected must transcend the brief and insecure career of an animal organism. There must, in short, be some form of continued personal life after death.

This is to say that the burden of evil – the burden of physical pain, mental suffering, and of man's manifold inhumanity to man – imprints upon human life as a whole a tragic character if that life ends in each individual case at physical death. For when we are trying to think about the human situation as a whole we must not be content to reckon it only in terms of our own fortunate and exceptional experience but in terms of the general experience of mankind through the world and across the centuries. When we try to form this global picture we see that life has been for most people an experience of suffering relieved by occasional flashes of happiness. It is characterized by unfulfilled possibilities, unrealized potentialities, great good which is glimpsed from afar but never attained. And this is one of the meanings, even though not the only meaning, of the word 'tragedy'.

3. HUMANISM AND THE PROBLEM OF EVIL

How does the christian view of our human situation differ from the humanist view, if not by the former's emphatic denial that man's existence is in the end irredeemably tragic? Christian faith asserts that our life has its meaning within the great *Divina Commedia* of the creation of perfected finite spiritual life, and that it is good not only because of the present elements of happiness and joy within it but also because it is in process towards a universal fulfilment of limitless value. Thus whilst in the humanist vision man's existence as a whole is seen as largely tragic, in the christian vision it is seen as ultimately good; in the words of Mother Julian of Norwich, 'all shall be well and all shall be well, and all manner thing shall be well'.[18] Christian faith is a final optimism because it sees the human story in its relation to God – God who, as we read in the New Testament, is *agape*, love.

Thus the issue between religion and humanism hinges upon the agony endured by men and women in generation after generation, whether through human cruelty or indifference or through the frailty of the human organism and its liability to pain in an environment which includes famine, drought, violent storms and earthquakes, animal predators and the other hazards of nature. The issue is whether the incalculable weight of suffering which has been borne during the hundred or so millennia of man's prehistory and history down to the present time, and as it seems likely to continue in the future, is or is not sheer meaningless, unredeemed and unredeemable suffering.

Now since a final bringing of good out of evil in the triumphant climax of the *Divina Commedia* does not belong to this earthly life, it can only happen – if it happens at all – beyond it. And so I conclude that the question of immortality forms a vital crux between Humanism and Christianity. For the idea of immortality (still in the minimal sense of our life not being terminated by bodily death) is an essential basis for any view which could count towards a solution of the theological problem of human suffering. Such a 'solution' must consist, not in denying the reality of suffering, but in showing how it is to be justified or redeemed. But what would it mean to justify, or redeem, the world's suffering? Presumably it would mean showing it to be rationally and morally acceptable either in itself or in relation to a future which will render it worthwhile. But the notions of the 'acceptability' and 'worthwhileness' of someone's suffering are highly ambiguous: acceptable or worthwhile from whose point of view? There seem to be three possibilities, two of which do not and one of which does require man's immortality. The first is a religious justification, but one which is compatible (as in ancient hebrew religion) with man's being a mortal creature, briefly endowed with conscience and the awareness of his Maker but, like the other animals, destined to return to the dust of the earth. It might be said that the experiences of such a fleeting creature, including his pains, travails and agonies as well as his joys, are justified in the eyes of his Creator. For if God wishes to create such beings, to observe their lives, and graciously to enter into personal communication with them during their brief careers, his omnipotent wish might be said to be its own justification. As St Paul asked, 'Will what is moulded say to its moulder, "Why have you made me thus?" Has the potter no right over the clay?'[19] This, then, is the first kind of justification that is possible for human suffering, namely that it should be part of a situation which is willed by an all-powerful creator; this is a justification which need not involve human immortality.

The second possibility is more humanistic. There might be a justification of human suffering through the ages from the point of view of a more ideal humanity or super-humanity in the future which will have evolved out of the painful process of human life as we know it. Individuals perish for ever in generation after generation; but the species goes on and from it there may develop a higher humanity which will justify the lower forms out of which it has come. Such a justification would function in a way analogous to that in which we ourselves regard the harsh struggle for survival through which the human species has evolved as being justified by its human end-product. This, too, would not involve individual immortality.

Whether these first two kinds of justification are morally acceptable depends upon a fundamental judgement concerning the worth of the individual human person. Kant focused the attention of the modern world upon this value judgement when he presented it as a basic moral principle, a form of the categorical imperative, that humanity is always to be treated, whether in one's own person or in the person of any other, never simply as a means but always at the same time as an end.[20] And the acceptability of these two putative justifications of human suffering depends upon whether individual persons are to be valued as ends in themselves or may properly be treated purely as means to some further end. Although it took Christianity a long time to clarify and is taking even longer for it to implement its valuation of individual personality, perhaps its chief contribution to the life of the world has been its insistence that each human being is equally a child of God, made for eternal fellowship with his Maker and endowed with unlimited value by the divine love which has created him, which sustains him in being, and which purposes his eternal blessedness. Thus, in spite of so many failures in christian practice, Christianity teaches that the human individual is never a mere means, expendable in the interests of some further goal, but is always an end in himself as the object of God's love. A humanist would not of course use this religious language in expressing his own valuation of individual human life; but nevertheless humanists oppose acts of genocide, injustice and racial discrimination on the ground that these deny to other human beings the intrinsic worth and dignity which we each claim for ourselves. There can of course be no proof of any such fundamental valuation. But for all who adopt this christian-humanist attitude to mankind the two possible justifications of human suffering which I have thus far outlined must be entirely unacceptable. For they imply a view of the individual human personality not only as expendable in the sense that he can be allowed to pass out of existence but, more importantly, as exploitable in the sense that he can be subjected to any extent and degree of physical pain and mental suffering for a future end in which he cannot participate and of which he knows nothing. This is a dangerous doctrine because, as B. H. Streeter pointed out, 'if the Divine righteousness may lightly "scrap" the individual, human righteousness may do the same'.[21] The individual's lack of any significant personal moral status or value is a corollary of the suggestion that his involuntary sufferings, however extreme they may be, are justified if they form part of a process which produces a good end, even though that end is entirely separate from the individual's own brief existence. Dostoyevsky voices the inadequacy of this approach when he makes one of his characters say, 'Surely I haven't suffered simply that I, my crimes and my sufferings, may manure the soil of the future harmony for somebody else. I want to see with my own eyes the hind lie down with the lion and the victim rise up and embrace his murderer. I want to be there when every one suddenly understands what it has all been for.'[22] Thus the only morally acceptable justification of the agonies and heartaches of human life must be of a third kind in which the individuals who have suffered *themselves* participate in the justifying good and are themselves able to see their own past sufferings as having been worthwhile. And this is the third kind of justification, to which the argument now leads us.

At this point, if we are to avoid being led off immediately along a major false trail, we must distinguish between, on the one hand, the idea of compensation in the form of future happiness enjoyed to balance past misery endured, and on the other hand the very different idea of the eventual all-justifying fulfilment of the human potential in a perfected life. There has always been something morally unattractive about the idea of the compensatory joys of heaven. It suggests a comparatively low level of ethical insight centred upon the notion of justice as exact reciprocity, 'an eye for an eye and a tooth for a tooth', a certain quantum of pleasure cancelling out a certain quantum of pain. The individual is treated as though he were a creditor in a hedonic bank, whose needs are adequately met by ensuring a mathematical balance. He is not seen as a free personal will capable of growth and of the exercise of positive acceptance, understanding and forgiveness. But surely the individual would be much more truly valued for his own sake as a living end in himself by a justification of the pains and sorrows through which he has passed in terms of a fulfilment which is a state of his own self and of the human community of selves of which he is a part. The good that comes about, and that justifies all that has occurred on the way to it, is then the personal growth and perfecting, the spiritual maturation to a state of full humanity, the free awareness and acceptance of the divine love which has brought men and women through so many sorrows to their Father's house. Such a justification treats each individual as an end in himself within a kingdom of ends, both because it functions as a justification in his own estimation and because the good on which it depends is a state of which the individual himself is to be a part.

Now it is clear that this third kind of justification of human suffering presupposes the individual's survival of bodily death under conditions in which it is possible for him to undergo further personal growth and development. What these conditions might be will be considered later. The point of the present argument is that any morally acceptable justification of the sufferings of humanity is bound to postulate a life after death. Attempted justifications which refuse to take this step fail under the criterion of universal love: only a fortunate few are regarded as ends in themselves, the less fortunate mass being treated as involuntary means to an end of which they are not aware and in which they do not participate. And the issue between a humanistic and a religious view of our human situation crystallizes at this point in their disagreement as to whether or not the universe is such that human suffering is to be finally justified. Humanism says that it will never be justified (in the only morally acceptable sense of this word), and thus presents man's situation as a whole as a tragic scene involving an immensity of unredeemed and unredeemable suffering and of unfulfilled and unfulfillable potentiality. The religions, on the other hand, say that our human situation is not ultimately tragic because it is leading to a universal fulfilment of such worth that in relation to it all human suffering will be rendered manifestly worthwhile.

We are now at the heart of the theodicy problem, where it meets the problem of man's destiny. The crucial question is whether any human fulfilment could provide a morally acceptable justification for the creation of a world containing all the suffering and all the wickedness which our world contains. I have been arguing that it *is* possible for a history including great evils to be rendered worthwhile by bringing about a sufficiently great good. But the issue is so important that this answer must be tested by confronting it with its direct denial. For it can be questioned whether *any* fulfilment, however good, in which men might eventually participate could ever render worthwhile the worst of human sufferings. Dostoyevsky has put the negative case in an unforgettable chapter of *The Brothers Karamazov*. The whole chapter (and indeed the entire novel) should be read; but the point comes through with great force in the following:

'It was in the darkest days of serfdom at the beginning of the century, and long live the Liberator of the People! There was in those days a general of aristocratic connections, the owner of great estates, one of those men – somewhat exceptional, I believe, even then – who, retiring from the service into a life of leisure, are convinced that they've earned absolute power over the lives of their subjects. There were such men then. So our general, settled on his property of two thousand souls, lives in pomp, and domin-eers over his poor neighbours as though they were depen-dants and buffoons. He has kennels of hundreds of hounds and nearly a hundred dog-boys – all mounted, and in uniform. One day a serf boy, a little child of eight, threw a stone in play and hurt the paw of the general's favourite hound. "Why is my favourite dog lame?" He is told that the boy threw a stone that hurt the dog's paw. "So you did it". The general looked the child up and down. "Take him". He was taken – taken from his mother and kept shut up all night. Early that morning the general comes out on horse-back, with the hounds, his dependents, dog-boys, and huntsmen, all mounted around him in full hunting parade. The servants are summoned for their edification, and in front of them all stands the mother of the child. The child is brought from the lock-up. It's a gloomy cold, foggy autumn day, a capital day for hunting. The general orders the child to be undressed; the child is stripped naked. He shivers, numb with terror, not daring to cry . . . "Make him run," commands the general . . . and he sets the whole pack of hounds on the child. The hounds catch him, and tear him to pieces before his mother's eyes! . . . I believe the general was afterwards declared incapable of administering his estates. Well – what did he deserve? To be shot? To be shot for the satisfaction of our moral feelings? Speak, Alyosha!'

'To be shot', murmured Alyosha, lifting his eyes to Ivan with a pale, twisted smile . . .

'Listen! If all must suffer to pay for the eternal harmony, what have children to do with it, tell me, please? It's beyond all comprehension why they should suffer, and why they should pay for the harmony. Why should they, too, furnish material to enrich the soil for the harmony of the future? I understand solidarity in sin among men. I understand solidarity in retribution, too; but there can be no such solidarity with children. And if it is really true that they must share responsibility for all their fathers' crimes, such a truth is not of this world and is beyond my comprehension . . . I understand, of course, what an upheaval of the universe it will be, when everything in heaven and earth blends in one hymn of praise and everything that lives and has lived cries aloud: "Thou art just, O Lord, for Thy ways are revealed". When the mother embraces the fiend who threw her child to the dogs, and all three cry aloud with tears, "Thou art just, O Lord!" then, of course, the crown of knowledge will be reached and all will be made clear. But what pulls me up here is that I can't accept that harmony. And while I am on earth, I make haste to take my own measure. You see, Alyosha, perhaps it really may happen that if I live to that moment, or rise again to see it, I, too, perhaps, may cry aloud with the rest, looking at the mother embracing the child's torturer, "Thou art just, O Lord!" but I don't want to cry aloud then. While there is still time, I hasten to protect myself and so I renounce the higher harmony altogether. It's not worth the tears of that one tortured child who beat itself on the breast with its little fist and prayed in its stinking outhouse, with its unexpiated tears to "dear, kind God"! It's not worth it, because those tears are unatoned for. They must be atoned for, or there can be no harmony. But how? How are you going to atone for them? Is it possible? By their being avenged? But what do I care for avenging them? What do I care for a hell for oppressors? What good can hell do, since those children have already been tortured? And what becomes of a harmony, if there is hell? I want to forgive. I want to embrace. I don't want more suffering. And if the sufferings of children go to swell the sum of suffering which was necessary to pay for truth, then I protest that the truth is not worth such a price . . . I would rather be left with my unavenged suffering and unsatisfied indignation, *even if I were wrong*. Besides, too high a price is asked for harmony; it's beyond our means to pay so much to enter on it. And so I hasten to give back my entrance ticket, and if I am an honest man I am bound to give it back as soon as possible. And that I am doing. It's not God that I don't accept, Alyosha, only I most respectfully return Him the ticket'.

'That's rebellion,' murmured Alyosha, looking down.

'Rebellion? I am sorry you call it that,' said Ivan earnestly. 'One can hardly live in rebellion, and I want to live. Tell me yourself, I challenge you – answer. Imagine that you are creating a fabric of human destiny with the object of making men happy in the end, giving them peace and rest at last, but that it was essential and inevitable to torture to death only one tiny creature – that baby beating its breast with its fist, for instance – and to found that edifice on its unavenged tears, would you consent to be the architect on those conditions? Tell me, and tell the truth.'

'No, I wouldn't consent,' said Alyosha softly.[23]

Dostoyevsky is surely right in seeing deliberate human cruelty – rather than any of the pain-producing aspects of nature – as the worst form of evil. But there is more to be said and pondered than even he considers. Two immensely important facts have to be brought into relation with the fact of wickedness – the experience of freedom and the achievement of forgiveness. The acts of savage and sadistic inhumanity which Dostoyevsky describes – which can certainly be matched outside the pages of a novel – can be taken as showing the cruel character of the power which has created a universe in which such things happen. But they can also be taken as showing the tremendous importance which that power attaches to our own character as free and responsible moral agents. If human beings were not free to be cruel, they would never *be* cruel, but they would also not be free or, therefore, moral beings. Thus the question is whether a good human fulfilment, the realization of which requires man's freedom, can render worthwhile the whole process of freely interacting human lives which ultimately leads to this fulfilment but which includes on the way the fearful misuse of freedom in acts of wickedness and cruelty. Such a state of human fulfilment would necessarily involve an ultimate universal forgiveness for the cruelties, injustices, and inhumanities which men have inflicted upon one another in their earthly lives. Dostoyevsky imagines such a final heavenly reconciliation and rejects it:

'I don't want the mother to embrace the oppressor who threw her son to the dogs! She dare not forgive him! Let her forgive him for herself, if she will, let her forgive the torturer for the immeasurable suffering of her mother's heart. But the sufferings of her tortured child she has no right to forgive; she dare not forgive the torturer, even if the child were to forgive him!'[24]

Dostoyevsky is evidently thinking of this meeting taking place when the general is still the same cruel (or perhaps insane) person who committed the appalling brutality; and he is thinking of forgiveness as a condoning of the general's behaviour. But forgiveness does not mean condoning, still less approving, the unspeakably brutal act that was committed. Pascal was right when he said, 'Time heals griefs and quarrels, for we change and are no longer the same persons. Neither the offender nor the offended are any more themselves. It is like a nation which we have provoked, but meet again after two generations. They are still Frenchmen, but not the same.'[25] In Dostoyevsky's case this means forgiving and accepting the perfect person whom the perpetrator of the terrible act has ultimately become. In the doubtless long course of this perfecting he may well have suffered fearful purgatorial consequences of his own cruelty – not divine punishments, but the effect of his actions encountered in his own conscience. His perfecting will have involved his utter revulsion against his own cruelty and a deep shame and sorrow at the memory of it. At the end of this hard creative process he will be the same person in the sense that he will remember how he treated the serf boy, and will feel ashamed and sorry and in desperate need of forgiveness. But in another sense he will no longer be the same person; for he will have changed in character into someone who is now morally incapable of behaving in such a way and who is, in comparison with his former self, 'a new creature'. In these circumstances, is forgiveness impossible or wrong? Would unforgiveness really be admirable at the termination of such a process of soul-making? Surely not; and certainly the idea of an ultimate universal mutual forgiveness, which even includes those who have committed history's most brutal and inhuman crimes, is in harmony with the deepest insights of the christian faith.

Could such ultimate forgiveness be part of an acceptance of the creative process as a whole, including the almost limitless pain and suffering that it has involved? Can we conceive of completed and perfected persons, having arrived at the state of full intensity of existence, full consciousness of reality, and fullness of joy in being, looking back upon the long, chequered story of human freedom in all its grandeur and all its misery, its agony and tragedy and failure as well as its moments of happiness and glory, and seeing it as worthwhile as the road by which they have at last come to this fulfilment? I believe so. I am not suggesting that it will be seen *sub specie aeternitatis* that each particular evil experienced by human beings was specifically necessary to the bringing about of this fulfilment. What was necessary was human freedom; and the particular detailed course that man's history has taken, as the expression of human freedom, is not necessary but contingent. The specific misuses of freedom which have so largely constituted human history were not necessary in order that mankind should move through the exercise of freedom to an eventual full humanization and perfection. But it was necessary that there should be genuine human freedom, carrying with it the possibility of appalling misuses; and all these inhumanities of man to man are part of the contingent form which the story of human freedom has in fact taken.

The conclusion to which all this points is that to say that human existence taken in its totality is a *Divina Commedia*, rather than an almost limitless tragedy, is to say that it leads to a good fulfilment which presupposes man's continued individual existence beyond death. This is the basic religious argument for 'immortality'.

NOTES

1. F. A. E. Crew, 'The Meaning of Death', in *The Humanist Outlook*, ed. A. J. Ayer, pp. 257–8.
2. ibid., p. 257.
3. ibid., pp. 259–60.
4. Arnold Toynbee, 'The Relation between Life and Death, Living and Dying', in *Man's Concern with Death* by Arnold Toynbee and others, p. 264.
5. See Hume's letters written during his last illness. For example, five days before his death he wrote to the Comtesse de Boufflers, 'I see death approach gradually, without any anxiety or regret' (J. H. Burton, *The Life of David Hume*, vol. II, p. 514). The day after Hume's death his physician wrote to Adam Smith: 'He continued, to the last,

perfectly sensible, and free from much pain or feelings of distress. He never dropped the smallest expression of impatience; but, when he had occasion to speak to the people about him, always did it with affection and tenderness. I thought it improper to write to you to bring you over, especially as I heard that he had dictated a letter to you desiring you not to come. When he became very weak, it cost him an effort to speak; and he died in such a happy composure of mind that nothing could exceed it' (ibid., vol. II, p. 515). See also James Boswell's 'An Account of My Last Interview with David Hume, Esq.', printed as Appendix A in Norman Kemp Smith's edition of Hume's *Dialogues concerning Natural Religion*.

6. For example, Lucretius, *On the Nature of the Universe*, book III; Marcus Aurelius, *Meditations*, book II.

7. For a standard modern expression of this view, see Corliss Lamont, *The Illusion of Immortality*; and for an older version, E. S. P. Haynes, *The Belief in Personal Immortality*.

8. *Mysticism and Logic*, pp. 47–8. In 1962 Russell commented in a letter that whilst he regarded the style of this essay as 'florid and rhetorical', nevertheless 'my outlook on the cosmos and on human life is substantially unchanged' (*The Autobiography of Bertrand Russell*, vol. III, pp. 172–3).

9. *Of Human Bondage*, condensed from ch. 106, pp. 653–5. On the relation of Philip's life and experiences to Somerset Maugham's, see the section on '*Of Human Bondage* as an autobiographical novel' in Richard A. Cordell's introduction.

10. ibid., p. 655.

11. For example, Isaac Asimov's *Foundation* trilogy.

12. Barbara Ward and René Dubos, *Only One Earth*, p. 35.

13. *Get Off Their Backs*, pp. 3–4.

14. *A Blueprint for Survival* (vol. 2, no. 1 of *The Ecologist*, 1972), p. 47.

15. *The Guardian*, 25 September 1973, p. 19.

16. *Buddhist Scriptures*, p. 186.

17. Erich Fromm, 'Values, Psychology, and Human Existence', in *New Knowledge in Human Values*, ed. A. H. Maslow, p. 156.

18. Mother Julian of Norwich, *The Revelations of Divine Love*, ch. 27, p. 92.

19. Romans 9: 20–1.

20. Immanuel Kant, *Grundlegung zur Metaphysik der Sitten*, pp. 66–7 (*The Moral Law*, p. 96).

21. B. H. Streeter, *Immortality*, p. 85.

22. Fyodor Dostoyevsky, *The Brothers Karamazov*, part II, book V, ch. 4, p. 289.

23. *The Brothers Karamazov*, from part II, book V, ch. 4.

24. ibid., p. 291.

25. *Pensées*, p. 37 (Brunschvicg's ed., no. 122).

Part III

CHRISTIAN
APPROACHES

CHAPTER 9

New Testament Views of the After-Life

I. THE RESURRECTION OF JESUS

So long as we do not insist upon any dogmatic definition of its precise nature, we can assert that beyond all reasonable doubt what has come to be called 'the resurrection of Jesus' was a real occurrence. For it can hardly be questioned that something immensely impressive, and in that sense undeniably real, happened shortly after Jesus' death to restore and enhance his disciples' faith in him as their living Lord and Master. If their life-situation had not been transformed by some powerfully moving event it seems very unlikely that the tiny Jesus-movement within Judaism would long have survived the execution of its leader and that there would today, nearly two thousand years later, be a christian community numbering hundreds of millions. Something must have happened to give Jesus' disciples new heart and spirit, so that they were (according to Luke) 'together in one place' in Jerusalem at the feast of Pentecost, fifty days after his crucifixion, ready to be 'filled with the Holy Spirit' and to proclaim publicly concerning one who had recently been executed, 'This Jesus God raised up, and of that we all are witnesses.'[1] And they referred to that which had transformed the world for them as the resurrection of Jesus, now revealed to them in supernatural glory and power.

It is however impossible for us today to be sure in precisely what the resurrection event consisted. Even the word 'resurrection' has to be used as a conventional name rather than as a description. For we do not know whether the lively faith of the apostolic circle was evoked by the coming forth of a miraculously revivified body from the grave, or by a series of visions (and perhaps auditions) of Jesus as a glorified figure of exalted majesty. Any kind of return of or encounter with the dead would, in the minds of Jesus' contemporaries, tend to become categorized as a resurrection; and except among a sophisticated minority this meant a physical resurrection. Despite the colossal difficulties which such a picture creates for the modern mind, the first-century jewish readers of Matthew's gospel could be expected to believe that at the time of Jesus' crucifixion 'the tombs also were opened, and many bodies of the saints who had fallen asleep were raised, and coming out of the tombs after his resurrection they went into the holy city and appeared to many'.[2] This, like Jesus' own resurrection, would be thought of as a foretaste of the universal rising of the dead to which most Jews looked forward. Bodily resurrection was the prevailing popular hebrew conception of life after death[3] and in whatever form Jesus may, as Christians believe, have manifested himself to his disciples on easter day the story of his appearing would have been drawn by this conception into the form provided by the resurrection model.

We cannot, then, learn with any certainty from the use of the word 'resurrection' in what the event itself consisted. There is a spectrum of possibilities. Did the dead body of Jesus come forth from its grave to resume a fully physical life? Or was it somehow changed in the tomb so that whilst retaining some physical attributes – including shape, solidity, and the capacity to speak and eat – it took on other contra-physical attributes such as the capacity suddenly to materialize and dematerialize at points in space? Should we draw upon the stories of super-natural powers developed by great spiritual masters of the east enabling them to exert an extraordinary control over their own bodies and even to materialize and dematerialize at will, and think of Jesus' resurrection as exhibiting an extreme form of this kind of psychic power?[4] Or did the resurrection consist in visions seen by some of Jesus' disciples shortly after his death? If so, were the visions produced in their minds by the living spirit of Jesus? Did the resurrection appearances thus belong to the category, familiar in the annals of psychical research, of 'veridical hallucinations' in which telepathically received information[5] is presented to consciousness in the form of visions? Or – moving further along the range of possibilities – instead of there having been either perceptions or visions, did the resurrection take place entirely on the inner plane of the disciples' faith? Was it a resurrection of their faith, or its elevation from a faith in Jesus as their earthly leader to faith in Jesus as God's chosen messenger, later becoming expressed in more readily comprehensible stories of visions and voices? And if so, is this powerful resurgence of faith to be attributed to the activity of the living spirit of the Lord; or to purely natural causes, such as wishful thinking and self-deception? Or to his spirit working through some such psychological mechanism?

Any view according to which the event which evoked the faith of the post-easter community was a real interaction after his death between Jesus and the disciples should be acceptable in principle to christian faith today. However, within the wide range of such views the two which have seemed most probable to Christians are the rising from the tomb of Jesus' mysteriously transformed body, and the seeing by some of his disciples of a vision or visions of their exalted Lord. A considerable debate has taken place over the years concerning the bodily or visionary, physical or psychological or para-psychological, character of the resurrection. But what is chiefly important for Christians is to see that neither the reality nor the religious significance of the resurrection event depends upon the outcome – if indeed there will ever be a definitive outcome – of that debate. The essential features of the resurrection gospel recorded in Acts are that God had raised up Jesus, giving him power and authority ('exalted at the right hand of God'[6]), and that Jesus was alive ('having loosed the pangs of death, because it was not possible for him to be held by it'[7]). Both aspects of the message are based upon the glorified Lord showing himself to some of his disciples; and whether he showed himself as a material body, which could (had this been technically possible in the first century) have been photographed and tape-recorded, or as a seen vision and a heard voice which were utterly real and vivid experiences, but nevertheless not available to cameras and tape-recorders, is relatively unimportant. If their living Lord revealed himself to the disciples as a supernaturally shining presence, of whose sublime love and transcendent authority they were overwhelmingly conscious, this would be an event of decisive, indeed absolute, significance. That this presence was or was not at the same time a physical object could neither add to nor detract from the experienced reality and transforming impact of such an encounter with the risen Lord. I therefore do not think that it should, from the standpoint of christian faith, be regarded as a centrally important question whether the resurrection event involved the reanimation of Jesus' dead body and its emergence from the tomb.

If this estimate of faith's detachment from the question of visions versus a bodily resurrection is accepted, the Christian is free to weigh the historical evidence without fear or prejudice. Because the evidence is complex, and the weighing of it a matter of probable judgement whose outcome is not ultimately important, I shall not attempt to adjudicate the issue but will merely rehearse some of the main considerations on either side and suggest the tentative conclusion to which they seem to me to point.

The case for presuming a bodily resurrection is based on the gospel narratives. These undoubtedly present the risen Christ as the revivified body from the tomb, with the marks of crucifixion upon him,[8] and depict him as eating,[9] and as inviting doubting Thomas to touch him.[10] It is however generally held by those who accept the case for a bodily resurrection that whilst the raised body was that which had been buried, it had nevertheless undergone a profound transformation and was now in a 'glorified' state, no longer subject to all the conditions governing ordinary objects in space. For the risen Jesus could at will become physically present within a locked room and could disappear at will.[11] Nevertheless the body which appeared and disappeared, and was alive in glorious power, had come from the tomb. That the tomb was in fact empty is evidenced by the story put about by the authorities that the disciples had stolen the body;[12] and by the consideration that it would have been impossible for the disciples at Pentecost, less than two months after Jesus' crucifixion, publicly to have proclaimed his resurrection in Jerusalem, within a mile or so of the tomb, if his body had still been there and able to be produced.

On the other hand the case for supposing that the resurrection event consisted in waking visions of the living Lord experienced by some of the disciples is largely based on the earliest New Testament reference to the resurrection, which is not in any of the gospels but in one of St Paul's letters.[13] Here

Paul recites what is apparently an official christian list of the resurrection appearances, but does not refer to the story of the empty tomb. Of course he could both have known of the empty tomb stories and regarded them as sound and yet not thought them relevant to his purpose. But on the other hand he was writing to counter doubts within the corinthian church (set in a hellenic rather than a hebrew environment) about the resurrection of the dead; and therefore one might think that the evidence of Jesus' empty tomb would in fact have been relevant. At any rate, on the face of it the evidence of Paul's reference to the resurrection is that, at the time when he was writing, the accepted tradition was about visions of the Lord, first to Peter then to other believers. Again, Paul clearly includes his own encounter with the risen Jesus on the Damascus road as the last of these appearances. For his claim to be an authentic apostle rested upon his being a first-hand witness to the fact of the resurrection. In the descriptions of this encounter in Acts[14] Paul is reported as speaking of a blinding light surrounding him and a voice which said, in reply to his question, 'I am Jesus of Nazareth, whom you are persecuting.' There is no reference to an embodied presence or even to a visual appearance other than the blinding light. Thus – the argument runs – at the earliest point at which we have access to the developing gospel tradition it did not include any empty tomb stories; and St Paul's subjective experience was understood (at least by Paul himself) as an instance of a resurrection appearance. On this view, the entire cycle of stories about the burial, the tomb, the miraculous removal of the stone, the angels, and the appearance of Jesus himself in the garden – indeed possibly the whole Jerusalem tradition – represents a legendary development. Jesus' body was probably placed in a common grave for executed criminals, and short of an elaborate exhumation it would seven weeks later, at Pentecost, have been impossible to establish anything corresponding to the empty tomb of the developed tradition.

But the New Testament evidence is even more varied and confusing than appears when we thus organize it around the question of a bodily resurrection versus visions. It shows indications of considerable growth and development unchecked by any firm core of tradition beyond the simple proclamation that Jesus is risen as the glorified Lord: 'God exalted him at his right hand as Leader and Saviour';[15] 'God has highly exalted him and bestowed on him the name which is above every name.'[16] The resurrection message within the original apostolic preaching (if this is what we have in Acts and the earlier epistles) is that since his death Jesus has revealed himself in glory, invested with a quasi-divine authority and power to save. But by the time when the gospels began to be written, some thirty to thirty-five years later, this message had been elaborated into a catena of stories, some however incompatible with others, of the empty tomb and of appearances and words of the risen Lord. There is the Jerusalem cycle of stories, in the earliest version of which in Mark's gospel, ending at 16: 8, the women find the tomb empty and are told by a 'young man' that Jesus has risen and has gone into Galilee, where the disciples are to follow him. It is only in the later gospel narratives that appearances in Jerusalem are added, together with a wealth of elaboration, much of which has the air of legend. Thus in Matthew there is the earthquake; the angel, 'his appearance like lightning', rolling back the stone that closed the tomb; the guards who 'became like dead men'; and the story that at the time of the crucifixion numerous bodies came forth from their tombs and were seen in Jerusalem.[17] In Luke the angel at the tomb has become two,[18] and we have the mysterious encounter with Jesus on the Emmaus road – mysterious because the disciples do not recognize their Lord until he breaks the bread, whereupon he vanishes; followed by an appearance in Jerusalem and then Jesus' ascension from Bethany. In Luke all this happens within the space of twenty-four hours, thus excluding the possibility of appearances in Galilee. But there is also the galilean tradition telling of appearances of Jesus to his disciples – to eleven on a mountain, according to Matthew (28: 16–20), or to Peter and six others by the Sea of Tiberias according to John (21: 1–3). It is impossible to conflate the Jerusalem and Galilee cycles, in view of Luke's timetable of events. But there are other problems also. Who first saw the risen Lord? According to Paul (1 Corinthians 15: 5) and Luke (24: 34) it was Peter; but according to Matthew and John it was two women (Matthew 28: 1–10) or one (John 20: 14). Did Jesus impart the Holy

Spirit to the disciples when he appeared in a locked room on the evening of easter day (John 20: 22), or some fifty days later at Pentecost (Acts 2)? After the discovery of the empty tomb, did the disciples go immediately to Galilee (Mark 16: 7), or remain in Jerusalem where, according to John, a second appearance occurred eight days after the first (John 20: 26)? Did the resurrection appearances begin and end on the same day (Luke 24), or were they spread over forty days (Acts 1: 3)?[19]

It is evident both that these various strands of tradition are incapable of being fully harmonized, and that the New Testament shows a development from a simple proclamation of the living reality of the glorified Lord to detailed stories of his bodily presence and speech, characterized by progressive degeneration from history to legend. Thus any extrapolation from the series of narratives back towards that which actually happened moves from the more elaborate towards the more simple. In the earliest experience and understanding of the disciples there was probably no distinction between Jesus having 'risen' and his being 'glorified', 'exalted', 'ascended to the right hand of the Father'.[20] The conviction, which was at the heart of the early gospel, that Jesus lives as exalted Lord and that men can find salvation through him, could thus have had as its simplest and perhaps most likely basis a vision or visions, perhaps only momentary, of Jesus as a majestic figure shining in supernatural light – an experience which may perhaps be reflected in the transfiguration story.

Less than this could hardly have launched the movement which sprang up so vigorously after Jesus' death, and more is probably not required to account for it. The resurrection may have been a bodily event, and the body may have mysteriously materialized and dematerialized; there may have been angels, earthquake and guards fainting; there may have been lengthy discourses by the risen Christ to his disciples, terminated after some weeks by his ascension into the air. But the gospel that Jesus lives, exalted by God to a glorious role in the process of man's salvation, does not depend upon the historicity of any of these problematic elements of the New Testament tradition.

2. JESUS' RESURRECTION AND THE BELIEF IN
A LIFE AFTER DEATH

To what extent is the resurrection of Jesus the basis of the christian belief in a life after death? It has often been said – though more in sermons than in considered contributions to theology – that whereas others may believe in a life to come on the basis of uncertain philosophical arguments or dubious spiritualistic phenomena, the Christian knows that death is not the end because he knows that Jesus rose from the grave:

> Jesus lives! thy terrors now
> Can no longer, death, appal us . . .
> Jesus lives! henceforth is death
> Entrance-gate to life immortal . . . [21]

But the idea that Jesus' resurrection provides the Christian's sole ground for belief in a life after death cannot be sustained historically. From at least the end of the second century the large majority of believers have, in so far as they have accepted the doctrines of their church, affirmed the immortality of the soul on grounds not directly connected with Jesus' resurrection. For it has long been the teaching of the roman church, although not formally defined as a dogma until the fifth Lateran Council (1512–17), that the soul is immortal;[22] and from the time of Calvin until recently the same doctrine has been held within the reformed churches. Further, the belief in the resurrection of the dead was not created by the resurrection of Christ. On the contrary, it is likely that Jesus' manifestation of himself to his disciples after his death came to be known as his 'resurrection' because this was already an accepted category of religious thinking. In the first century AD the Pharisees, and the mainstream of Judaism, affirmed the doctrine of the future resurrection, although the more conservative Sadducees rejected it as a heretical innovation. In spite of his strong condemnation of the Pharisees for the insincerity and hypocrisy shown by many of them, Jesus agreed with them on the question of the resurrection. This comes out for example in his controversy with certain Sadducees who put to him the trick question about the woman who married a man, and then after his death married his brother, and so on to the seventh brother: whose husband would she be in the resurrection? Jesus replied, 'Is not this why you are wrong, that you know neither the scriptures nor the power of God? For when they rise from the dead, they neither marry nor are given in marriage, but are like angels in heaven. And as for the dead being raised, have you not read in the book of Moses, in the passage about the bush, how God said to him, "I am the God of Abraham, and the God of Isaac, and the God of Jacob"? He is not God of the dead, but of the living; you are quite wrong.'[23] Since the Sadducees were an aristocratic party we may presume that Jesus' first disciples, who were apparently mostly galilean fishermen and other artisans, were not of their persuasion but would be believers in the resurrection of the dead. And St Paul was a strict Pharisee before his conversion on the Damascus road.[24] It was thus almost inevitable that resurrection should have been the category in which they understood the easter visions and proclaimed Jesus' glorified existence to the world. There would be a natural transition in their minds from 'We have seen the Lord.' to 'God has raised Jesus from the dead', and a ready path in the imaginations of second- and third-generation believers from this to 'an angel of the Lord descended from heaven and came and rolled back the stone . . . '

Thus Jesus' disciples believed in life after death before and independently of his resurrection; and much christian theology has since affirmed the immortality of the soul on grounds which do not rely on the easter message. Jesus' resurrection does of course support and confirm belief in the continuity of man's life beyond physical death; but it is probably only in the modern period, when the assurance of survival has waned, that it has occurred to anyone to point to Jesus' resurrection as a primary ground for belief in a life to come.

In recent, particularly protestant, discussions a strong contrast has been drawn between the ideas of the resurrection of the body and the immortality of the soul. The difference which has been stressed does not hinge upon the term 'immortality' as indicating *unending* existence; for the resurrection is also thought of as a resurrection to life everlasting. The contrast emphasized is between natural immortality as the property of an inherently perduring soul and an immortality

which depends upon a particular act of God in raising the
individual from the dead. On the one view, the human self
is secure in its unlimited existence whether there be a God or
not; and death is not the final end towards which our lives have
to be lived but only a natural transition, like walking out of one
room into another or taking off one suit of clothes to don
another. On the other view, man is inherently mortal, made out
of the dust of the earth, and can have no life beyond the blank
wall of death unless God wills to recreate him on the other side
by a miracle of divine power. In facing death we face total
destruction and non-existence; and only faith in the gracious
goodness of God gives hope beyond the grave. Oscar Cullmann,
in his influential lecture *Immortality of the Soul or Resurrection
of the Dead?*, sees these contrasting outlooks symbolized in the
deaths of Socrates and Jesus – Socrates (as depicted in Plato's
Phaedo) facing death with a serene certainty of the immortality
of his real self, in contrast with Jesus who 'began to be greatly
distressed and troubled' and who prayed 'Father, . . . remove
this cup from me.'[25] Cullmann says,

> Only he who apprehends with the first Christians the horror
> of death, who takes death seriously as death, can comprehend
> the Easter exultation of the primitive Christian community
> and understand that the whole thinking of the New Testa-
> ment is governed by belief in the Resurrection. Belief in the
> immortality of the soul is not belief in a revolutionary event.
> Immortality, in fact, is only a *negative* assertion: the soul
> does *not* die, but simply lives on. Resurrection is a *positive*
> assertion: the whole man, who has really died, is recalled to
> life by a new act of creation by God. Something has hap-
> pened – a miracle of creation! For something has also
> happened previously, something fearful: life formed by God
> has been destroyed.[26]

A radical distinction between the immortality of the soul
and the resurrection of the body would be valid as part of a
distinction between a non-theistic and a theistic metaphysic:
the view that man, as a natural, not-divinely-created being is
inherently immortal does indeed contrast with the view that
he has been made by God as a mortal creature who would
perish if God did not hold him in existence by divine power.

But on the other hand, if we posit the reality of God the difference between immortality and resurrection, as variations within a theistic picture, becomes quite secondary. For if God has created souls of such a nature that they do not perish with the body, their capacity to survive bodily death is a gift of divine grace. It is as truly a gift of God's grace as would be his recreation of beings whom he had made naturally mortal. These are two different ways in which the Creator can bestow unending life upon his creatures. But in either case we are dependent upon him for our existence, both now and hereafter. For those theists who hold that the soul is naturally immortal also hold that the omnipotent God could if he wished abolish the souls that he has made. Their immortality does not give them independence over against their Maker, but only sets them outside the natural mortality of physical organisms.

Yet another contrast seems to be implied in the distinction between the immortality of the soul and the resurrection of the dead – that between a disembodied and an embodied after-life. However, we can only test this implication by spelling out the two possibilities much more fully; and when we do this, in chapters 14 and 15, it will appear that the contrast is much less considerable than at first appears.

3. JESUS' TEACHING ABOUT THE AFTER-LIFE

The New Testament scholar, Henry Cadbury, has written some wise words of caution on the use of Jesus' scattered sayings about the life after death:

> The afterlife was taken for granted by Jesus and by his hearers generally. He did not need to impress it or correct it. It was not for him or them a question of hesitation or debate. It is therefore an assured ingredient of his perspective. By the same token his allusions do not allow us to reconstruct any very definite or circumstantial impression of this future. They were innocently unprecise, intimations rather than descriptions, and were employed in connection with other matters on which Jesus had something emphatic and significant to say.[27]

About all that we can say with full assurance is that, in agreement with contemporary Judaism with the notable

exception of the Sadducees, Jesus affirmed the future resurrection and judgement of the dead. The individual's existence did
not end with his death: he would be raised again to appear
before the judgement-seat of God, or of his messiah, and
thereafter to live for ever in the divine Kingdom or (perhaps)
survive in Gehenna or be destroyed altogether.

Was the resurrection of the dead to be a raising of earthly
bodies to live again in this world; or a creation of heavenly
bodies to live in a heavenly world? The expectations expressed
in the earliest (second-century BC) apocalyptic literature was
that the messianic age would be an unending kingdom of God
on earth and that the righteous who had died and were now
'asleep' would be raised to take their places within it. Thus the
resurrection involved the bringing forth of the revivified dead
from their graves. This picture lingered on as the prevailing
popular conception of resurrection well into the christian era.
We see it at work, for example, in the curious epicycle to
Matthew's account of Jesus' crucifixion, referred to above, in
which he says that the earth shook and rocks were split, and
'the tombs also were opened, and many bodies of the saints
who had fallen asleep were raised, and coming out of the tombs
after his resurrection they went into the holy city and appeared
to many'.[28] The 'saints' whom Matthew has in mind were
probably 'devout Jews of the type of Simeon (Lk. 2), or even
patriarchs, prophets, and martyrs',[29] and their emergence was
no doubt thought of by Matthew and his original readers as a
first burst of the imminently expected general resurrection,
caused by the dramatic inbreaking of the future in Jesus' own
death and resurrection – which Matthew likewise presents as
the coming forth of his revivified body from the tomb.

But on the other hand the ideas expressed in many of the
jewish apocalyptic writings of the first century BC had been
more sophisticated. To quote R. H. Charles, 'Whilst some
taught, as the writers of I Enoch 91–104 and the Psalms of
Solomon, that there would be no resurrection of the body at
all but only of the spirit, others, as the writer of the Parables,
said that there would be a resurrection of the body, but that
this body would consist of garments of glory and of light
(I Enoch 62: 15, 16), and that the risen righteous would be of
an angelic nature (51: 4). Thus we find that the doctrine of the

resurrection which was current amongst the cultured Pharisees in the century immediately preceding the Christian era was of a truly spiritual nature.'[30] Jesus' words in his controversy with the Sadducees are in line with this more spiritual conception. For he says that 'when they rise from the dead, they neither marry nor are given in marriage, but are like angels in heaven'.[31] Thus Jesus' teaching seems to point to some kind of 'spiritual body' – an idea later developed by St Paul. The presence of this thought side by side in the gospels with that of the resurrection of the physical body, with no indication on the writers' part of any awareness of a tension between them, was to be a source of confusion in christian eschatology, as we shall see in the next section.

A second confusion concerned the relation between future resurrection and future judgement. In the parable of the sheep and the goats[32] the judgement coincides with the coming of the Son of man in his glory. On the other hand two of Jesus' sayings (both in Luke) support the idea that after the death of the individual his (disembodied) soul goes to 'Abraham's bosom', or 'Paradise', or sheol, having already been judged – presumably at the moment of death. One is the parable of Dives and Lazarus, in which the righteous poor man is 'carried by the angels to Abraham's bosom'[33] whilst the unrighteous rich man finds himself in torment. This situation, which clearly implies a divine assessment of their lives, is prior to the resurrection; for the rich man's brothers are still living on earth.[34] The other saying is Jesus' word to one of the two criminals who were crucified with him, 'Truly, I say to you, today you will be with me in Paradise.'[35] We need not be concerned about whether Paradise is an ultimate heavenly state or only 'a superior suburb of Sheol'.[36] The point at the moment is the implication that a divine judgement has already taken place.

We shall see in the next section how the early christian theologians harmonized these various apparently divergent indications within a single picture – though inevitably a cumbersome picture which was always in danger of falling apart. But it would be a mistake to attribute their system to Jesus. He was not concerned with systematic theology but with the vital 'existential' import of his convictions about God and about the future. He was concerned with eschatology only as bearing upon men's lives now. As another New Testament scholar emphasizes, 'there is no interest in disclosing mysteries of death and what lies beyond. Rather, the references to death function as sanctions. They suggest the serious consequences of today's decision; they mark out the horizon against which Jesus expects his hearers to act. Because Jesus and his hearers shared views of death he could use them to undergird the urgency of his appeal.'[37]

4. THE AFTER-LIFE BELIEFS OF THE EARLY CHRISTIANS

In the first century BC and the first century AD there was a pervasive sense among the Jews that the world was in a desperate state, with God's chosen people chafing under pagan rule and the divine purpose being flaunted and mocked. In this darkness men of faith yearned for the long-prophesied coming of the Lord's anointed, the messiah, to inaugurate God's glorious new age on earth. Jesus clearly shared this general hope, and out of his overwhelming sense of the reality and living presence of God he proclaimed that the great Day was about to dawn. For he lived in an intense awareness of God, conscious of the limitless divine love reaching out to men and women through his own compassion for them, and of God's power pulsating through his hands in acts of healing. Reasoning that 'if it is by the Spirit of God that I cast out demons, then the kingdom of God has come upon you',[38] Jesus proclaimed, 'The time is fulfilled, and the kingdom of God is at hand; repent, and believe in the gospel.'[39] The machinery of the great eschatological clock was already in motion to strike the last hour of history, and for those who could hear its movements and sense the impending End all else paled into utter insignificance. Men were living in the final moments of the present Age – even though these might span years of earthly time – and each could now find salvation by turning from the past, organized as it was around his own ego, to the future in which the ego and its concerns would be lost in the glorious life of God's Kingdom.

After Jesus' death and resurrection the early christian community expected the imminent Day of the Lord, which it came to understand as the time when Jesus would come again in glory as Son of man. This would also be the moment of the resurrection of the dead. No doubt many – indeed probably most – of them had been accustomed to think of the resurrection as the revivification of entombed corpses, and continued to think in these terms.[40] But the only deliberate teaching to be found within the New Testament about the nature of the resurrection (apart from Jesus' words to the Sadducees[41]) is that in which St Paul distinguishes between the natural or animal body (*soma pseukikon*) and the spiritual body (*soma pneumatikon*):

> What you sow does not come to life unless it dies. And what you sow is not the body which is to be, but a bare kernel, perhaps of wheat or of some other grain. But God gives it a body as he has chosen, and to each kind of seed its own body. For not all flesh is alike, but there is one kind for men, another for animals, another for birds, and another for fish. There are celestial bodies and there are terrestrial bodies; but the glory of the celestial is one, and the glory of the terrestrial is another. There is one glory of the sun, and another glory of the moon, and another glory of the stars; for star differs from star in glory. So is it with the resurrection of the dead. What is sown is perishable, what is raised is imperishable. It is sown in dishonour, it is raised in glory. It is sown in weakness, it is raised in power. It is sown a physical body, it is raised a spiritual body. If there is a physical body, there is also a spiritual body.[42]

Hundreds of pages have been written in exegesis of this passage and of the chapter of which it is a part. But the main options reduce to two, a transformed earthly body or a new heavenly body, respectively described by M. E. Dahl as the 'traditional' view and the (contemporarily) 'accepted' view.[43] The former holds that in the resurrection the corpse will be raised from its grave, but changed in the process along with its environment.[44] There will be a new heaven and a new earth, inhabited by glorified bodily beings on the model of Jesus' resurrection body, which bore the marks of crucifixion but was so fully subject to Jesus' will that he could disappear in one place and appear in another in a way impossible to an ordinary physical being. Nevertheless it is insisted that Jesus' risen body was the body that had lain in the tomb, and likewise that in the general resurrection men will rise in their earthly bodies, though now transfigured. Thus this view affirms a strong continuity between the natural and the spiritual body: as the seed has mysteriously become the wheat – instead of perishing and something else being created in its place – so the physical body is mysteriously transformed into a body of glory.

In contrast with this, what has become a widely accepted view in modern times holds that the resurrection body is a new and different body given by God, but expressing the personality within its new environment as the physical body has expressed it in the earthly environment. The physical frame decays or is burned, disintegrating and being dispersed into the ground or the air, but God re-embodies the personality elsewhere. Indeed, it is stressed that by 'the body' St Paul does not mean the physical organism in distinction from the mind, but (usually) 'the whole personality'[45] considered as having both an outer or objective and an inner or subjective aspect. In attempting to discuss Paul's thought today we are thus in the difficulty of using the word 'body' to refer both in a more limited sense to the physical frame and also in a more comprehensive sense to the total psycho-physical personality. To avoid this difficulty let us speak of the latter simply as the person. Paul is then saying that the earthly person – earthly because his life is the life of a physical body which is part of this fallen and dying world – perishes but that God raises up a person who is the same and yet different because his life is the life of a new body in a new environment. Or using Paul's language elsewhere, there is an 'outer nature' and an 'inner nature'[46] which jointly constitute the person. The outer nature, which is part of the world, ceases at death, so that the person no longer exists in our present world; but God recreates him with a new outer nature integral to another world. There is thus genuine personal continuity; but whereas the individual was formerly organically related to this world he is now organically related to another.

I do not profess to know which of these views, if indeed either of them,[47] Paul himself intended; but something like the latter of the two seems to me to be a coherent possibility, and later I shall try to spell this possibility out further in order to test its viability.[48]

The early Christians, then, expected a general resurrection which probably most of them continued to think of in physical terms although we see a more spiritualized conception in Jesus' words to the Sadducees and in St Paul's discussion in 1 Corinthians 15. Thus a material and earthly picture of the resurrection existed in tension with a more spiritual and heavenly picture. The tension had in fact already been present within jewish thought for several generations. As long ago as the fourth century BC the earliest doctrine of the resurrection 'taught that the righteous nation of Israel and the righteous individual – alike the quick and the dead – would be recompensed to the full in the *eternal* Messianic kingdom *on earth*. But the synthesis thus established as early as the fourth century BC hardly outlived the second . . . ; for the earth had at last come to be regarded as wholly unfit for the manifestation of the *eternal* kingdom of God, and to such a kingdom and none other could the hopes of the righteous individual be directed. The Messianic kingdom was still expected, but one only of temporary duration. Henceforth not the [earthly] Messianic kingdom, but heaven itself or paradise became the goal of the hopes of the faithful in death.'[49] This compromise between the claims of earth and heaven provided a pattern for the faith of the early church at about the end of the New Testament period.

The first generation of Christians expected the return of Jesus in glory in their own lifetime, as they believed that their Master had taught;[50] although he had also taught that the exact day was known only to God and would come suddenly and without warning, like a thief in the night.[51] In the interval before the great day dawned the prophets and saints of old and the recently slain martyrs of the christian brotherhood were thought of either as lying asleep in hades,[52] conceived as a kind of limbo or antechamber between heaven and hell, or as already experiencing bliss or torment after an individual judgement which would later be publicly ratified at the parousia.[53] The dead would then rise from their tombs to join the living before the judgement-seat. This, at least, is the broad picture, although quite important details differ as between different New Testament writings (and indeed probably, in the case of Paul, between earlier and later writings by the same hand[54]). For example, some passages suggest that only the righteous, or only those who believe in Jesus, will be raised,[55] whilst others suggest that *all* men are to be raised.[56] Assuming the latter, and therefore also the great assize at which just and unjust are to be separated 'as a shepherd separates the sheep from the goats',[57] the Messiah would thereafter rule in glory in Jerusalem during the last phase of earthly history, and then finally the life of the blessed would be taken up into the eternal heavens. Thus the end state was not to be a heaven on earth but a new 'earth' in heaven.

A version of this eschatology is vividly depicted in the last book of the New Testament, the Revelation to John. On the great Day an angel comes down from heaven and binds Satan and throws him into a pit, which is sealed for a thousand years. The first resurrection then takes place in which the saints are raised to participate in triumph in Christ's kingdom on earth: 'I saw the souls of those who had been beheaded for their testimony to Jesus . . . They came to life again, and reigned with Christ a thousand years.'[58] At the end of the thousand years Satan is to be released and (the narrative wavers between the past, present and future tenses) 'will come out to deceive the nations which are at the four corners of the earth . . . their number is like the sand of the sea. And they marched up over the broad earth and surrounded the camp of the saints and the beloved city.'[59] However, the hosts of evil are destroyed by fire from heaven, and 'the devil who had deceived them was thrown into the lake of fire and brimstone where the beast and the false prophet were, and they will be tormented day and night for ever and ever'.[60] There then occurs the second or general resurrection and the universal judgement: 'And I saw the dead, great and small, standing before the throne, and books were opened. Also another book was opened, which is the book of life. And the dead were judged by what was written in the books, by what they had done . . . and if anyone's name was not found written in the book of life, he was thrown into the lake of fire.'[61]

Finally, heaven and earth pass away and a new heaven and a new earth take their place. What might be meant by this? For 'John' and his first- and second-century readers heaven

ånd earth (together with hell beneath the earth) filled different
parts of the same space, with heaven just beyond the moving
spheres which held the stars. Thus a new heaven and earth
meant a new two-storeyed spatial universe. This conception
cannot be translated directly into terms of modern cosmology.
We can however ask what might be meant by a new physical
universe? Are we to think of this one transformed? Or is such
talk simply a way of saying that the resurrection life is an
embodied existence in another space? We are told that on the
new earth there is no more death;[62] there is perpetual day with
no night;[63] and the holy city is described in poetic language as
being made of precious metals and stones symbolizing an
inconceivable beauty and worth.[64] Thus the new universe is
not, like this one, a process of temporal change – birth and
death, growth and decay – and the new earth is not a planet
circling a sun, and the new Jerusalem is not a city that we can
picture except in fairy-tale terms. Such a state of affairs is not
this world transformed, but a new and different environment
altogether. For if the 'transformation' of this world is sufficiently radical it becomes meaningless to describe the end-
product as the present world renewed. It is a 'new earth' only
in the sense that it is a new situation, a different environment,
another 'world'. Further, this other world is not composed of
the same matter as our present earth and is not at any distance
or in any direction from our sun and its planets. What the
writer is saying is that redeemed and perfected human beings
will find themselves in an ultimate situation in which God will
be known as an all-pervasive presence. The redeemed will live
consciously in the ambience of him 'in whom they live and
move and have their being'.[65] For the writer does not describe
a vision of God but describes a totally God-oriented existence
in an environment which expresses throughout the divine
goodness: 'he will wipe away every tear from their eyes, and
death shall be no more, neither shall there be mourning nor
crying nor pain any more, for the former things have passed
away' (21: 4). This at least is the main theme of the vision. But
complete consistency is not to be found here any more than
elsewhere in the New Testament, and later 'John' says that
the redeemed 'shall see his [God's] face', adding that 'his name
shall be on their foreheads' (22: 4). A spiritual interpretation

of this symbolic language, bringing it into focus with the vision as a whole, might be that the lives of the redeemed are totally responsive to God's presence (his name on their foreheads) and their thus living consciously in God's presence is their 'seeing' him.

So we find in the New Testament a diversity of thought, within the ambiguous framework of belief in 'the resurrection', ranging from cruder and more popularly comprehensible ideas of the rising of the just to a renewed existence which belongs to the future history of this world, to notions of life in spiritual bodies and in a new environment which is altogether other than this earth, even though we can only conceive it in glorified earthly terms. The millennial (or chiliastic) expectation which linked these ways of thinking together was gradually abandoned (though continuing down to the present day in the margins of the christian world), leaving the main weight of later christian eschatology on the thought of the eternal life of the soul in 'heaven'.

NOTES

1. Acts 2: 32.
2. Matthew 27: 52–3.
3. Cf. H. A. Guy, *The New Testament Doctrine of the 'Last Things'*, p. 115.
4. Some instances are cited in Arthur Ford, *The Life beyond Death*, pp. 149–51.
5. 'Information' in the cybernetic sense of input from an external source.
6. Acts 2: 33.
7. ibid., 2: 24.
8. Luke 24: 39–40; John 20: 20.
9. Luke 24: 41–3; John 21: 13.
10. John 20: 24–9.
11. Luke 24: 31, 36.
12. Matthew 28: 11–15.
13. 1 Corinthians 15: 3–8. This is dated about AD 50, whereas the earliest gospel, Mark, was probably written shortly before AD 70.
14. Chs. 22, 26.
15. Acts 5: 31.
16. Philippians 2: 9.
17. Matthew 27: 52–3.

18. Luke 24: 4–5.

19. These and other similar questions are carefully analysed by Willi Marxsen, who concludes that 'at the time when the evangelists were writing their Gospels, there was no longer a unified view in the primitive church about the mode of the Easter happening. This does not seem to have played the decisive part then which is often ascribed to it today. For if people had been really interested in the mode of the resurrection, this would surely have been depicted in uniform terms' (*The Resurrection of Jesus of Nazareth*, pp. 75–6). On the narratives in general, see R. H. Fuller, *The Formation of the Resurrection Narratives*.

20. Cf. Gunther Bornkamm, *Jesus of Nazareth*, p. 183.

21. Christian Gellert (1715–69).

22. Denzinger, *Enchiridion Symbolorum*, 738 (*The Church Teaches*, p. 149).

23. Mark 12: 24–7. Cf. Matthew 22: 23–32; Luke 20: 27–38. For comment on the markan passage, see D. E. Nineham, *Saint Mark*, pp. 319–21.

24. Acts 23: 6; Philippians 3: 5.

25. Mark 14: 33, 36. I do not however believe, with Cullmann, that Jesus, with his intense sense of the reality and presence of God, can have feared death as such. But it should be remembered that whilst Socrates and Jesus were both executed, they were executed in very different ways. Socrates faced what was probably the most humane method of judicial execution that has ever been practised down to the present day. At whatever moment he chose during the appointed day he had to drink a poison which would cause a quick and painless death; and he did so in the company of devoted and admiring disciples. Jesus faced a violent, long-drawn-out and excruciatingly painful death – indeed it was the prolonged exposure to pain, heat and thirst that caused the victim's death – in deliberately humiliating circumstances, deserted by his shattered disciples, surrounded by jeering enemies and with despairing wellwishers watching in the background. The natural shrinking from this prospect, which he overcame only with great courage, expressed his genuine humanity; and we may presume that Socrates, who shared the same human nature, would not have been exempt from a like shrinking in the same circumstances.

26. Oscar Cullmann, *Immortality of the Soul or Resurrection of the Dead?*, pp. 26–7. *Immortality and Resurrection*, ed. Krister Stendahl, p. 19. For a critique on biblical grounds of Cullman's thesis, see George W. E. Nickelsburg, Jr, *Resurrection, Immortality, and Eternal Life in Intertestamental Judaism*, appendix.

27. Henry J. Cadbury, 'Intimations of Immortality in the Thought of Jesus', in *Immortality and Resurrection*, ed. Krister Stendahl, pp. 139–40.

28. Matthew 27: 52–3.

29. A. J. Grieve, *Peake's Commentary on the Bible*, p. 722.

30. R. H. Charles, *Eschatology*, p. 295.

31. Mark 12: 25. But in using this passage, note Eduard Schweizer's cautionary suggestion that it is not mostly authentic teaching of Jesus, but early christian polemic (*The Good News according to Mark*, pp. 245–9).

32. Matthew 25: 31–46.

33. Luke 16: 22. The story of Dives and Lazarus has rabbinic parallels and was apparently originally derived from an egyptian folk-tale. See, e.g., G. B. Caird, *The Gospel of St Luke*, p. 191.

34. Luke 16: 28. The parable ends: 'If they do not hear Moses and the prophets, neither will they be convinced if someone should rise from the dead' (16: 31). The saying has not been heeded by those Christians who have exaggerated the significance of Jesus' resurrection in establishing both his divinity and the reality of eternal life. George B. Caird has commented well: 'Let us suppose that tomorrow you were confronted with irrefutable evidence that an acquaintance whom you had good reason to believe dead had been seen alive by reliable witnesses. You would certainly feel compelled to revise some of your ideas about science, but I doubt whether you would feel compelled to revise your ideas about God. I doubt whether you would conclude that your acquaintance was divine, or that a stamp of authenticity had been placed on all he ever said or did, or even that he would not yet, at some time in the future, have to die' ('The Christological Basis of Christian Hope', in *The Christian Hope*, p. 10).

35. Luke 23: 43.

36. David Edwards, *The Last Things Now*, p. 38.

37. Leander E. Keck, 'New Testament Views of Death', in *Perspectives on Death*, p. 37.

38. Matthew 12: 28.

39. Mark 1: 15.

40. There is second-century evidence of this in 2 Clement, 9, and the First Apology of Justin Martyr, 18.

41. Mark 12: 24-7, discussed on p. 183.

42. 1 Corinthians 15: 36–44.

43. M. E. Dahl, *The Resurrection of the Body*.

44. Dahl cites Pelagius, Ambrosiaster, Chrysostom, Theodoret, Primasius, St Thomas, Calvin and Bengel.

45. Dahl, op. cit., p. 94. Cf. J. A. T. Robinson, *The Body*, pp. 27–9. See also, more generally, Robinson's *In the End, God*.

46. 2 Corinthians 4: 16.

47. Dahl adds a third interpretation of his own, according to which the resurrection body is 'somatically identical' with the present physical body (op. cit., p. 94). But the notion is not spelled out and the phrase remains little more than a slogan: it is not made clear how somatic identity differs from the kind of identity postulated in what Dahl calls the currently 'accepted' view.

48. See chapter 15.

49. R. H. Charles, *Eschatology*, p. 364.

50. Mark 9: 1; Matthew 16: 28; Luke 9: 27. R. H. Charles says that 'there is not a single writer of the New Testament . . . who does not look forward to the personal return of Christ in his own generation' (*Eschatology*, p. 387). On the other hand it remains a matter of dispute whether Jesus himself taught this. See, e.g., T. F. Glasson, *The Second Advent*, ch. 7.

51. Matthew 24: 50; 1 Thessalonians 5: 2–3.

52. 1 Corinthians 15: 20, 51; 1 Thessalonians 4: 15.

53. Luke 16: 22–3; 23: 43. Philippians 1: 23 also suggests a heavenly state prior to the general resurrection.

54. On the development of Paul's eschatology, see, e.g., D. E. H. Whiteley, *The Theology of St Paul*, pp. 244–8.

55. e.g.: 'those who are accounted worthy to attain to that age and to the resurrection from the dead' (Luke 20: 35); 'the resurrection of the just' (ibid., 14: 14).

56. e.g.: 'there will be a resurrection of both the just and the unjust' (Acts 24: 15); 'all who are in the tombs will hear his voice and come forth, those who have done good, to the resurrection of life, and those who have done evil, to the resurrection of judgment' (John 5: 28–9).

57. Matthew 25: 32.

58. Revelation 20: 4. St Augustine explains the biblical basis of millenarianism (which he rejects) in *The City of God*, book 20, ch. 7. According to 2 Peter 3: 8, 'with the Lord one day is as a thousand years'. Therefore, as God created the world in six days and rested on the seventh, its history is to run for six thousand years with a rest for the saints, their earthly rule, during the seventh millennium.

59. Revelation 20: 8–9.

60. ibid., 20: 10.

61. ibid., 20: 12–15.

62. ibid., 21: 4.

63. ibid., 21: 25.

64. On the details of the symbolism, see G. R. Beasley-Murray, 'The Contribution of the Book of Revelation to the Christian Belief in Immortality', in *Scottish Journal of Theology*, vol. 27, no. 1 (January 1974), pp. 80–5.

65. Acts 17: 28.

CHAPTER 10

Later Christian Thought

1. THE CHANGING THEOLOGICAL SCENE

The early christian eschatological hope contained within it tensions and anomalies which later thought was to remove or soften by gradual processes of de-emphasis and reinterpretation. One was the imminent expectation of the parousia within the lifetime of those then living, an expectation which became increasingly at variance with the facts. As time went on without the parousia occurring, and as more and more believers 'fell asleep', the sense of living in the last hours of a dying Age gradually faded and the church had to adjust itself to the prospect of an indefinitely long future in this world. This in turn underlined the anomaly of the double judgement. Those who had died were often thought of, in the light of the parable of Dives and Lazarus, as being now in paradise or hades, and thus as having been individually judged at the time of their deaths. But a second universal and public judgement was nevertheless supposed to await them at the great assize on the Last Day.[1] When this was still expected at any moment no great problem seems to have been felt about the state of the departed during the interim period. But as the Last Day distanced itself into the remote future the thought of a second judgement naturally also faded within the christian imagination. The sentence pronounced upon the individual as he passed out of this life became the real crisis upon which men's hopes and fears were fixed, and the popular christian view came to be that each man as he died went to heaven (directly or via purgatory) or to hell.

A second tension was that between, on the one hand, the expectation of an earthly kingdom of God, generally thought of as the thousand years' reign of the saints, and on the other hand the feeling which existed among some of the Jews around the turn of the eras that the ultimate fulfilment of God's good purpose could not be encompassed within the conditions of[1] earthly existence.[2] Paul was presumably expressing such a view when he wrote that 'flesh and blood cannot inherit the kingdom of God'.[3] This same tension appears in the distinction between the ideas of the 'resurrection of the body' and the 'resurrection of the flesh'. In pauline thought the 'body' usually referred to the total personality, with its inner and outer aspects, whilst the 'flesh' came in the early church to refer to the physical organism. Accordingly whilst 'the resurrection of the flesh' meant the revivification of a corpse, 'the resurrection of the body' meant the raising of the total personality to the new life in a new 'spiritual' body.

In the earliest period there were undoubtedly different levels of understanding of the future resurrection, some believers sharing Paul's more sophisticated view and others holding to the continuing popular conception of the revivification of corpses which is witnessed to, for example, by the story in Matthew 27: 52–3 of the bodies of the saints of old coming forth from their graves and being seen in the streets of Jerusalem. As a result of several co-operating causes the equation of the 'resurrection of the body' with the 'resurrection of the flesh' came to prevail within the church, and the phrase *resurrectionem carnis* became part of the 'Apostles' Creed' which has been used by virtually all Christians down to the present day.[4] On the other hand this affirmation, largely formed by factors peculiar to the earliest centuries of the church's life – such as the millenarian expectation (which required an earthly resurrection) and the struggle against Gnosticism (and thus against spiritualizing notions) – cohered with the idea of the far distant Judgement when souls which had long been waiting for the great Day would be reunited with their bodies. By the medieval period this picture had been replaced in the minds of ordinary believers by that of the soul, individually judged at death, gravitating directly to its eternal destiny, and the resurrection of the earthly flesh tended to go out of focus in the christian imagination. It remained the official belief, adhered to by the professionals, that at the Last Day souls will reanimate their bodies, raised from their graves before the great assize; but in popular belief the two judgements had in effect merged into one. In this conflation of the individual judgement at death with the universal judgement at the end of the world faith was following (perhaps unconsciously) not only the logic of the imagination but also the logic of the intellect; for once the individual's eternal fate has been settled, and he has begun to enjoy or endure his appropriate destiny, the second judgement becomes an anti-climax, if not an empty form. And so, whilst official statements of christian doctrine – catholic, anglican and reformed alike – continued until the present century to present the complete traditional scheme, the ordinary christian believer had long since been thinking simply of 'going to heaven' or 'going to hell' or 'being in purgatory' from the time of death onwards.[5]

It was, accordingly, natural for the hour of death to be seen as the decisive moment at which the soul's destiny was determined. To die in a state of grace, having repented and confessed one's sins, however great they might be, was to be bound for heaven; whilst to die in one's sins meant eternal damnation. The emphasis was thus not upon living but upon dying. For any life, however evil, could be redeemed by a good death; and any life, however relatively blameless, could be spoiled for ever through dying in a state of sin. Hence the importance of the 'art of dying'; and hence also the late medieval pictures of angel and devil hovering in rivalry around the death-bed, each hoping to snatch the soul away in accordance with its condition in the final moment of life. Shakespeare presents this state of mind in Hamlet's hesitation to kill his father's murderer whilst the latter is at prayer:

> Now might I do it pat, now 'a is praying!
> And now I'll do 't. And so 'a goes to heaven;
> And so am I reveng'd? That would be scann'd.
> A villain kills my father, and for that,
> I, his sole son, do this same villain send
> To heaven . . .
> No.
> Up, sword, and know thou a more horrid hent;
> When he is drunk asleep, or in his rage,
> Or in th' incestuous pleasure of his bed,
> At game a-swearing, or about some act
> That has no relish of salvation in 't.

Then trip him, that his heels may kick at heaven,
And that his soul may be as damn'd and black
As hell, whereto he goes . . . [6]

Going back to the earlier phases of this shifting of the theological scenery, what Augustine was to stigmatize as the 'ridiculous fancies' of millenarianism – an initial selective resurrection inaugurating the thousand years' earthly rule of Christ and his saints, followed by a second general resurrection and judgement – gradually faded from the christian imagination during the third, fourth and fifth centuries.[7] Augustine exerted his immense authority against the Chiliasts or Millenarians, arguing not that the expectations expressed in the Revelation to John were mistaken but that the passage in question does not mean what it says. Although Augustine's procedure here is peripheral to our present concern it is nevertheless interesting to watch him at work reinterpreting scriptural passages whose plain meaning he rejects. In this case he offers a Bultmann-like demythologization of the 'first' resurrection, describing it as a spiritual resurrection consisting in the rising to faith of those souls who believe in Jesus and are baptized in his name.[8] The thousand years' reign of the saints thus becomes the earthly life of the redeemed in the church during the present age;[9] and accordingly as the year AD 1000 approached, the augustinian timetable created a widespread uneasiness in face of the impending end of the world. According to Augustine the second and general resurrection, unlike the first, was to be a literal bodily event when 'the dust of bodies long dead shall return with incomprehensible facility and swiftness to those members that are now to live endlessly'.[10] However, in treating of the judgement Augustine is bothered by the difficulty of visualizing it concretely. The text speaks of the book of life out of which men are to be judged. But 'if this book be materially considered', says Augustine, 'who can reckon its size or length, or the time it would take to read a book in which the whole life of every man is recorded? Shall there be present as many angels as men, and shall each man hear his life recited by the angel assigned to him? In that case there will be not one book containing all the lives, but a separate book for every life. But our passage requires us to think of one only.'[11]

Accordingly he suggests that we should understand the text to be speaking of 'a certain divine power, by which it shall be brought about that everyone shall recall to memory all his own works, whether good or evil, and shall mentally survey them with a marvellous rapidity, so that this knowledge will either accuse or excuse conscience, and thus all and each shall be simultaneously judged'.[12] After this judgement, in which each man judges himself in the light of God's presence, the world is to be consumed by fire and remade into a new earth in which the blessed shall live for ever whilst the wicked endure perpetual torment.

Thus the broad development within Christianity consisted in a shift of scene from earth to heaven (and hell); with divine judgement coming forward to the moment of each individual's death; and with a corresponding change of emphasis from body to soul. It was however a soul still visualized in bodily terms. How else could one imagine it? And so in all the medieval pictures of the dead, whether in 'Abraham's bosom' awaiting the Last Judgement, or being conducted by angels up to heaven or driven by demons with whips and pitchforks down to the fires of hell, souls appear as bodily men and women – usually naked in the case of the damned and clothed in the case of the redeemed.

2. HELL

Augustine's magisterial presentation of the christian myth – the drama of creation, fall, salvation, heaven and hell – dominated the imagination of the west for the next thousand years and more. His understanding of the final state of man perhaps has its most enduring expressions in Dante's *Divine Comedy* (which, according to Boase, 'rapidly, at least in educated circles, became an authoritative statement about the after-life'[13]) and Milton's *Paradise Lost*. The doctrines which lie behind these great works of art were normative within the church until recent times and broadly represent what the rest of the world, looking at Christianity as a whole over its two thousand years of existence, sees as its teaching concerning the life to come.

Augustine insists at great length and with many pre-scientific analogies that the damned are embodied and are able

to burn everlastingly in literal flames.[14] Of course the idea of
bodies burning for ever and continuously suffering the intense
pain of third-degree burns without either being consumed or
losing consciousness is as scientifically fantastic as it is morally
revolting. There is indeed an evident incongruity, if not self-
contradiction, in the very notion of perpetual torment; for the
sheer monotony of the continuous pain would produce
diminishing returns of agony. Thus Milton's Mammon,
advising resignation in hell, not unreasonably holds out the
hope that

> Our torments also may in length of time
> Become our elements, these piercing fires
> As soft as now severe, our temper changed
> Into their temper; which must needs remove
> The sensible of pain.[15]

It was no doubt to repair this flaw in the system of eternal
punishment that the pious imagination introduced an element
of contrast. Thus Milton in his description of hell speaks of a
frozen continent:

> Thither, by harpy-footed Furies haled,
> At certain revolutions all the damn'd
> Are brought; and feel by turns the bitter change
> Of fierce extremes, extremes by change more fierce,
> From beds of raging fire to starve in ice
> Their soft ethereal warmth, and there to pine
> Immovable, infix'd, and frozen round,
> Periods of time; thence hurried back to fire.[16]

And Dante includes ample movement and variety in his
tremendous picture of hell, including the detail of the thief
who is bitten by poisonous snakes, whereupon he bursts into
flame and crumbles to ash –

> But as he lay on the ground dispersedly,
> All by itself the dust gathered and stirred
> And grew to its former shape immediately.[17]

In such ways as these ingenuity sought to defend a fantasy
which is, happily, intrinsically incredible – the endlessly
prolonged torture of human consciousnesses.

In the seventeenth, eighteenth and nineteenth centuries the christian mind gradually awoke from these nightmare imaginings of eternal pain and misery.[18] There had of course, since the time of Origen, been a small underground stream of belief in universal salvation. But any relaxation of the dogma that the wicked are destined to suffer unending torment was regarded as so manifestly subversive of morality that when, in the seventeenth century, some theologians began to see difficulties in the dogma they hesitated to discuss the matter publicly lest they should weaken the moral bulwarks of society.[19] The questioners were in any case in a small minority; amongst most of their brethren there was still a firm belief in the reality of hell and its relevance to our present life both as an ethical sanction[20] and as a motive for the missionary movement.[21] Even in the mid-nineteenth century one who was far from being a traditional hell-fire theologian, the great tractarian E. B. Pusey, could preach about the terrors of hell in these terms:

> This, then, is the first outward suffering of the damned, that they are purged, steeped in a lake of fire. O woe, woe, woe! Woe unutterable, woe unimaginable, woe interminable! . . . You know the fierce, intense, burning, heat of a furnace, how it consumes in a moment anything cast into it. Its misery to the damned shall be that they feel it, but cannot be consumed by it. The fire shall pierce them, penetrate them: it shall be, Scripture says, like a molten 'lake of fire', rolling, tossing, immersing, but not destroying.[22]

Between the moral outlook of that sermon and the general ethical outlook of today, both inside and outside the christian church, there is a great gulf fixed.[23] On Pusey's side of the gulf theology was exempt from moral criticism and the theologian could with a good conscience attribute to God an unappeasable vindictiveness and insatiable cruelty which would be regarded as demonic if applied analogously to a human being; whereas today theological ideas are subject to an ethical and rational criticism which forbids the kind of moral perversity indulged by Pusey. The objections to the doctrine of eternal torment which once seemed so weak and now seem so strong are well known: for a conscious creature to undergo physical and mental torture through unending time (if this is indeed conceivable) is horrible and disturbing beyond words; and the thought of such torment being deliberately inflicted by divine decree is totally incompatible with the idea of God as infinite love; the absolute contrast of heaven and hell, entered immediately after death, does not correspond to the innumerable gradations of human good and evil; justice could never demand for finite human sins the infinite penalty of eternal pain; such unending torment could never serve any positive or reformative purpose precisely because it never ends; and it renders any coherent christian theodicy impossible by giving the evils of sin and suffering an eternal lodgment within God's creation. Accordingly contemporary theologians who do not accept the doctrine of universal salvation usually speak of the finally lost as passing out of existence rather than as endlessly enduring the torments of hell-fire.

3. PURGATORY

The basic conception of purgatory – which also goes back embryonically to Paul[24] – is that of an intermediate state between our present existence and the eternal heavenly life. This idea has been developed and elaborated within roman catholic theology as the next stage for such as die in a state of venial sin or who still have to undergo further temporal punishment for mortal sin. Those who, at the time of their death, are already fit to participate in the ultimate divine glory are immediately translated into the presence of God. But the great majority of those destined by grace for heaven (whether this be all men or only some) are too imperfect to enter it immediately; and purgatory comprehends the range of further experiences through which they face the consequences of their own sins and become purified in character and prepared for the beatific vision. In this purgatorial stage they can be helped, as can men on earth, by the prayers of others; and as a stage of the after-life in which the dead are aided by the prayers of the living the idea of purgatory goes back to Old Testament Judaism[25] and was taken over by the early Christians as part of their jewish heritage, being well established within the church by the second century.[26]

In the late medieval world, and particularly in the fifteenth and sixteenth centuries, the saying of masses for souls in purgatory, paid for by the living, became a major ecclesiastical industry; and the sale of indulgences, supposed to remit specified periods of purgatorial suffering, was a gross fraud which provoked the violent condemnation of Martin Luther and precipitated the Reformation. This is a tale of 'old, un-happy, far-off things, and battles long ago' which there is no need to rehearse today; but it brought the idea of purgatory into a disrepute among Protestants from which it only began to recover in the late nineteenth century under such aliases as 'the intermediate state' and 'progressive sanctification after death'. A rehabilitation of the notion was much to be desired; for the basic concept of purgatory as that of the period between this life and man's ultimate state seems unavoidable. The gap between the individual's imperfection at the end of this life and the perfect heavenly state in which he is to participate has to be bridged; and purgatory is simply the name given in roman theology to this bridge. In the next chapter, however, when distinctive roman catholic contributions to the theology of death are examined, I shall suggest that this function of 'purgatory' is frustrated in official catholic thought by the accompanying dogma of the 'final decision' at the moment of death, and needs to be expanded into the idea of a continued person-making process in other spheres beyond this world.

4. HEAVEN

Christian thought about heaven, as the final state of the blessed, has been immensely varied, though always tending at its best to be deliberately reticent and open-ended. The most basic conception is that human personalities, made perfect, will enjoy an existence which is totally oriented to God. This has generally been described in terms either of the worship of God or of a beatific vision of the divine Reality. Although both these themes are encompassed within the christian tradition and mingled together in its language they stand in some degree of tension with one another – a tension which may however, as we shall see later, contribute towards the develop-ment of a global theology of death.

The notion of heavenly worship has been pictured in christian hymns about 'those endless Sabbaths the blessed ones see'[27] and the saints 'casting down their golden crowns around the glassy sea':[28]

> Now, with triumphal palms, they stand
> Before the throne on high,
> And serve the God they love amidst
> The glories of the sky.[29]

Again:

> The Lamb's apostles there
> I might with joy behold;
> The harpers I might hear
> Harping on harps of gold.[30]

The original fount of all such language is the last book of the New Testament, the Revelation to John. Its imagery is however more profound than most of the hymns which it has inspired. In the new Jerusalem there is no need of temples because God is present with his people in the person of Christ, the Lamb. Accordingly the worship of the saints is not expressed in singing psalms and playing harps but in the life of the holy city as a community wholly responsive to God. The social and interpersonal character of human existence is not only acknowledged but brought to its perfection in this ideal society. However, deep conceptual difficulties emerge when we try to visualize a society of perfected individuals in a totally stress-free environment from which pain, sorrow and death have been banished. The basic problem is to conceive of a worthwhile human existence in a situation in which there can be no needs, lacks, problems, perils, tasks, satisfactions or, therefore, purposes. I shall suggest later that this converges with other difficulties inherent in the idea of the immortal ego to suggest a pareschatological doctrine of many successive lives in many worlds and an eschatology in which ego-hood is finally transcended in a state of human unity which can be characterized, on the trinitarian model, as one-in-many and many-in-one.[31]

However, this is to look beyond the established christian tradition, which assumes that the saints in glory persist for ever as separate and distinct individuals. Within this common assumption two tendencies have appeared. On the one hand there has been a concern for the mutual recognition of those in heaven and the consequent reunion of families and friends parted by death. This could be illustrated from innumerable sources, but I shall use a minor nineteenth-century work, C. R. Muston's *Recognition in the World to Come, or Christian Friendship on Earth Perpetuated in Heaven* (2nd ed., 1831). The writer argues from both reason and scripture that personal recognition must be possible in the life of heaven. He claims for example that continued personal identity, involving continuity of one's individual embodied character and memory, such as is implied by the idea of judgement, also implies the possibility of recognition. And turning to the Bible he cites (along with a number of other passages) Jesus' saying that 'many will come from east and west and sit at table with Abraham, Isaac and Jacob in the kingdom of heaven'[32] and asks, not unreasonably, how if the redeemed cannot recognize these three great patriarchs they will know that they are sitting down with them.[33] And all the imagery, for example in death-bed scenes in nineteenth-century novels, of 'going to join' parents, or brothers or sisters who have died early, presupposes the continuity of distinctive individuality and personal relationships. On the other hand, another tendency appeals to Jesus' statement concerning resurrected persons that 'they neither marry nor are given in marriage, but are like angels in heaven'.[34] This suggests a very far-reaching change. It 'abrogates not only [the] essential human faculty of sexual love and relationship and the need for procreation but even the very survival of family ties. The earthly relationships do not appear to be translated into Heaven.'[35] And so this other development has de-emphasized personal continuity from earth to heaven and has stressed instead that the life to come will be different in ways which are at present unknowable to us and which render nugatory all speculations that seek to peer beyond the veil.

This latter emphasis borders upon the other great theme of christian eschatology, the beatific vision of the Godhead, an idea which reached its full doctrinal development in the medieval period. However, the basic thought is not distinctively medieval but is as old as Christianity, and indeed older. The notion of a direct and transforming awareness of the divine Reality had already excited the religious mind of the ancient world, so that the promise of such a *gnosis* latent within the christian gospel soon began to be drawn out. As K. E. Kirk says, 'Christianity came into a world tantalized with the belief that some men at least had seen God, and had found in the vision the sum of human happiness; a world aching with the hope that the same vision was attainable by all.'[36] Jesus had said, 'Blessed are the pure in heart, for they shall see (*opsontai*) God';[37] Paul had spoken of seeing face to face;[38] and in the Revelation to John it is said that the saints in heaven will see (*opsontai*) the face of God.[39] The hope for the vision of God on earth, as man's highest good, was soon appropriated by the hermits who retired to live the ascetic life in solitude in desert places, and then by the monks and nuns who formed the monastic communities. The doctrine of the two lives – the higher, contemplative life of the celibate, and the lower life of ordinary men and women in the secular world – goes back as far as Origen in the early third century, was formalized by Jerome and Ambrose in the fourth century, and has continued within the roman church until now. Today, although still official doctrine, it has in practice been partly superseded by the ideal of redemptive christian involvement in the life of the world.

The theology of the eschatological vision of God begins with Irenaeus, in the second century, who taught that 'men therefore shall see God, that they may live, being made immortal by that sight and attaining even unto God'.[40] There was however little discussion of what 'seeing God' means until Thomas Aquinas, working within the framework of aristotelian philosophy, described the *visio dei* as the intellectual knowledge of the divine substance.[41] This is not a literal seeing, but 'since we reach the knowledge of intelligible things from sensible things, we also take over the names proper to sense knowledge for intellectual knowledge, especially the ones which apply to sight, which, compared to the other senses, is more noble and more spiritual, and so more closely related to the intellect. Thus it is that this intellectual knowledge is called vision.'[42] Such a 'vision of the divine substance is the ultimate end of every intellectual substance':[43] it involves seeing all things in God and seeing them not successively but in the total simultaneity of eternity.[44] However, Aquinas also speaks of the *visio dei* in temporal terms: for its felicity endures perpetually; it cannot be lost; nor can the blessed voluntarily abandon it.[45] Again, Aquinas meets what might be called the problem of heavenly boredom, which itself presupposes a temporal form of experience, by saying that:

> nothing that is contemplated with wonder can be tiresome, since as long as the thing remains in wonder it continues to stimulate desire. But the divine substance is always viewed with wonder by any created intellect, since no created intellect comprehends it. So, it is impossible for an intellectual substance to become tired of this vision. And thus, it cannot, of its own will, desist from this vision.[46]

The beatific vision is described in thoughtful catholic writings in a profound and open-ended way which can contribute importantly, I shall suggest in chapter 22, to an eschatology comprehending the convergent indications of both west and east. It is said, for example, that in the beatific vision God will not be known as a presence over against ourselves but as a reality apprehended in the direct way in which we know ourselves: 'God will not remain outside us. He will be within our mind itself, and there we shall see him. The nearest approximation to such knowledge on earth is our knowledge of ourselves. We know ourselves because we are ourselves; we are present to ourselves in our innermost being . . . We must not, therefore, imagine God in the Beatific Vision as some outside Object to look at, but as dwelling within the very essence of our soul, and thus being perceived from within by direct contact.'[47] Again, in an analogy much used by some of the christian mystics: 'Throw a bar of iron into a blazing furnace and leave it there till it is molten metal in the midst of the fire, and the eye can no longer see the iron. As that iron knows the fire, so shall we know God. Our innermost being will thrill and throb in unison with God's life, and we shall be fully conscious of it.'[48]

There is a wealth of spiritual insight within these various and even sometimes incompatible christian pictures of heaven – as the Kingdom of God, the ideal community of perfected men and women; as involving continued personal identity and mutual recognition; and yet as transcending the categories of this world; as a dynamic life, presupposing change and time, and yet as participation in eternity, beyond all temporal successiveness; and finally as the beatific vision in which the finite spirit knows God directly as the ultimate reality of all being. But whilst these insights have been able to float together down the stream of christian devotion and hope, they cannot easily be fitted together into a single conception of the final state of man. I shall argue later, however, that a distinction between pareschatology and eschatology can enable these various elements of christian belief to find their place within the resulting more complex total picture.

5. CHRISTIAN ATTITUDES TO DEATH[49]

Two rather different attitudes, cohering with two rather different types of theology, appear with the expressions of christian piety in the face of death. In the earliest days there seems to have been so vivid a sense of the reality and love of God, and of Christ as having overcome death, that those who had died were thought of as having gone forward into a greater fulfilment and joy. 'The departed has "gone to God", is "received or accepted by God", "lives with Christ", "is among the angels", "among the saints", "refreshed and joyful among the stars".'[50] However, Paul had planted within the growing seed of christian thought the idea (already familiar within Judaism) that death is a punishment for sin: 'as sin came into the world through one man [Adam] and death through sin, and so death spread to all men because all men sinned . . . '[51] In Paul's own writings this thought always occurs in the context of the good news that Christ has overcome death on our behalf: 'the wages of sin is death, but the free gift of God is eternal life in Christ Jesus our Lord'.[52] It was above all Augustine, in the fifth century, who first wove the dark themes of guilt, remorse and punishment into the tremendous drama of creation, fall, incarnation, heaven and hell which has dominated the christian imagination in the west until within the last hundred years or so. In this picture our mortality is an expression of our sinfulness, and it is only by the free mercy of the divine judge that we may hope to escape from the wrath to come.

Augustine taught that 'the first men were so created that if they had not sinned, they could not have experienced any kind of death; but that having become sinners, they were so punished with death, that whatsoever sprang from their stock should also be punished with the same death'.[53] Moving across the centuries and touching only the peaks of christian thought, Anselm in the eleventh century, in his immensely influential *Cur Deus Homo?*, wrote:

> That also [man] was so created as that he was not under the necessity of dying, may hence be easily proved, since, as we said before, it is contrary to the wisdom and justice of God that He should compel man, whom He made upright for everlasting happiness, to suffer death for no fault. It follows, therefore, that had man never sinned, he never would have died.[54]

And Thomas Aquinas,[55] and later John Calvin,[56] likewise affirmed the same doctrine.

On this view our mortality is not an aspect of the divinely intended human situation, but is an evil, a state that ought never to have come about, a disastrous consequence of man's turning away from his Maker. Death is a punishment, and the emotions which appropriately reverberate around it are those of guilt and sorrow, remorse and fear. Man is born in sin, deserving eternal torment, and is saved from it only by faith in the redeeming blood of Christ, shed to avert the divine condemnation. The atmosphere is one of doom, horror and dread.

However, we have seen that among the early Christians, before negative implications began to be drawn from positive insights, there was a more hopeful attitude to death; and this attitude has recurred throughout christian history, although usually not integrated into the dominant and official theology. Alongside the dark, punitive conception of the meaning of death there has always been the very different picture of human life as a pilgrimage, with bodily death as the end of one stage of that pilgrimage and, by the same token, as a passing on to another stage. This picture has in it a glint of gold, a note of fulfilment, of triumph, even of adventure in face of death, which is perfectly caught in John Bunyan's passage about the passing of that great pilgrim, Mr Valiant-for-truth:

> After this it was noised abroad that Mr Valiant-for-truth
> was taken with a summons by the same post as the other,
> and had this for a token that the summons was true, That
> his pitcher was broken at the fountain. When he understood
> it, he called for his friends and told them of it. Then said he,
> I am going to my fathers, and tho' with great difficulty I am
> got hither, yet now I do not repent me of all the trouble I
> have been at to arrive where I am. My sword I give to him
> that shall succeed me in my pilgrimage, and my courage and
> skill to him that can get it. My marks and scars I carry with
> me, to be a witness for me that I have fought his battles
> who now will be my rewarder. When the day that he must
> go hence was come, many accompanied him to the riverside,
> into which as he went he said, Death, where is thy sting?
> And as he went down deeper he said, Grave, where is thy
> victory? So he passed over, and all the trumpets sounded
> for him on the other side.[57]

This pilgrim attitude to death is not really at home within
the official augustinian understanding of our mortality as a
divinely inflicted punishment for sin. A more congenial
framework can however be found within the history of
christian thought, though for most of the time only as a minority report overshadowed by the dominant augustinian tradition.
The alternative goes back through strands of eastern Christianity to the early hellenistic Fathers, and has been developed
more fully in the modern period since it reappeared in the
work of the great nineteenth-century protestant thinker,
Friedrich Schleiermacher. On this view man was not created
in a finitely perfect state from which he then fell, but was
initially brought into being as an immature creature who was
only at the beginning of a long process of growth and development. Man did not fall disastrously from a better state into one
of sin and guilt, with death as its punishment, but rather he is
still in process of being created. Irenaeus, in the second
century, provided a vocabulary for this teleological conception
when he distinguished between the image (*imago*) and the
likeness (*similitudo*) of God in man. Man as he has emerged
from the slow evolution of the forms of life exists as a rational

and personal creature in the image of God. But he is still only the raw material for a further stage of the creative process by which man, the intelligent animal, is being brought through his own free responses to his environment to that perfection of his nature which is his finite likeness to God.[58]

From this point of view the wide gap, marked by the doctrine of the fall, between man's actual state and the state intended for him in God's purpose, is indeed a reality. But the ideal state, representing the fulfilment of God's intention for man, is not a lost reality, forfeited long ago in 'the vast backward and abysm of time', but something lying before us as a state to be attained in the distant future. And our present mortal embodied earthly life is not a penal condition, but a time of soul-making in which we may freely respond to God's purpose and become, in Paul's phrases, 'children of God' and 'heirs of eternal life'. For such a theology the proper function of our earthly existence, with its baffling mixture of good and evil, is to be an environment in which moral choices and spiritual responses are called for, and in which men and women are being formed in relationship to one another within a common world. This theology prompts an understanding of the meaning of life as a divinely intended opportunity, given to us both individually and as a race, to grow towards the realization of the potentialities of our own nature and so to become fully human. Life is thus aptly imaged in terms of the ancient picture of an arduous journey towards the life of the Celestial City. This pilgrimage crosses the frontier of death; for its end is not attained in this life, and therefore if it is to be attained at all there must be a further life, or lives, in which God's purpose continues to hold us in being in environments related to that purpose.

NOTES

1. The idea of the two judgements, an individual one at death and a universal one at the resurrection, may have been learned from Zoroastrianism.

2. Cf. R. H. Charles, *Eschatology*, p. 295.

3. 1 Corinthians 15: 50.

4. Cf. J. G. Davies, 'Factors Leading to the Emergence of Belief in the Resurrection of the Flesh', in *Journal of Theological Studies*, vol. XXIII, part 2 (1972).

5. On an unorthodox variation, christian mortalism – the view that the soul either sleeps until the Day of Judgement, or is annihilated and then re-created – see Norman T. Burns, *Christian Mortalism from Tyndale to Milton*.

6. *Hamlet*, act III, scene 3.

7. For a brief history of millenarianism, see the *Encyclopædia of Religion and Ethics*, 'Eschatology'.

8. *The City of God*, book 20, chs. 6, 10.

9. ibid., book 20, chs. 8–9.

10. ibid., book 20, ch. 20, p. 742.

11. ibid., book 20, ch. 14, p. 733.

12. ibid.

13. T. S. R. Boase, *Death in the Middle Ages*, p. 54.

14. *The City of God*, book 21, chs. 2–8, 23.

15. *Paradise Lost*, book II, ll. 274–8.

16. ibid., book II, ll. 596–603.

17. *The Divine Comedy*, book I, canto 24, ll. 103–5.

18. This awakening is admirably traced, as it occurred in Britain, in D. P. Walker, *The Decline of Hell*, and Geoffrey Rowell, *Hell and the Victorians*.

19. Cf. D. P. Walker, *The Decline of Hell*, ch. 1.

20. Cf. Walker, op. cit., ch. 1.

21. Cf. Rowell, op. cit., pp. 190–2.

22. Quoted by Rowell, op. cit., p. 108.

23. There are however still a few Christians on the far side of the gulf. For example, René Pache in *The Future Life*, a french work translated by the Moody Bible Institute of Chicago, says on the basis of Luke 16: 19–31 that 'immediately after leaving this world: the wicked suffer; they are fully conscious; they are in entire possession of their memory; no one can comfort them; there is no possibility of their leaving the place of torment; they are entirely responsible for not having listened in time to the warnings of the Scriptures. Who would not shudder before such a horrible fate as this?' (p. 42).

24. 1 Corinthians 3: 17. Cf. Luke 12: 46–8.

25. Cf. 2 Maccabees 12: 39–45.

26. Cf. *Encyclopædia of Religion and Ethics*, vol. XI, pp. 837–8.

27. 'O what their joy and their glory must be', by John Mason Neale (1818–66), from Abelard.

28. 'Holy, holy, holy, Lord God Almighty!', by Reginald Heber (1783–1826).

29. 'How bright these glorious spirits shine!', by William Cameron (1751–1811).

30. 'Jerusalem on high', by Samuel Crossman (1624–83).

31. See chapters 20 and 22.
32. Matthew 8: 11.
33. op. cit., pp. 98–102.
34. Mark 12: 25.
35. Ulrich Simon, *Heaven in the Christian Tradition*, p. 217.
36. K. E. Kirk, *The Vision of God*, p. 54.
37. Matthew 5: 8.
38. 1 Corinthians 13: 12.
39. Revelation 22: 4.
40. *Against Heresies*, book IV, ch. 20, para. 6.
41. *Summa contra Gentiles*, book III, ch. 53.
42. ibid. (*On the Truth of the Catholic Faith*, book III, part 1, pp. 181–2).
43. ibid., ch. 59 (p. 195).
44. ibid., ch. 60.
45. ibid., ch. 62.
46. ibid. (p. 205).
47. J. P. Arendzen, 'Heaven or the Church Triumphant', in *The Teaching of the Catholic Church*, vol. II, pp. 1253–4.
48. ibid., p. 1254. Cf. pp. 444–5 below.
49. Some paragraphs in this section are taken, with permission, from my essay, 'Towards a Christian Theology of Death', in *Dying, Death and Disposal*, ed. Gilbert Cope.
50. Ulrich Simon, *Heaven in the Christian Tradition*, p. 219.
51. Romans 5: 12.
52. ibid., 6: 23.
53. *The City of God*, book 13, ch. 3.
54. *Cur Deus Homo?*, book 2, ch. 2.
55. *Summa Theologica*, part I, q.97, art 2. For other roman catholic statements see Denzinger, *Enchiridion Symbolorum*, 101, 175, 788, 789.
56. *Institutes*, book II, ch. 1, para. 6.
57. John Bunyan, *The Pilgrim's Progress*, towards the end of part II.
58. Cf. my *Evil and the God of Love*, part III.

CHAPTER 11

Contemporary Protestant Views

1. JÜRGEN MOLTMANN

The currently influential 'theology of hope' professes to re-establish eschatology, after a period of neglect, as the central theme of christian theology. Jürgen Moltmann, in his book *Theology of Hope: On the Ground and the Implications of a Christian Eschatology*, argues that eschatology ought not to be an appendix to the body of doctrine; rather, the whole of christian theology should be eschatological. 'From first to last, and not merely in the epilogue, Christianity is eschatology, is hope, forward looking and forward moving, and therefore also revolutionizing and transforming the present.'[1] This quotation reveals Moltmann's main concern in developing a theology of hope, a concern which is indicated by the other name which he gives to his programme – political theology. He wants to show the power of the christian gospel as a source of earthly hope, in competition with marxist and other secular philosophies of progress or of revolution. As Moltmann says in one of his essays, 'in the past two centuries, a Christian faith in God without hope for the future of the world has called forth a secular hope for the future of the world without faith in God . . . The messianic hopes emigrated from the church and became invested in progress, evolution, and revolutions . . . We have arrived at a moment in history that provokes the question: Should there now be a parting of ways in history, so that faith aligns itself with the past and unfaith with the future? I think that we can overcome this present dilemma only if Christians begin to remember the "God of Hope", as he is witnessed to in the promissory history of the Old and New Testaments, and thus begin to assume responsibility for the personal, social, and political problems of the present.'[2]

This is (in my view) a valid and important task: I am wholly in favour of the claim of 'political theology' that the gospel has historical implications and that it offers a ground of hope amidst the struggle for social, political, economic and racial justice. But what is chiefly interesting, from the point of view of our concern in this book, is that whilst Moltmann recognizes that such a hope must be based on an eschatological faith, that basis is in practice relegated to the periphery of his thought and reduced to a mere uncritical use of biblical mythology. The result is that all the problems facing christian eschatology in the twentieth century are systematically ignored.

Moltmann's doctrine of the 'end' is threefold. First, he expects the return of Christ in glory. 'When we speak of the "future of Jesus Christ", then we mean that which is described elsewhere as the "parousia of Christ" or the "return of Christ".'[3] This cannot be anticipated at any particular date because it is a free divine act. 'The return of Christ does not come "of itself", like the year 1965, but comes from himself, when and as God will according to his promise.'[4] If Moltmann does not intend the Sècond Coming to be interpreted literally, as it is in the New Testament and in much of the thought of the church through the ages, he gives no hint of any such critical discrimination. He appears to be making a straight pre-critical appeal to traditional apocalyptic imagery. Second, Christ's Second Coming will inaugurate his earthly reign, to which we look forward in the 'eschatological expectation of the all-embracing lordship of Christ for the corporeal, earthly world'.[5] Once agɑin Moltmann uses the biblical imagery without betraying any awareness of the immense critical problems which it involves for the modern Christian. Third, after the return and the earthly reign of Christ there will supervene the final consummation of the universe in which God will at last be all in all. For 'even the coming world lordship of Christ over all his enemies can once again be eschatologically surpassed, in that not even his lordship is in itself the eternal presence of God, but has an eschatologically provisional character in which it serves the sole and all-embracing lordship of God'.[6] For the righteousness of God 'refers not merely to a new order for the existing world, but provides creation as a whole with a new ground of existence and a new right to life. Hence with the coming of the righteousness of God we can expect also a new creation.'[7] As with the other two eschatological symbols of the Second Coming and the reign of the Messiah, the idea of the 'new heavens and a new earth in which righteousness dwells'[8] is used by Moltmann as a straight biblical image. He makes no attempt to analyse its meaning or to spell out its implications. He does however claim, with characteristic rhetoric, that 'the cosmic ideas of Christian eschatology are therefore not by any means mythological, but reach forward into the open realm of possibilities ahead of all reality, give expression to the "expectation of the creature" for a *nova creatio*, and provide a prelude for eternal life, peace and the haven of the reconciliation of all things'.[9]

In this reversion to uncriticized biblical imagery Moltmann is turning his back on the task of formulating a coherent and credible christian expectation concerning the future of the individual and of the race beyond the continuation and termination of their present earthly life. It seems to me paradoxical that such a renunciation of the theologian's responsibility in this sphere should have been presented as the triumph of eschatology within christian thought!

2. PAUL TILLICH

The most distinctive new protestant thinking about the last things takes the form of what I shall call recapitulation theories, which suggest that man's immortality is the eternal presence of his earthly life within the divine memory. As it happens, the first thinker to suggest a view of this kind was (so far as I know) the very individual spanish catholic writer Miguel de Unamuno, who said in his *Tragic Sense of Life* (1913), 'If there is a Universal and Supreme Consciousness, I am an idea in it; and is it possible for any idea in this Supreme Consciousness to be completely blotted out? After I have died, God will go on remembering me, and to be remembered by God, to have my consciousness sustained by the Supreme Consciousness, is not that, perhaps, to be?'[10]

The idea was not taken up within catholic thought. It has however been independently developed by a number of recent protestant thinkers. Paul Tillich was the first such to sponsor, though in his case cloudily and unclearly, such a recapitulation conception of immortality. In the third volume of his *Systematic Theology* he defines eternal life as the end of history in the sense of its inner aim or *telos*,[11] this being something quite distinct from its temporal end. The end as *telos*, Tillich says, 'is not a moment within the larger development of the universe (analogously called history) but transcends all moments of the temporal process'.[12] History, and human beings as parts of it, may however enter into eternal life; for 'the ever present end of history elevates the positive content of history into eternity at the same time that it excludes the negative from participation in it'.[13] However, 'the transition from the temporal to the eternal, the "end" of the temporal, is not a temporal event . . . Time is the form of the created finite . . . and eternity is the inner aim, the *telos* of the created finite, permanently elevating the finite into itself.'[14] And then Tillich goes on to offer what he describes as the bold metaphor of man's immortality within the 'eternal memory'. This eternal divine memory is selective. Like human memories it tends to remember the good and to forget the bad. And its selectivity can provide a partial solution to the vexing problem of evil. 'If we apply again the metaphor of "eternal memory," we can say that the negative is not an object of eternal memory in the sense of living retention. Neither is it forgotten, for forgetting pre-supposes at least a moment of remembering. The negative is not remembered at all. It is acknowledged for what it is – non-being. Nevertheless it is not without effect on that which is eternally remembered. It is present in the eternal memory as that which is conquered and thrown out into its naked nothingness (for example, a lie).'[15] So far this seems to mean that what an existing thing ought to be, or that which is inherently good in it, is eternal and that in so far as the thing is what it ought to be it may be said to participate in eternity by being 'remembered' by God.

How does this work out in relation to the question of human existence or non-existence after death? Tillich says that 'for the individual participation in Eternal Life, Christianity uses the two terms "immortality" and "resurrection" '.[16] In developing this aspect of the subject, however, he says mutually contradictory things which cancel each other out and offer the reader little more than an experience of intellectual confusion. On the one hand he rejects the notion of the continued life of an individual beyond the grave. This emerges when he raises the problem of those who, often through no fault of their own, 'are unable to reach a fulfilment of their essential *telos* even to a small degree, as in the case of premature destruction, the death of infants, biological and psychological disease . . . '[17] 'From the point of view which assumes separate individual destinies,' he says, 'there is no answer at all. The question and the answer are possible only if one understands essentialization or elevation of the positive into Eternal Life as a matter of universal participation . . . '[18] Accordingly, we are not to think in terms of separate individual destinies. But only a little later Tillich asserts that the 'self-conscious self cannot be excluded from Eternal Life'[19] and even that 'eternal fulfilment cannot be denied to the biological dimension and therefore to the body'.[20] But then again he adds that 'the participation of the centred self is not the endless continuation of a particular stream of consciousness in memory and anticipation. Self-consciousness, in our experience, depends on temporal changes both of the perceiving subject and of the perceived object in the process of self-awareness. But eternity transcends temporality and with it the experienced character of self-consciousness.'[21] And so we are left with the thought of embodied self-conscious beings who are nevertheless devoid of any stream of consciousness. In face of such unresolved contradictions the reader can only suffer in silence! I therefore turn to the not altogether dissimilar, but much more lucidly presented, theory of the process theologian Charles Hartshorne.

3. CHARLES HARTSHORNE

According to Hartshorne human immortality means that after we are dead our lives will be perpetually remembered by God.[22] This is a form of what has been called social immortality, immortality achieved by influencing the lives of others who come after us. Such was the kind of immortality that Shakespeare envisaged in his eighteenth sonnet,

> Nor shall Death brag thou wanderest in his shade,
> When in eternal lines to time thou growest:
> So long as men can breathe, or eyes can see,
> So long lives this, and this gives life to thee.[23]

The late President John Kennedy, for example, still exists vividly in the memories of very many of us; whilst on the other hand the anonymous roman soldier of the first century whose helmet is in the museum has only an exceedingly dim and shadowy social immortality – for no one now knows anything about him beyond the bare fact that there once was a roman soldier who owned this helmet. Thus ordinary social immortality is a very variable quantity, and necessarily one that diminishes through time. We all live on a *little* in the memory of others, but usually only a little and only for a comparatively brief period.

But Hartshorne's new concept of social immortality is much stronger than this. According to him all men live on in memory totally and for ever; for they live on in the complete and infallible memory of God. Everything that has ever happened is treasured with one-hundred-per-cent accuracy in the divine awareness. Each human life, from the cradle to the grave, stands totally recorded in God's memory and has an immortal existence in this form. 'In short', says Hartshorne, 'our adequate immortality can only be God's omniscience of us. He to whom all hearts are open remains evermore open to any heart that ever has been apparent to Him. What we once were to Him, less than that we never can be, for otherwise He Himself as knowing us would lose something of His own reality . . . Hence, if we can never be less than we have been to God, we can in reality never be less than we have been . . . Death cannot mean the destruction, or even the fading, of the book of one's life; it can mean only the fixing of its concluding page. Death writes "The End" upon the last page, but nothing further happens to the book, by way of either addition or subtraction.'[24] And to Hartshorne it is an inspiring thought that one's life is going to be preserved in this way for ever, contributing perpetually to the consciousness of God. Thus 'all of one's life can be a "reasonable, holy, and living sacrifice" to deity, a sacrifice whose value depends on the quality of the life, and this depends on the depth of the devotion to all good things, to all life's possibilities, neither as mine nor as not mine but as belonging to God's creatures and thus to God'.[25] So, 'the true immortality is everlasting fame before God'.[26]

By way of comment, I think we should be clear, first, that this is not a doctrine of immortality in the sense of a doctrine about the continuance of human life after bodily death. Hartshorne says, in one of the passages I have quoted, 'What we once were to [God], less than that we can never be, for otherwise He Himself as knowing us would lose something of His own reality . . . Hence, if we can never be less than we have been to God, we can in reality never be less than we have been.'[27] But this reasoning contains a truly magnificent ambiguity. It may mean, innocently, that God's original consciousness of a man when he was alive is retained with complete accuracy in the divine memory; in other words, God never forgets. Or it may mean, far from innocently, that the man himself can never be less than he was in life, since he is thereafter eternally remembered by God – with the implication that the state of being remembered as having lived constitutes as full and real an existence as the state of being alive. But this latter is manifestly false. The difference between the two states is all-important. On Hartshorne's view there is no human *life* after death, no continued consciousness, no continued interaction with other people and with an environment. What continues to exist is not you or me, or anything that is in any way different from and yet continuous with our present earthly existence, but simply someone else's memory of our lives – that someone else being God. But to be alive in any ordinary sense of the word is not only to be remembered, but also to be capable of remembering, and of creating fresh and different material for memory. On Hartshorne's view the book of a man's life is closed at death, so that nothing can thereafter be added to it or subtracted from it, although the book itself is eternally preserved in the heavenly library which is the universal divine memory. *We* do not exist in an after-life; but after we have ceased to exist the record of our lives will exist as part of the continually expanding cosmic record – in eastern terms, the *akashic* record – of everything that has occurred in the whole universe throughout past time. This, I repeat, is not a doctrine of man's immortal life; for the fact that the divine mind contains a full record of your life or mine no more involves your or my immortality than the population records in a national computer bank give life to the millions of people in the past to whom these records refer.

As a second comment, it seems to me pertinent to ask whether the theme of life as process, change, development and growth is as adequately expressed in Hartshorne's theory as it is in the doctrine of the continued existence of the living human personality after bodily death. For Hartshorne's doctrine postulates, after all, a static, frozen immortality. The last page of the book of life has been filled and all that happens subsequently is that the completed volume is preserved for ever, unchanged and unchangeable. Hartshorne's notion is not, it is true, static in every respect. He holds that the divine memory of a man's life is taken up into God's response to that life, thus forming a new synthesis which itself enters into all subsequent moments of the divine consciousness through unending time. For God, according to process theology, is a temporal reality undergoing continual change in the form of growth towards an ever fuller perfection. And so as objects now of God's contemporary awareness, and later of his memory, our lives are contributing to the content of the divine mind. 'In this sense', says Hartshorne, 'we can interpret "heaven" as the conception which God forms of our actual living, a conception which we partly determine by our free decisions but which is more than all our decisions and experiences, since it is the synthesis of God's participating responses to these experiences. It is the book which is never read by any man save in unclear, fragmentary glimpses; but is the clearly given content of the divine appreciation.'[28] But the element of process and change which Hartshorne introduces at this point does not alter the fact that there is, on his theory, no continuing life, no new experiences and choices, no personal consciousness, beyond bodily death. In contrast to this the traditional teaching (at least in one of its forms) involves a dynamic view of immortality, in which the person continues as a living centre of consciousness, receiving new impressions, making fresh choices and decisions, interacting with a new environment and continuing to move, as a free creature in a divinely ruled universe, towards the perfect fulfilment of his own nature in the ultimate Kingdom of God.

My third comment arises out of the last; and it concerns the problem of evil. On Hartshorne's view not only is all the good that has been realized in human experience immortalized within the divine memory, but also and equally all the evil – all the cruelty, hatred and malevolence, all the pain, suffering and misery of the ages. This is all equally perpetuated in the divine consciousness. It is as though God's eternity were filled with a continual playing over again and again of the records of this world. Evil is eternalized together with good, and presumably in the same proportions as before. There is no final resolving of evil in the gradual creation of an ultimate good. In contrast to this, an older christian theology sees our temporal existence as moving towards a far distant goal in which good will finally have been brought out of evil and evil itself will have been left behind in the dead part. On this view evil will not be immortalized, as it is in Hartshorne's theory, in the static hell formed by the eternal retention of evil in the divine memory. And if we are tempted to say – with Tillich – that the divine memory simply forgets all the evil in us and remembers only the good, this will not avoid the difficulty. For it will then no longer be *us* whom God remembers. He will not be remembering real people, because real people are a mixture of good and evil; and if everything in us that is less than perfect were blotted out of the divine consciousness, there would be very little of us left! In contrast to such speculations the strand of christian tradition that I shall later want to draw upon speaks of real people being drawn towards their perfection in an existence which extends far beyond this present life.

4. WOLFHART PANNENBERG

The last form of recapitulation theory that I want to examine is that of Wolfhart Pannenberg, one of the most significant of the post-barthian theologians on the continent of Europe, in his *What is Man? Present-day Anthropology in the Light of Theology*, which was first published in 1962, with a third edition in 1968. Pannenberg's theory is a subtle and interesting one. Man's self-centredness (by which Pannenberg means *Ichbezogenheit* in contrast to *Weltoffenheit*) is the source of his sinfulness; and as a consequence of it man experiences the world in temporal terms, divided into past, present and future. But God on the other hand is conscious in a single comprehensive 'present' of what is thus fragmented within our human experience,[29] and this unity of all events in a single divine moment is eternity, which Pannenberg also describes as the 'truth' or 'reality' (*Wahrheit*) of time. Accordingly the content of eternity is identical with that of time. Nothing further happens in eternity, for this is simply time experienced as a non-temporal whole. Let me at this point quote from Pannenberg:

> The truth of time lies beyond the self-centredness of our experience of time as past, present, and future. The truth of time is the concurrence of all events in an eternal present. Eternity, then, does not stand in contrast to time as something that is completely different. Eternity creates no other content than time. However, eternity is the truth of time, which remains hidden in the flux of time. Eternity is the unity of all time, but as such it simultaneously is something that exceeds our experience of time. The perception of all events in an eternal present would be possible only from a point beyond the stream of time. Such a position is not attainable for any finite creature. Only God can be thought of as not being confined to the flow of time. Therefore, eternity is God's time. That means, however, that God is present to every time. His action and power extend to everything past and future as to something that, for him, is present.[30]

Thus eternal life is more appropriately pictured by the idea of the resurrection of the dead than by that of the immortality of the soul, for it consists in our present earthly life in all its bodily concreteness, though seen in a radically new perspective: 'The life that awakens in the resurrection of the dead is the same as the life we now lead on earth. However, it is our present life as God sees it from his eternal present. Therefore it will be completely different from the way we now experience it. Yet, nothing happens in the resurrection of the dead except that which already constitutes the eternal depth of time now and which is already present for God's eyes – for his creative view! Thus through the bridge of the eternal depth of our lifetime we are, in the present, already identical with the life to which we will be resurrected in the future.'[31]

Proceeding on this basis Pannenberg is able to speak of

judgement as the pain of eternity, caused by the consciousness of the eternal loss of our right relationship to God and of the proper fulfilment of our own nature. It is the experience of a negative eternity. Of the individual under judgement Pannenberg says, 'he will not simply become nothing; he will be destroyed in the face of his infinite destiny, that is, his destiny to a total, healed life'.[32] This suggests a conception of the state of those for whom eternity is spent under God's judgement as one in which they are eternally conscious of their earthly life in its true character, as God has always seen it, namely as a tragic and wilful self-enclosed cutting of oneself off from the life-giving reality of God's activity. There is however, Pannenberg adds, the possibility before us now in this life of a different experience of eternity, in which it will not only be judgement but also, beyond this, eternal life. This is the hope of those who are 'in Christ', those whose lives have become linked by faith to Jesus. 'Then in the eternal concurrence of our existence, community with Jesus will drown out and transform the discords . . . Only for the person who is in community with Jesus does the resurrection mean eternal life as well as judgment.'[33]

So far, a reader might well suppose that Pannenberg is thinking of the continued existence of human consciousness after bodily death in a new relationship with God in which the individual participates – either as a heavenly or as a hellish experience – in the divine view of his own now completed earthly life. This would, thus far, be an intelligible conception. But it can hardly be Pannenberg's meaning. For he insists in a number of places that the notion of the soul or the mind persisting after the decease of the body has to be ruled out as impossible: 'In the sense of the concept that a part of man continues beyond death in an unbroken way, the idea of immortality cannot be held . . . The inner life of our consciousness is so tied to our corporeal functions that it is impossible for it to be able to continue by itself alone.'[34] It follows that the experience of seeing one's life as God sees it, as a simultaneous whole, is not a post-mortem experience; for the human consciousness cannot, according to Pannenberg, continue after the death of the physical body. Does it occur in the instant of dying, as a final moment of truth in which we review our life

as a totality and become conscious of its meaning? Pannenberg
does not give this answer either. On the contrary, he says,
'the whole of his existence never enters into the self-consciousness of his ego during his lifetime, because each person forgets
and suppresses many things. But even the portentous preview
of a person's own death and of the path toward it does not
enable him to attain the totality of his own existence. Even for
the dying person the totality of his existence still remains
hidden. If it is to involve us at all, the wholeness of our
existence can only be represented as an event beyond death.'[35]
Again, 'The unity of our life in the eternal concurrence of all
events can . . . enter into our life only after death, with the
resurrection of the dead.'[36] It cannot, however, be the post-
mortem experience of a disembodied consciousness; for
Pannenberg has ruled this out. Is he then thinking of a literal
future bodily resurrection of the dead in this world? Since the
content of the resurrection life is identical with that of our
present life, would the one be a repetition of the other – but
accompanied by a new subjective awareness of its meaning?
This is no doubt a conceivable understanding of the resurrection of the dead. It would however be surprising for Pannenberg to take such a doctrine seriously when he has so confidently invoked 'scientific impossibility' in vetoing the idea of
the mind's survival of death: the resuscitation of corpses seems
no less impossible.

    Can any assistance be gained at this point from the fact,
which Pannenberg stresses, that a conception of the life to
come can only be an earthly metaphor?[37] 'Naturally', he says,
'the concept of a future judgment is merely a metaphor
(*Gleichnis*), like the hope of resurrection itself and like every
other idea that reaches out beyond death.'[38] However, the
metaphorical or symbolic character of eschatological language
does not void the questions when and where the indescribable
experience of participating in God's vision of our earthly lives
takes place. These require literal and not metaphorical
answers. But they do not receive such answers in Pannenberg's
pages.

    There are also purely theological difficulties in Pannenberg's
position, whether interpreted in terms of earthly resurrection
or of some kind of unearthly experience. For I think it is clear

that Pannenberg's is a theory of what I have called the recapitulation' type, in that it permits of no new actions and consequently no further development of character beyond death. The difference between our life as we now experience it in time and as we shall know it as resurrected beings in eternity is that in the latter we are to share God's view of it. This provides the basis for a strong, and indeed terrifying, conception of judgement and hell. But as presented by Pannenberg it involves the difficulty of any view which makes salvation depend exclusively upon the saving encounter with Jesus. Such a doctrine can only apply to those who have lived to responsible maturity during the centuries since Jesus lived and in the lands in which his gospel has been known. It cannot apply – consistently with the reality of God's universal love – to those who have lived before Jesus or outside the influence of historic Christianity; and yet these of course constitute the large majority of the human race.

There is also a difficulty about the other side of Pannenberg's theory, namely the doctrine of eternal life or heaven which it entails. The content of eternity, according to Pannenberg, can only be that of our temporal lives. But suppose that this content is a life lived in desperate poverty and degradation, in ignorance and superstition, in starvation, disease and weakness, and in the misery of slavery or oppression? Suppose that it is a poor stunted life, devoid of joy and nobility, in which the good possibilities of human existence remain almost entirely unfulfilled? Or suppose it is the life of a hermit who has only participated minimally in the human community; or again, an evil career, only redeemed by conversion in its last moments. How is such a life, even though it also contains a moment of saving faith in Christ, to be significantly different and better as the content of eternal life? Can God's good gift of eternal life be simply a consciousness of this life seen now *sub specie aeternitatis*?[39] Is this the best form of eternity that omnipotent love can devise? I suggest that in the case of those whose earthly lives have been almost empty of moral, physical, aesthetic and intellectual good it is not a credible conception of the eternal life in Christ that they should simply experience that same earthly life as a whole instead of receiving it serially through time. Its evils will still be evils; and indeed they may in their accumulated totality seem even more evil than when known one by one. The discords cannot, I suggest, be worked into an eternal harmony without the making of more and different music.

NOTES

1. *Theology of Hope*, p. 16.
2. 'Hope and History', in *Theology Today*, October 1968, p. 370.
3. *Theology of Hope*, p. 227.
4. ibid., p. 194.
5. ibid., p. 164.
6. ibid., p. 163.
7. ibid., pp. 204–5.
8. 2 Peter 3: 13.
9. *Theology of Hope*, pp. 214–15.
10. *The Tragic Sense of Life*, p. 149.
11. *Systematic Theology*, vol. III, p. 394.
12. ibid.
13. ibid., p. 397.
14. ibid., p. 399.
15. ibid., p. 400.
16. ibid., p. 409.
17. ibid.
18. ibid.
19. ibid., p. 413.
20. ibid., p. 414.
21. ibid.
22. Hartshorne's eschatology is to be found in his essay 'Time, Death and Everlasting Life', in *The Logic of Perfection*, with a summary in 'A Philosopher's Assessment of Christianity', in *Religion and Culture*, ed. Walter Leibrecht, pp. 177–8. There are important clarifications in Hartshorne's 'The Immortality of the Past', in *The Review of Metaphysics*, vol. VII, no. 1 (September 1953). See also Peter Hamilton, *The Living God and the Modern World*, pp. 108–41; W. Norman Pittenger, *Process Thought and Christian Faith*, ch. 4, and 'The Last Things' in a Process Perspective; and David Edwards, *The Last Things Now*, pp. 88–91.
23. 'The Elizabethans', says Theodore Spencer, 'seem to have dreaded nothing so much as the possibility that future generations might not know they had lived' (*Death and Elizabethan Tragedy*, p. 135).
24. *The Logic of Perfection*, pp. 252–3.
25. ibid., p. 257.

26. ibid., p. 259.
27. ibid., pp. 252-3.
28. ibid., p. 258.
29. Cf. Karl Barth, *Church Dogmatics*, vol. III, part 2, para. 47, e.g. pp. 438, 526.
30. W. Pannenberg, *What is Man?*, p. 74. Pannenberg has presented an essentially similar view in *Theology and the Kingdom of God*, and, briefly, in 'Can Christianity do without an Eschatology?', in *The Christian Hope* by G. B. Caird and others, and in *The Apostles' Creed*, pp. 174-5. The wider theological significance of his doctrine of eternity is brought out in Allan D. Galloway, *Wolfhart Pannenberg*, pp. 93-8. Eberhard Jüngel proposes a somewhat similar view to Pannenberg's in *Death*, pp. 121-2.
31. *What is Man?*, p. 80.
32. ibid., p. 79.
33. ibid., p. 81.
34. ibid., pp. 49-50. Again, 'This concept of the undying continuation of the soul while the body perishes has become untenable today' (*Jesus – God and Man*, p. 87).
35. *What is Man?*, pp. 79-80.
36. ibid., p. 81.
37. ibid., p. 52.
38. ibid., p. 80.
39. A recent modification of Pannenberg's position is hinted at by E. Frank Tupper, who quotes Pannenberg as writing in a personal communication in 1971, 'I would not speak today as I did then of a standpoint outside the flow of time but rather of the absolute future of God' (*The Theology of Wolfhart Pannenberg*, p. 289). But the eschatology to be based upon this later idea remains to be developed.

CHAPTER 12

Contemporary Catholic Views

1. KARL RAHNER

Despite the intense ferment in roman catholic thought which lay behind the second Vatican Council, and which has gone on since in relation to such distinctively roman doctrines as papal infallibility, as well as in such areas as the doctrines of the church and the laity, the nature of revelation and the development of dogma, and such moral issues as birth-control, there has been no comparable ferment in eschatology. The only major new work has been that of Karl Rahner, followed up, and linked back into the tradition, by Ladislaus Boros.

In his treatise *On the Theology of Death*[1] Rahner suggests that the soul, which in this life is exclusively related to one particular bit of the world, namely a human body, is at death released from that limitation and becomes related instead to the world as a whole. 'In death', he says, 'the soul becomes *nicht akosmisch, sondern allkosmisch* – not acosmic, but pan-cosmic.'[2] The starting-point of Rahner's theory is the traditional catholic doctrine that death is the separation of soul from body. But this, he says, need not be understood, as it has been by a long christian tradition formed under the influence of neoplatonism, as meaning that the soul becomes detached from matter, acosmic, totally out of this world and no longer related to the space-time continuum. For even in this present life our bodies are not entirely autonomous pieces of matter but elements in the continuous system of nature. The matter inside our skins is as truly part of the world as the matter outside it, influencing and being influenced by all the rest of nature. Accordingly, 'since the soul is united to the body, it clearly must also have some relationship to that whole of which the body is a part, that is, to the totality which constitutes the unity of the material universe'.[3] And the conception of death which Rahner offers is that the termination of the soul's special relationship to an individual body enables it to enter instead into relation with the entire material cosmos. This new relationship, which was always implicit in the body's continuity with its physical environment, is realized at death, and its exclusive interaction with an individual organism is superseded by interaction with the entire realm of matter.

Rahner suggests that life at the sub-human levels consists in the informing of matter by 'life-entelechies', and that the death of an animal or, presumably, of a plant is not the cessation of that entelechy but 'the surrender of the entelechial relation at a certain space-time point in the world, while the entelechial powers persist as constituents of the universe'.[4] One might perhaps fill out this suggestion a little by saying either that the life-entelechies correspond to individual members of a plant or animal species and become repeatedly reincarnated in new individuals; or alternatively that in pre-human evolution there are entelechies of species rather than of individuals, each entelechy informing at any one moment a great number of living pieces of matter which are the contemporary members of the species. However, to return to the more developed entelechy which is a human soul, Rahner's suggestion is that at death this becomes 'pancosmic', related to the entire material universe. The soul's relationship to the physical creation is 'not abolished, but is rather, for the first time, perfected, becoming a fully open, pancosmic relationship, no longer mediated by the individual body'.[5] This cannot be understood however, he says, 'as meaning that at death the entire world becomes the "body" of this particular soul precisely in the way in which its own body was its own'.[6] Nor, he says, 'is it a case of the omnipresence of the soul in the whole cosmos'.[7] Rather 'the soul, by surrendering its limited bodily structure in death, becomes open towards the universe and, in some way, a co-determining factor of the universe precisely in the latter's character as the ground of the personal life of other spiritual corporeal [i.e. human] beings'.[8] Rahner's view seems to be that the world has an inner spiritual aspect as well as an outer physical aspect, and that the quality of this spiritual aspect is affected by that of the souls which enter pancosmically into it. Rahner's suggestion would thus provide a basis for the traditional catholic idea that the moral quality of

each individual's life, when completed, influences this world.[9]
He also suggests in passing that his hypothesis might help to
explain certain parapsychological phenomena.[10]

Rahner makes use of his idea of the pancosmic life of the
soul after death at an important further point in his theology.
This is in his explanation of the way in which the death of
Christ has redeemed the world. He points out that the
traditional catholic atonement doctrine, based upon Anselm's
notion of satisfaction, does not make it clear why it was
specifically through Christ's *death* that men were redeemed
rather than, for example, through his life. And yet scripture
insists that it was specifically Christ's death that has redeemed
the world.[11] And so Rahner draws upon his theory of 'the
opening out of a pancosmic relation of the spirit'[12] at death.
Being truly human (as well as truly divine), Christ died a
human death, and it is therefore true of him, as of other men,
that at death his soul entered into the pancosmic state. Christ
as spirit entered into 'the intrinsic, radically unified, ultimate
and deepest level of the reality of the world'[13] – this going
down of the Christ-spirit into the depths of the cosmos being
traditionally symbolized by his descent into hell. The result of
this is that the Christ-spirit, restricted during the period of the
incarnation to exerting an influence in one place at a time, is
now able to influence the world as a whole, changing the
environment in which men have ever since lived. So Rahner
says:

> We have already remarked that it is in death, and only in
> death, that man enters into an open, unrestricted relation-
> ship to the cosmos as a whole, that he is integrated, as a
> constant and determining factor, into the world as a whole,
> through his own total reality achieved in his life and death
> . . . [It] is through his death that man in some way introduces
> as his contribution the result of his life into the radical, real
> ground of the unity of the world. Applying this hypothesis
> of the metaphysical anthropology of death to the death of
> Christ, we must say that through Christ's death, his spiritual
> reality, which he possessed from the beginning, enacted in
> his life, and brought to consummation in his death, becomes
> open to the whole world and is inserted into this whole

world in its ground as a permanent determination of a real ontological kind.[14]

There are two other implications of his theory which Rahner mentions but which we need not I think dwell upon here. One is that his hypothesis 'would also render more readily intelligible the doctrine of purgatory'[15] in that the soul's wrong relationship to the created order, developed during the present life, will after this life be experienced and suffered as a wrong relationship to nature as a whole. The other is that his hypothesis illuminates the idea that at the end of time, in the resurrection of the just, the redeemed will receive glorified bodies. This, he suggests, will be a 'corporeality which . . . though concrete, remains open for maintaining or entering into free and unhampered relations with everything. In this way the glorified body seems to become the perfect expression of the enduring relation of the glorified person to the cosmos as a whole.'[16]

I turn now from the exposition of Rahner's theory to comment upon it. I have already suggested that in this highly speculative field the only way to assess theories is by trying to spell out their meaning and implications as fully as possible. We shall then at least discover whether we have before us a viable possibility or merely a medley of ideas incapable of being developed into a clear hypothesis. As it stands in Rahner's book his theory is only a sketch, and our task is accordingly to see whether it is capable of expanding into a coherent conceptual structure or only into a larger confusion.

It is I think a central implication of Rahner's theory that the environment of which a departed spirit is conscious and in relation to which it lives is still *this* world, so that no idea of 'the next world' or of 'another world' or worlds is required. The departed remain earth-bound: they have no other sphere of operation than this physical universe and world. Let us try to think out more fully some of the details of this picture.

As a first attempt, it is possible to visualize individual souls being at death poured back, as it were, into a common stock of soul-life which is related as a whole to the world as a whole. The kind of picture that presents itself to those who tend to think visually is of a large reservoir of liquid into which little phials of variously tinted fluid, representing individual human souls, are from time to time being poured, each to some small extent affecting the colour of the whole. The general soul-life, into which individual lives are at death emptied, is somehow conscious of the world and somehow influences the world. Thus in the case of the death of Christ, the Christ-soul has altered the character of the world into which subsequent generations have been born by being poured into and transforming the pancosmic soul-life – somewhat as a powerful chemical element, added to a body of fluid, may change the character of the entire volume of fluid. On this interpretation Rahner would be invoking something akin to the widespread eastern notion of the sea of spirit from which drops are temporarily withdrawn to form individual souls, but to which they return when they leave the body, losing thereby their separate consciousness and personal identity.

This would, at first sight at any rate, be one possible way of understanding Rahner's 'pancosmic state'. However, this is not what Rahner intends. For he insists upon the continued individual and personal identity of each soul after death. He says that 'the personal, spiritual soul does not perish when the structure of the body is dissolved, but maintains its personal, spiritual life',[17] and he speaks at another point of 'the survival of man's conscious personal existence'[18] as an affirmation of faith to which he is committed. For the traditional ideas of the resurrection of the dead and of the life of heaven and hell presuppose continued personal identity. We must therefore adjust the picture that we derive from Rahner's theory to include distinct individual consciousnesses in the pancosmic state.

Accordingly a second possible way of construing his notion of pancosmic existence sees it as the post-mortem state of the continuing individual personal consciousness. Each soul retains its identity but becomes somehow aware of the world as a whole and somehow influences the character and course of the world as a whole.

When we look at this suggestion more closely, however, I think we shall find difficulties in it. We may consider the pancosmic state both from the point of view of the action of the world on the soul, in enabling the soul to be conscious of it, and from the point of view of the action of the soul upon the world, in influencing the course of events within the world.

To take the first point first: a universal or pancosmic consciousness would not be limited by a particular spatial perspective and by selective sense organs, but would be aware of the entire physical universe as from every perspective at once. This might well be the description of a divine consciousness; but the question is whether it is compatible with the existence of finite human consciousnesses continuous with those of this life. For our separate individuality is constituted precisely by its borders, in virtue of which we are not universally cognitive but know the world within the limitations of a particular perspective, and within this perspective through highly specialized and selective sensory organs. If everything going on everywhere poured into my mind quite indiscriminately, the character of my consciousness would be so totally different that it is doubtful whether I could be said to be the same person, or indeed to be a finite mind at all. For if the boundaries of individual consciousness were removed at death, the series of perceptions from a particular locality in space, and of volitions in which we act at the place where we are, and the growing chain of memories arising out of such particularized experience, would all be dissolved. The frontiers of the mind would be abolished, and with them the structure of a finite individual ego. It thus appears to me that the notion of pancosmic consciousness is incompatible with the continued existence of the bounded consciousnesses of now living human beings. Essential marks of personal identity would have been obliterated.

There are at least equal difficulties with regard to the pancosmic soul's influence upon the world. Rahner points out that his theory might be used to account for certain parapsychological phenomena.[19] He does not say what types of paranormal event he has in mind. It would seem however that he must be thinking of the various kinds of poltergeist effect and of mediumistic phenomena, concerning which it is a possible hypothesis that discarnate souls are directly influencing parts of the physical world – whether inanimate objects or a medium's body. For if the pancosmic soul is related to the entire material universe so as to be able to affect its state, it may be possible for it to produce poltergeist effects, materializations, and direct voice and trance mediumship. Thus the production of such paranormal events could provide an outlet for the energies of pancosmic souls. The problem however is not so much whether they could do this, as whether there is anything else that they could do. How might they be occupied when *not* producing paranormal raps and movements of objects and communicating through mediums with the still embodied inhabitants of earth? Does Rahner think of them as influencing the weather, or the growth of crops, or what? For on Rahner's theory souls in their pancosmic state have no other environment in which to express themselves, and to which to react, than *this* world. And so if there are thousands of millions of discarnate souls now in the pancosmic state, acting upon this world, it ought to be possible for us to discern some signs of their activity. For in so far as they are more than merely passively conscious of the world their existence becomes, on Rahner's theory, an empirical hypothesis subject to observational testing.

But it would not be easy to point to the tangible effects of the influence on the world of departed souls. In particular, in the case of the redeeming effect of the death of Christ, it should be possible, on Rahner's theory, to indicate those features of the human environment which have been transformed since approximately AD 30; but he would be a bold historian who would venture to do this.

I think however that one can see what Rahner might say in reply at this point. I think he would say that souls in the pancosmic state do not act in the world in any sense that entails volitions causing local changes in the dispositions of matter. For it is an established catholic doctrine, to which Rahner fully subscribes, that at death the decisions and actions which determine a man's eternal destiny come to an end. As Rahner says, 'the fundamental moral decision made by man in the mundane temporality of his bodily existence, is rendered definite and final by death'.[20] Beyond death, then, there are no more free, responsible, character-forming decisions, and accordingly no actions expressing such decisions. Rather the spiritual quality of the soul, in the condition in which it is at the time of bodily death, is somehow contributed to the inner or entelechial side of the developing physical universe. Thus the soul becomes, to quote Rahner's words again, 'a co-determining factor of the universe precisely in the latter's character as the ground of the personal life of other spiritual corporeal beings' so that the soul 'by this real ontological and open relation to the whole cosmos, might come to have a direct influence within the world'.[21]

Does this help? I hardly think so. The hypothesis is still excessively unclear. What is it that souls, when functioning as co-determining factors in the universe, help to determine? Presumably, some of the events which constitute the history of the physical universe. But what events? Whether the answer specifies predictable events, such as the rotation of the seasons, or less usual occurrences – such as coincidences, accidents, and unexpected healings – the causal connection between the realm of pancosmic souls and such earthly events remains wholly obscure.

2. LADISLAUS BOROS

Despite its besetting vagueness Rahner's hypothesis of the pancosmic state of the soul after death has been adopted by a number of roman catholic scholars, among them Ladislaus Boros, who has supplemented it with a restatement of the traditional doctrine (also accepted by Rahner[22]) that the individual's eternal destiny is settled at the moment of death. Boros develops this into the notion of the 'final decision' for or against God made by the soul in the moment of dying.[23] This is, however, no ordinary moment. It is a 'metaphysical moment'[24] which 'occurs neither before nor after death, but *in* death'.[25] It is thus neither the last moment of this life nor the first moment of the life to come; for 'the moment of death, the transition itself, is – when looked at from the subsequent condition – the last moment of the preceding condition, and – when viewed from the preceding condition – the first moment of the succeeding condition'.[26] Further, it is a non-temporal 'moment'; for 'death as an instantaneous transformation can only occur in a non-temporal transition'.[27] And yet within this non-temporal transition an event, an act of decision, takes place. Thus the moment of dying has as its content an act of choice, for 'the moment of death offers an opportunity for decision';[28] and yet on the other hand it is not a temporal moment, for 'the moment of death is a non-temporal transition'.[29] It is thus far from clear that in this notion of a non-temporal moment in which a decision nevertheless occurs Boros has succeeded in establishing a meaningful starting-point for his theory of the final decision.

However, the traditional idea that there are no further spiritual choices and decisions after death does not depend upon Boros's paradoxes, and our main concern is to be with the former and more fundamental idea. This is the doctrine of 'the unalterability of the state we reach through death':

> A human existence that has passed through death has reached a final state in which no further change is possible in its basic tendency. At death a man's final figure with the destiny it deserves is irrevocably attributed to him. Once beyond death no more decisions altering the course of one's existence can be made. Death makes human decision irrevocable. One's decision as regards God now becomes final, permanent, unchangeable being.[30]

It appears to me that there is both truth and error in this doctrine; and if we can disentangle them our investigation into death and eternal life will thereby be carried a step forward.

The truth in the idea is that it must be possible for man *eventually* to arrive at a final, permanent and irreversible state in which he has confronted reality and found his eternal home within it. It must be possible for us, in Boros's words, 'to open ourselves up to the absolute';[31] and since 'a decision like this realizes once and for all the whole extent of man's essential dynamism, completely transforming it into being, existence with this unhampered decision reaches the state in which all its possibilities of decision in regard to its last end are exhausted, and this is the domain of ultimate finality'.[32] To be endlessly on the way to nowhere would be ultimately meaningless. We have to posit an arrival as well as a journey – or else the journey is not a genuine journey; and to arrive involves a 'final decision' on our part, a definitively chosen stance in relation to the ultimate. It does not however follow that this definitive disposition of the self must take the form of a single momentary act of decision, whether at death or later; the decision may perhaps be made in the course of a long series of choices in this life and in a further life or lives to come. But the basic notion has to be accepted, within any religious understanding of man and his destiny, that there is an eventual freely chosen or accepted outcome of our existence in time.

The error, however, in the traditional doctrine is its insistence that man's final destiny must be settled at the moment of earthly death. Such an insistence, although intended to give spiritual meaning and gravity to this life, in fact undermines its spiritual significance. For if everything depends upon our state at the moment of death, the succession of small and large decisions that go to make up the rest of our lives is thereby reduced in importance. It is true that catholic theologians are at pains to stress that, in Boros's words, 'the final decision is being prepared the whole time, growing out of the most trivial decisions right in the midst of the obscurities and conflicting claims of life'.[33] But nevertheless these daily decisions cannot directly add up to the state in which we face God; for it is acknowledged that a death-bed repentance, or a death-bed lapse from grace, can supersede a lifetime of evil or good activity; the whole trend of a life can be reversed in the final decision.

The essential meaninglessness in relation to eternity which this entails for our present life comes out most clearly in Boros's discussion of the problem posed by the deaths of unbaptized infants. The older (though not biblical and never dogmatically defined) doctrine was that such infants go to 'limbo', a state in which they are eternally excluded from the beatific vision of God, but in which on the other hand they are not conscious of this exclusion and so can enjoy a 'natural beatitude'. This idea has been under increasing criticism among roman catholic thinkers, and is rejected by Boros because of the self-contradictoriness of the notion of an exclusion from man's proper and intended end which is nevertheless not experienced by a spiritual being as pain or suffering. He offers his hypothesis of the final decision as one which avoids the necessity to resort to this notion of limbo. 'It must not be forgotten', he says, 'that infants who die before they come to the use of their mental and spiritual faculties, are nevertheless creatures endowed with spirit, and they, like all other human beings, awake in death to their full liberty and complete knowledge . . . In death the infant enters into the full possession of its spirituality, i.e. into a state of adulthood that many adults themselves never reach during their lifetime. The result of this is that no one dies as an infant, though he may leave us in infancy. The decision of these "infants" . . . was concentrated into one single moment and their decision developed at once into an eternal state.'[34]

The implication of this is that the soul's final decision can be made with equal validity at the end of a long life or as a newly born baby or even as a foetus in the womb. The pilgrimage of decades is concentrated into a single metaphysical 'moment' of spiritual decision. In by-passing existence *in via*, the pilgrimage of responsible life in time, the unborn or newly born infant thus misses nothing in his relationship to God. But surely such a doctrine empties the present life of its religious significance. Indeed, it even suggests that those who die in the womb are more fortunate than those who survive to face the trials and temptations of life – an implication which surely generates far greater problems than it solves. We cannot be content with a theory which gives meaning to death by depriving this life of its meaning.

But it is not only Boros's own special conception of the 'final decision', but any doctrine which freezes our relationship with God at the point of bodily death, that fails under this criterion. We must reject the traditional doctrine, both catholic and protestant, of the unalterability of the soul's state beyond death, the doctrine that there can be no 'second chance' of salvation beyond this life, no new and different moral decisions, and no further personal growth or development in response to further experiences. The doctrine excludes a prolongation of life beyond the grave; and the theological criticism of such an exclusion can be presented both negatively and positively. Negatively, the criticism is that it would be profoundly unjust to many that their final destiny should be determined by what they are able to become in this life. For – leaving aside the fact that a considerable proportion of all the human beings who have been born have died in infancy, their mind and character not sufficiently developed for them to make a spiritual choice of eternal significance – it is evident that the varying circumstances of human birth and environment make it much easier for some and much harder for others to come in the course of their lives into a right relationship with God. The soul born to a bad genetic inheritance (perhaps, for example, with the extra Y chromosome which is said to have a significant statistical correlation with a tendency to violent criminality), or to unloving and irreligious parents, or in a situation of desperate competition for the means to survive, or under all these handicaps at once, cannot be said to enjoy the same auspicious spiritual circumstances as one born to favourable genetic, parental and environmental conditions. And the problem created by the unequal conditions of human birth would be at its maximum, and indeed at an intolerable maximum, if each individual's eternal destiny depended upon the state into which he had come by the end of his earthly career.

This is the negative side of the coin. The positive side is the need for more than this present life if a divine purpose of person-making, through the human being's free responses, is to continue to its completion. For it is evident that the great majority of men and women – perhaps all – come to the end of their present life without having attained to perfect humanity. Most make some progress during their lives towards a radically un-selfcentred existence; but many others become locked by harsh pressures into a self-enclosed egoism; and many others again have died in infancy without ever launching out upon the adventure of creation. Thus if responsible life – the exercise of freedom through time in an environment which demands responses – is the basis of the person-making process, and if the divine intention in initiating this process is that it shall be carried through to completion, it follows that responsible life must continue beyond bodily death.

The only alternative would seem to be that in the moment of death the individual is instantaneously transformed into a perfected person, the stages of his further personal development being all concentrated into an instant. But if X, in the very incomplete and imperfect state in which he is at the time of his death, is suddenly perfected by divine fiat, in a momentary transformation, the resulting perfect being will no longer be X. God would have de-created X and created a new and very different person in his place. And if he can do this consistently with his creative purpose, he can presumably do it equally in the case of individuals who die in old age, in middle age, in youth, in infancy, at birth, or in the womb. But in that case the experience of temporal existence serves no necessary purpose, and this life loses its significance as a sphere in which the divine intention is at work.

I believe, therefore, that the notion of a final decision at the moment of death determining the individual's eternal destiny must be emphatically rejected. Its rejection enables pareschatology – the doctrine of man's existence between bodily death and the ultimate state – to receive proper attention. Christian theology has need of the possibilities thus opened up in dealing, above all, with the topic of universal salvation.

NOTES

1. Karl Rahner, *On the Theology of Death*, reprinted in *Modern Catholic Thinkers: An Anthology*, ed. A. Robert Caponigri. See also Rahner's article on 'Death', in *Sacramentum Mundi*, vol. II, and 'Ideas for a Theology of Death', in *Theological Investigations*, vol. XIII.
2. Karl Rahner, *On the Theology of Death*, p. 20.
3. ibid., p. 18.
4. ibid., p. 21.
5. ibid., pp. 23–4.
6. ibid., p. 21.
7. ibid., pp. 21–2.
8. ibid., p. 22.
9. ibid., pp. 22–3.
10. ibid., p. 21.
11. ibid., p. 60.
12. ibid., p. 58.
13. ibid., p. 64.
14. ibid., p. 63.
15. ibid., p. 24.
16. ibid., pp. 25–6.
17. ibid., p. 17.
18. ibid., p. 27.
19. ibid., p. 21.
20. ibid., p. 27.
21. ibid., pp. 22–3.
22. ibid., pp. 26–7; 'Ideas for a Theology of Death', p. 174.

23. Ladislaus Boros, *The Moment of Truth: Mysterium Mortis*. For a bibliographical note, as well as useful critical comments, on recent catholic writings on the idea of the 'final decision', see Gisbert Greshake, 'Towards a Theology of Dying', in *Concilium*, vol. 4, no. 10 (April 1974), pp. 81–5.

24. *The Moment of Truth*, p. 3.

25. ibid., p. 4.

26. ibid., p. 5.

27. ibid.

28. ibid.

29. ibid., p. 23.

30. ibid., p. 86. Another recent catholic writer who reaffirms that death ends our *status viatoris*, and who does so in terms of the idea of the final decision, is Josef Pieper, *Death and Immortality*, chs. 5–6.

31. *The Moment of Truth*, p. 94.

32. ibid.

33. ibid., p. 104.

34. ibid., pp. 109–10.

CHAPTER 13

Universal Salvation

1. GOD'S LOVE AND MAN'S FREEDOM

The debate between the universalist and the non-universalist has for some time languished in a largely repetitive and unproductive phase; and the only kind of case for universal salvation, or case against it, that is likely to be of interest today is one which tries to escape from this impasse. What follows is intended as a probe at least in the direction of such an escape.

But in order to attempt to dissolve the stalemate we must first take note of the forces which form it. The situation is that nearly all of us today would like to accept the universalist view but find ourselves hindered by the apparent impossibility of reconciling it with the reality of human freedom. We seem in fact to be faced by a logical antinomy, with formally valid arguments establishing two contradictory conclusions.

The customary proof of universalism runs as follows: The God whom we worship is a God of love, whose gracious purpose is to save all men. God's relation to the universe, as its creator and ruler, is such that he is able to fulfil his purposes. Therefore all men will in the end be saved. However, confronting this reasoning is an equally perspicuous disproof. This does not deny the premiss that it is God's loving purpose to save all men. But it adds another premiss which apparently prohibits us from drawing the universalist conclusion. This additional premiss is that God has endowed us with a genuine freedom, so that we cannot be saved without our own positive and voluntary response to him. No doubt God could by omnipotent power override the human will; but so long as he affirms man's existence as a free and responsible being he cannot fulfil his saving purpose without man's free co-operation. It therefore remains possible that some will fail to co-operate and will instead become so hardened in a self-enclosed blindness as never to respond to God. Accordingly we are not entitled to make the positive affirmation that all *will* eventually be saved.

This is the antinomy. On one side is the omnipotent divine love intending man's salvation. If that divine intention is never fulfilled, then God is not after all the sovereign lord of his own universe: he is a limited God, defeated by an evil which he has permitted to exist but which he cannot now overcome. And on the other side is our human freedom. If man is saved against his will, or without his will, then he does not after all make a free, personal response to his Maker. In forcing man into his kingdom God would have turned the human thou into an it.

Is there any hope of resolving the antinomy? Let me first say something about the New Testament evidence and then turn to the question of human freedom in relation to the divine saving activity.

2. THE NEW TESTAMENT EVIDENCE

In the New Testament we find two different and apparently conflicting sets of utterances, supporting the two sides of the antinomy. But as we note their different settings and functions we can, I think, see how the two sets of utterances may both be true and thus how the antinomy may be resolved, so far at least as scripture is concerned.

On the one hand we have sayings of Jesus in which the real possibility is set before us that we may so conduct ourselves as to be finally and eternally rejected by God. These sayings have sometimes been thought to be much more numerous than they are. This has resulted from a failure to distinguish between these rather rare sayings and the much larger group in which post-mortem rewards and punishments are referred to in general but without any suggestion that they are eternal and thus without any indication that they entail a final division between the saved and the lost. For example, Jesus contrasted the fates of the poor and the rich, saying to the former, 'Your reward is great in heaven', and to the latter, 'But woe to you that are rich, for you have received your consolation';[1] but we have no warrant to treat this as asserting an eternal felicity and torment in heaven and hell. Or again, when he said, 'Woe to you, scribes and Pharisees, hypocrites! for you devour widows' houses and for a pretence you make long prayers;

therefore you will receive the greater condemnation',[2] the condemnation in question is apparently one that is to come on the day of judgement; but again we have no warrant for assuming that it will be a sentence of *eternal* punishment. Indeed, the very notion of a greater condemnation suggests a range of punishments and not a simple dichotomy between infinite penalty and infinite reward. In another of Jesus' sayings a fitting of the punishment to the crime is hinted at – namely in the advice to come to terms with your adversary whilst you are in the way with him, lest he have you put in prison: 'I say to you, you will never get out till you have paid the last penny.'[3] Since only a finite number of pennies can have a last one we seem to be in the realm of graded debts and payments rather than of absolute guilt and infinite penalty. This comes out also in the parable of the debtors, which ends: 'And in anger his lord delivered him to the jailers, till he should pay all his debt. So also my heavenly Father will do to every one of you, if you do not forgive your brother from your heart.'[4] Once again, only a finite debt can ever be paid in full.

And indeed, if we look at the matter in a rational and ethical light we can see that the divinely ordained moral order of the world would be extremely crude if all the judgement sayings were rightly held to involve eternal heaven and hell. If the universe is to train mankind ethically, then its reactions to our misdeeds must be more discriminatingly proportioned to the varieties of human motivation than is permitted by the awarding of eternal salvation or eternal damnation for each human action. A penal code in which the only punishment available was the death penalty would have minimal value as an instrument of moral education. For it would always be true that 'one might as well be hung for stealing a sheep as a lamb'. Does it not, then, seem altogether more likely that the divinely appointed moral order of the universe is one in which fulfilment and frustration respectively are brought about by right- and wrong-doing – not indeed from day to day, or even from year to year, but over much longer periods – and that these consequences are morally proportionate and thus directed to a constructive purpose? If so, it must be a mistake to interpret in terms of unending and therefore non-educative and non-redemptive punishment those judgement sayings of Jesus which are equally capable of being understood in terms of temporal and therefore potentially educative and redemptive suffering. Exegetically, the mistake consists in lumping together two different classes of sayings, one fairly numerous and the other extremely sparse, and then interpreting the larger group by means of the smaller.

Having distinguished these two sets of sayings, we find that the smaller group – those concerning eternal loss and punishment – consists, so far as the synoptic tradition is concerned, strictly of only one item and, on a less strict criterion, of either two or three. The single clear case occurs in the parable of the sheep and the goats, preserved in Matthew's gospel. To those who have failed to feed the hungry, give drink to the thirsty, clothe the naked, help the sick, and visit the prisoners, on the day of judgement the Son of man says, 'The curse is upon you: go from my sight to the eternal fire that is ready for the devil and his angels.' And the parable ends: 'And they will go away into eternal punishment, but the righteous into eternal life.'[5] This is the only passage in the recorded teachings of Jesus in the synoptic gospels in which eternal punishment is threatened and a final and permanent division is asserted between the saved and the damned. However, the preceding parable in Matthew, the parable of the talents, can perhaps be grouped with this for our present purpose, although the word 'eternal' does not occur in it. But it ends: 'Cast the worthless servant into the outer darkness; there men will weep and gnash their teeth.'[6] Apart from these there is only the saying concerning the sin against the Holy Spirit. This occurs in all three synoptic gospels and reads in the marcan version: 'But whosoever blasphemes against the Holy Spirit never has forgiveness, but is guilty of an eternal sin.'[7]

It is perhaps further worth noting, in connection with the synoptic gospels, that the theme of judgement and the atmosphere of threat and impending punishment are most prominent in Matthew's gospel and are almost completely absent from Mark's, in which the puzzling saying about the sin against the Holy Spirit stands by itself. On the generally accepted theory of marcan priority the evidence of source criticism thus points away from the originality of the judgement sayings as we have them in the later gospel of Matthew, and towards their emergence within the life of the church during the post-apostolic age of persecution, when the christian community might only too naturally have been receptive to the thought that its persecutors will face a fearful doom in the future.

The Fourth Gospel sets itself apart from the Synoptics on this matter. It shows signs of an important development in the church's understanding of Jesus' teaching from the reticence of the synoptic period towards the confident double-destiny theology which has prevailed during the greater part of christian history. For whilst there are in the Fourth Gospel many sayings in which eternal life is offered to all who respond in faith to Christ, without any accompanying threats to those who do not, there are other sayings confronting us with the parallelism of eternal life and eternal death: for example, 'He who believes in the Son has eternal life; he who does not obey the Son shall not see life, but the wrath of God rests upon him',[8] and 'those who have done good, to the resurrection of life, and those who have done evil, to the resurrection of judgement'.[9]

However, in the Fourth Gospel the notion of a free human response to Christ upon which men's eternal destinies depend is obscured and indeed undermined by the disconcerting idea that mankind is already irrevocably divided into two races, children of God and children of the devil, the former of whom are to enjoy eternal life and the latter to undergo eternal death. This is expressed at several points. For example, Jesus says to 'the Jews', 'He who is of God hears the words of God; the reason why you do not hear them is that you are not of God.'[10] Again, 'The works that I do in my Father's name, they bear witness to me; but you do not believe, because you do not belong to my sheep.'[11]

Now this quite explicit two-races conception is no more acceptable to the modern non-universalist than it is to the modern universalist. In practice both treat it as at best hyperbole and at worst an unchristian idea which arose within the church during the early periods of persecution. Thus the Fourth Gospel cannot be used in evidence on either side of our contemporary debate; for in it the issue does not concern human freedom and responsibility but rather a predestination involving a fixed and impassable gulf between those marked from birth for eternal life and those marked from birth for eternal death. If, despite the contrary witness of the synoptic gospels, this is indeed the teaching of Jesus, then the antinomy that we are now attempting to resolve does not arise; and in taking the antinomy seriously we have already tacitly set aside the johannine doctrine in favour of the earlier picture of Jesus' teaching in the Synoptics.

Thus the confident assertion that Jesus threatened, or predicted, eternal torment is not so securely based as has often been assumed. It may be that Jesus was an innovator, departing at this point from contemporary jewish ideas, and that the extreme paucity of explicit references in his recorded teaching to an eternal hell is an indication of this. Such a possibility would not lessen the significance of Jesus' warnings about real pains and sorrows to be endured as the consequences of evil actions now. It may well be that – as the eastern concept of karma suggests – we are all the time creating good and bad future experiences for ourselves. But what is far from certain is that Jesus defined the bad consequence of evil deeds as eternal and therefore unredemptive suffering. However, the case which I now wish to develop does not depend upon this uncertainty. It is compatible with the possibility that Jesus *did* indeed threaten eternal punishment. Although I do not regard it as at all certain that he did so, I am nevertheless prepared to suppose this for the sake of argument. Let us then assume, hypothetically, that our Lord did confront his hearers with the real danger of irreversible disaster and eternal torment. And let us now set beside this the biblical warrant for the other side of the antinomy.

For there are statements coming to us from the earliest thinking of the church which point fairly clearly to the final salvation of all men and indeed to the restoration of the entire created order. These occur mainly in the writings of St Paul. He speaks of a universal fall in Adam paralleled by a universal restoration in Christ. 'As in Adam all die, so also in Christ shall all be made alive' – where the second 'all' can hardly have a narrower domain than the first (1 Corinthians 15: 22).[12] Again, 'It follows, then, that as the issue of one misdeed was condemnation for all men, so the issue of one just act is acquittal and life for all men' (Romans 5: 18). Again, 'For in making all mankind prisoners to disobedience, God's purpose was to show mercy to all mankind' (Romans 11: 32). Again, Paul defines 'God's hidden purpose' as 'that the universe, all in heaven and on earth, might be brought into a unity in Christ' (Ephesians 1: 10). And yet again, the author of 1 Timothy speaks of 'God our Saviour, whose will it is that all men should find salvation and come to know the truth' (2: 4).

There are of course also non-universalist passages in St Paul, as for example in the discussion of predestination in Romans 9 or in 2 Thessalonians 1: 8–9. Thus one can quote Paul on either side of the debate. I would not in fact claim with confidence that he was a universalist; though I suggest that sometimes as he wrote about the saving activity of God the inner logic of that about which he was writing inevitably unfolded itself into the thought of universal salvation.

However, let us now bring together Jesus' threats of eternal punishment, reported above all in Matthew's gospel, and those of Paul's statements which point to the final restoration of all things in Christ.

These two sets of statements differ not only in their content but also in the type of utterance that they are; and it is this latter difference which suggests the possibility of their ultimate compatibility. They belong to quite different situational contexts and fulfil quite different functions. St Paul was writing theology in and for the christian community, whilst Jesus was wrestling with individual men and women, trying to win them back from self-destructive sinfulness. St Paul was standing back in thought in order to try to see things as a whole and to relate all human life and history to the universal purpose of God. In contrast the teaching of Jesus is, in the jargon of our own day, existential. It is not academic teaching seeking primarily to illuminate the theoretical reason, but practical and personal admonition and exhortation aimed at converting the hearer's heart and moving his will. Jesus was neither propounding a theological theory nor defining theological doctrines. He was preaching to contemporary men and women, warning and challenging them with vivid parables and images. He was standing with them in the flow of human life at a certain moment in time, trying to get them to wrench them-

selves round in the direction of their lives and open their
hearts to one another as fellow children of the heavenly Father.
In this situation he was in effect saying: If you go on like this,
heedless of your neighbour, you will come to absolute disaster;
for this way of living ends in spiritual self-destruction.[13] In the
parable of the sheep and the goats, for example, in which the
threat of eternal damnation occurs most explicitly, Jesus was
warning his hearers of the fearful danger that envelops
loveless and self-enclosed minds – the danger that in failing to
meet and serve the neighbour in his need one will forfeit one's
own membership of the human race and become lost in an
outer darkness. He was saying bluntly to all who are living in
selfish disregard of human need: If you go on like this you will
be damned. But in speaking in this way Jesus was not discussing the general question whether anyone ever has remained
or ever will remain in this state beyond the point of no return.
As a relatively trivial analogy, a parent might tell his child,
who has been raising false alarms about fires and burglars, a
story about what happens to children who do this – one day,
he might say, there is a real fire, and they perish in it because
no one any longer takes their cries for help seriously. Such a
story would be told as a warning, and with the object of preventing the prophecy contained in it from ever coming true.
May not Jesus' preaching to men and women who are heading
towards destruction have been intended to have a like effect?
If so, his grave warnings, uttered in the existential mode to
actual individuals in their concrete life-situations, do not
necessarily conflict with St Paul's indications, in the more
detached theological mode, of a final universal salvation. It may
well be true at a given point within the temporal process that
unless you repent you will surely perish, and yet also true as a
statement arrived at from other grounds, about human
existence as a whole, that in the end all will turn from their
wickedness and live. The two truths are formally compatible
with one another because the one asserts that something will
happen if a certain condition is fulfilled (namely, permanent
non-repentance) while the other asserts that this same thing
will not happen because that condition will not in fact be
fulfilled. The two truths are thus compatible as the truth of
utterances occurring in quite different contexts and fulfilling

quite different functions. If we meet them both within the rich variety of the New Testament, then we must accept them both. But in doing so we should accept them for what they are – the one a challenging warning addressed to individuals; and the other a theological proposition about humanity as a whole seen in relation to God's ultimate providence.

Are we however in all this saying, presumptuously, that Jesus thought that some men will be damned but that the christian theologian can know better? No, we are not saying this. We are saying that when Jesus declared that various people whom he was addressing were going to be damned unless they repented he was speaking existentially, within the situation and in an attempt to change it. He was concerned for and was dealing with concrete individuals, not formulating general theological truths. And when the theologian, on the basis of an irresistible inference from the divine love and power, declares as an implicate of his faith that God will in the end succeed in saving all his human creatures, he is abstracting from the concrete personal situations both of himself and others and speaking theologically – that is, speaking logically about God.

I believe we may therefore conclude that if there was a dominical threat addressed to particular individuals that if they did not repent they would reap eternal damnation, this threat is not incompatible with universalism. The danger which Jesus declared so starkly is a most real danger: unless you repent you will inevitably come to total and irretrievable misery and frustration. But it does not follow from the fact of this danger that you or I or anyone else is in fact never going to repent and be saved.

3. THE PROBLEM OF HUMAN FREEDOM

But if universalism is not ruled out by the biblical evidence we next have to ask whether it is compatible with the reality of human freedom. Most of us today have travelled far enough from Augustine and Calvin to believe that the heavenly Father of Jesus' teaching *wants* to save all men. We can no longer accept the dark doctrine of double predestination with its negation of the central christian message of the love of God. If such words as 'good' and 'loving' are rightly applied to God at all, in however analogical or symbolic a way, we cannot but believe that God desires and intends the salvation of all mankind. The only question is whether he is able to fulfil his intention – or more precisely whether we can, consistently with the reality of our own freedom and responsibility, make the universalist affirmation that God *will* succeed in fulfilling his loving purpose. For if we are to remain free personal creatures it is clear that God cannot coerce us into saving faith, either by a direct force overcoming our wills or even by the hidden operation of the Holy Spirit working in the depths of our unconscious selves. So long as we are free beings standing responsibly before our Maker there must be the possibility of our opposing and refusing him; and so long as there is this possibility it cannot be known in advance that all men are indeed going to be saved.

This argument, which in its own terms is so clear and decisive, rests I now want to suggest upon a vulnerable premiss. This premiss is that God can only ensure that all men will eventually be saved if he is prepared if necessary to coerce some of them, however subtly. Otherwise, the presupposition is, there can be no grounds on which to affirm with certainty the future salvation of all. The only possible route to that conclusion, it is assumed, lies through the idea of divine omnipotence overruling the wayward wills of men. But what is overlooked in this argument is that the christian doctrine of creation offers an alternative route to the universalist conclusion. For it authorizes us to hold that in creating our human nature God has formed it for himself, so that – to draw upon another strand of Augustine's thought – our hearts will be restless until they find their rest in him. Indeed, it is worthwhile going back to the original form of Augustine's famous statement: ' . . . *quia fecisti nos ad te, domine, et inquietum est cor nostrum donec requiescat in te.*'[14] Thou hast made us *ad te*, towards thyself. In other words, God has so made us that the inherent gravitation of our being is towards him. We have here the notion of an inner *telos* of human nature, a quest of man's whole being for his own proper good – a notion that goes back through a long intellectual tradition to Aristotle. In christian terms it is the idea of the divine structuring of human nature, through the forces by which man has been made, for a relationship with God which is the basis of man's own ultimate good. This capacity for God is the image of God within us; and the perennial theological question to which it has given rise in both ancient and modern times is whether that image has been destroyed by the fall, so that man's nature is now no longer structured towards God, or whether on the contrary man still has this God-given capacity to be addressed by and tendency to respond to his Maker. Very roughly, and with numerous crossings of party lines, the former has been the catholic and the latter the reformed view. If it were necessary to choose between them I should myself opt for the catholic view at this point. But for many of us today the issue does not take this form, since the doctrine of the fall on which it turns is no longer acceptable, and accordingly the question whether the fall has resulted in total or only partial depravity does not arise. In distinction from both the typical catholic and the typical protestant positions the eastern christian outlook, especially as we find it in the early greek Fathers, such as Irenaeus, is much more readily adaptable for use today. On this view man was not created as a finitely perfect being who then fell disastrously into sin and misery. Rather he was created as an immature and imperfect creature who was to grow in grace through time from the *imago dei*, which is the capacity for God, to the finite *similitudo* or 'likeness' to God, which is the perfection of our nature in relation to him. This development is possible precisely because man's nature is not neutral or alien towards his Maker, like that of a stone or a demon, but is inwardly structured towards him, so that man will find at the same time his own perfecting and his right relationship to God. Thus God does not have to coerce us to respond to him, for he has already so created us that our nature, seeking its own fulfilment and good, leads us to him. The notion of divine coercion is set aside by the fact of divine creation.

If then we affirm the openness of human nature towards the reality to which the religions of the world are responses, the question of the relation between man's freedom and God's saving will ceases to be a version of the old conundrum about the immovable post and the irresistible force. A better analogy may perhaps be found in the relationship between a psychia-

trist and the patient whom he is seeking to free from inner
blockages and inhibitions which are preventing him from
confronting reality and from being and doing what he really
wants to be and do. The divine therapy is a matter of healing,
of enabling us to fulfil our own selves and to become more
truly what our own nature cries out to be. The present life
sees the beginning of this process of the bringing of human
personality to maturity and wholeness, though the progress
which different individuals make is extremely varied, ranging
from a great deal (in the saints) through rather little (in most
of us) down to none at all or even less than none. We must
suppose that beyond this life the process continues in other
environments offering other experiences and challenges which
open up new opportunities of response and growth.

Our analogy suggests that we need not even rule out the
possibility of more direct operations of divine grace, corresponding in their effect to that of the chemical and electric-
shock treatments used in our psychiatric hospitals. For although
these are almost a form of surgery, treating the patient for the
time being as a physical object rather than as a person, yet
their purpose and their result (when successful) is not to
diminish but to restore and enhance his own freedom and
responsibility. They are a form of direct action to undo the
effects of past mistakes; and their outcome is to make it again
possible for the patient to come to terms with reality for himself. No one else can make the essential inner act of confrontation for him; but sometimes the therapist can do something
to make this possible which the patient had become incapable
of doing for himself. Then the natural appetite for life and
health operates again, prompting him to begin to relate himself
rightly to the world in which he lives. In an analogous way the
divine therapist may perhaps dissolve inhibiting blockages and
distortions in order that the inherent need of our nature may
eventually lead us freely to respond to him. Perhaps this
speculation reflects the element of truth in the objective
theories of the atonement. For in their different languages –
whether it be that of the payment on our behalf of a debt
which we could never have paid, or the bearing in our stead
of a penalty that would have destroyed us, or the overcoming
of demonic powers from whose thrall we could never have

freed ourselves – these ancient theories were all saying that God in Christ has done something to make possible again for us a blessed future which had become otherwise impossible.

When we consult the psychiatrists about their end of this analogy their testimony varies; but some at least would say that they seem to meet in some patients an apparently endless capacity for resistance to being helped towards a fuller personal health. This witnesses to the fact that in the actual conditions in which psychiatric therapy has to be practised – with limited time, limited influence over environmental conditions, and limited knowledge and skill on the doctor's part – it is not always successful. But in using a psychiatric analogy for God's grace we have to try to think away these limitations. We have to suppose, not a human but a divine therapist, working not to a limited deadline but in unlimited time, with perfect knowledge, and ultimately controlling instead of being restricted by the environmental factors. In so far as we can conceive of this, do we not find that it authorizes an unambiguously good prognosis?

What I have argued thus far, then, is that since man has been created by God for God, and is basically oriented towards him, there is no final opposition between God's saving will and our human nature acting in freedom; and that accordingly the universalist argument is not after all undermined by the fact of human freedom.

But now let us press a stage further and ask, would not a divine structuring of man's nature, such that in coming to God he is achieving his own human fulfilment, amount to a divine determining of man? I have suggested that man has been made by God so that he will in the free out-working of his own nature eventually come to love and worship his Maker. But is not this simply to say, in effect, that his response to God has been predetermined by the way in which he has been created?

I suggest that this question presupposes – wrongly – that human beings have or could have chosen their own basic nature. But both the universalist and the non-universalist have to reckon with the fact that to be created at all is to be subject to an ultimate arbitrariness and determination. This is true whether we have been created by the natural processes of the physical universe or by God working through these natural processes. In either case it is true that we have come into being through the operation of forces other than ourselves. In other words, we are creatures – contingent, dependent beings. And not only is the fact that we exist a result of the operation of forces beyond ourselves, but the fact that we exist with a certain nature. For there is no existing in general; all the constituents of a world are particular and specific. It would thus be meaningless to postulate a divine ordination that nature shall produce man, with the proviso that he is to have no specific nature. For man to have come into existence is for a creature to have evolved with a given set of characteristics, with specific powers and potentialities, with a definite structure of capacities, instincts, drives, needs and tendencies. And our freedom can only be a freedom within the basic situation of our being the kind of creatures that we are in the kind of world in which we are. It can only be the freedom of beings who are – without their choice – of a certain determinate kind. This is true not only of the race as a whole, which has emerged as the distinctive species *Homo sapiens*, but also of each individual, born at a particular time, as male or female, conditioned by a particular group and culture and with a particular genetic inheritance guiding his development. That the basic conditions of our existence are thus set by forces beyond ourselves must be presupposed in any viable concept of human freedom. The problem of free will does not hinge upon whether we are created beings (i.e. the product of forces other than ourselves) but upon whether as created beings we have any significant freedom. For any human actions exemplifying our concepts 'free' and 'responsible' must in the nature of the case be the actions of beings who have been created and formed by forces beyond themselves. Thus the principle that to be created is *ipso facto* to be unfree would merely serve to nullify the language of personal agency.

But if our ordinary and operative notion of human freedom is compatible with our having been brought into existence by forces outside ourselves, it must be compatible with our having been brought into existence by the will of God. And this would seem to hold equally whether our nature embodies a religious bias or not. If the human mind did not tend to interpret life religiously it would be no less true that man is a creature with a nature given to him rather than chosen by him. Thus we should no more be arbitrarily determined from beyond ourselves as religious than as non-religious animals. Hence it is, I suggest, a mistake to think that if God has structured our nature towards himself, so that our hearts are restless until they find their rest in him, he has thereby prevented us from being free and responsible agents. Any usable notion of human freedom must be compatible with our having been created with the nature that we actually have. Thus there is no conflict between man's freedom as anyone has seriously conceived of it and the fact that human beings have been brought into existence, with their specific nature, by forces other than themselves.

And yet there is still perhaps a difficulty. Granting that the fact of the divine creation of man does not in general negate man's freedom, yet can man be said to be free specifically *in relation to God* if his nature is such that it will sooner or later lead him to God? If God has made man for himself then surely, it might be said, man cannot ultimately be free *vis-à-vis* his Maker, however free he may be in other respects.

At this point, if our thought is not to revolve in circles, we must firmly confront the options before us and choose between them. What are the alternatives which we are comparing with the universalist picture? There seem to be two: first, that man should have been created as religiously neutral – that is to say, without any gravitational pull towards God; the second, that he should have been created as a religious being but that God should then have refrained from actively seeking to draw men to himself. And the question that we have in each case to ask is whether we should then be more truly free in relation to God than we are on the universalist hypothesis.

First, then, would man without any religious tendency be more free in relation to God than man endowed with this Godward bias? In order to answer this question we have to try to imagine man emerging as a non-religious animal in this world. We have, that is to say, to imagine him without those aspects of his nature which have given rise to the religions of mankind – without the sense of cosmic wonder or numinous awe or of his own dependent finitude; without any sense of the transcendent and without any propensity to respond with worship to the idea of that which is supremely valuable;

without indeed any tendency to form the concept of gods or of God and without the ability to reason from contingency and teleological order to at least the possibility of non-contingent being and ordering intelligence. And when we do imagine such a completely non-religious *Homo sapiens* it is clear that he would have a very different freedom in relation to God. He would be free *from* God instead of being free *for* God. God would simply be outside his cognitive range. He would not be mentally equipped to think of and to worship a supreme Being. And assuming – as we are doing in this discussion – that there *is* a supreme Being, we must say that man would have the freedom not to know and worship God instead of the freedom to know and worship him. But this would not be, formally, a greater freedom, nor would it be, materially, as desirable a freedom to have. Thus there does not seem to be any proper sense in which man as a religiously neutral creature could be said to be more free, or more truly free, in relation to his Maker.

But what of the second possibility? Suppose that God had made us for himself, with a bias of our nature towards him, but had not actively sought to draw us to himself – so that it remained an entirely open question whether we ever came to him. Suppose that he had refrained from working as the divine therapist, but had left us to ourselves, allowing a real (and not merely a theoretical) possibility that we should for ever fail to attain to the wholeness of our nature. This is a coherent supposition. We can conceive of our Maker not seeking actively to bring all men freely to himself. We are, then, postulating a God who creates but who does not perfect or redeem his creation. He is inactive, deistic rather than theistic, in relation to his creatures. What we are supposing is the falsity of the christian message of the love of God who is ever at work to seek and to save those who are lost; and the question is now whether we should in this case be more truly free in relation to God than we are if he is actively trying to save us by every means compatible with our existence as free personal beings. It seems that the question answers itself: so long as the divine saving activity does not negate or undermine our freedom, so long as we remain responsible personal beings in relation to God, we can only rejoice that he is so working that we shall

eventually attain to the perfecting of our nature in his eternal
kingdom.

Thus the investigation returns to its starting-point. Everything depends upon whether God can in fact carry his saving
work to completion without undermining our status as
autonomous finite persons. And I have already argued, on the
basis of the christian doctrine of the creation of our human
nature, that we may properly believe that he can.

Two further possible difficulties should be briefly noted.
First, if we have the picture of human life continuing after
bodily death in other environments containing experiences
and challenges which offer new opportunities of response and
growth, must we not add that those other environments will
also offer new opportunities for refusal and diminishment?
How, then, is a mere temporal extension of human existence
going to bring about the qualitative change of salvation? It
must I think be granted that temporal extension as such cannot
do so. But the outcome of the previous argument, in so far as
it is valid, is relevant at this point. If there *is* continued life
after death, and if God *is* ceaselessly at work for the salvation
of his children, it follows that he will continue to be at work
until the work is done; and I have been arguing that it is
logically possible for him eventually to fulfil his saving purpose
without at any point overriding our human freedom.

But, second, we may ask, concerning the idea which I
introduced of more direct operations of divine grace in the
future life, why should God postpone these to future environments instead of employing them in the present life? In
response to this question I would suggest that the notion of
such 'direct operations' or 'shock treatments' permits of
degrees and that some degrees of it *do* occur in this present
life. That is to say, there are traumatic experiences in which an
individual is turned round and made to see things significantly
differently. Indeed, a religious conversion sometimes takes
this form. A person may feel buffeted by life's circumstances
or carried irresistibly along by the current of events, or con-
strained by a truth that is dawning upon him, and yet also
feel after passing through this experience that he is more free
and more firmly in touch with reality than he was before. If we
grant that this happens in the present life, and that it may

happen perhaps in other and more powerful ways in the life or lives to come, then the question that has been raised is really the broader question as to why the process of human soul-making takes as long as it does, instead of half or a quarter or a hundredth as long. This is a question which we cannot answer and which furthermore the non-universalist is no more able to answer than the universalist. We do not know why the time-scale of God's dealings with us is as it is. When we question such basic circumstances we are in effect asking why God has made man as *man*, living on the human time-scale, and not as angel or animal. We do not know why; but we are equally in ignorance at this point whether we are universalists or not. I therefore do not feel that these considerations, puzzling though they are, constitute an argument against universalism.

And so the conclusion which now seems to me to be warranted is this: the faith that God has made us for fellowship with himself, and that he so works in his creative power as to enable us to reach that fulfilment, carries with it the faith that in the end all human life will, in traditional theological language, be 'saved'. We must thus affirm the ultimate salvation of all mankind; and the faith in which we affirm this is that in which we have affirmed God's saving love and sovereign power. In faith we affirm God's love as both a present and an eternal reality; and as it looks to the future this becomes a faith in the universal triumph of the divine love, when God shall be 'all in all' and the entire creation shall have become his kingdom. If we prefer to give the name of hope to christian faith when it refers to the future, we may; for christian faith and christian hope are the same response to God in Christ, expressed in different tenses.

4. KARL BARTH ON UNIVERSALISM

Finally, there is one further obstacle in the way of the universalist doctrine which I should like briefly to note. This has been set forth by Karl Barth. There are in some of his later works, written during his last two or three decades, indications of a sympathy with universalism. We find this, for example, in his remarkable 1956 essay on the humanity of God.[15] And in the treatment of election in volume II, part 2 of the *Church*

Dogmatics there are statements to the effect that on the cross
Christ has borne God's rejection of the ungodly, so that no
one else can any longer be rejected. However, Barth has
nevertheless insisted, and some of the Barthians have insisted
even more emphatically, that he was not a universalist. He
was not a universalist because although he rejected the doctrine
of a double predestination to heaven and hell, and gladly
acknowledged the real possibility that God will save all men,
and although he did not see such a possibility as incompatible
with human freedom, nevertheless he held that because of
God's own sovereign freedom we must never positively assert
that he *will* do this. Such an assertion would infringe the
divine autonomy and impugn the Deity's total independence
of the world. Because he is absolutely free *vis-à-vis* his creation
we cannot even say that God's love must express itself towards
mankind in salvation rather than in reprobation. Because of
the absolute divine independence and freedom we may not
propound a doctrine of God's goodness and love and then
proceed to draw the universalist conclusion from it. As Barth
says, 'If we are to respect the freedom of divine grace, we
cannot venture the statement that it must and will finally be
coincident with the world of man as such (as in the doctrine
of the so-called *apokatastasis*). No such right or necessity can
legitimately be deduced. Just as the gracious God does not
need to elect or call any single man, so He does not need to
elect or call all mankind';[16] or again in another place, 'Even
though theological consistency might seem to lead our
thoughts and utterances most clearly in this direction [i.e. in
the direction of universalism], we must not arrogate to ourselves that which can be given and received only as a free
gift.'[17]

But in his desire to acknowledge without qualification the
absoluteness of the divine freedom is Barth not in his own
thought limiting that freedom? In forbidding God to allow us
to make valid inferences about him is not Barth in effect
legislating for the Deity? For he is saying that in order to be
sovereignly free God *must* remain, in relation to us, arbitrary
and unpredictable. But in that case the Lord of the universe is
not free to reveal his love to man so definitively that we can
rest upon it and draw inferences from it; not free to make

promises upon which he means us to rely; not free to act consistently and therefore predictably in relation to his creation. Surely in insisting that we cannot presume to know, from the divine self-revelation in Christ, what God is like and what he will do, Barth is over-protecting the Creator's freedom. He is applying to God an anthropomorphic conception of freedom which denies to the Creator the ultimate freedom to commit himself to man in a revelation of divine love which is to be taken so seriously that in the light of it we know that 'all shall be well, and all shall be well, and all manner of thing shall be well'. Is there not even something presumptuous about a theology which forbids us so to respond to God's self-revelation that we rely upon it and rejoice in it and proclaim it with its final implications as good news for all mankind?

In short, then, it does not seem to me that the barthian embargo upon drawing the universalist conclusion should be heeded.

NOTES

1. Luke 6: 23-4.
2. Matthew 23: 14.
3. ibid., 5: 26.
4. ibid., 18: 34-5.
5. ibid., 25: 41, 46.
6. ibid., 25: 30.
7. Mark 3: 29.
8. John 3: 36.
9. ibid., 5: 29.
10. ibid., 8: 47.
11. ibid., 10: 25.
12. The interpretation of this as meaning, 'As all who are in Adam (i.e. all men) die, so all who are in Christ (i.e. some men) will be brought to life' (cf. D. E. H. Whiteley, *The Theology of St Paul*, p. 271), would put this passage at variance with its parallels in Romans 5: 18 and 11: 32.
13. Cf. William Strawson, *Jesus and the Future Life*, p. 141.
14. *Confessions*, book I, ch. 1.
15. Karl Barth, *The Humanity of God*.
16. *Church Dogmatics*, vol. II, part 2, p. 417.
17. ibid., vol. IV, part 3, first half, p. 477.

Part IV

WESTERN
AND EASTERN
PARESCHATOLOGIES

CHAPTER 14

The Survival of the Disembodied Mind

1. A MIND-DEPENDENT WORLD

Although the dualist belief that after bodily death the mind continues to live goes back in western thought at least to Plato, it has usually been a somewhat undefined belief, developed only in mythological terms. What might it be like to be a consciousness without a body? What would one be conscious of? How might different people recognize one another? How might they communicate together? The notion of the survival of the disembodied mind has long been in need of being turned into an intelligible hypothesis, and it is something of a scandal that it should have had to wait until the twentieth century for this to be done. However, it has now been done by the philosopher H. H. Price in a long and important paper, 'Survival and the Idea of "Another World" '.[1]

Price's theory can be stated in three stages. First, he suggests that post-mortem perceptions will be of the same general kind as perceptions in dreams. That is to say, they will be mind-dependent, and will be formed out of mental images acquired during one's embodied life. These will include images of one's own body as seen and felt by oneself and of a surrounding material environment. The result will, from the experient's point of view, be the perception of a 'real' and solid world in which he exists as a bodily being. This world may however differ from our present world in the kinds of way in which the sequence and arrangement of events in our dreams is liable to differ from that of waking life, by exhibiting on occasion discontinuities and all sorts of sudden elisions and transformations. For the laws of the post-mortem world will not be those of physics but of psychology, since our survival (according to the hypothesis we are considering) will be a psychological rather than a physical survival.

Second, whereas our dreams are private experiences in which other 'people' are only appearances that are not animated by independent centres of consciousness, there may in the post-mortem world be real communication and interaction with other minds by means of what in this life we call extrasensory perception. There may be continual telepathic activity, producing visual and auditory images, so that the resulting experience is just like that of seeing other people and hearing them talk. There may likewise be tactile images, and images of taste and smell. There may in fact be a coherent three-dimensional world which we inhabit jointly with other persons. Or rather, there may be a number of such worlds, formed by communities of individuals whose minds are somehow telepathically linked together and correlated to sustain a common environment – perhaps people who share common memories or who have similar attitudes and interests. Accordingly there may not only be many different post-mortem worlds but, from the moral and aesthetic points of view, higher and lower such worlds.

Third, the next world will be fashioned by the power of our desires. Thus Price says of the supposed inhabitants of the world to come, 'Their memories and their desires would determine what sort of images they had. If I may put it so, the "stuff" or "material" of such a world would come in the end from one's memories, and the "form" of it from one's desires.'[2] But Price cautions us against assuming that such a realm of wish-fulfilment would necessarily be unqualifiedly pleasant. For these dreams would reveal with unerring accuracy the real character of our desires, including those that are repressed during our present life. There may be ground here for apprehension and misgiving, as Hamlet realized:

> For in that sleep of death what dreams may come,
> When we have shuffled off this mortal coil,
> Must give us pause.[3]

They might well be purgatorial or even hellish dreams, rather than heavenly ones. We might discover that some of our desiring was repugnant to our better nature, and that much of it was trivial and only capable of producing a world that soon became unutterably boring. But then we might perhaps sooner or later be prompted by these purgatorial experiences to desire something better, to hunger and thirst after righteousness, and thus to gravitate by the power of our own desiring to other and higher worlds, and perhaps even eventually to enter into what christian tradition has called the vision of God. Or again, as an alternative possibility more in keeping with eastern modes of thought, it might be that eventually desire becomes satiated and dies and that our individual personal life fades with it, absorbed into a supra-personal state of nirvana.

Thus within his basic hypothesis of psychological, as distinguished from physical, survival Price works with two principles – first, the mind-dependent character of the post-mortem world (or worlds), and second, its (or their) formation by the power of human desire. It appears to me that these principles generate a whole spectrum of possible forms of psychological survival, ranging from a solipsistic version at one extreme to a view at the other which borders upon the apparently quite different notion of the resurrection or reconstitution of the psycho-physical person. Price's own conception stands about in the middle of this spectrum – about halfway between a private-mental-worlds picture and a bodily-resurrection picture. There is however in his theory a tension between the idea of the formation of a post-mortem world by the power of desire and the idea that such a world is common to many minds in virtue of telepathic links between them. I shall suggest that the wish-fulfilment principle is only fully at home within a theory of private worlds and that it becomes increasingly difficult to accommodate as we move along the spectrum. And sooner or later it becomes so awkward an element that one is ready to consider what might be gained and what lost by jettisoning it.

At one extreme, then, there is the picture of a plurality of private mental worlds each created by the individual's own desires. We can call this the solipsistic picture, using the adjective in an epistemic rather than in an ontological sense. That is to say, any number of people might be severally and simultaneously in this state, but each would exist in isolation and with no interaction or communication between them. Each one's stream of experiences would be like a prolonged dream, and might well comprise both agreeable and disagreeable phases as his desires, at present limited in their expression by an environment that is independent of his

wishes, compete to produce objects to satisfy them. Wish-
fulfilment would thus create all sorts of sensual, aesthetic and
intellectual delights. There might also however, as Price
reminds us, be painful conflicts between excessive, cruel, or
perverted desires on the one hand, and a yearning for sanity,
decency, or normality on the other, such conflicts perhaps
creating agonizing nightmares. However, in the course of time
such conflicts might eventually work themselves out. Again,
as Price likewise suggests, a revulsion might develop against
the emotional poverty of many of our existing desires and a
consequent elevation of the quality of our conative life; or
alternatively a satiety and eventual cessation of desire. All
this would I think constitute the picture of a state of affairs in
which the individual consciousness could properly be said to
have survived physical death, though – it must be stressed –
only in isolation, as a windowless monad.

Would it be proper to speak of the individual in this situation
as still *living*? This depends upon how we choose to define life.
But a more important task than the assigning of a label is that
of describing and analysing the situation in question. The
individual would not in the ordinary sense of the words be
interacting with other people within a common environment
or having new experiences which add new and different images
to his memory store. But on the other hand he would not have
ceased to exist: for he would certainly exist from his own point
of view! He would be conscious and would be undergoing
experiences, but he would not be interacting with realities
external to his own mind. This amounts only to a very
truncated sense of being alive, in comparison with normal
waking life. Would it however be enough to permit the continued progress of the self in the fulfilling of its potentialities?
Let us ask at this point the very odd and difficult question
whether there could in dreams, including post-mortem
'dreams', be real moral choices and hence the possibility of
moral growth. If (as may well be the case) our dreams are
psychologically determined events, then we shall in our dream
life have only the illusion of free choices. But if on the other
hand our dreams are not fully determined, then it appears to
be a coherent hypothesis that in a prolonged dream one might
have to make ethical decisions and that there might accordingly

be the possibility of development of character. This would however require both that there are other 'people' in the dream, and that the dreamer is not aware that they are 'people' only within inverted commas; and indeed that he is not aware that he is dreaming. He must regard the 'persons' with whom he is having to do as independent centres of consciousness and will, and must regard the situations in which he is called upon to make moral choices as 'real life' situations. Given these conditions it seems possible to suppose that the individual, solipsistically situated though he is, might develop morally and, speaking now from a theistic point of view, might move closer to or further from God. If these conditions apply to the post-mortem world of our first picture, then it would seem that its inhabitants would indeed in a significant sense be alive. And on the face of it there does not appear to be any conclusive reason why these conditions should not apply: the encounters with other 'people' might be sufficiently vivid and sufficiently coherent and extended to be taken as real despite any odd dream-like features that the environment might display. There would however – we cannot help noticing – be an element of delusion or deceit in the situation which may well jar against our views concerning the way in which a divinely created universe ought to be conducted. Man is essentially a social creature, existing and developing as a person in interaction with other persons; and yet in the post-mortem world that we are now imagining his social environment would be unreal and his commerce with other people delusory. This consideration must, surely, count to some extent at least against a theory of this kind.

So in this first possible picture, human survival is the survival of individuals each living his or her own solipsistic dream life. It seems conceivable however that they might each develop in their separate dream-like existences towards a condition of moral perfection at which they could enter into a further and different state – such as that referred to in christian tradition as the vision of God. Or alternatively they might perhaps eventually become purged of all desire and gradually cease to have any existence as distinct psychic entities.

This first picture fully embodies Price's two principles,

namely the mind-dependent character of the post-mortem world and its formation by the power of human desire. But in Price's own discussion this first picture only appears in outline as a contribution to the more complex picture of a *public* post-mortem environment sustained by telepathic contact between different people. Here the solipsistic situation is transcended by the sharing by many minds in the imaging of a common world. Their thoughts so influence one another that they are each conscious, from their appropriate different perspectives, of the same environment and of one another as visible and tangible embodied persons within it. Thus there is real interpersonal relationship and interaction, which could give rise to real ethical issues and constitute a sphere of genuine moral activity and progress. The element of delusion which we noted in the first picture does not reappear here.

2. THE CREATIVE POWER OF DESIRE

At this point however we notice the tension which I have already mentioned between the notion of a common world and the wish-fulfilment theme. For the latter points to a solipsistic rather than a public after-life. Surely only a plurality of private worlds could permit each individual to experience a post-mortem environment appropriate to his own individual mixture of desires, such as is indicated by Price when he says, 'Each man's purgatory would be just the automatic consequence of his own desires.'[4] Thus it is not easy to combine the two suggestions that the post-mortem world is created by human wishes and that it is common to a great number of people. For desires inhere in individuals, and at the level of ordinary everyday wishes at any rate it may be presumed that no two individuals' and certainly no large community of persons' desires coincide sufficiently to be capable of being fulfilled in identically the same state of affairs. I do not believe that we can in fact imagine a coherent world created by the desires of a multitude of different people out of the material of their several sets of earthly memories. For the different wishes of different individuals would, left to themselves, produce different features and states of the environment. Imagine a situation involving, one would think, a minimum of conflict of desires: suppose a devoted husband and wife on holiday sitting comfortably side by side on the seashore. Still, one of them might wish for a calm sea for bathing, the other for tremendous waves for surfing; she might in the course of the afternoon wish she were in a dress shop in Paris, whereas he would be disconcerted by her sudden disappearance to fulfil that wish; he might desire that they should be entertained by a troupe of dancing girls, she be quite content that they are not; and so on. But if it is hard to suppose an exact, continuous and detailed correlation of desires even between two individuals who are harmoniously related to one another, it becomes virtually impossible to suppose such a correlation between great multitudes of miscellaneous people populating one and the same world.

Nevertheless it may still be possible to retain the wish-fulfilment principle in a modified form within the picture of a common and public world. But to do so we must, I think, abandon the notion that each individual's desires are sovereign in the creation of his own post-mortem environment. We can however instead conceive, at least in general terms, a situation in which the memories and desires of a number of minds – and these could number thousands or millions – are pooled to produce a common environment. Each would contribute to the world in which they all live, though this would not be exclusively based upon any one individual's memories or express exclusively any one individual's wishes. The desires which determine its character would represent a composite result produced by the cancellings out and mutual reinforcements of the multitude of individual desires, so that in perceptible content such a world might be analogous to a 'generic picture' formed by the superimposition of a great number of individual photographs.

Along these lines one could suppose a single post-mortem world, formed by the memories and desires of all the human beings who have died since man began, this world developing gradually as new sets of memories are contributed to the common stock and changing if and as the prevailing pattern of human desires changes. Or one could suppose, as Price does, a number of separate worlds created by groups of people with sufficiently similar memories or desires or both. There must in that case, it would seem, be a class structure in the life to come, with high-brow and low-brow worlds; military worlds always in a state of war; heavenly harems always in a state of uxorious activity; unending holiday camps; perpetual conspiracies and revolutions; endless classical concerts or philosophical seminars – in short a paradise for every taste.[5] There might also, as a slightly more complex possibility, be a rotation of seasons formed by the tendency of one's interests to alternate, these different human climates, or a selection of them, succeeding one another to form a balanced cosmic year, which perhaps eternally repeats itself. Or there might instead be a spiral effect in the revolving aeons, with an evolution taking place in the quality of human consciousness and thus in the character of the environments which it creates.

The notion of a single world beyond death, whose character is the resultant of the emotions, desires and memories of the entire human race is thus far consonant with a prominent Old Testament theme, that of the corporate unity of the race, within which individuals exist as cells in a larger social organism – though of course in the Old Testament literature the race was generally thought of only in restricted tribal terms. On the other hand the relatively more individualistic outlook of the New Testament, and to a much greater extent again of post-Renaissance western thought, is more consonant with the notion of a hierarchy of heavens existing at different spiritual (rather than cultural) levels. St Paul may possibly have had something like this in mind when he wrote, presumably referring to himself, 'I know a man in Christ who fourteen years ago was caught up to the *third heaven* – whether in the body or out of the body I do not know, God knows.'[6]

3. A THEOLOGICAL CRITICISM

There is however a general theological consideration which I now want to mention that operates, to some extent at least, against theories envisaging a post-mortem world shaped by human desires, whether individual or corporate. This consideration, if we choose to heed it, would lead us yet further from the solipsistic end of the theory-spectrum and away from the use of the wish-fulfilment principle. The consideration that I have in mind has been formulated mainly in connection with the theological problem of evil, where it appears within one of the two major christian traditions of theodicy, going back to the thought of Irenaeus towards the end of the second century AD. According to this, the purpose of our earthly existence is that men should develop morally and spiritually from the state of intelligent social animals towards a quality of being which represents the perfecting of our human nature; and this world is intended to be an environment in which such growth can take place. Now it is essential to this person-making process that the world should *not* be plastic to our human wishes but should constitute a given natural order with its own stable character and 'laws' in terms of which we must learn to live. For it is by grappling with the demands of an objective environment of which we are ourselves a part, presenting us with work to be done, problems to be solved, difficulties to be met and hardships to be endured, that human intelligence and character have developed. Again, it is through men's needs and claims in relation to one another as they face the disciplines and hazards of their natural environment that morality has developed. And it would seem that a world which is to function in this way, as the scene for the creation of a valuable quality of human personality, cannot be formed by men's desires but must on the contrary have its own fixed structure, independently of human wishes.[7]

Now it is evident that if a person-making process is taking place in this life, that process is seldom (if indeed ever) completed by the time of bodily death. In some people the creative process makes considerable progress during their earthly existence, in most only a little, and in some none at all or less than none. Indeed, of all the thousands of millions of human beings who have lived since human life can be deemed to have begun, a considerable proportion have died in infancy or at any rate well before completing a full human span. Thus if the person-making process is ever to be carried through it seems that it must necessarily continue beyond bodily death. And this appears to require a real continuation of human life as a formative process. This consideration, in so far as it is valid, does not of course tell decisively against the type of theory advocated by Price; but it does I think tell to some extent against it. For Price's theory involves an important distinction between the present life and any future ones, a distinction that does nothing to reinforce but which on the contrary would tend to weaken the irenaean picture. The distinction in question is that whereas the present life is one in which our individual nature is being formed by our grappling, in interaction with others, with the problems of an objective and challenging environment, any future lives are to have a radically different character. Instead of a world that is given to us and to which we must adapt ourselves, we shall (on Price's theory) inhabit a world created, perhaps corporately, by our own minds and expressing, again perhaps corporately, our own desires. Could such a world continue the person-making process begun on earth? It seems clear at any rate that it could not continue precisely the same process, since it was integral to this that the environment had its own fixed character, independent of human desires. All that a wish-fulfilment world would seem able to do in the way of character-formation would be to refine and purify the structure of desires and dispositions that had already been developed on earth. If I may use again Hartshorne's analogy between the living of a life and the writing of a book,[8] there could in the world to come be a correcting of what had already been written but no continued primary authorship. There could be no writing of a second volume which begins where the first had left off and which produces its own novel developments and surprises. But the latter possibility is far more congenial to the irenaean type of theodicy even though the former may perhaps not be absolutely incompatible with it.

Thus the considerations flowing from this particular theological standpoint tend to lead one away from the wish-fulfilment aspect of Price's theory. They are however compatible with the mind-dependence aspect, providing we understand this in a way which allows the phenomenal world to be objective in relation to the minds which are conscious of it. This of course was precisely what Bishop Berkeley advocated in his own distinctive form of metaphysical idealism. Price refers to Berkeley at the end of his discussion, pointing out that in Berkeley's philosophy 'material objects are just collections of "ideas", though according to Berkeley the will which presents these ideas to us is the will of God, acting directly upon us in a way which is in effect telepathic'. And he poses the intriguing question, 'Could it be that these idealist metaphysicians have given us a substantially correct picture of the next world, though a mistaken picture of this one?'[9] Now a conception of the world to come on strictly berkeleian lines would agree with Price's in postulating psychological survival, but would differ from his in retaining the idea of an objective environment which is not plastic to our wishes. If God has created our present world to be (so far at least as it concerns mankind) a place of soul-making, perhaps he also creates another world or worlds for the continuation of the same process. We should have to say of such a world that it exists in its totality in the divine consciousness, whilst different parts and aspects of it are imparted to the minds of individual men and women according to the perspectives which they severally occupy within it. There is no reason why such a world or series of worlds should be limited in content to the images stored up in men's memories of their earthly lives or, in its formative principle, to the range of current human desires. Its possibilities would be open-ended; and this is perhaps an advantage in such a theory. For it can then accommodate the religious sense that there are vast depths of reality totally beyond our present range of experience – 'as it is written, "What no eye has seen, nor ear heard, nor the heart of man conceived, what God has prepared for those who love him" '.[10]

But given a berkeleian account of a post-mortem world (or worlds) we must go on to ask why this should not also apply to our present world; or alternatively, why a non-berkeleian account should not apply to the next world as well as to this. We have noted Price's speculation that the understanding of reality developed by idealist metaphysicians might be true of the next world although not of the present one. But why make any such invidious distinction? Why should this world differ from any other worlds in fundamental character? For a theist of the irenaean point of view, who holds that both worlds exist through the creative activity of God to serve the same purpose of person-making, it must seem likely, unless there are reasons to suppose the contrary, that both will have the same basic nature. They may lead ultimately to a further and radically different state, eternal rather than temporal, symbolized by such ideas as heaven, nirvana, the kingdom of God, and the *visio dei*; but if we are thinking of that which lies more immediately beyond death, as the next stage of the creative process, there is a prima facie case at least for expecting it to have a like metaphysical status with our present world. Two assumptions are I think at work when this prima facie view is rejected. One is the assumption that Berkeley's theory is not true of this world; and the other is the assumption that the next world cannot be a material world. Each of these presuppositions can of course be questioned; and I do not wish to press the claims of berkeleian metaphysics. But some kind of physicalist conception of the 'next world' remains a possibility and will be explored in the next chapter and again in chapter 20.

One important conclusion that emerges from Price's paper is that as soon as we try to conceive of the post-mortem existence of the disembodied mind we find that this is not after all truly disembodied. If there is no physical body inhabiting a physical world, then the mind must supply its own 'dream' body inhabiting a 'dream' world, the latter being as real to those who experience it as the former. For continued personal identity would seem to require the continuation of a finite consciousness, aware of an environment from a particular perspective within it, and able to exercise volition in relation to that environment. The very notion of an environment seems to presuppose space, filled with a variety of objects, and interaction with that environment seems to presuppose that we are embodied as one of the space-filling objects. We have already noted the attempt of Karl Rahner to find an alternative to this in the idea of the pancosmic state of the soul after death, and have found this obscure to the point of unintelligibility.[11] Thus when the notion of the survival of the disembodied mind is developed it turns out not after all to be a radical alternative to the possibility of an embodied post-mortem existence, but rather a special form of that possibility.

NOTES

1. *Proc. SPR*, vol. 50, part 182 (1953), reprinted in *Classical and Contemporary Readings in the Philosophy of Religion*, ed. John Hick, from which the quotations in this chapter are cited; and in *Brain and*

Mind, ed. J. R. Smythies, which also contains critical discussions. There is a further such discussion in H. D. Lewis, *The Self and Immortality*, ch. 8. There is a valuable treatment of the neighbouring topic of disembodied existence in its relation to this world in Terence Penelhum, *Survival and Disembodied Existence*.

2. op. cit., p. 385.

3. Shakespeare's *Hamlet*, act III, scene 1, ll. 66–8.

4. op. cit., p. 390.

5. Swedenborg's conception of the life to come included this feature. See Signe Toksvig, *Emanuel Swedenborg: Scientist and Mystic*, ch. 23.

6. 2 Corinthians 12: 2–3.

7. Cf. my *Evil and the God of Love*, ch. 16.

8. See above, p. 218.

9. op. cit., p. 393.

10. 1 Corinthians 2: 9.

11. Chapter 12, section 1.

CHAPTER 15

The Resurrection of the Person

I. THE IDEA OF RESURRECTION

'I believe', says the Apostles' Creed, 'in the resurrection of the body and the life everlasting.' The resurrection of the body, or of the flesh, has been given a variety of meanings in different ages and different theological circles; but we are not at present concerned with the history of the concept.[1] We are concerned with the meaning that can be given to it today in terms of our contemporary scientific and philosophical understanding.

The prevailing view of man among both contemporary scientists and western philosophers is that he is an indissoluble psycho-physical unity. The only self of which we know is the empirical self, the walking, talking, acting, sleeping individual who lives, it may be, for some sixty to eighty years and then dies. Mental events and mental characteristics are analysed into the modes of behaviour and behavioural dispositions of this empirical self. The human being is described as an organism capable of acting in the high-level ways which we characterize as intelligent, resentful, humorous, calculating and the like. The concept of mind or soul is thus not that of a 'ghost in the machine' but of the more flexible and sophisticated ways in which human beings behave and have it in them to behave. On this view there is no room for the notion of soul in distinction from body; and if there is no soul in distinction from body there can be no question of the soul surviving the death of the body. Against this background of thought the specifically christian and jewish belief in the resurrection of the body, in contrast to the hellenic idea of the survival of a disembodied soul, might be expected to have attracted more attention than it has. For it is consonant with the conception of man as an indissoluble psycho-physical unity and yet it also offers the possibility of an empirical meaning for the idea of life after death.

St Paul is the chief biblical expositor of the idea of the resurrection of the body. His basic conception, as I understand it, is this. When someone has died he is, apart from any special divine action, extinct. A human being is by nature mortal and subject to annihilation at death. But in fact God, by an act of sovereign power, either sometimes or always resurrects or reconstitutes or recreates him – not however as the identical physical organism that he was before death, but as a *soma pneumatikon* ('spiritual body') embodying the dispositional characteristics and memory traces of the deceased physical organism, and inhabiting an environment with which the *soma pneumatikon* is continuous as our present bodies are continuous with our present world. We are not concerned here with the difficult exegetical question of how precisely Paul thought of the resurrection body but with the conceptual question as to how, if at all, we can intelligibly think of it today.

2. THE 'REPLICA' THEORY

I wish to suggest that we can think of it as the divine creation in another space of an exact psycho-physical 'replica' of the deceased person.

The first point requiring clarification is the idea of spaces in the plural.[2] In this context the possibility of two spaces is the possibility of two sets of extended objects such that each member of each set is spatially related to each other member of the same set but not spatially related to any member of the other set. Thus everything in the space in which I am is at a certain distance and in a certain direction from me, and vice versa; but if there is a second space, nothing in it is at any distance or in any direction from where I now am. In other words, from my point of view the other space is nowhere and therefore does not exist. But if there *is* a second space, unobservable by me, the objects in it are entirely real to an observer within that space, and our own world is to him nowhere – not at any distance nor in any direction – so that from his point of view it does not exist. Now it is logically possible for there to be any number of worlds, each in its own space, these worlds being all observed by the universal consciousness of God but only one of them being observed by an embodied being who is part of one of these worlds. And the idea of bodily resurrection requires (or probably requires) that there be at least two such worlds, and that when an individual dies in our present world in space number one he is either immediately or after a lapse of time re-created in a world in space number two.[3]

In order to develop this idea more fully I shall present a series of three cases, which I claim to be logically possible of fulfilment.

We begin with the idea of someone suddenly ceasing to exist at a certain place in this world and the next instant coming into existence at another place which is not contiguous with the first. He has not moved from A to B by making a path through the intervening space but has disappeared at A and reappeared at B. For example, at some learned gathering in London one of the company suddenly and inexplicably disappears and the next moment an exact 'replica' of him suddenly and inexplicably appears at some comparable meeting in New York. The person who appears in New York is exactly similar, as to both bodily and mental characteristics, to the person who disappears in London. There is continuity of memory, complete similarity of bodily features, including fingerprints, hair and eye coloration and stomach contents, and also of beliefs, habits, and mental propensities. In fact there is everything that would lead us to identify the one who appeared with the one who disappeared, except continuous occupancy of space.

It is I think clear that this is a logically possible sequence of events. It is of course factually impossible: that is to say, so long as matter functions in accordance with the 'laws' which it has exhibited hitherto, such things will not happen. But nevertheless we can imagine changes in the behaviour of matter which would allow it to happen, and we can ask what effect this would have upon our concept of personal identity. Would we say that the one who appears in New York is the same person as the one who disappeared in London? This would presumably be a matter for decision, and perhaps indeed for a legal decision affecting such matters as marriage, property, debts, and other social rights and obligations. I believe that the only reasonable and generally acceptable decision would be to acknowledge identity. The man himself would be conscious of being the same person, and I suggest that his fellow human beings would feel obliged to recognize him as being the one whom he claims to be. We may suppose, for example, that a deputation of the colleagues of the man who disappeared fly to New York to interview the 'replica' of him which is reported there, and find that he is in all respects but one exactly as though he had travelled from London to New York by conventional means. The only difference is that he describes how, as he was listening to Dr Z reading a paper, on blinking his eyes he suddenly found himself sitting in a different room listening to a different paper by an american scholar. He asks his colleagues how the meeting had gone after he had ceased to be there, and what they had made of his disappearance, and so on. He clearly thinks of himself as the one who was present with them at their meeting in London. He is presently reunited with his wife, who is quite certain that he is her husband; and with his children, who are quite certain that he is their father. And so on. I suggest that faced with all these circumstances those who know him would soon, if not immediately, find themselves thinking of him and treating him as the individual who had so inexplicably disappeared from the meeting in London; and that society would accord legal recognition of his identity. We should be extending our normal use of 'same person' in a way which the postulated facts would both demand and justify if we said that the person who appears in New York is the same person as the one who disappeared in London. The factors inclining us to identify them would, I suggest, far outweigh the factors disinclining us to do so. The personal, social, and conceptual cost of refusing to make this extension would so greatly exceed the cost of making it that we should have no reasonable alternative but to extend our concept of 'the same person' to cover this strange new case.

This imaginary case, bizarre though it is, establishes an important conceptual bridgehead for the further claim that a post-mortem 'replica' of Mr X in another space would likewise count as the same person as the this-world Mr X before his death. However, let me strengthen this bridgehead at two points before venturing upon it.

The cyberneticist, Norbert Wiener, has graphically emphasized the non-dependence of human bodily identity through time upon the identity of the physical matter momentarily composing the body. He points out that the living human body is not a static entity but a pattern of change: 'The individuality of the body is that of a flame rather than that of a stone, of a form rather than of a bit of substance.'[4] The pattern of the body can be regarded as a message that is in principle capable of being coded, transmitted, and then translated back into its original form, as sight and sound patterns may be transmitted by radio and translated back into sound and picture. Hence 'there is no absolute distinction between the types of transmission which we can use for sending a telegram from country to country and the types of transmission which at least are theoretically possible for transmitting a living organism such as a human being'.[5] Strictly, one should not speak, as Wiener does here, of a living organism or body being transmitted; for it would not be the body itself but its coded form that is transmitted. At other times, however, Wiener is more precise. It is, he says, possible to contemplate transmitting 'the whole pattern of the human body, of the human brain with its memories and cross connections, so that a hypothetical receiving instrument could re-embody these messages in appropriate matter, capable of continuing the processes already in the body and the mind, and of maintaining the integrity needed for this continuation by a process of homeostasis'.[6] Accordingly Wiener concludes that the telegraphing of the pattern of a man from one place to another is theoretically possible even though it remains at the present time technically impossible.[7] And it does indeed seem natural in discussing this theoretical possibility to speak of the bodily individual who is constituted at the end of the process as being the same person as the one who was 'encoded' at the beginning. He is not composed of numerically the same parcel of matter; and yet it is more appropriate to describe him as the same person than as a different person because the matter of which he is composed embodies exactly the same 'information'. Similarly, the rendering of Beethoven's ninth symphony which reaches my ears from the radio loud-speaker does not consist of numerically the same vibrations that reached the microphone in the concert hall; those vibrations have not travelled on through another three hundred miles to me. And yet it is more appropriate to say that I am hearing this rendering of the ninth symphony than that I am hearing something else.

The kind of transmission which Wiener envisages differs of course from my case number one in that I have postulated no machinery for coding and decoding, and no procession of radio impulses proceeding from London to New York and requiring a certain elapse of time for their journey. It differs even more radically from the notion of resurrection as 'replication' in another space, since *ex hypothesi* in this case no physical connection between the two spaces, as by radio impulses, is possible. But if we abstract from all questions of practical logistics, Wiener's contribution to the present argument is his insistence that psycho-physical individuality does not depend upon the numerical identity of the ultimate physical constituents of the body but upon the pattern or 'code' which is exemplified. So long as the same 'code' operates, different parcels of matter can be used, and those parcels can be in different places.[8]

The second strengthening of the bridgehead concerns the term 'replica' which, it will be observed, I have used in quotes. The quotes are intended to mark a difference between the normal concept of a replica and the more specialized concept in use here. The paradigm sense of 'replica' is that in which there is an original object, such as a statue, of which a more or less exact copy is then made. It is logically possible (though not of course necessary) for the original and the replica to exist simultaneously; and also for there to be any number of replicas of the same original. In contrast to this, in the case of the disappearance in London and re-appearance in New York it is not logically possible for the original and the 'replica' to exist simultaneously or for there to be more than one 'replica' of the same original. If a putative 'replica' did exist simultaneously with its original it would not be a 'replica' but a replica; and if there were more than one they would not be 'replicas' but replicas. For 'replica' is the name that I am proposing for the second entity in the following case. A living person ceases to exist at a certain location, and a being exactly similar to him in all respects subsequently comes into existence at another location. And I have argued so far that it would be a correct decision, causing far less linguistic and conceptual disruption than the contrary one, to regard the 'replica' as the same person as the original.

Let us now move on to a second imaginary case, a step nearer to the idea of resurrection. Let us suppose that the event in London is not a sudden and inexplicable disappearance, and indeed not a disappearance at all, but a sudden death. Only, at the moment when the individual dies a 'replica' of him as he was at the moment before his death, and complete with memory up to that instant, comes into existence in New York. Even with the corpse on our hands it would still, I suggest, be an extension of 'same person' required and warranted by the postulated facts to say that the one who died has been miraculously re-created in New York. The case would, to be sure, be even odder than the previous one because of the existence of the dead body in London contemporaneously with the living person in New York. And yet, striking though the oddness undoubtedly is, it does not amount to a logical impossibility. Once again we must imagine some of the deceased's colleagues going to New York to interview the person who has suddenly appeared there. He would perfectly remember them and their meeting, be interested in what had happened, and be as amazed and dumbfounded about it as anyone else; and he would perhaps be worried about the possible legal complications if he should return to London to claim his property; and so on. Once again, I believe, they would soon find themselves thinking of him and treating him as the same person as the dead Londoner. Once again the factors inclining us to say that the one who died and the one who appeared are the same person would far outweigh the factors inclining us to say that they are different people. Once again we should have to extend our usage of 'same person' to cover the new case.

However, rather than pause longer over this second picture let us proceed to the idea of 'replication' in another space, which I suggest can give content to the notion of resurrection. For at this point the problem of personal identity shifts its focus from second- and third-person criteria to first-person criteria. It is no longer a question of how we in this world could know that the 'replica' Mr X is the same person as the now deceased Mr X, but of how the 'replica' Mr X himself could know this. And since this raises new problems it will be well to move directly to this case and the issues which it involves.

The picture that we have to consider is one in which Mr X dies and his 'replica', complete with memory, etc., appears, not in America, but as a resurrection 'replica' in a different world altogether, a resurrection world inhabited by resurrected 'replicas' – this world occupying its own space distinct from the space with which we are familiar. It is, I think, manifestly an intelligible hypothesis that after my death I shall continue to exist as a consciousness and shall remember both having died and some at least of my states of consciousness both before and after death. Suppose then that I exist, not as a disembodied consciousness but as a psycho-physical being, a psycho-physical being exactly like the being that I was before death, though existing now in a different space. I have the experience of waking up from unconsciousness, as I have on other occasions woken up from sleep; and I am no more inclined in the one case than in the others to doubt my own identity as an individual persisting through time. I realize, either immediately or presently, that I have died, both because I can remember being on my death-bed and because my environment is now different and is populated by people some of whom I know to have died. Evidences of this kind could mount up to the point at which they are quite as strong as the evidence which, in the previous two pictures, convinces the individual in question that he has been miraculously translated to New York. Resurrected persons would be individually no more in doubt about their own identity than we are now, and would presumably be able to identify one another in the same kinds of ways and with a like degree of assurance as we do now.

3. IDENTITY FROM WORLD TO WORLD

But if it be granted that resurrected persons might be able to arrive at a rationally founded conviction that their existence is *post-mortem*, how could they know that the world in which they find themselves is in a different space from that of their pre-mortem life? How could such a person know that he is not in a number-two type situation in which he has died and has been re-created somewhere else in the same physical universe –

except that the 'replica' is situated, not in New York, but on a planet of some other star?

It is no doubt conceivable that the space of the resurrection world should have properties which are manifestly incompatible with its being a region of physical space as we know it. But on the other hand, it is not of the essence of the notion of a resurrection world that its space should have different properties from those of physical space. And supposing it not to have different properties it is not evident that a resurrected individual could learn from any direct observations that he was not on a planet of some sun at so great a distance from our own sun that the stellar scenery visible from it does not correlate with that which we now see. And indeed, it is not essential to the conception of resurrection which I am presenting that God's re-creation of us should in fact take place in another space rather than elsewhere in this space. There are however probable arguments in favour of the plural space hypothesis. The main ground that a resurrected person would have for believing that he is in another space would be his belief that case-one and case-two type events would be incompatible with the 'laws' of the space in which he was before death. Thus although such 'replication' is logically conceivable within our space we have good reason to believe that it does not in fact occur. But on the other hand we have no experience to indicate that 'replication' does not (or does) occur as between different spaces; and we should I think therefore be strongly, and reasonably, inclined to opt for the latter hypothesis.

I have already acknowledged that there can be no scope for our normal second-person and third-person criteria of personal identity in the case of 'replication' in another space, except as between persons in that space. For the notion of life in a resurrection world that is spatially unrelated to this world is not simply an extrapolation of the conditions of our present existence. The resurrection world is not just further away from Europe than, say, America is but is not at any distance, great or small. Consequently it is impossible to travel from the one to the other. Thus the ways in which we come to judge that our vanished or our deceased colleague has been re-created in New York cease to be available when the question shifts to his re-creation in another space. Nevertheless we can still ask this question: Suppose we believe, on whatever grounds (say, revelation), that such 'replicas' do indeed come into existence as indicated in the hypothesis, how could we best describe the situation? Should we say that 'replica' Mr X is the same person as Mr X, or that he is a different person, or that it is uncertain whether he is the same or a different person? We are supposing it to be the case that after my death someone comes into existence in another space who is physically and psychologically indistinguishable from me, and who thus has all the memories that I have had up to the moment of death plus, as time goes on, further post-mortem memories. To believe that this happens would be to believe that we are faced with a new situation which may well require us to adjust some of the concepts with which we have hitherto operated. But this is a familiar enough kind of requirement. Indeed, the growth of the scientific understanding of the universe has involved a continuous evolution of our concepts, as well as occasional theoretical revolutions made possible by the formation of new concepts – and all this in response to the demands of the facts. If we were not willing to face the possibility of conceptual development and change we should, as a race, have remained at the level of primitive savages. Thus if the universe – in the sense of the range of possible objects of human consciousness – turned out to be more extensive and more complex than our present science assumes, we should I hope be more likely to enlarge our system of concepts than to close our minds to the facts.

What reconceptualization, then, would be appropriate given the phenomena outlined in our hypothesis?

I suggest that if we knew it to be a 'law of nature' that re-creation or 'replication' occurs in another space, we should be obliged to modify our concept of 'same person' to permit us to say that the 'replica' Mr X in space two is the same person as the former Mr X in space one. For such an extension of use involves far less arbitrariness and paradox than would be generated by saying either that they are not the same person or that it is uncertain whether they are the same person. They have everything in common that they could possibly have, given that they exist successively in different spaces. They are physically alike in every particular; psychologically alike in every particular; and the Mr X stream of consciousness, memory, emotion and volition continues in 'replica' Mr X where it left off at the death of earthly Mr X. In these circumstances it would, I submit, be wantonly paradoxical to rule that they are not the same person and that the space-two 'replica' ought not to think of himself as the person whose past he remembers and whom he is conscious of being.

Terence Penelhum has discussed this concept of resurrection and suggests that although the identification of resurrection-world Mr X with the former earthly Mr X is permissible it is not mandatory. He argues that in my cases number two and number three (and probably number one also) it would be a matter for decision as to whether or not to make the identification. The general principle on which he is working is that there can only be an automatic and unquestionable identification when there is bodily continuity. As soon as this is lost, identity becomes a matter for decision, with arguments arising both for and against. He concludes that although 'the identification of the former and the later persons in each of the three pictures is not absurd', yet 'in situations like these it is a matter of decision whether to say that physical tests of identity reveal personal identity or very close similarity. We can, reasonably, decide for identity, but we do not have to. And this seems to leave the description of the future life in a state of chronic ambiguity.'[9] In response to this I would agree, and have indeed already acknowledged, that these are cases for decision. Indeed, I would say that *all* cases other than ordinary straightforward everyday identity require a decision. Even physical identity, as such, is no guarantee against the need for decisions, as is shown by such imaginary cases as that of the prince whose consciousness, memory, and personality is transferred into the body of a cobbler, and vice versa.[10] Thus all cases outside the ordinary require linguistic legislation. My contention is not that the identification of resurrection-world Mr X with the former this-world Mr X is entirely unproblematic, but that the decision to identify is much more reasonable, and is liable to create far fewer problems, than would be the decision to regard them as different people.

4. TIMES AND SPACES[11]

But if the notion of spaces in the plural, and of resurrection as psycho-physical re-creation after death in another space, is accepted as meaningful, how can we understand the time relationship between the two spaces? Is not time so closely linked with space that the this-world series of events would have to be temporally as well as spatially unrelated to the resurrection-world series of events? And in that case how could someone be said to appear in the resurrection world *after* he had died in this world? Alan Olding has posed the problem:

> To speak about the simultaneity of events in the two different worlds presupposes that bodies in the two different worlds might be temporally related even though they are not spatially related, and it is not clear that this is possible. Consider, for example, a nebula in our own universe that explodes. An astronomer observing the event, and knowing how far away the nebula is from us, can calculate how long ago the explosion took place. But suppose a similar explosion occurs in the resurrection world and we ask *our* astronomer how long ago it occurred. He would not know where to begin. This is not simply because he has not been able to observe the explosion, but rather because it is logically impossible for him to have the relevant data to perform the calculation. The nebula is no distance away from him, meaning not that it is on top of him but that it is not spatially related to him . . . But now it seems to make no sense to say that the resurrection body appears at the same time as the physical body dies. No time elapses between the death of the physical body and the appearance of the resurrection body, not because the two events are simultaneous but because they are not temporally related.

That the two worlds are not temporally related has further disastrous consequences for Hick. In particular, problems arise when we attempt to ascribe memory to the resurrection person for, we might think, it is a logically necessary condition of memory that it refers to the past. Hick says of the resurrection person: 'He remembers dying; or rather he remembers being on what he took to be his

death-bed, and becoming progressively weaker until, presumably, he lost consciousness'. But the resurrection person
cannot remember being on his death-bed, because the
death-bed scene is not a past event. It is an event that occurs
in another world![12]

There is undoubtedly a problem here. But it appears to me
that what Olding's argument establishes is not the logical
impossibility of there being singular time and plural spaces,
but the impossibility of synchronizing clocks and calendars as
between two such spaces. Why should there not be a single
time sequence in which events can occur simultaneously in
different spaces, even though within each space the measurement of time must be in relation to physical movements
peculiar to that space? Presumably the divine mind, conscious
of all spaces and of the elapse of singular time, would be aware
of the temporal relationship between events in different spaces.
But the inhabitants of a given space could only be aware of the
continuity of time through spaces as an inference from their
own memories of life in another space. It could then be the
case that 'replica' Mr X in space two comes into existence
subsequently to the death of Mr X in space one, although the
only direct evidence of this available to him is his own
memory. Reversing Olding's conclusion: he remembers
dying, and therefore his dying must have been a past event.

5. MULTIPLE REPLICATION?[13]

A further difficulty has been raised, based upon the logical
spectre of the existence of two or more identical resurrection
Mr X's.[14] If it makes sense to suppose that God might create
a second-space reproduction of Mr X, then it makes sense to
suppose that he might create two or more such second-space
reproductions, namely X^2, X^3, etc. However, since X^2 and X^3
would then each be the same person as X^1, they would both
be the same person; which is absurd. Thus the existence of X^3
would prohibit us from identifying X^2 as being the same
person as X^1. Further, it has been argued by J. J. Clarke that
the bare logical possibility of X^3 has the same effect. Speaking
of several Hicks, H1, H2 and H3, he says, 'It is not even
necessary to suppose that God has *actually* created H3, for the

mere *possibility* of his doing so is as much a threat to H2's identity as is H3's actual existence. If the actual *existence* of H3 alongside H2 obliges us to refrain from identifying H2 as Hick, then the mere *possibility* of H3 ought similarly to restrain us from conferring identity. This is pinpointed by the fact that if H3 became reconstituted some while after H2, one would have to say that for a while H2 *could* conceivably have been H1, but then on H3's arrival in the resurrection world this identification ceased to be possible. This is incoherent.'[15] That is to say, so long as it is true that it could turn out, through the arrival of H3, that H2 was not after all identical with H1, that identification is not permissible. Accordingly, since there cannot be two or more re-created X's, there cannot be one re-created X. Applying his argument, appropriately, to myself, Mr Clarke concludes: 'Since multiples of re-embodied Hick cannot enter the resurrection world, then neither can one.'[16]

It might perhaps be thought that this difficulty has been avoided by so defining 'replica' that there cannot at any given time be more than one 'replica' of the same individual. As was said above, if there were two or more they would not be 'replicas' but replicas. But whilst this is, I believe, the correct conception of the entity whose existence would constitute the resurrected existence of a deceased individual, it does not obviate the 'if not two, then not one' argument. For if there were two (or more) identical post-mortem persons, none of them could be 'replica' Mr X, and thus their existence would render 'replication' impossible.

We are asked, then, to contemplate the idea of God re-creating Mr X, not as a 'one off' act but as the re-creation of a plurality of 'Mr X's', each starting life in the world to come as a re-creation of the earthly Mr X, complete with his memories, etc. I think it must be granted that if this were to happen our present system of concepts would be unable to deal with it. We should simply not know how to identify the multiple 'Mr X's'. Our concept of 'the same person' has not been developed to cope with such a situation. It can tolerate a great deal of change in an individual – the changes, for example, that occur as between the baby, the young man, the middle-aged man and the very old man. And I have argued that it could if necessary tolerate gaps in occupancy of space (an instantaneous quantum jump from one point in space to another, or divine de-creation at one place and re-creation at another), or even in occupancy of time (a person ceasing to exist at t^1 and existing again after a, preferably short, time lapse at t^2). But one thing that it will not tolerate is multiplicity. A person is by definition unique. There cannot be two people who are exactly the same in every respect, including their consciousness and memories. That is to say, if there were a situation satisfying this description, our present concept of 'person' would utterly break down under the strain.

The question, then, is whether we can properly move from the premiss that there cannot be two beings in the world to come each of whom is the same person as Mr X in this world, to the conclusion that there cannot be *one* being in the world to come who is the same person as Mr X in this world. And it seems clear to me that we cannot validly reach any such conclusion. Suppose that last week I was in New York and now I am in London. It would be absurd for someone to argue that since there cannot now be *two* JH's in London who are the same person as JH in New York last week, therefore there cannot be *one* JH in London now who is the same person as JH in New York last week! I freely grant that if there were two resurrection 'Mr X's' neither of them could be identified as the same person as the earthly Mr X, and that therefore, so far from there being two, there would not even be one. But I deny that the unrealized logical possibility of their being two resurrection 'Mr X's' makes it logically impossible for there to be one. It is a conceptual truth that if there were one resurrected 'Mr X' there could not be another; but this truth does not prohibit there being one and only one. The fact that if there were two or more 'Mr X's', none of them would be Mr X, does not prevent there being the only kind of resurrected 'Mr X' that could exist, namely a single one.

In other words, it is impossible for the universe in which we are to have incompatible characteristics. If we are in a universe in which an individual can die and be re-created elsewhere, then we are not in a universe in which an individual can die and be multiply re-created elsewhere. But this fact does not show, or even tend to show, that we cannot be in the first kind of universe.

This point can be reinforced by applying it to the idea of de-creation and re-creation within this world. Suppose that, as in my original case number one, Mr X suddenly disappears from a meeting in London and suddenly appears at a meeting in New York, the one who appears being in every respect, including consciousness of being Mr X and possession of the Mr X memories, indistinguishable from the one who disappears. I maintain that this is manifestly a logically possible occurrence; but on the 'if not two, then not one' principle it is excluded. For suppose God decided, after de-creating Mr X in London, to re-create him in New York not merely once but twice. There would then be two Mr X's – which is absurd. But it would be equally absurd to argue that because a multiple re-creation is impossible, a single re-creation is impossible. The fact that we should not know what to say, and should indeed be linguistically helpless, if the universe switched to being one in which there were two or more identical re-created individuals, does not annul the logical possibility that we are in a universe in which there can be one-for-one re-creations. It is not possible in this case to show that there cannot be an x by showing that there could not be two or more x's.

It is in fact possible to conceive of a great number of situations and worlds in which our present understanding of personal identity would fail to apply and in which we should simply not know what to say. But these do not properly tell against the claim that our ordinary concept of 'the same person' can be applied, extended but not disrupted, to the resurrection situation which I have described. It is not an acceptable form of argument that because all manner of other conceivable situations would be unintelligible, or would undermine some of our basic concepts, therefore the possibility that I have outlined is to be rejected as either unintelligible or impossible. It has to be considered on its own merits. And I hope that this discussion has in fact established the conceivability of resurrection as the divine re-creation of the individual after his earthly death as a total psycho-physical 'replica' in another space. This can however, in relation to our present knowledge, be no more than a logical possibility; and if in due course we each discover that this possibility is realized we shall undoubtedly also discover that our present bare outline of it is filled out in ways which we do not foresee. That the basic notion of psycho-physical re-creation can only be the beginning of a full picture becomes evident when we remember that an exact 'replica' of a dying man at his last moment of life would be a dying man at his last moment of life! In other words, the first thing that the resurrection body would do is to expire. For we have thus far supposed that the body being replicated is one whose heart is failing, or whose breathing is being fatally obstructed, or which is in the terminal stage of cancer – or whatever other condition is the immediate cause of death. If, then, life is to continue in the post-mortem world we must suppose a change in the condition of the resurrection body. But what might be the nature of such a change? Could we, for example, suppose that the resurrection body, instead of being identical in form with the earthly body at the moment of death, is a 'replica' of it at some earlier point of life, when it was in full health and vigour?[17] No doubt we can conceive of this; but the cost would be high. For if we envisage the resurrection body as 'replicating' the individual in the physical prime of his life at, let us say, around the age of thirty or perhaps twenty-five, he will presumably lose in the resurrection all the memories and all the development of character that had accrued to him on earth since that age. It would seem, then, that we must think of the resurrection body as being created in the condition of the earthly body, not necessarily precisely at the last moment of physical life (which can be defined in several different ways), but perhaps at the last moment of conscious personal life. And then, instead of its immediately or soon dying, we must suppose that in its new environment it is subjected to processes of healing and repair which bring it into a state of health and activity. In the case of old people – and most people die in relatively old age – we might even conceive of a process of growing physically younger to an optimum age.

The reason for postulating full initial bodily similarity between the resurrected person and the pre-resurrection person is to preserve a personal identity which we are supposing to be wholly bound up with the body. If the person is an indissoluble psycho-physical unity, it would seem that he must begin his resurrection life as identically the person who has just died, even though he may then proceed to undergo changes which are not possible in our present world.

This, at least, represents the simplest model for a resurrection world. But this model is only the most accessible of a range of possibilities. It is conceivable that in the resurrection world we shall have bodies which are the outward reflection of our inner nature but which reflect it in ways quite different from that in which our present bodies reflect our personality. In supposing this we have already begun a process of speculation which we cannot profitably pursue. The consideration of logically coherent extrapolations can take us as far as the bare idea of divine reconstitution in another world which is not spatially related to our present world; but beyond this only creative imagination can paint pictures of the possible conditions of such a world and of human life within it.

NOTES

1. On this, see chapter 9, section 4.
2. The conceivability of plural spaces is argued by Anthony Quinton in an important article to which I should like to draw the reader's attention: 'Spaces and Times', in *Philosophy*, April 1962.
3. See below, pp. 284–5.
4. Norbert Wiener, *The Human Use of Human Beings*, p. 91.
5. ibid.
6. ibid., p. 86.
7. ibid., p. 92.
8. For a discussion of Norbert Wiener's ideas in this connection, see David L. Mouton, 'Physicalism and Immortality', in *Religious Studies*, March 1972.
9. *Survival and Disembodied Existence*, pp. 100–1.
10. Locke's *Essay concerning Human Understanding*, book II, ch. 27, para. 15.
11. Much of this section repeats, with the editor's permission, material first published in 'Resurrection Worlds and Bodies', in *Mind*, July 1973.
12. 'Resurrection Bodies and Resurrection Worlds', in *Mind*, October 1970, pp. 584–5.
13. Much of this section repeats, with the editor's permission, material in 'Mr Clarke's Resurrection Also', in *Sophia*, October 1972.
14. This spectre was first raised in a different context by Bernard Williams in 'Personal Identity and Individuation', in *Proc. Aristot.*

Soc., 1956–7, reprinted in *Problems of the Self*, particularly pp. 8–11. Williams's article provoked a valuable discussion in *Analysis*, with articles by C. B. Martin (March 1958), G. C. Nerlich (June 1958 and October 1960), R. C. Coburn (April 1960), Bernard Williams (December 1960), and J. M. Shorter (March 1962). See also: Robert Young, 'The Resurrection of the Body', in *Sophia*, July 1970.

15. J. J. Clarke, 'John Hick's Resurrection', in *Sophia*, October 1971, p. 20.

16. ibid., p. 22.

17. In some medieval christian books about death it was stated that the blessed 'would be in the full vigour of their age, for at the Resurrection of the Dead they would have the same age as that of Christ at his death, thirty-two years and three months, regardless of the age at which they died' (T. S. R. Boase, *Death in the Middle Ages*, pp. 19–21). Cf. Aquinas, *Summa Theologica, III* a (Suppl.), Q81, art. 1.

CHAPTER 16

Reincarnation – the Basic Conception

1. REINCARNATION AND THE PROBLEM OF EVIL

The idea that we have lived many times before and must live many times again in this world seems as self-evident to most people in the hindu and buddhist east as the contrary idea that we came into existence at conception or birth, and shall see the last of this world at death, seems self-evident to almost everyone in the christian and post-christian west. In India, at least from the age of the Upanishads onwards,[1] the related ideas of karma and rebirth have been accepted by all religious traditions other than Islam and Christianity – hindu (both vaishnavite and shaivite), buddhist, jain, parsee (i.e. zoroastrian) and sikh – and by all the main schools of philosophy except the medieval materialists (Carvakas). The idea was accordingly seldom debated in classical indian literature,[2] and whilst modern indian writings offer abundant popular apologetic for it there has so far been surprisingly little philosophically sophisticated examination and appraisal.[3] This lack is evident, for example, even in the Proceedings of the First All-India Seminar held by the Centre of Advanced Study in Philosophy at the University of Madras in 1965, devoted to the subject of 'Karma and Rebirth'.[4] On this occasion twenty-seven of India's leading philosophers presented papers which together sought to provide detailed expositions and critical analyses of the concepts of karma and rebirth. But whilst the book contains a good deal of valuable historical information, and includes virtually all the arguments that have ever been presented for reincarnation, very few of the papers attempt a rigorous critical discussion and the proceedings as published accordingly represent a notable non-confrontation with the acute philosophical problems involved.

This tendency among indian thinkers to be blind to difficulties involved in one of their own basic positions is matched by a corresponding phenomenon in the west. For western religious thinkers have seen equally little reason to provide arguments for their own assumption that a new human soul is created, or emerges, for every new baby born. That this must be what happens has usually seemed so evident to orthodox christian theologians that they have not stopped to examine or defend its plausibility. Thus east and west have been able to see clearly the presuppositions lodged in the other's eye, whilst each has accepted without criticism the dogma that was all the time blocking its own intellectual vision; and only the interaction of eastern and western thinkers in joint discussions and conferences, individually and in groups, is gradually enabling us each to examine our own presuppositions as critically as we are accustomed to examine those of others.

Accordingly if a westerner is to understand the eastern belief in rebirth in a way approximating to that in which an oriental understands it, he must first try to see the problematic side of our prevailing western dogma. For from a theological and cultural distance the assumption of the semitic religions – Judaism, Christianity and Islam – that souls are not eternal and that a new soul comes into existence whenever a new empirical human life begins, seems utterly unreasonable, implausible and unattractive. So far as fundamental points of view can be expressed as arguments, this is because the western dogma by implication attributes the inequalities of our human condition, ultimately, to the will of the Creator. We must therefore dwell a little upon these inequalities in order to appreciate what is, from an alternative point of view, the sheer enormity and indeed moral impossibility of our tacit western assumption concerning them.

The differences in men's lots are of two kinds: there are immense variations both in the genetic inheritance which makes us each what we are as human individuals and also in the outer or environmental circumstances amidst which our lives are set.

We are not concerned here with what might be described as value-neutral human differences, such as those between the sexes, the races, and the pigmentations of mankind, except to the unhappy extent to which in particular historical contexts these have themselves come to constitute arbitrary advantages or disadvantages in the quest for human fulfilment and happiness – as for example it has been, and is, in many societies a disadvantage in respect of civil rights and educational and cultural opportunities to be a woman or to be black. Under such conditions these natural differences have become part of the injustice of human circumstances. But in addition to these differences we are born, as a result of predetermining genetic factors, with healthy or unhealthy bodies; constitutionally energetic or feeble; whole, lacking a limb, or deformed; seeing or blind; intelligent, stupid or mentally defective; and perhaps also with innate temperaments ranging from the most elevated and sensitive to the most brutish, gross and material-istic; from the happy, outward-going and loving type of personality to the miserable, grasping and selfish; from the most adventurous to the most timid; from the artistically inclined to the totally philistine; and so on through the almost limitless range of variations on the pluriform theme of human nature. And with all these innate differences men have been destined to live in immensely different circumstances according as they are born in one period of history or another and in one part of the world or another. It makes a great difference to the possibilities of human life whether one is born into a highly developed culture or into a primitive tribe, into an affluent or a poverty-stricken society, into a prosperous or a poor family; in time of peace or in time of chaos and bloodshed; in a period of settled civilization in which life can be enjoyed and the values of human existence appreciated, or in a time of anarchy and violence in which man's life is (in Hobbes's phrase) 'poor, nasty, brutish and short'. Consider the differences between birth into the dirt and starvation of an english urban slum in the nineteenth century and birth in the same period into one of the rich aristocratic families; into an illiterate outcaste family living in a mud hut in rural India in the twentieth century, or into a cultivated and wealthy brahmin family; in continental Europe during the violence and terror of the Thirty Years War or in the settled peace of the roman empire in the period of the Antonines; in a refugee family deprived of home, savings and the likelihood of work, or as the heir to a maharaja's palace and a private fortune. And so on through an endless range of examples that offer themselves from the ongoing human story.

We do not need to enter here into the question of the relative strengths of the influences exerted upon human character by inheritance and environment respectively; the important point is that both alike are factors imposed upon the individual rather than chosen by him. A qualification, or complication, is required to this statement in that some people are born in such fortunate circumstances that they have the power to change their environment for the better, usually by moving to a place where more favourable conditions prevail. Some, for example, live within a social and economic system in which it is possible to abandon an occupation or status for a better one; and some are endowed with sufficient freedom, vitality, imagination and money to enable them to emigrate to another region or country; and so on. But the great majority of human beings have never enjoyed any such privilege. They have been born into a firm 'slot' within a tribal, feudal or caste or class society, and have been so entirely moulded by their social environment as to be incapable of transcending or changing it. Thus it remains true for the great majority of human beings that our basic environmental circumstances – the time and place of our birth, with all that is consequent upon them – no less than our genetic make-up, are given to us rather than chosen by us.

Amidst all these permutations and combinations of factors forming the inner constitutive and the outer environing conditions of a human life, we have (on the prevailing western view) individually deserved neither our good nor our bad fortune. We have not created by our own free actions either the favourable or the unfavourable make-up of our genetic code; and we have not earned the fortunate or the unfortunate conditions in which our lives are set. Neither our inner constitution nor our outer circumstances are in any way appropriate to what we have hitherto been or done – for we did not exist at all prior to our birth as the particular individuals that we are, living in the particular place and in the particular historical period in which we have been born.

On a purely naturalistic view these inequalities would simply have to be accepted as details of the natural order, neither fair nor unfair, just nor unjust. If one seed is blown by the wind to take root in the shade and grows into a weak, stunted tree whilst another is blown on to well-watered fertile ground in the open sunlight and grows into a tall and healthy tree, there is no unfairness of treatment. For no one is 'treating' them; they are both parts of the same universal system of physical cause and effect. And if human life is likewise wholly a part of this same system then the variations among humans, as among animals and plants, can have no moral significance. But if, on the other hand, the religious claim is well founded that man's life is established by a higher spiritual power or process, then these disparities of human life take on an inescapable moral significance. It becomes appropriate to ask why they occur and to consider whether they are just or unjust. And on the western assumption that we have had no previous existence and have been brought into being *ab initio* in our present state of inequality, the human scene seems cruelly unfair. No justice is apparent in the fact that one has been formed, by act or permission of the spiritual power behind nature, as mentally defective, another with a strong and lucid intelligence; one blind or crippled, another whole; one to be a down-trodden slave, worked to death in an underground mine, another to live at ease and inherit the riches of human culture. These gross inequities can only be held, from a detached and impartial standpoint, to be utterly unjust and morally indefensible.[5]

This is the way in which the indian mind sees our western religious assumption of the creation of a new soul for each human birth; and it would be hard to deny that a prima facie case at least has been made out against this assumption. The insight embodied in this criticism must not be disregarded in our final reckoning.

The alternative assumption of the religions of indian origin is that we have all lived before and that the conditions of our present life are a direct consequence of our previous lives. There is no arbitrariness, no randomness, no injustice in the inequalities of our human lot, but only cause and effect, the reaping now of what we have ourselves sown in the past. Our essential self continues from life to life, being repeatedly reborn or reincarnated, the state of its karma, or the qualitative sum of its volitional activity, determining the nature of its next earthly life. As R. K. Tripathi of Banaras Hindu University says, 'The law of karma along with the doctrine of rebirth has the merit of solving one great problem of philosophy and religion, a problem which is a headache to the western religions and which finds no satisfactory solution in them. The problem is: How is it that different persons are born with an infinite diversity regarding their fortunes in spite of the fact that God is equally good to all? It would be nothing short of denying God to say that He is whimsical. If God is all-Goodness and also All-Powerful, how is it that there is so much evil and inequality in the world? Indian religions relieve God of this responsibility and make our *karmas* responsible.'[6]

We must consider later whether the idea of reincarnation does indeed offer a solution to this vexing problem or whether it merely postpones and conceals it. But first we must see what the reincarnation thesis involves, both in the more popular form of the transmigration and rebirth of the human self, and in the more complex forms developed in vedantic and buddhist philosophy. The present chapter will be concerned with the former and the next two with the latter.

2. A REINCARNATION HYPOTHESIS

We are concerned now, then, with the idea of the transmigration of the soul, in the sense of the conscious character- and (in principle) memory-bearing self, from body to body. We read in the Bhagavad Gita, 'As a man casts off his worn-out clothes and takes on other new ones, so does the embodied self cast off its worn-out bodies and enters other new ones.'[7] On this conception it is possible to say that I – the I who am now conscious; who has various psychological characteristics, such as a strong interest in philosophy; and who is now composing these sentences – have lived before and will live again in other bodies. It must accordingly be in principle possible for me now to remember my past lives, even though in fact the traumas of death and birth generally erase such memories, repressing them to a deep and normally inaccessible level of the unconscious. (That we have 'buried memories' lodged in the unconscious is proved by their retrieval under both psycho-analysis and hypnosis.) Occasionally however ordinary people do for some reason seem to remember fragments of a recent life. I shall return to these reputed memories in chapter 19.

But whatever their evidential value they are important conceptually as indicating what is meant by the doctrine of rebirth. Let me therefore now try to formulate a reincarnation hypothesis on the basis of these claimed memories of previous lives.

Consider the relation between the John Hick who is now composing these sentences, whom I shall call JH[50], and John Hick at the age of three, whom I shall call JH[3]. The main differences between them are, first, that JH[50] and JH[3] do not look in the least like one another and, second, that their conscious selves are quite different. As to the first difference, no one shown a photo of JH[3] would know, without being told, that it is a photo of JH[50] as he was forty-seven years ago, rather than of almost anybody else at the age of three. For there is very little similarity of appearance between these two visible objects. And as to the second difference, if one were to hear a tape-recording of the three-year-old JH revealing his thoughts in words and other noises one would I hope feel that JH[50] has a very different mind. No doubt the same basic personality traits are present in both the child and the man, but nevertheless the one conscious self is very different from the other – so much so that a comparison of the two would never by itself lead us to conclude that they are the same self. There are, accordingly, immense differences between JH[3] and JH[50] from the points of view both of physical and of psychological description. But nevertheless JH[50] does have at least one fragmentary memory of an event that was experienced by JH[3]. He remembers being told when his sister, who is nearly three years younger than himself, was born. Thus there is a tenuous memory link connecting JH[50] with JH[3] despite all the dissimilarities which we have noted between them; and this fact reminds us that it is possible to speak of memory across the gap of almost any degree of physical and psychological difference.[8]

Now let us see if we can say the same of someone who apparently remembers a previous life. To spell this out in terms of a well-known case: Lugdi, who was born in 1902, who lived in Muttra and who married Kedar Nath Chaubey, was (presumably) very different as regards both physical and psychological description from Shanti Devi who was born in

1926 and lived at Delhi. But Shanti Devi had (or claimed to have) certain memories of people and events experienced by Lugdi, which memories are said to have been confirmed by impartial investigators.[9] And our reincarnation hypothesis is that despite the differences between them they are in fact the same person or self, in a sense comparable with that in which JH^{50} is the same person as JH^3. In speaking in this way of the same person being born in 1902 in one part of India, later dying, and then being born again in 1926 in another part of India, we are presupposing the existence of a continuing mental entity which we may call the self or the person. The hypothesis we are considering is that just as JH^{50} is the same person as JH^3, though at a later point in the history of that person, so also Shanti Devi is the same person as Lugdi, though at a later point in that person's history. The big difference – concerning which we have to ask whether it is *too* big a difference – is that these are not now earlier and later points in the same life but in two successive lives. They are, as it were, points in different volumes of the same multi-volume work instead of in different chapters of the same volume.

If there are, as is claimed, at least a small number of cases of individuals who genuinely remember a previous life, these could be presented within either of two general theories. One theory would be that reincarnation is confined to the few exceptional cases in which memories of a former life are in fact experienced; and the other, that these cases are rare only in respect of memory but that everyone has lived before whether they have previous-life memories or not. From the point of view of one who has denied any kind of body-mind separability even a single case of reincarnation would have decisive significance. But at the present stage of the argument of this book, in which we are considering different pareschatologies, reincarnation as a rare and exceptional event would have comparatively minor significance. It could be that within a general pattern of human survival there are rare individual deviations consisting of small detours which some follow before rejoining the main stream. If this is so, it would certainly be a fact of interest; but it should not divert us from our attempt to spell out possible conceptions of the generally prevailing pattern. We ought therefore to concentrate upon the theory that *all* people, and not just a few special individuals, are subject to rebirth; and not only once, or even two or three times, but innumerable times. If there are indeed verifiable cases of memories of previous lives we shall then see these against the background of a universal process of reincarnation which however normally proceeds without producing conscious recollections.

3. THE PROBLEM OF PERSONAL IDENTITY

Let us therefore focus upon the belief that all human selves have lived many times before, even though the great majority, even perhaps some 99.9%, have no memory of any such previous lives. The claim is that just as JH[50] is the same person as JH[3], and would still be the same person even if JH[50] had not happened to remember an incident experienced by JH[3], so we are all of us the same self as innumerable apparently other selves of whom we have no knowledge or memory, who have lived one after the other in the past. And the question that I now want to raise concerns the criterion or criteria by which someone living today is said to be the same person as someone who lived, let us say, five hundred years ago, of whom he has no knowledge or memory. This is the problem that John Locke raised with his characteristic trenchant common sense:

Let any one reflect upon himself, and conclude, that he has in himself an immaterial spirit, which is that which thinks in him, and in the constant change of his body keeps him the same; and is that which he calls himself: let him also suppose it to be the same soul that was in Nestor or Ther-sites, at the siege of Troy, (for souls being, as far as we know any thing of them, in their nature indifferent to any parcel of matter, the supposition has no apparent absurdity in it,) which it may have been as well as it is now the soul of any other man: but he now having no consciousness of any of the actions of Nestor or Thersites, does or can he conceive himself the same person with either of them? Can he be concerned in either of their actions? attribute them to himself, or think them his own, more than the actions of any other man that ever existed? So that this consciousness not reaching to any of the actions of either of those men, he is no more one self with either of them, than if the soul or immaterial spirit that now informs him had been created and began to exist when it began to inform his present body, though it were ever so true that the same spirit that informed Nestor's or Thersites's body were numerically the same that now informs his. For this would no more make him the same person with Nestor, than if some of the particles of matter that were once a part of Nestor were now a part of this man; the same immaterial substance, without the same consciousness, no more making the same person by being united to any body, than the same particle of matter, without consciousness, united to any body, makes the same person.[10]

For when we remove the connecting thread of memory, as we are doing in our present hypothesis (which is to apply to the 99.9% who have no previous-life memories), we have taken away one, and a very important one, of the three strands of continuity which constitute what we normally mean by the identity of a particular human individual through time. A second strand is bodily continuity, an unbroken existence through space and time from the newly born baby to the corpse in the coffin. It may be that none of the atoms that composed the baby's body are now part of the adult's body. But nevertheless a continuously changing physical organism has existed, and has been in principle observable, composed from moment to moment of slightly different populations of atoms, but with sufficient overlap of population and of configuration from moment to moment for it to constitute what we mean by the same organism. However, this strand of bodily continuity is also taken away by our rebirth hypothesis. For there is no physical connection between someone living in India today and someone who lived, say, in ancient Greece two and a half thousand years ago. Nor does it even seem to be claimed by the doctrine of rebirth that there need be any bodily resemblance; for it is said that one is sometimes born as a man, sometimes as a woman,[11] sometimes in one and sometimes in another branch of the human race;[12] and sometimes indeed, according to one version of the doctrine, as an animal or perhaps as an insect.

Thus all that is left to be the bearer of personal identity is the third strand, which is the psychological continuity of a pattern of mental dispositions. It is this that now has to carry all the weight of the identity of two persons, one of whom is said to be a reincarnation of the other. For the only connection left, when memory and bodily continuity are excluded, is that of the psychological profile of personal character. It is claimed that B, who is A reincarnated, has the same personality traits as A. If A was proud and intolerant, B will be proud and intolerant. If A becomes in the course of his life a great artist, B will start life with a strong artistic propensity. If A was kind and thoughtful, B will be kind and thoughtful. But much now depends, for the viability of the theory, upon the *degree* of similarity that is claimed to exist between the total personalities of A at t^1 and B at t^2. Many people are kind and thoughtful, or have artistic temperaments, or are proud and intolerant; but so long as they are distinct bodily beings with different streams of consciousness and memory the fact that two individuals exhibit a common character trait, or even a number of such traits, does not lead us to identify them as the same person. Indeed, in the case of people living at the same time, to do so would be a direct violation of our concept of 'same person'. In the case of people who are not alive at the same time such an identification is not, to be sure, ruled out with the same *a priori* logical definitiveness. But nevertheless it is beset with the most formidable difficulties. For the similarity between $A(t^1)$ and $B(t^2)$ must in most cases be so general as to be capable of very numerous exemplifications, since A and B may be of different races and sexes, and products of different civilizations, climates and historical epochs. There can be *general* similarities of character found in such qualities as selfishness and unselfishness, introverted or extroverted types of personality, artistic or practical bents, and in level of intelligence, between let us say a female tibetan peasant of the twelfth century BC and a male american college graduate of the twentieth century AD. But such general similarities would never by themselves lead or entitle us to identify the two as the same person. Indeed, to make an identity claim on these grounds, in a case in which there is neither bodily continuity nor any link of memory, would commit us to the principle that all individuals who are not alive at the same time and who exhibit rather similar personality patterns are to be regarded as the same person. But in that case there would be far too many people who qualify under this criterion as being the same individual. How many people in each generation before I was born had character traits similar to those that I have? Probably many hundreds of thousands. On this basis alone, then, it would never have occurred to anyone that I am the same person as some particular individual in the past. On this basis I could equally well be a reincarnation of any of many thousands of people in each former generation. Thus this criterion of character similarity is far too broad and permissive; if it establishes anything it establishes too much and becomes self-defeating.

It may however be replied to this objection that although people normally have no recollection of their former lives, nevertheless there is an unconscious thread of memory linking each life with one and only one series of previous lives. This continuously lengthening thread of memory picks out from all the lives lived in the past those which constituted the previous existences of a particular present individual, though these memories remain latent until a final moment of total recall as the reincarnating soul at last attains to enlightenment. When we speak of the individual who lived, say, a hundred years ago and who was *me* in a previous incarnation, we are accordingly speaking of a uniquely identified individual whose experience is totally recorded in the same memory chain that is now recording my own experiences. For memory, whether conscious or unconscious, does not link me with the lives of all those in the past who share certain character traits with me but only with one particular life or succession of lives.

With the memory link restored in this way, reincarnation stands thus far as a viable hypothesis. I shall discuss in chapter 19 various problems connected with this memory link, but will conclude the present chapter by returning to the initial claim that the idea of rebirth solves the problem of the inequality of human birth and circumstances. I suggest that the solution offered is not after all a real one. For either there is a first life, characterized by initial human differences, or else (as in orthodox hindu belief) there is no first life but a beginningless regress of incarnations, in which case the explanation of the inequalities of our present life is endlessly postponed and never achieved. For we are no nearer to an ultimate explanation of the circumstances of our present birth when we are told that they are consequences of a previous life if that previous life has in turn to be explained by reference to a yet previous life, and that by reference to another, and so on in an infinite regress. One can affirm the beginningless character of the soul's existence in this way; but one cannot then claim that it renders either intelligible or morally acceptable the inequalities of our present lot. The solution has not been produced but only postponed to infinity. And if instead we are to postulate a first life (as Hinduism does not) we should then have to hold either that souls are created as identical psychic units or else as embodying, at least in germ, the differences that have subsequently developed. If the latter, the problem of human inequality arises at the point of that initial creation; if the former, it arises with equal force with regard to the environment which has produced all the manifold differences that have arisen between initially identical units. Thus if there is a divine creator he cannot escape along any of these paths from an ultimate responsibility for the character of his creation, including the gross inequalities inherent within it. And if there is no creator, but only a universal and beginningless process of rebirth, that process, again, cannot be characterized as just or good.

NOTES

1. There have been debates among historians of indian thought as to whether the karma-rebirth conception is or is not pre-upanishadic; and the prevailing view today seems to be that it is not found in the vedic hymns of the aryan conquerors, but was probably a fundamental belief of the ancient inhabitants of India and was adopted in due course by the Brahmins who wrote the Upanishads. See, e.g., E. Geoffrey Parrinder, *The Indestructible Soul*, p. 78. See also J. F. Staal, *Advaita and Neoplatonism*, pp. 51-3.

2. The materialist school of the Carvakas did criticize the rebirth doctrine, and provoked replies; but this source of criticism died out by the late medieval period. Ninian Smart describes the arguments used in his *Doctrine and Argument in Indian Philosophy*, ch. 12.

3. One of the first such attempts has recently been published – G. C. Nayak, *Evil, Karma and Reincarnation*.

4. *Indian Philosophical Annual*, 1965.

5. Cf. Swami Nikhilananda, *Man in Search of Immortality*, p. 22.

6. R. K. Tripathi, *Problems of Philosophy and Religion*, pp. 108–9.

7. II, 22, trans. R. C. Zaehner, p. 133.

8. On the limitations of memory, however, see chapter 20, section 4.

9. The case is described by Ian Stevenson, *The Evidence for Survival from Claimed Memories of Former Incarnations*, in *Journal of the American SPR*, April and July 1960, reprinted as a booklet, pp. 17–18. Stevenson also cites some of the literature discussing the case.

10. *An Essay concerning Human Understanding*, book II, ch. 27, para. 14. Leibniz made essentially the same point when he asked, 'What good would it do you, sir, to become king of China on con-dition of forgetting what you have been? Would it not be the same thing as if God at the same time he destroyed you created a king in China?' (*Philosophischen Schriften*, vol. IV, p. 300).

11. 'It [the soul] is not female, nor is it male; nor yet is it neuter. Whatever body it takes to itself, by that it is held' (*Svetashvatara Upanishad*, V, 10 (*The Principal Upanishads*, p. 741)).

12. What I am calling the more popular conception of reincarnation has been very fully developed in Theosophy, and in C. W. Lead-beater's *The Soul's Growth through Reincarnation* the successive incarnations of a number of different souls are described. One such is 'Erato' who in his most recent incarnation was John Varley (1850–1933), an English landscape-painter and a disciple of Madame H. P. Blavatsky, founder of the Theosophical Society. Erato's last 17 lives are described, beginning with one in 19,245 BC in Chaldea. We are told in volume I that in these 17 lives Erato was a man on 10 occasions and a woman on 7, and was at different times a Chinese, an Indian, a European, a Japanese, an Eskimo, a South American, an Egyptian, and an inhabitant of the now submerged continent of Atlantis. (Incidentally, we are also told that his average length of life was 55½ years, and that the average period between his incarnations was 1264 years. An average life-span of 55½ years is surprising in view of the fact that the average expectation of life has only risen to this level in developed countries during little more than the last hundred years.)

CHAPTER 17

The Vedantic Theory of Reincarnation

I. THE VEDANTIC PHILOSOPHIES

We turn now to the more complex and subtle conception of karma and rebirth developed in philosophical Hinduism, and particularly in the Vedanta. In its essentials this theory is common both to the Vedanta and to the other orthodox schools of indian philosophy,[1] so that in examining it we are dealing with a central concept of indian religious thought. The buddhist variation will be discussed in the next chapter.

Vedantic philosophy itself falls into two main streams – the monistic (*advaita*: non-dualist) and non-theistic system, whose great creative synthesizer was Shankara (AD 788–820); and the 'qualified non-dualist' (*vishishtadvaita*[2]) theistic stream, whose outstanding thinker was Ramanuja (11th century AD, his precise dates being unknown). Within their different metaphysical frameworks both teach essentially the same theory of karma and rebirth; but we must briefly note the broad features of their respective 'pictures of the universe' before examining the common doctrine of reincarnation which occurs within them.

In the monistic system the ultimate reality, Brahman, is pure undifferentiated consciousness or, as is also said, a trinity of being-consciousness-bliss (*satcitananda*). Nirguna Brahman, or Brahman-in-itself, is indescribable and beyond all qualities, including personality; but Saguna Brahman, or Brahman as known to man, is God (Isvara), the permanent personification of Reality in relation to personal creatures. The creative power of Brahman, *maya*, expresses itself in the existence of the universe, in which the Infinite Consciousness is associated with *maya* to constitute a plurality of finite consciousnesses, the *jivas* or *jivatmans*. These finite consciousnesses, being products of *maya*, are wrapped in the illusion of separateness from the one universal consciousness, Atman/Brahman.

Accordingly *jivatmans* are the pure consciousness of Brahman qualified or limited by *maya*. In an often used vedantic simile, Atman is like space and the individual *jivas* like space in jars.[3] When the jars are destroyed the space which they enclosed remains part of space. Likewise the *jivas* merge into the infinite Atman when the ignorance (*avidya*) which constitutes their finite boundaries is removed in enlightenment (*moksha*).

There are, then, a limitless number of individual *jivas*; and yet this plurality and individuality is ultimately illusory, for when different *jivas* attain to consciousness of themselves as Atman the distinction between them ceases to exist: all *jivas* as Atman or Brahman are one and the same. And the theory of karma and rebirth is concerned with the *jiva* and its evolution from the state of illusion to true self-consciousness. For the innumerable souls, as 'sparks of divinity'[4] which have become illusorily separated from their source, ground, and identity in Brahman, are being gradually purged of this illusion through a succession of rebirths in a process which is eventually to culminate in the attainment of *moksha* (or *mukti*), liberation, the realization of identity with the sole ultimate Reality, Brahman, unspoiled by an illusory sense of separate identity – a conception which has affinities in the west in Orphism, Neoplatonism and Gnosticism and in the recent theology of Paul Tillich.

This is the broad picture painted by the monistic philosophy of advaita Vedanta. From the alternative starting-point of hindu theism (*vishishtadvaita*) the Ultimate Reality, beyond even Brahman, is personal, the *Bhagavan* (Lord), and is variously known as Isvara, or Vishnu, or Krishna. He has created the multitude of *jivas*, this creative act being thought of as his *lila*, the divine play or sport. That is to say, the creation of the multitude of finite souls is an expression of the super-abundant exuberance and energy of the infinite divine life. *Samsara*, the round of rebirths, is not a purposive activity directed eschatologically to an end beyond itself but is, like a dance or a piece of play, an end in itself. As such it is beginning-less and endless – a divine breathing out and then breathing in again of the realm of *maya* (*maya* being ultimately simply the exercise of divine creativity), within which souls are gradually moving through illusion towards conscious communion with

God. But as non-purposive movement the cyclical life of the creaturely universe will have no end or completion: there is no thought of an eschaton in which God's purpose will have been finally fulfilled. Each *jiva* may eventually attain to liberation, worshipping and reflecting the glory of God; but as there is an infinite number of them the liberation of each still leaves an infinity of souls in the never-ending process of *samsara*.

From these two starting-points, monistic and theistic, both systems recognize the present existence of an unlimited multitude of living *jivas*, and develop their doctrine of karma and rebirth as an account of the path along which these are destined to go.

2. THE JIVA (SOUL)

We must therefore now look more closely at the hindu concept of the *jiva* or *jivatman*. It seems best, following many indian scholars (including S. Radhakrishnan and T. M. P. Mahadevan[5]), to render *jiva* and *jivatman* as 'soul'. The term 'soul' has of course been used to refer to any of a whole family of notions, named by such terms as 'self', 'higher self', 'elusive self', 'psyche', 'mind', 'ego', 'I', 'transcendental unity of apperception', 'metaphysical subject', etc., and there is no single clearly defined western concept of soul available for comparison with the *jiva*. But since the concept of the *jiva* does not stand at any greater distance from some of the soul family of concepts than these do from each other, it can be less misleadingly seen as another member of this family – even though a fairly remote cousin to some other members – than as an entirely different and unrelated concept with no parallels or affinities to justify even a cautious and commentary-protected translation. I shall accordingly use 'soul' as the english version of the two interchangeable sanscrit terms *jiva* and *jivatman*.

The soul, then, in hindu thought is eternal in that it is, illusion apart, identical with the eternal Brahman/Atman. But as *jiva* – that is, as illusorily separate individual – it is asserted to have existed eternally into the past though not, as a separate entity, to continue eternally into the future. In respect of temporal endurance it is thus the obverse of sempiternal, sempiternity being defined in western theology as the status of the soul as created, and thus having a beginning, but as enjoying thereafter an unending existence. The *jiva* is not, or at any rate need not be, eternal into the future because there lies before it the possibility of attaining to the enlightenment which liberates it from the cycle of rebirths. But on the other hand it is insisted that the soul is eternal into the past. For it is claimed that the theory offers a religiously satisfying explanation of the inequalities and apparent injustices of human life as we find it; and if these were to be traced back to an initial state of inequality, the responsibility for all the evils suffered by mankind would ultimately have to rest upon the creator (Isvara) or the source (Brahman). Only if the series is infinite, and therefore without any first member, can the hindu mind be satisfied that each *jiva* is responsible for its own mixture of suffering and joy; for it is the karma (i.e. action) of its previous lives that has formed the conditions of its present existence. I have already argued that in fact such a conception does nothing to justify the present inequalities of our human experience.[6] It merely points for their justification to a previous life, from which we are then referred to a yet earlier life, and so on in a regression which never terminates and therefore never produces its promised justification. Nevertheless despite this evident difficulty it is a deeply rooted indian belief that the doctrine of rebirth does in fact solve the twin problems of human inequality and suffering.

There are, then, an infinity of souls existing beginninglessly throughout past time. But I, the conscious self who am now composing these sentences, and you, the conscious self now reading them, are not – or rather are not consciously – two of these eternal souls. We are psycho-physical egos, illusorily distinct persons of the kind which exist only in this realm of *maya*. Whereas the psycho-physical ego is a man or a woman, the *jiva* is neither male nor female.[7] Again, whereas the psycho-physical ego is not normally conscious of the eternal past of the *jiva* which in a sense it is, there are depths of the *jiva* in which all this past experience is recorded. Each psycho-physical ego is thus a temporary expression or organ or instrument of an eternal soul, one indeed of the succession of such expressions which constitute the successive rebirths of that soul. For that the soul is involved in *maya* means that it has become enclosed in a set of 'bodies' or coverings, thought of on the analogy of a number of sheaths successively enclosing the blade of a sword and all having to be discarded before the blade is free.

3. THE LINGA SHARIRA (SUBTLE BODY)

There are three of these 'bodies' or sheaths; the gross body (*sthula sharira*), the subtle body (*suksma sharira* or *linga sharira*) and the causal body (*karana sharira*). So far as the essential logic of the idea of rebirth is concerned we can conflate the latter two into one, the subtle body, and concentrate upon the relation between this and the gross body. This latter is the physical organism which begins to be formed at conception and begins to disintegrate at death. But it is survived by the subtle body, which then influences the development of another physical body as its next vehicle of incarnation. It must however at once be added that the phrase 'subtle body' is liable to mislead the western reader. For the subtle body is not, in the philosophically more sophisticated versions of the theory, conceived of as a material entity in the western sense of 'material'.[8] It does not occupy space, and accordingly it has no shape or size, and is indeed not a body at all in the normal western sense of the term. It is however material in the quite different sense given by the fundamental indian dichotomy between consciousness (*cit*) and everything that lacks consciousness (*acit*) and is called *prakrti*, nature or matter – this being identical with *maya*.[9] In western terms, the subtle body must accordingly be described as a mental rather than as a physical entity; and indeed one hindu expositor speaks of it simply as 'the psychical part of the psycho-physical organism',[10] and another says, 'The subtle body is called mind because mind is the chief factor of the subtle body.'[11] It is composed, according to the traditional doctrine, of seventeen elements – the cognitive intellect (*buddhi*), the deliberative mind (*manas*), the five powers of perception, the five powers of activity, and the five vital forces. But so far as its function in the theory of rebirth is concerned we may describe the *linga sharira* as a mental entity or substance which is modified by, or which registers and thus (metaphorically) 'embodies' the moral, aesthetic, intellectual and spiritual dispositions that have been built up in the course of living a human life, or rather in living a succession of human and perhaps also non-human lives.

These modifications of the subtle body are called *samskaras*, impressions. But they are not thought of on the analogy of static impressions, like marks on paper, but rather as dynamic impressions, modifications of a living organism expressed in its pattern of behaviour. We ordinarily think of the human mind and personality as being modified in all sorts of ways by its own volitions and responses to experience. A repeated indulgence in selfish policies reinforces one's egoistic tendencies; a constant exercise of the discipline of precise thought makes for more lucid and exact thinking; devoted attention to one or other of the arts quickens and deepens one's aesthetic sensibilities; spiritual meditation opens the self to the influence of its spiritual environment; and so on. These familiar facts can be expressed by saying that the *linga sharira* is the seat of the various emotional, spiritual, moral, aesthetic and intellectual modifications which are happening to us all the time in the course of our human existence. Such modifications are most adequately characterized in contemporary western categories as mental dispositions and I shall follow a number of indian philosophers in making this equation.

We have already noted that the subtle body belongs to the material (*prakrti*) side of the fundamental dichotomy between consciousness and *prakrti*; and it is for this reason that it is appropriate in the context of indian thought to call it a body; for as finite, changeable, and devoid of consciousness[12] it has more in common with the physical body than with consciousness. To appreciate this we have to conceive of thoughts, emotions and desires as things, and as things that are capable of existing apart from consciousness as dispositional energies able, when linked with consciousness, to guide action. Through like grouping with like in mutual reinforcement, such dispositions form relatively stable and enduring structures whose 'shape' is the character of the person whose thoughts have formed it. Such a dispositional structure survives the extinction of consciousness in death and continues to exist as an entity, the subtle body or *linga sharira*, which will later become linked to a new embryo. So Anima Sen Gupta says, 'When a man dies, his thought-energy in the form of *samskaras* do not get scattered in space; but this energy remains stored up in the subtle body.'[13] And it is this subtle body, this bundle of *samskaras*, that is reincarnated. The subtle body may accordingly be characterized as a psychic organism consisting of a structure of mental dispositions, but differing from a 'person' in that it lacks self-consciousness. It is thus very close to what C. D. Broad has called the 'psychic factor'.[14] Broad developed his concept of the psychic factor to provide a possible explanation of the phenomenon of trance mediumship. When an individual dies the mental aspect of his being persists, not however as a complete conscious personality but as a constellation of mental elements – dispositions, memories, desires, fears, etc. – constituting a psychic factor which may hold together for a considerable time or may soon disintegrate into fragments. Broad suggests that such a psychic grouping, sufficiently cohesive to be identified as consisting of the memories and dispositional character of a particular deceased individual, may become connected with a medium in a state of trance, thus generating a temporary conscious personality which is a conflation of certain persisting mental elements of the deceased and the living structure of the medium. The theory of reincarnation can be seen as taking this concept further – as indeed Broad himself noted[15] – and claiming that the psychic factor which separates from the body at death subsequently becomes fused, not with the developed life-structure of a medium (though this also need not necessarily be excluded) but with the still undeveloped life-structure of a human embryo. It then influences the growth of the embryo, as a factor additional to its genetic inheritance. As P. S. Sastri says, 'The parents provide the physical body; and the subtle body comes with the self from its previous incarnations.'[16] However, not all the dispositions or *samskaras* (and in any case not normally the memory dispositions) are re-embodied on each occasion, but only those which are especially dominant and demanding of further activity and expression.

4. KARMA AND THE MANY SPHERES OF EXISTENCE

It must be added, in further filling out the hindu picture, that in addition to this world of physical bodies there are held to be many other higher and lower realms or planes of existence in which *jivas* can live in their other 'bodies'. In these various heavenly, purgatorial, and hellish spheres the *jiva* reaps the

consequences of good and evil deeds done in this world. Thus
its experiences in these other realms reflect the good and bad
desert of its preceding life. But it is only in the physical body,
and therefore only on this earth, that the soul is able to exercise
its limited but real freedom and responsibility and thus to
undergo further stages of development towards the ultimate
self-awareness of *moksha*. It must therefore return repeatedly
to earthly life until it attains to its final liberation.

In addition to punishments (and rewards) undergone in the
subtle body in non-physical realms, there may be regressive
incarnations in animal, bird, fish, and insect bodies,[17] popularly
conceived of as punishments but more philosophically regarded
as being due to some overmastering disposition of a brutish
and elemental kind which can most easily work itself out in the
life of an animal supposedly characterized by that quality:
for example, an obsessively gluttonous character might expend
his excess of gluttony through the life of a pig. In such cases,
however, it would be misleading (if not meaningless) to say
that the human glutton has been reborn as a pig; rather, part
of a continuing *linga sharira*, a part consisting of an over-charge
of gluttonous appetite, has been incarnated in the life of a pig
whilst the rest remains temporarily inactive.

In general, the relation between the sub-human and human
spheres is depicted as a hierarchy of lower and higher forms
of life through which souls progress towards the human level,
at which alone liberation (*moksha*) is possible. Thus a soul now
embodied in human life has in the far distant past been
through innumerable embodiments in the animal kingdom;
and the animals, insects, birds and fishes around us are all
bearers of evolving psychic life within the same universal
process in which we, as rational creatures, are playing our own
part. Thus they too are all ultimately expressions of Brahman.
This is the theoretical foundation for the hindu ideal of respect
for life in all its forms, and for the vegetarianism practised by
many Hindus.

These extensions of the scope of the doctrine of rebirth into
both the animal kingdom and the heavenly spheres, although
not originally developed for this purpose, suggest a reply to
the difficulty posed by the current population explosion.[18] For
if there were a finite and constant number of souls each

producing its own succession of embodied selves one would expect the world's population to be more or less stable. But in fact it has been growing through recorded history and has during the present century been mushrooming at a tremendous rate; and this might seem to be inconsistent with the reincarnation theory. However if, as hindu tradition teaches, there is an unlimited number of souls, only a portion of the careers of each of which is occupied by successive incarnations in this world, the remainder being spent in various other spheres of existence, then one can suppose that our present rapid expansion of population corresponds to a sharp increase (of unknown cause) in the proportion – if one can speak of proportions within an infinite number – of the total who are currently on earth. Or again, taking account of the idea of animal incarnations, one can suppose that what is happening in the human population explosion is that an increasing number of karmic histories are moving up out of animal into human life. Or one could combine these two speculations, calling upon each to account for part of the phenomenon to be explained. The problem of reconciling such explanations with the natural causes at work – for example, decreasing infant mortality and increasing life expectancy due to the progress of medical science – is part of the wider problem of reconciling a reincarnational account of the circumstances of human life and character with the sciences of genetics and ecology.[19]

The process of the working out of the soul's karma through a series of earthly lives is not thought of, by many hindu thinkers at least, as a consciously directed process. It is thought of as proceeding automatically, in accordance with a system of moral and psychic law, comparable with natural law, without having to be planned or guided by anyone. This is as true in the theistic *vishishtadvaita* systems as in the non-theistic *advaita* systems; for according to the former the world of *maya* which Isvara has created by emanation out of his own being is an autonomously functioning karmic process. The dynamic within this process is desire or appetite directed towards the world of *maya*, and it is this that leads the soul on from life to life until all desire has at last ended, releasing us from the egoistic appetites which bind us to the realm of *maya*. Other hindu thinkers, however, attribute an important part to God

(Isvara) in presiding over the mechanism of reincarnation, and see him as fulfilling the role of an unlimited moral intelligence continuously designing the course of each individual's career and the complex interactions of the multitude of karmic histories.[20] Indeed, the need for such an intelligence to direct the process of karma has been used in *saivite* teaching as an argument for the existence of God.[21]

5. GROUNDS FOR BELIEF IN REINCARNATION

We may now ask in what sense, and on what grounds, such an account of the hidden workings of the universe is affirmed to be true. Is the doctrine of reincarnation being put forward as a claim about what is actually happening, or as a symbolic or mythological idea which is devoid of factual content?

We have seen that at one point at which empirical confirmation or disconfirmation might have seemed possible, namely in relation to the changing size of the world's human population, the theory's internal elaboration avoids a confrontation. But there is another point at which it could be presented as a factual claim which connects with the circumstances of human life. For is not each karmic history supposed to form a gradual moral and spiritual progress, with some advance normally taking place in each successive incarnation? This question applies with special force to the evolutionary picture of *samsara* painted by Sri Aurobindo, one of the great modernizers of hindu thought. 'The true foundation of the theory of rebirth', he says, 'is the evolution of the soul, or rather its efflorescence out of the veil of Matter and its gradual self-finding.'[22] Again, 'What we are is a soul of the transcendent Spirit and Self unfolding itself in the cosmos in a constant evolutionary embodiment of which the physical side is only a pedestal of form corresponding in its evolution to the ascending degrees of the spirit, but the spiritual growth is the real sense and motive.'[23] But should we not in that case expect a gradually rising moral and spiritual level of human life to make itself evident over the centuries as the procession of evolving souls moves slowly upwards? Ought not the general spiritual state of mankind today to be observably superior to its state one thousand, or two thousand, years ago? If this is indeed a correct understanding of the implications of the rebirth hypothesis, is any such spiritual progress through the ages in fact discernible? There has undoubtedly been progress of several kinds. There has for example been an immense accumulation of scientific knowledge and technological know-how. But has there been any comparable, or even less than comparable, moral and spiritual progress? Regretfully, I am inclined to think not. And the lack of it, if it is indeed lacking, might prompt one to prefer the alternative idea that the spiritual growth of each individual takes place in other realms beyond this world rather than through successive earthly lives, an idea which is developed further in chapter 20.

On the other hand the evolutionary picture of *samsara* as a gradually ascending movement could be developed in a way which avoids any immediate test by historical observations. For it could be said that each soul produces a phenomenal self only once every, say, three thousand years, so that the moral and spiritual progress of a karmic history cannot yet be evident within the short span of our human records. It may thus be claimed that such progress is in fact taking place along the axis of earthly history as each among the revolving population of souls returns again and again, but that this progress is not yet sufficient to be registered in man's historical consciousness. However, such progress, it might be said, will become evident when it has accumulated sufficiently, so that the doctrine remains at this point open to future observational confirmation.

The more traditional vedantist view, however, is that there will never be any discernible spiritual progress in the realm of *maya*. There is only an unending cycle of births and deaths, with no direction or pattern, *samsara* being conceived non-eschatologically as purposeless and endless – except in the sense that the individual soul can escape from it, so that for the liberated consciousness *samsara* eventually ceases to exist. Here we have the ancient upanishadic teaching of the emanation of finite existence from Brahman and its return to Brahman – a divine breathing out and then breathing in again of the phenomenal world, each occurrence of the world, or *kalpa*, including entire cycles of karma to be lived out and endured. Here, it might seem, we have a metaphysical picture of reality which entirely eludes empirical testing. And within this picture reincarnation is itself an idea to which no verification procedure could ever be appropriate. The case for adopting it would not then rest upon the sense that it is supposed to make of the facts of human experience. It would rather depend upon the recommending of a wider system of religious ideas, namely the vedantic philosophy as a whole, which includes reincarnation as an element within it.

However at this point a reference, characteristic of indian in distinction from western philosophy, is made to the direct experience of those who have attained release or enlightenment (*mukti*, *moksha*). They have detached their minds from the material world, cutting the cords of valuation and desire which bind the rest of us to our earthly environment. As a result of this inner liberation and consequent realization of their identity with the eternal Atman they now for the first time see reality with a vision undistorted by illusion. And such enlightened souls still in this world (*jivanmuktas*) can, we are told, vouch for the truth of the vedantic picture of the universe.[24] Again, as a closely related claim, the practice of yoga (which is a method of developing spiritual capacities) can enable one to enter into higher states of consciousness in which aspects of reality that lie beyond the scope of the discursive intellect are opened to the mind's view. On the basis of these higher cognitions the yogi is able to declare the true nature of man and of the universe of which he is a part. Such claims are entirely consonant with the distinctive indian understanding of philosophy as a method of attaining to direct experience of reality. For in India philosophy has always been conceived as an existential path to salvation by knowledge rather than as a detached exercise in theory-construction or conceptual clarification. From this point of view the ultimate appeal is not to the deliverances of reason inspecting the logical relations between propositions but to the direct spiritual insight of enlightened souls.

It is very difficult for the non-enlightened and the untrained in yoga to know what to make of this proposed ground of belief. He cannot, without impugning the cognitive value of religious experience, deny the propriety in principle of such an appeal. He cannot therefore deny the right of one who enjoys a rare form of cognitive experience to take account of it when forming his own beliefs. If the *jivanmukta's* or the yogi's experience is sufficiently coherent and lasting then, in so far as the one who enjoys this experience is a rational person, he is rationally entitled to believe what his special experience leads him to believe, providing this is not excluded by internal inconsistency or challenged by contradiction with what he already has good reason to believe on other grounds. In the case of the kind of metaphysical knowledge said to be revealed in *moksha*, or in the yogic experience of deep meditation, internal consistency is not hard to achieve, nor is it hard to avoid contradiction with other fields of knowledge - unless of course it is held to be an item of such knowledge that there are no metaphysical realities. Accordingly, one who appeals to his own personal experience of insight achieved in a higher state of consciousness, whether that of the *jivanmukta* or of the yogi, is in a strong position so far as the basis of his own personal belief is concerned.

However, the more difficult question, and for most of us the more important one, is not whether the *jivanmukta* or the yogi himself can claim to have good grounds for believing what he believes, but whether others who do not share his special experience are thereby provided with a sufficient reason for adopting that belief. In considering this we have to look beyond the claim, for example, that the extremely complex picture of reality presented in the writings of Sri Aurobindo reflects his own personal experience in higher states of consciousness and thus has behind it the authority of direct spiritual vision. For the comparative study of revelations reminds us that a like claim is made for the very different teachings of the Buddha, the Enlightened One *par excellence*; and, on a level more comparable with that of Sri Aurobindo, for the teachings of Ramakrishna; and again for the theosophical teaching said to have been imparted to Madame Blavatsky by mahatmas in Tibet. These latter two, it is true, share with Aurobindo's philosophy a basic vedantic framework of thought; but their distinctive contributions differ, and each school of thought is regarded by the others as eccentric and misleading. Thus the appeal to special knowledge received in higher states of awareness is to some extent vitiated by the existence of a plurality of rival deliverances allegedly from the same transcendent source.

But more broadly, individuals in many different ages and cultures have attained to *moksha* in the basic sense of reaching the goal of the spiritual life, often described in the east as the realization of unity with Ultimate Reality and in the west as perfect reconciliation with God and union with his will, accompanied in each case by peace, bliss, and insight into reality. In their different ways Gautama the Buddha, Jesus the Christ, Mohammed, St Francis, Guru Nanak, Ramakrishna, may all be described as *jivanmuktas*, souls who were free from the domination of the world and were in harmony with reality. And surrounding them is a great cloud of supporting witnesses – muslim Sufis, hindu Bhaktas, christian and buddhist saints and mystics. As we listen to the world-wide company of those who have spoken about the divine Reality out of direct personal experience we find that they have conceptualized their experiences in many different and often incompatible ways, each in accordance with his own environing tradition and culture. It thus seems an inevitable conclusion that as well as expressing an authentic spiritual experience their teachings also include culture-relative philosophical concepts and theological theories. Are we then to hold that all these concepts and theories are validated by the fact that some among those who have learned to use them have attained to *moksha*, or to fellowship with God? Does the grace of sainthood, or the attainment of *moksha*, or of salvation, entail that all the saint's or the *jivanmukta's* metaphysical beliefs are true? No such conclusion is necessary; and since it would create difficult problems concerning the conflicting truth-claims of the different theological traditions it is to be rejected. And having rejected it we shall be chary of the appeal to yogic experiences and to the enlightenment of the *jivanmukta* as a guarantee of any one of the descriptions of the structure and process of the universe that have been promulgated on this basis.

There is one further ground offered in the context of the indian religious tradition for belief in reincarnation – namely that it is a revealed truth. It is part of *sruti*, the eternal verbalized wisdom contained in the Vedas and Upanishads.

Written revelations constitute the core of a number of great religious traditions – not only the Vedas and Upanishads as the core of Hinduism, but the Bible as the core of Christianity (and within it the 'Old Testament' as the core of Judaism), the Koran as the core of Islam, the Granth as the core of Sikhism, and so on. And in each case the acceptance of a particular scripture as an infallible authority is a function of commitment (including the commitment that often results from attachment by birth) to a particular religious community and its faith. Thus whilst the appeal to the authority of the scriptures is in order within a community of faith it lacks force beyond the borders of that community. What are sacred texts to the in-group are to the outside world the ancient religious writings of an alien culture. If they carry authority it is not that of divine oracles but such appeal as the writings themselves, as human literature, are able to make to the mind and conscience of the reader. Accordingly the fact that, for Hindus, *sruti* endorses and indeed guarantees the belief in reincarnation cannot function as a decisive argument in the context of trans-cultural and inter-religious discussion.

Another more empirical set of arguments commonly used claims that various phenomena of human life, otherwise inexplicable, become intelligible when understood in terms of reincarnation. It is said that the newly born infant's instinct to suck must have been learned in previous lives;[25] that the universal human fear of death presupposes a knowledge derived from having approached death many times before;[26] that love at first sight, and quickly formed friendships, are explained by the individuals having been lovers or friends in a previous life;[27] that 'infant geniuses' and striking precocity in children can only be explained if we assume that they are using skills and knowledge already acquired in other lives;[28] that the differences between children of the same parents require us to postulate the existence of souls with already developed characters.[29] But none of these arguments is particularly impressive to those not already predisposed to the idea of reincarnation. The baby's instinct to suck and the adult's fear of death have direct survival value and can readily be explained as evolutionary developments. Love at first sight is so personal and individual an experience as to be indeed something of a mystery – but hardly more so than love which is not at first sight. The differences between children of the same parents are explicable by the processes of genetic inheritance. The child genius – Mozart composing minuets before he was four; Beethoven playing in public at eight and publishing compositions at nine; Handel giving concerts at nine; Schubert composing at eleven; Chopin playing concertos in public before he was nine; and many more – may well be instances of exceptionally fortunate genetic combinations.

There is however, it must be granted, a residual mystery in human individuality; and some have assumed that this mystery can be removed by postulating reincarnation. Thus M. Yamunacharya says,

> Take an individual child that is born. No one can aver that the child has a psyche which is a *tabula rasa*. The child brings with it certain innate endowments which constitute its individuality apart from the instinctual apparatus which it inherits in common with all children, and even with all animals. There are many elements in the composition of the child's nature which can, of course, be traced to heredity. They become traceable to the parents of the child. They include both physical peculiarities and temperamental elements. Physical features are inherited including the body build. Even some psychological features become inherited. But according to Indian thinkers, the individuality of the child can never be exhaustively traced to the parental elements thus inherited by the child . . . The individual child that is born is, according to this hypothesis, a product not merely of the father-element and the mother-element, but also of another incalculable factor which constitutes its uniqueness and individuality as a person. This element comes from a source different from those traceable to heredity. This is said to be the element of individual Karma.[30]

But if we seek to account for the ultimate individual uniqueness of the empirical self by reference to the contribution of the reincarnating *linga sharira*, have we really advanced towards a genuine explanation? For (as was noted above[31]) if the element of unique individuality is traced back to a previous life, and then to one before that, and so on, we either come eventually to a first life in which the problem still confronts us in its full force, or else the series of lives is without beginning and we have merely substituted one mystery for another. Thus reincarnation's supposed elucidation of the mystery of individuality is spurious; at best the solution has been indefinitely postponed and at worst the problem has been concealed.

6. A FACTUAL HYPOTHESIS?

We may now apply these various considerations to the question, Does the affirmation of the doctrine of reincarnation constitute a factual assertion, which either corresponds or fails to correspond with reality, or is it the painting of a metaphysical picture without factual confent, such that its truth or falsity makes no difference to the course of actual or possible human experience? Does the belief in reincarnation have the logical character of a factual truth-claim, or only of an illuminating myth – comparable for example with the christian myth of the fall of man from a state of original perfection?

The answer would seem to be that the doctrine of reincarnation, in some forms, makes sufficient connection with actual or possible human experience to constitute it a factual claim. For the assertion that we may eventually attain to a level of consciousness in which we remember all our previous lives offers something analogous to Christianity's 'eschatological verification' of the reality of God by participation in the finally manifest Kingdom of God.[32] It is important to the possibility of such a verification of reincarnation that the lives which are thus remembered are linked together in a karmic series in which the circumstances of each new life arise out of the character of the previous members of the series. For it is this karmic connection that singles out a particular set of lives as constituting the successive incarnations of the same soul. Otherwise the eschatological consciousness, which the last individual in the series is to share, might be aware of any number of lives, contemporaneous as well as successive. Indeed, we can conceive of an unlimited consciousness in which memories are lodged of all the human lives that have ever been lived. (This is indeed entailed by Charles Hartshorne's conception of human immortality discussed in chapter 11.) Then *all* human lives, however different from their own several points of view, would be connected via a higher consciousness in which they are remembered. It would then be proper to say of *any* two lives, contemporaneous as well as non-contemporaneous, that the one individual is a different incarnation of the other. However, developed in this way the idea of rebirth would no longer assert an individual reincarnating person or entity, but would become instead a mythological expression of the unity of mankind throughout the ages in the sight of God or of the Infinite Consciousness.

It is also important for the possibility of an eschatological verification of reincarnation that the memory of previous lives is memory of those lives as experienced 'from within' and not merely as observed 'from without'. At this point the hindu philosophical tradition is ambiguous. For it is stressed that there is a new empirical self in each incarnation. The distinction between the temporary empirical self and the permanent atman is symbolized in the upanishadic figure of the two birds sitting on different branches of the same tree, the one observing the other, the observer being the real and eternal self and the observed being the temporary empirical self.[33] In this 'picture' the eternal self is aware of the series of empirical selves which constitute its successive incarnations, although they (with the exception of the last one) are not aware either of it or of one another. But it seems that on this view the eternal self is aware of its incarnations only as an external observer of them. For it did not in fact undergo those past sets of experiences so as to be able to remember them 'from within'. It was not the conscious subject of those lives. Each was experienced by a different empirical consciousness, which underwent that one life and no other. Interpreted in this way, the reincarnationist claim is that there is a supernormal consciousness which has witnessed the past lives constituting the particular karmic series which includes my own life, and that a future member of the series – namely the last one – will merge into that supernormal consciousness. This is a conceivable state of affairs. But it leaves open the question how it can best be described. Let us name the first person in the series A and the last Z. The question is whether we are to say that B–Z are reincarnations of A. If we do, we shall be implicitly stipulating the following definition of 'reincarnation': given two or more distinct and non-contemporaneous human lives, if there is a higher consciousness which is aware of them all, then each later individual in the series is defined as being a reincarnation of each earlier individual in the series. But reincarnation so defined is a concept far removed from the idea that if I am A, then *I* shall be repeatedly reborn as B–Z; or that if I am Z, *I* have repeatedly lived before as A–Y.

But on the other hand there is another strand of hindu thought which suggests a somewhat different interpretation. For it is sometimes said that the full memory of each successive life, as experienced 'from within', accumulates in the reincarnating being and is lodged at a deep unconscious level within each of the new empirical selves which it produces. These memories can, in principle, be brought to consciousness, and there are said to be yogic techniques for doing this. The experience of remembering one's former lives would then perhaps be analogous to that of waking from the restricted world of a dream and suddenly becoming possessed of the memories of one's waking life. For the relationship between the usually limited life of a dream, and the waking life of the one whose dream it is, is asymmetrical. The waking person may remember many dreams, within each of which he was only conscious of that particular dream and was unaware of himself either in other dreams or in waking life. In this analogy the many lives of the reincarnating soul are comparable with the many dreams of the total self, and the final state of the soul remembering its long series of incarnations is comparable with the consciousness of the waking self remembering its many dreams. Such an interpretation of reincarnation is however perhaps more clearly developed within the buddhist philosophy, in which the continuing soul or atman – symbolized by the bird on the higher branch watching the other bird, the empirical self, on the lower branch – is denied, and that which includes many births is simply a flow of mental life in which conscious and unconscious characteristics, including memory, are carried forward. We therefore now turn to the buddhist conception of rebirth.

NOTES

1. 'Orthodox' in the sense of recognizing the revelatory authority of the Vedas, the six recognized orthodox schools being: Samkhya, Yoga, Vaishesika, Nyaya, Vedanta and Mimansa.

2. I am omitting diacritical marks from sanscrit transliterations.

3. Shankara, *Brahmasutrabhasya*, I, i, 5 (*Sacred Books of the East*, vol. 34, pp. 51–2). Cf. *Vivekachudamani*, 565, p. 210.

4. Cf. *Mundaka* Upanishad, II, 1, 1.

5. S. Radhakrishnan, *The Bhagavadgita*, introductory essay; T. M. P. Mahadevan, 'The Advaita Conception of Man', in *Religion and Society*, vol. 7, nos. 3 and 4 (1960).

6. pp. 308–9.

7. Cf. *Svetashvatara* Upanishad, V, 10.

8. There are however some writers who refer to it as material (though composed of a very 'subtle' kind of matter) in the western sense of being extended in space and thus having shape and size. Such writers often identify the *linga sharira* with the 'etheric' or 'astral' body which some people claim to be able to see. Thus the Theosophist, Annie Besant, wrote that 'the Linga Sharira, or Astral Double, is the ethereal counterpart of the gross body of man' (*Death – and After?*, p. 22). Again, for the Jains karma is a physical substance, 'an aggregate of very fine imperceptible material particles' (Ram Jee Singh, 'Karmic Idealism of the Jainas', in *Indian Philosophical Annual*, 1965, p. 21). See also p. 422, n. 12.

9. *Svetashvatara* Upanishad, IV, 10.

10. S. S. Suryanarayana Sastri, 'The Doctrine of Re-Incarnation in Educational Work', in *Indian Philosophical Annual*, 1965, p. 165.

11. S. Radhakrishnan, *The Principal Upanishads*, p. 273.

12. Sankara, *Vakyavritti*, Sloka 20.

13. 'Karma and Rebirth', in *Indian Philosophical Annual*, 1965, p. 115.

14. C. D. Broad, *The Mind and Its Place in Nature*, pp. 536ff. In his later *Lectures on Psychical Research*, pp. 415ff., Broad refers to this as the 'ψ-component'.

15. *The Mind and Its Place in Nature*, p. 551.

16. 'Karma and Rebirth', in *Indian Philosophical Annual*, 1965, p. 120.

17. *Chandogya* Upanishad, V, 10, 7: 'Those whose conduct here has been good will quickly attain a good birth, the birth of a Brahmin, the birth of a Ksatriya or the birth of a Vaisya. But those whose conduct here has been evil will quickly attain an evil birth, the birth of a dog, the birth of a hog or the birth of a Candala ("untouchable")' (*The Principal Upanishads*, p. 433).

18. The objection did not have to wait for the current population explosion but was put forward in the third century by Tertullian in his critique of the idea of reincarnation (*A Treatise on the Soul*, ch. 30).

19. See further, on this problem, chapter 19, section 5.

20. e.g., R. K. Tripathi, *Problems of Philosophy and Religion*, p. 134.

21. Cf. Ninian Smart, *Doctrine and Argument in Indian Philosophy*, pp. 152–3.

22. Sri Aurobindo, *The Problem of Rebirth*, vol. 16, p. 86.

23. ibid., p. 121.

24. The enlightened individual's claimed memory of former lives will be further discussed in chapter 19, section 4.

25. *Indian Philosophical Annual*, 1965, pp. 109, 161.

26. ibid., p. 109.

27. Leslie Weatherhead, *The Case for Re-Incarnation*, p. 10.

28. *Indian Philosophical Annual*, 1965, p. 164; Leslie Weatherhead, *The Christian Agnostic*, pp. 211–12.

29. *Indian Philosophical Annual*, 1965, p. 110.

30. M. Yamunacharya, 'Karma and Rebirth', in *Indian Philosophical Annual*, 1965, pp. 67–8.

31. pp. 308–9.

32. Cf. my *Faith and Knowledge*, ch. 8.

33. *Mundaka* Upanishad, III, 1, 1.

CHAPTER 18

The Buddhist Conception of Rebirth

I. THE 'NO SOUL' DOCTRINE

To a great extent the buddhist conception of reincarnation – which is essentially the same in the theravada and mahayana teachings – is similar to the vedantic; and it will therefore not be necessary to repeat the discussions and arguments of the last chapter but only to take note of the distinctive feature of the buddhist doctrine which leads many contemporary buddhist scholars to prefer the term 'rebirth' to 'reincarnation'. This is its association with another and even more fundamental doctrine, that of *anatta* (sanscrit, *anatman*: 'no soul', 'egolessness'). This formulates one of the three basic features of all existence: everything is characterized by *anatta* ('no soul'), *anicca* ('transitoriness', 'process'), and *dukkha* ('suffering', 'unsatisfactoriness'). These three concepts turn out to be variations on the same theme, though each with its own emphasis and, in the case of *anatta*, with an additional polemical significance. Thus *anatta* must be understood in its context of what Wijesekera[1] calls the three signata (*tilakkhana*) of existence.

The most fundamental of these is *anicca* ('transiency', 'impermanence', 'process'. Literally: the negative prefix *a* plus *nicca*, 'permanent'). The Buddha's teaching is pervaded by a tragic sense – which is indeed characteristic of indian religious thought as a whole – of the insubstantial and transient nature of all temporal existence. To be born is already to have begun to die. Everything that comes to be passes away. Even the most apparently solid and enduring realities are secretly in process of dissolution. 'Whatever is of the nature to uprise, all that is of the nature to stop.'[2] And as a philosopher the Buddha saw this universal transiency as arising from the fact that everything, all distinguishable entities and processes (*sankharas*[3]), are composite. Each is a long- or short-lived pattern formed in the ceaseless flow and swirl of universal change. And the Buddha held – again within a common pattern of indian thought – that such brief, contingent and unstable patterns cannot be ultimately real or finally valuable. To change is to be imperfect, insubstantial, tainted with illusoriness, and therefore not a fitting object of valuation or desire. Thus after describing in terms of splendid hyperbole the wealth and glory of the great king of Kusavati (who was Gautama himself in a former life) – his royal city surrounded by seven ramparts of gold, silver, beryl, crystal, agate, coral, and gems; this surrounded by seven rows of palm trees made of similar precious stones and metals; his magnificent palace; his 84,000 wives, chief of whom was the Pearl among Women; his 84,000 dependent cities; his 84,000 elephants; and so on – the Buddha points out that all of these belonged to a long-vanished previous life and that the great kingdom with all its wealth and glories is now only a memory:

> See, Ananda, how all these things are now past, are ended, have vanished away. Thus impermanent, Ananda, are component things; thus transitory, Ananda, are component things; thus untrustworthy, Ananda, are component things. Insomuch, Ananda, is it meet to be weary of, is it meet to be estranged from, is it meet to be set quite free from the bondage of all component things![4]

And the Sutta ends with the refrain:

> How transient are all component things!
> Growth is their nature and decay;
> They are produced, they are dissolved again;
> To bring them all into subjection – that is bliss.[5]

We must not however think of this poignant sense of the fleeting character of all human glory, achievement and happiness as stemming from a peculiarly buddhist or even a peculiarly indian mentality; for it is a universal theme, expressed as much in western as in eastern literature. Shakespeare's sonnets are full of it:

> Like as the waves make towards the pebbled shore,
> So do our minutes hasten to their end;
> Each changing place with that which goes before,
> In sequent toil all forwards do contend.

Nativity, once in the main of light,
Crawls to maturity, wherewith being crown'd,
Crooked eclipses 'gainst his glory fight,
And Time that gave doth now his gift confound.
Time doth transfix the flourish set on youth,
And delves the parallels in beauty's brow,
Feeds on the rarities of nature's truth,
And nothing stands but for his scythe to mow.[6]

And other western as well as eastern poets in every generation
have expressed a like sense of the transiency of human existence.

Further, the linking of transitoriness with the compounded-
ness of earthly things has also been an outcome of philosophical
analysis in both east and west. According to Plato it is because
all mundane things are composite, being temporary coalescences
of matter with Form or Idea, that they are inherently impermanent and must eventually dissolve away. The world of
change is essentially temporal and therefore ultimately unreal,
a mere moving shadow of eternity. Only the perfect and
changeless realm of the eternal Forms is fully real. Whether
the buddhist nirvana stands in the same contrast to transient
existence as the platonic Forms is a much disputed question
to which we shall come in chapter 21.

The buddhist *anatta*[7] ('no soul') teaching presents the
obvious difficulty that it has to be understood in a way which
is compatible with the doctrine of rebirth. And when we note
that this doctrine asserts the possibility of remembering one's
previous lives, this restricts the range of permissible interpretations of *anatta*. We cannot take it to be a denial of the
continuity through all these lives of that which remembers
them. Nor, on common-sense grounds, can we understand it
as a denial of the existence of the empirical self – the conscious,
remembering, responsible ego – even though sometimes it
seems to be precisely this. We read, for example, in the
writings of the great buddhist scholastic, Buddhaghosa:

> For there is suffering, but none who suffers;
> Doing exists although there is no doer;
> Extinction is but no extinguished person;
> Although there is a path, there is no goer.[8]

At first sight such verses seem to call in question something which it does not make sense to question, namely the existence of the questioner. But nevertheless we are not being asked to deny that there are, in the ordinary sense of the word, *persons* who have each been born on a certain day, and continue through time and eventually die, or that each of these thinks of himself as 'I' and of others as 'you' or as 'he', 'she' or 'they'. The buddhist book on the concept of *anatta* which lies on the desk before me has an author's name on the title page: it does not present itself as a bundle of thoughts which have come together by themselves. Buddhists have names and addresses, receive and answer correspondence, have careers, marry, take part in organizations, are subjects of obituary notices. Further, as I have already noted, the buddhist conception of rebirth entails the possibility, and in some cases the actuality, of memory of former lives. The Buddha himself, at the time of his enlightenment, recalled thousands of his previous lives;[9] and there are numerous cases in modern times, made use of in buddhist apologetics, of ordinary people who have apparently remembered fragments of an immediately preceding life. In such a case, when someone remembers an earlier life he speaks of what is being remembered as *his* own previous life. He does not recall its circumstances as one might recall a history learned at school but as one remembers one's own holiday of last year or one's school-days of forty years ago. Thus the empirical self – the conscious personality who acts in the present, plans for the future, and remembers past experiences (including, it may be, experiences in former lives) as moments through which he has lived – is treated by buddhist thought as being real. Acknowledging all this, buddhist writers explain that although in ordinary life we have to speak of the self, the concept is only a convenient fiction. Thus Nyanatiloka Maha-thera wrote that

> whenever the Buddha uses such terms as I, person, living being, etc., this is to be understood as conventional speech (*vohara-vacana*), hence not correct in the highest sense (*paramattha-vacana*). It is just as speaking of the 'rising' and 'setting' of the sun, though we know thoroughly well that this does not correspond to reality. Thus the Buddha

teaches that, in the ultimate sense, amongst all these psycho-physical phenomena of existence there cannot be found any eternal or even temporary ego-entity, and hence that all existence of whatever kind is something impersonal, or *anatta*.[10]

However, to suggest that the empirical self is a conventional fiction, like the rising of the sun in the post-copernican world, hardly bears examination. The upward movement of the sun is a visual appearance. But if we use this as an analogy for the self we shall quickly run into logical difficulties. Thus V. F. Gunaratna writes:

> [The mind] is a stream of successive thoughts which are continually arising and passing away from moment to moment. Each thought is succeeded by another with such a rapidity as to give the mind a semblance of something stable and permanent. A stick burning at one end and turned rapidly round and round in the dark creates the illusion of a ring or circle of fire to onlookers at a distance who do not know what is actually happening . . . So it is with the mind where thoughts succeed each other with a much greater rapidity.[11]

But if it is the rapid succession of thoughts which creates the illusion of a persisting mind, as the rapidly moving flame creates the illusion of a fiery circle, in what consciousness is the illusion created? It cannot occur in a point-instant of consciousness, for it is a result of one and the same consciousness being aware of the successive positions of the burning stick, which follow one another so rapidly that instead of registering individually they are seen as a continuous ring of fire. Thus the consciousness which undergoes the illusion must itself endure through time. Accordingly it is impossible to character-ize all enduring minds as illusions created by rapid change; for there will still remain the enduring mind in which the illusion occurs!

But 'enduring' does not mean 'unchanging'. All physical and psycho-physical entities endure for a greater or shorter period of time, and all of them change, whether rapidly or slowly. A person does not differ in this respect from a tree or a table, and we see the unilluminating character of one sort of *anatta* doctrine if we form parallel no-tree, no-table, no-mountain, no-cat, etc., doctrines. For each of these things also exists in a series of states no two of which are totally alike. Two successive states of a rock are usually more alike than two successive states of a galloping horse; but nevertheless the one is changing as surely as the other. But a universal no-'x' doctrine would merely be a gratuitous and unproductive renunciation of the use of nouns. For we mean by 'tree' precisely the slowly growing or decaying object with its roots in the ground and its leafy branches in the air, and the fact that it changes through time does not make it any less a tree but is on the contrary an essential aspect of its tree-hood. We mean by 'table' something like the wooden object on which my papers are resting; and the fact that it is, from the physicist's point of view, a swarming universe of electrons and protons in perpetual motion does not make it any less a standard instance of what we mean by 'table'. And we mean by a person, the kind of thing of which John Smith is an instance; and the fact that persons are temporal creatures, continuously undergoing change, is already taken into account in our ordinary use of the word 'person'.

This realization brings us to another and more attractive interpretation of *anatta* as saying, not that there is no ordinary-language self, but that the mind or self or person is a wholly temporal reality, a living entity existing in its different states. Like everything else, the empirical self is a process and not a timeless unchanging entity. Throughout life, from womb to worm, his body is undergoing processes of growth, decay and repair – though large-scale alterations, as from the form of a baby to that of an adult, are generally slow. His stream of consciousness is a flux, changing momentarily. And the set of behavioural dispositions which constitutes his character is likewise in process of continuous modification, even though its major transformations usually occur imperceptibly. There is no empirical self or person, and no psycho-physical organism, outside this ceaseless flow of change.

The only flaw in this interpretation is that it represents the Buddha as asserting something which probably no one either in his own time or before or since has ever thought of denying.

That a human being is a living organism, with all that that implies even for the pre-scientific mind, has never been a matter of debate; and to reaffirm it can hardly have been the full meaning of a central teaching of the Buddha's.

But perhaps he was pointing to a deeper significance in this changing and transitory character of human existence. Perhaps as the great ethical teacher that he was the Buddha was trying to bring his hearers to a more living realization – in contemporary jargon, an existential awareness – of the contingent, secondary, dependent and fleeting status of the empirical self so that they might thereby be helped to escape from the self-centred standpoint of the 'beloved ego'. There are passages in the *Sanyutta-Nikaya* which suggest that the Buddha's concern is to warn against egoism and false stress upon 'me' and 'mine'. For example, he ends one conversation as follows:

> Thus, brother, should one know, thus should one see, so that in this body, together with its inner consciousness, and likewise in all outward objects, there be no idea of 'I' or 'mine', no leanings to conceit therein.[12]

Perhaps, then, meditation upon one's own transitoriness and imperfection is a means to the transcending of egoism. In that case the ethical significance of the *anatta* doctrine is a call to become morally *anatta*, selfless, moved by a universal love which does not discriminate between self and other. This is a theme to which we shall return in chapter 22.

But we have still to note the generally accepted interpretation of *anatta*, which is different in kind from this moral interpretation although compatible with it. It is generally agreed that the Buddha was rejecting some version of the *atman* concept which has always played a central role in indian philosophy apart from Buddhism. In brahminical or 'hindu' thought the infinite plurality of eternal souls (*jivas*) are each, in their deepest being – when the illusion of separate egohood is transcended – atman and identical with Atman, the one universal eternal Spirit, which in turn is one with Brahman, the Absolute beyond all human categories. Thus the *jiva* or atman is an individual 'spark of divinity' which, in its hidden identity with Brahman, exists eternally and unchangingly. This notion of an immutable atman, without beginning or end, which each of us ultimately is, is explicitly rejected by the Buddha's *anatta* doctrine. That it is the notion of an *immutable* soul that he is attacking is made clear in numerous texts which assume that anything worth calling a real self must be eternal, unchanging and blissful, and then proceed to show that no part of the empirical self fits such a description. For example,

> 'Now what think ye, brethren? Is body permanent or impermanent?'
> 'Impermanent, lord.'
> 'And what is impermanent, is that weal or woe?'
> 'Woe, lord.'
> 'Then what is impermanent, woeful, unstable by nature, is it fitting to regard it thus: "this is mine; I am this; this is the Self of me"?'
> 'Surely not, lord.'[13]

And the Buddha rejected this idea of the unchanging atman, presumably, because it is a piece of speculative metaphysics such as he always avoided and advised his disciples to avoid. He was an intensely practical and ethical teacher; and the self to which ethical suasions and injunctions are addressed is the empirical self. It is this self that must progressively strip itself of egoism, self-centred desire and clinging, including the basic clinging to its own separate ego-history.

How does all this agree or disagree with western and christian ideas? The Buddha's rejection of the brahminical atman would also operate against its nearest western equivalent in the theory of the soul as a substance which, being simple, is incapable of dissolution and therefore perpetually existent. This conception, with its consequent argument for immortality, appears in Plato's *Phaedo* and was later adopted into the thomist theology of the catholic church. It belongs, however, only to one strand – though a major one – of western thought. It has been by no means universally accepted, having been criticized on philosophical grounds, above all by Kant,[14] and having come in recent times to be generally rejected by Christians in the protestant tradition as being unbiblical.[15] It is unclear, moreover, whether the simple psychic substance constituting the soul of platonic and thomist philosophy is to be thought of as immutable. But with the possible exception of this platonic-thomist tradition, the view of man as a radically temporal creature, and thus both *anicca* ('transient') and *anatta* ('with no unchanging core'), probably commends itself to non-Buddhists – though not of course usually in the same terminology – as widely as to Buddhists. Indeed, the general doctrine of nature, including man, as process has long been familiar and widely accepted in the west; for the sciences show every aspect of nature to be continually in movement as a ceaseless play of energy; and the fundamental concept of space-time in relativity theory involves the totally temporal character of all physical existence. The history of the universe, so far as it is known to us, is one of the continual transformation of matter-energy in the evolution of galaxies and nebulae and, in our own tiny corner of space-time, in the geological evolution of the earth, the emergence of life, and the brief story of man.[16]

So far as christian thought in the reformed tradition is concerned, and the biblical view that lies behind it, there are striking similarities with the buddhist conception of the status of the empirical self. *Anatta* means negatively that the empirical self – the conscious, responsible, remembering ego – is not a self-existent substance. It exists only in time as an ever-changing process of consciousness, and there is no part of the self outside this ceaseless temporal flow. On the other hand, as a process this empirical self is said to continue through immense aeons until he attains to nirvana, which is the end of rebecoming. The christian biblical and reformed view of the empirical self – the same conscious, responsible, remembering ego – is likewise that he is not a self-existent substance but is dependent for existence from moment to moment on the active will of the Creator. He is wholly immersed in time, wholly a process sustained from beyond himself. Thus both religions affirm the radically temporal and inherently transitory nature of the human person. But beyond this similarity there is a difference. For theravada Buddhism, the perfecting of the empirical ego, its attainment of arhatship, leads to its cessation. For Christianity, on the other hand, the perfecting of the empirical self takes it beyond mortality into an eternal life lived in relation to God. The crux is the belief in a Reality transcending *samsara*, the process of nature. If there is only

samsara and the cessation of *samsara* then the empirical self
ceases with the ceasing of *samsara*. If there is a more ultimate
Reality beyond *samsara* then the perfecting of the empirical self
may consist in a shifting of its relationship and dependency
from the one to the other and a sharing in that eternal life. We
shall return in chapter 22 to this difference and to the further
question of a possible convergence beyond it.

The third of the three universal characteristics of existence
is perhaps the one most open to differing interpretations.
Dukkha is commonly put into English as 'suffering', 'sorrow',
'woe' or 'ill'. But, as Wijesekera points out, *dukkha* is variously
used in the pali canon in a narrow physical sense (pain), in a
narrow psychological sense (suffering), and in the general
philosophical sense in which it occurs in the Buddha's doctrine that all life is *dukkha* – for which Wijesekera and others
recommend the translation 'unsatisfactoriness'.[17] This unsatisfactoriness of all life is virtually equivalent to its transiency;
for in the Buddha's vision 'what is impermanent, that is
suffering (*dukkham*)'.[18] Again:

> 'Now what think ye, brethren? Is body permanent or
> impermanent?'
> 'Impermanent, lord.'
> 'And what is impermanent, is that weal or woe?'
> 'Woe (*dukkha*), lord.'[19]

Thus, as Wijesekera says, the 'characteristic of general Unsatisfactoriness is derived directly from the first characteristic
of Impermanence'.[20]

The Buddha's first Noble Truth, that all life is *dukkha*, is
often treated by western readers as an empirical statement to
the effect that every moment and aspect of human experience
is one of suffering, pain, sorrow or unhappiness and that there
is no joy or happiness to be found in human existence. That
this cannot be the meaning of the Buddha's words is shown by
his teaching about the five higher and lower states of existence
– the lower worlds, the animal kingdom, the spirit sphere,
human life, and the realm of the devas or higher spirits. In a
vivid analogy, the lower world of Niraya Hell is compared to
a pit of hot charcoal into which a traveller falls; animal existence
to a cesspool; existence in the spirit-sphere to coming under a

tree in a desert, but with sparse leaves and little shade; whilst human life is compared to coming under 'a tree growing on even ground, with dense leaves and foliage (giving) thick shade', where one 'is experiencing feelings that are abundantly pleasant';[21] whilst the deva-world is compared to a beautiful palace. This is clearly not an account of human existence as all pain and suffering. There is much suffering, but there is also much happiness; but both together are included under the statement that all life is *dukkha*. Here *dukkha* must be taken to mean, not incessant actual pain and suffering, but a general human condition of inescapable liability to these ills. Within the temporal span of a human life suffering is inevitable; and when it is not occurring to one person it is occurring to others. One man's happiness is balanced by another's sorrow; our joys are poignantly transient and insecure; and sooner or later disease, old age and death come to all. Thus the Buddha's disciple, Sariputta, told an enquirer, 'There are these three [modes of] feeling, friend – which three? Pleasant, painful, neutral feeling. Now these three modes are impermanent. And when it is discerned that that which is impermanent is painful (*dukkha*), blissful feeling is not present';[22] and the Buddha approved his answer.

Thus *dukkha* is the transitoriness and imperfection of human life, including both its happiness and its unhappinesses, its pleasures and its pains, seen comprehensively as a general state of Unsatisfactoriness. In a similar way the Christian may rejoice in all that is good in life and yet speak of man's sinful state and of the whole world as being 'fallen'. He does not mean that everything in it is evil and nothing good, but that it is a place of trial and of the slow and painful creation of personality rather than of perfection and fulfilment. We are in the midst of our pilgrimage, not at its end. Empirically, that which constitutes the world as 'fallen' is the presence of evil within it – the physical evil of pain, the psychological evil of suffering, and the moral evil of sin. In augustinian theology sin is seen as the original and continuing cause of pain and suffering; and here buddhist teaching differs significantly, not in denying the fact of moral evil, but in seeing *avijja* ('ignorance') as its deeper source. This is not so far removed, on the other hand, from the irenaean view within Christianity of sin and suffering as deriving from man's creation at an epistemic distance from God, this distance constituting the creature's freedom and autonomy in relation to the creator.[23] But on any view all mundane life is subject to evil, or to *dukkha*; and to escape from it (as, in very different ways, in augustinian Christianity and theravada Buddhism), or to turn it into good (as, again in very different ways, in irenaean Christianity and mahayana Buddhism), has always been a central concern of religion. In the yearning words of the pali canon,

> They're transient all, each being's parts and powers,
> Growth is their very nature, and decay.
> They are produced, they are dissolved again:
> To bring them all into subjection – that is bliss.[24]

2. THE MECHANISM OF REBIRTH

Man, then, is an essentially temporal creature (*anicca*), indeed temporal without remainder (*anatta*), and inherently vulnerable to evil (*dukkha*). And like every other distinguishable item of the world-process he is composite, a temporary and changing conjunction of elements. Human nature is analysed according to several different schemes in buddhist literature; but a fairly standard division is into five factors (*khandhas*): the physical body (*rupa*, literally 'form'); and the four mental elements of feeling, or hedonic tone (*vedana*); perception, or awareness, or recognition of sensation (*sanna*); the moral will and its accumulated character dispositions (*sankhara*), and the stream of consciousness (*vinnana*). Collectively these are termed *nama-rupa* (literally 'name-form'). *Citta* is also often used, being roughly equivalent to *vinnana*.[25]

At death the *nama-rupa* disintegrates. Its elements come apart and the psycho-physical individual which they have formed ceases to exist. He does not survive death, and he is not reborn to live again. That particular conjunction of elements which had held together for, say, seventy years is no more. But nevertheless an aspect of him does continue – not indeed eternally, but until it has finally expended itself, or become blown out (*nibbana*) at the end of many lives. That which thus continues through aeons of time, playing a part in the formation of individual after individual, consists of a system of character dispositions, the karmic deposit of former lives, animated and propelled onwards by the power of craving.

In the post-canonical pali writings the following question is asked:

> The King said: 'Revered Nagasena, who reconnects [i.e. is reborn]?'
>
> The Elder said: 'Name-and-shape (*nama-rupa*), sire, reconnects.'
>
> 'What, is it this name-and-shape itself that reconnects?'
>
> 'This name-and-shape does not itself reconnect, sire; but, sire, by means of this name-and-shape one does a lovely or an evil deed, and because of this deed another name-and-shape reconnects.'[26]

This life-craving system of dispositions which goes forward to give its basic character to a new embryo is essentially equivalent to the *linga sharira* of vedantic theory, discussed in the previous chapter. It is not a conscious self but a formation of non-conscious psychic elements. I noted that the *linga sharira* is roughly equivalent to C. D. Broad's 'psychic factor', and so it is not surprising that K. N. Jayatilleke, expounding the buddhist term, should speak of 'the *vinnana* – which may be the "psychic factor" (to borrow a term of Prof. C. D. Broad's) which survives physical death and by entering the womb helps in the development of a new individual'.[27] Buddhist philosophy has always recognized the subconscious and unconscious aspects of personal life, including both deep character dispositions and a craving for life which is analogous to the freudian concept of the libido.[28] It is in this area of the unconscious and subconscious that the continuant from life to life is to be found. But in the more precise identification of it the buddhist system becomes extremely complex and open to different interpretations. One might have expected that the aspect of the individual that is reborn would be the set of *sankharas* or karmically formed character dispositions. And indeed, essentially, it would seem that this is the case; but the terminology shifts confusingly among the different strata of the literature. That which rebecomes is called *vinnana*.[29] But this is not unambiguously the *vinnana* ('consciousness') which is one of the five components of the psycho-physical individual.

The *vinnana* which rebecomes is not consciousness as such, but something more like the unconscious dispositional state which constitutes the karmic deposit of the past. (As such it is called by Theravadnis the *bhavanga citta*; and also, more popularly, the *gandhabba*, 'ghost'.) The connection of this with *vinnana* ('consciousness') is possibly that it is the dying individual's last conscious thought that determines the nature of the next birth. This terminal moment of consciousness is charged with a craving for life and so constitutes a 'grasping force' which attached itself again at a new point to the stream of biological life.

The buddhist account of the beginningless process of human experience (*samsara*), the wheel of life, depicts it as a self-propelling, causal[30] cycle in which old age and death are produced by birth, which is produced by becoming, which is produced by grasping, which is produced by craving, which is produced by sensation, which is produced by contact with the world, which is produced by embodied existence (*nama-rupa*), which is produced by cognition.[31] (Since a cyclical process is being described, one could begin the description at any stage; and indeed the list itself, dividing up the cycle of existence in this particular way, could be varied without affecting its validity.) It was a central insight of the Buddha's that the craving which is the mainspring of the whole process is dependent upon the sense of separate hard-core ego-identity which the *anatta* doctrine, understood as an instrument of moral training, attacks. So long as we see and value from an egocentric standpoint we shall be driven by false desires, cling to false values, and seek to perpetuate our own separate existence with all the imperfection and liability to suffering that is inseparable from it. The cessation of this ego-existence is nirvana – to the consideration of which we shall come in chapter 21.

Returning now to the mechanism of rebirth, the first moment of thought in the new stream of life stands in direct causal sequence to the last moment of thought in the dying person, which thought thus determines the nature of the next birth. Accordingly:

In Buddhist countries, it is therefore the custom to recall to

the dying man's memory his good actions performed by
him, in order to rouse in him a happy pure karmical state
of mind, as a preparation for a favourable rebirth. Or, his
relations let him see things (robes or other offerings) which
they, for his good and benefit, wish to offer to the Sangha,
the community of monks, saying: 'This, we shall offer to
the Sangha for your future good and welfare'. Or they may
let him hear a religious sermon, or a recital of a Sutta, very
often the *Satipatthana Sutta*.[32]

The first thought of the new life stream, which is the
immediate successor to the last thought of the dying individual,
is thus sometimes called the 'relinking consciousness'. This
first 'thought' is however not necessarily a conscious thought,
and indeed in the case of an embryo clearly it cannot be. It is
rather a complex dispositional impulse, carrying a set of basic
character traits and a store of unconscious memories, all
powered by the craving for existence. It might thus be better
to speak, not of a first thought, but of the first moment in the
mental life of the new individual. That this first moment must
be the immediate successor to the last moment of the mental
life of the expiring person, without hiatus, follows from the
anatta doctrine, with its denial of any empirical self other than
the continuous stream of (conscious and unconscious) mental
life.

However, this immediate rebirth or rebecoming is not
necessarily into our earthly world; and indeed, only a minority
of births are into human life.[33] Rebecoming may occur in any
of the many 'worlds' – the *kama*-worlds (sense worlds), which
include our earth, purgatory, and the nearer *deva* (angel)-
worlds; the *rupa*-worlds (worlds of visible form though not
sense) which are the further Brahma and supra-Brahma
spheres; and the *arupa*-worlds (incorporeal worlds of thought).
The fact that there are all these other 'worlds' makes it
intelligible both that rebirth on earth does not always follow
instantaneously upon death; and also (as we noted concerning
the parallel hindu doctrine) that the human population of the
globe has always been increasing and is today expanding in
explosive proportions – for it may be that the additional karmic
streams of life which are now being brought into our world

have hitherto been carrying on their existence in these other spheres.

3. IS REBIRTH AN ESSENTIAL BUDDHIST DOCTRINE?

Having noted the buddhist conception of the process of rebirth let us raise a question which may be as startling to some buddhist readers as parallel questions raised earlier in the book may have been to some christian readers. Is the belief in rebirth essential to Buddhism? Or could it be abandoned without thereby undermining the remainder of the buddhist system? I am raising this question in terms of the logic, not the psychology, of belief. Psychologically, it is hardly conceivable that so ancient and widespread a concept, and one that is so deeply woven into the fabric of buddhist culture, could be jettisoned. It might however be capable of the kind of reinterpretation which has been applied to various equally venerable christian concepts and beliefs – for example the fall of man, which was formerly accepted as history and is now seen by most educated Christians as a profound religious myth; or the concept of original sin, which depends upon the doctrine of the fall. Having seen that certain elements of his tradition are mythological it then becomes the theologian's task to try to discern the positive meaning of the myth. I shall in a later section venture to suggest what might be the positive meaning of the idea of rebirth if it is accepted as being mythologically rather than literally true.

Is it, then, for Buddhism just a contingent fact, brought to light by memories of past lives, that we live again and again; or is the process of rebirth deducible from and logically integral to the wider body of buddhist belief?

The answer depends upon whether we are thinking of the narrower idea of rebirth (i.e. a series of literal births within the biological process of this world) or the wider idea of rebecoming (i.e. the continuation after death of the individual system of dispositions, whether in this or other 'worlds'); for as Jayatilleke says, 'rebirth is only a special case of re-becoming when a person comes back to an earth-life'.[34] This wider concept of rebecoming (*punabbava*, literally 'existence again') is clearly essential to Buddhism. For *samsara* entails that the individual bundle of dispositions, constituting the karmic

deposit of its past history, continues its processive existence in
one form or another through aeons of time until its craving for
existence is exhausted and it attains to nirvana. But to designate
this basic buddhist theme the word 'rebecoming' is more
appropriate than 'rebirth'. For birth, as the beginning of a new
animal life-span, is only one form of rebecoming. The way in
which the term 'rebirth' is used in much of the literature has
tended to obscure this important distinction and to reduce the
wider concept to the narrower. Accordingly 'rebirth' has generally been treated as an alternative term to 'reincarnation' in
referring to the process whereby human beings are born again
and again to live further human (or other animal) lives. The reports of individuals who are said to remember fragments of a
past life, often discussed in support of the buddhist doctrine
of rebirth,[35] have also helped to fix the meaning of the word
as signifying rebirth within the evolution of life on this earth.
But the idea that rebecoming must take the form of rebirth
from the womb is not a buddhist belief. The traditional buddhist
view is rather that it may take either this form or other forms
in the numerous purgatorial and heavenly 'worlds'. For the
Buddha himself taught that only a small minority of rebecomings are as human beings:

> Just as, monks, in this Rose-apple Land [i.e. India] trifling
> in number are the pleasant parks, the pleasant groves, the
> pleasant grounds and lakes, while more numerous are the
> steep, precipitous places, unfordable rivers, dense thickets
> of stakes and thorns, and inaccessible mountains, – just so
> few in number are those beings who, deceasing as men, are
> reborn among men. More numerous are those beings who,
> deceasing as men, are reborn in Purgatory, who are reborn
> in the wombs of animals, who are reborn in the Realm of
> Ghosts.[36]

In these other 'worlds' rebecoming is not a matter of being
born as a baby but rather of the stream of personal consciousness, which from the point of view of an earthly observer
terminates at death, continuing in another environment – as
in the Buddha's story of a great king: 'When the Great King
of Glory, Ananda, had died, he came to life again in the happy
world of Brahma.'[37] Or again, 'as that person fares along . . .

so will he arise, at the breaking up of the body after dying, in a good bourn, a heaven world'.[38]

I suggest then that from the point of view of the logic of the Dharma it is a question of fact, to be determined by appropriate observations, whether rebecoming sometimes or always takes the form of rebirth in this world. In the Buddha's and other arhats' reports of their own recollections of their former lives buddhist tradition contains strong reasons for supposing earthly rebirth to occur. But if these stories came to be given a mythological interpretation, and it were held that rebirth (as distinguished from rebecoming in other spheres) either never or only seldom occurs, this conclusion would not, I suggest, involve an abandonment of the central structure of buddhist faith. It would not, for example, affect the validity of the Four Noble Truths or the Eightfold Path to deliverance. Thus if scientific disproof of rebirth should at some future time be forthcoming, Buddhism would be able to adjust itself to such new knowledge as Christianity has – though not without great pains – adjusted itself to the knowledge of biological evolution. I am not predicting that this will happen; though I should think it possible that the growing influence of science and technology within the traditional buddhist cultures may gradually lead to belief in rebirth becoming a 'dead letter' – not officially repudiated and yet no longer seriously believed by most educated Buddhists. If this should happen, future buddhist thinkers may well find it proper to reconsider the status of the rebirth doctrine.

It is worth noting that to the extent that rebecoming in other 'worlds' is emphasized, rather than rebirth in this world, there is essential agreement between the pareschatologies of Buddhism and of Christianity in the irenaean tradition. It is true that these other 'worlds' are depicted in buddhist (as also in hindu) literature as places of reward, punishment, rest or purgation rather than as realms in which new moral and spiritual acts take place and in which progress towards nirvana is accordingly possible. They thus correspond, in christian thought, more to the purgatory of the augustinian-catholic tradition than to the continued person-making beyond death postulated by the irenaean type of theology. But if we want to imagine a Buddhism in which the doctrine of rebecoming has ceased to be associated with earthly rebirth, it will be one in which the idea of the other worlds has been developed to take over from this world the function of accommodating the many linked rebecomings which are to lead eventually to nirvana. It will be a doctrine (such as that to be outlined in chapter 20) of 'vertical' rather than 'horizontal' reincarnation.

4. KARMA AND MEMORY

Reincarnation, no doubt mainly in the popular form of the idea discussed in chapter 16, was very widely believed in the India into which Gautama the Buddha was born.[39] However, his own version, as we have examined it so far in the pali canon, was more subtle than this, as also was the developing vedantic conception. Indeed, the Buddha's doctrine does not differ from the latter as regards the nature and the propulsion of the life-to-life continuant but only in his rejection of the idea of the atman which lies behind, or above, or in the depths of the empirical self and which is ultimately one with the eternal and changeless divine Spirit – if he did indeed, as is generally held, reject this.[40] But so far as reincarnation or rebirth in this world is concerned, the Buddha and the Vedantists were in agreement that the link from one life to another is not the empirical or conscious self but a set of deep character dispositions and latent memories which somehow become attached to a new embryo to form a fresh empirical self. Thus, to the question whether the one who is born is the same person as the one who died, the answer can only be the Buddha's – both that he is and that he is not the same. In one sense they are the same person; for the basic character traits and latent memories of the one are carried over into and continue within the other. But in another sense they are different; for the earlier person dies in (let us say) old age with the memories, habits, fixity of character and failing powers of an old man whilst the later individual is born as a baby, without memories or habits, with an extremely pliable character-structure, and with mental and physical powers as yet undeveloped.

In reply to questions about personal identity within the rebirth process a simile is used in the *Milindapanha* which has ever since intrigued those who have considered it:

The King said: 'Revered Nagasena, does that which does
not pass over reconnect?'

'Yes, sire, that which does not pass over reconnects.'

'How, revered Nagasena, does that which does not pass over
reconnect? Make a simile.'

'Suppose, sire, some men were to light a lamp from (another)
lamp; would that lamp, sire, pass over from the (other)
lamp?'

'No, revered sir.'

'In the same way, sire, that which does not pass over
reconnects.'[41]

This simile offers itself for possible development in two
different directions, one of which links it to the Vedanta
whilst the other moves towards the thought of a common or
world karma – an idea which might well constitute the moral
content of a reincarnation myth. The issue turns upon the
notion of karma and upon whether or not this is linked with
memory. Karma, moral cause and effect, is the natural law of
the spiritual world whereby every action, including every
volition, has its appropriate effect: 'If one speaks or acts with
wicked mind, because of that, suffering follows one, even as
the wheel follows the hoof of the draught-ox . . . If one speaks
or acts with pure mind, because of that, happiness follows one,
even as one's shadow that never leaves.'[42]

The theme is not confined to religions which teach reincarnation; the christian scriptures, for example, also affirm that
'whatever a man sows, that he will also reap'.[43] Within the
present life the effects of action are felt both inwardly, in what
it does to the agent's own character, and outwardly in the world,
by contributing to the future circumstances in which he (and
hence, inevitably, to some extent others also) shall live. The
inward effects are obviously inseparable from the agent.
Every thought and choice helps to form his character-structure.
In acting kindly one reinforces and develops one's own kindli-
ness. In acting brutally one brutalizes oneself. Every volition,
important or trivial, does something to strengthen or to modify
one's own personal nature. As William James wrote,

> We are spinning our own fates, good or evil, and never to
> be undone. Every smallest stroke of virtue or of vice leaves

its never-so-little scar. The drunken Rip Van Winkle, in
Jefferson's play, excuses himself for every fresh dereliction
by saying, 'I won't count this time!' Well, he may not count
it, and a kind Heaven may not count it; but it is being
counted none the less. Down among his nerve-cells and
fibres the molecules are counting it, registering and storing
it up to be used against him when the next temptation comes.
Nothing we ever do is, in strict scientific literalness, wiped
out.[44]

This is the reflexive operation of the moral law of karma, seen
by James as physical as well as mental; and if the agent lives
a second or third or any number of lives, so long as he is the
same person he must take with him the character which he has
been forming and reforming in all his past volitions. For it is
the basic shape of this character that is said to be passed on
from life to life in the form of unconscious karmic energies
which transfer their operation from the dying person to a new
embryo.

It is less obvious however that the external effects, constituting what we may call circumstantial karma, always fall upon
the agent himself. It is claimed however that they affect the
agent by selecting the circumstances of his next birth. Thus
we read in the *Milindapanha*:

> The King said: 'Revered Nagasena, what is the reason that
> men are not all the same, some being short-lived, some
> long-lived, some weakly, others healthy, some ugly, others
> comely, some of few wishes, others of many wishes,
> some poor, others rich, some belonging to low families,
> others to high families, and some being weak in wisdom,
> others having wisdom?'
> The Elder said: 'But why, sire, are trees not all the same,
> some being acid, some salt, some bitter, some sharp,
> some astringent, others sweet?'
> 'I think, revered sir, that it is because of a difference in
> seeds.'
> 'Even so, sire, it is because of a difference in kammas
> [sanscrit: *karmas*] that men are not all the same, some
> being short-lived, others long-lived . . . '[45]

And if there is indeed a process of rebirth, it may be that the life-to-life continuant is directed to its new stage of existence by some law of affinity, so that each bundle of dispositions automatically connects itself with an appropriate embryo. But whether or not this is so, it remains certain that our actions have consequences in the world and that for the most part these affect other people more, or at any rate more directly, than ourselves. This fact is the basis of the idea of world karma to which we shall return later.

We must now bring in the question of memory. For it is the notion of individual karma *plus* memory that makes the idea of rebirth morally intelligible. Is there, then, a unique set of memories recording the experience of a series of successive lives, such that the latest and current individual in the series has, or may have, all the memories, whilst no one else can have any of the memories, comprising that particular set? Given such a continuous thread of memory it is morally intelligible that inner karma (the effects of one's actions on one's own character) should accumulate from life to life, and that the basic traits which show in the growing child should be the result of the volitions of previous existences. It is likewise morally intelligible that external karma (the effects of action upon the world), as well as affecting other people, should operate to select the basic circumstances of the next birth of the karmic continuant.

But all this is intelligible only if the *current* individual can remember the past lives whose harvest he is now reaping. He would then be in essentially the same situation as one who reaps the results of his own past action in the same life. If a man loses a leg in a motor accident caused by his own drunken driving he is conscious of a natural cause and effect which, although it may seem harsh, cannot be said to be arbitrary or unjust. And if he were born lame in one leg as a result of the same accident in his previous life, which he could still recall, he might again see his lot as an intelligible one. But suppose that he has no awareness at all of any previous lives. Suppose, as must normally be the case if rebirth is a universal process, all such memories are erased by the traumas of death and birth. In what sense can he then be said to be the person who was responsible for an accident of which he knows nothing and which occurred before he was born? It may be that certain psychic formations which were part of the previous individual are now part of him. But if they are not accompanied by memory, can they be said to constitute the same person? – 'the same immaterial substance, without the same consciousness', as Locke argued, 'no more making the same person by being united to any body, than the same particle of matter, without consciousness, united to any body, makes the same person'.[46]

I am not sure however that this argument is in the end valid. For it might be said that so long as the ever lengthening chain of memories of past lives is brought to consciousness sooner or later, it does not fundamentally matter that in the meantime it is in abeyance. Suppose that as a result of an accident caused by himself, in which a man loses a leg, he also suffers amnesia and can remember neither the accident nor the circumstances leading to it. And suppose that after ten years he recovers his memory. He would then see retrospectively what he had been unable to see during the intervening ten years, namely that his legless condition was the consequence of his own action. As C. J. Ducasse says, 'The supposition that, at *some* time, memory of earlier lives is recovered suffices to make rebirth of *one* person mean something different from death of one person followed by birth of *another* person.'[47] It seems reasonable to suppose that the memory which renders the operation of karma from life to life morally intelligible might be suppressed from consciousness through many lives so long as, either from time to time (perhaps in the intervals between earthly lives) or at the end of the karmic process, the unity of the whole series of lives is seen in retrospect. Such a picture is consonant with the buddhist conception of the self as a stream of conscious and unconscious mental life in which a gradually changing pattern of dispositional characteristics, including memory, is continually being passed on from one momentary state to the next. The rejection of the hindu doctrine of the permanent atman lying behind these momentary states and being conscious of them – as in the simile of the two birds[48] – ensures that any memories of earlier lives are memories of those lives as experienced 'from within' and not merely as observed 'from without'. For it is a continuing thread of memory 'from within' that is necessary to make the concept of rebirth morally significant.

We see here once again the crucial role of memory in any version of the reincarnation doctrine that is to be factually true or false and subject to the possibility of confirming or disconfirming evidence. I shall discuss this evidence in the next chapter. But there is also in buddhist literature the basis for a quite different use of the rebirth idea, at which we should now look, as a mythological expression of certain moral and spiritual realities.

5. REBIRTH AS A MYTHIC TRUTH

Let us return to the simile of the flames and add to it other similes which occur in the same section of the *Milindapanha*, but now without postulating a continuous memory linking successive lives. Karma, then, as it moves from death to birth, is likened to a flame from which another flame is kindled. The second flame is produced from the first and reproduces its character (i.e. shape, colour, brightness) and yet is a second flame and not a continuation of the existence of the first. Similarly a set of deep character traits transfers itself from a completed life to a new life; and the latter is a different person, yet bearing the same karma. Again, there is the simile of the verses:

> 'Do you remember, sire, when you were a boy learning some
> verse from a teacher of verses?'
> 'Yes, revered sir!'
> 'But, sire, does that verse pass over from the teacher?'
> 'O no, revered sir.'
> 'In the same way, sire, that which does not pass over (yet)
> reconnects.'[49]

And again, the simile of the mango stone:

> 'Suppose, sire, some man, having eaten a ripe mango, should plant the stone and a large mango-tree should grow from it and yield fruit; and that the man, having eaten a ripe mango from it too, should plant the stone and a large mango-tree should grow from it too and yield fruit. In this way no end to these trees can be seen. Even so, sire, what is born here dies here; having died here it uprises elsewhere;

being born there, there it dies; having died there it uprises elsewhere.'[50]

Now none of these similes restricts the operation of karma to a linear model, like the dots in a dotted line, in which a given 'bundle' of karma is transmitted from A to B (and only B), and then from B to C (and only C), and so on. For a flame can kindle many flames; a teacher can teach the same verse to many pupils; and a mango tree can produce many fruits. And so we must consider the possibility that, in the absence of threads of memory linking successions of lives, karma – that is to say, the effects of actions – should be thought of as more like the waves expanding from a stone thrown into a pond than to a linear succession like that of the kings and queens of England.

At this point however we must distinguish again between inner or character, and outer or situational, karma. Inner karma must by definition remain with the individual whose karma it is, since it is another name for his basic character. If after bodily death his life continues with actual or latent memory in other spheres, then his basic character or inner karma will of course continue as an aspect of him. If on the other hand he perishes totally at death then his character perishes also. It is however possible to suppose an intermediate case in which the system of his character dispositions, without even latent memory, persists and 'enters' into a fresh embryo. Unlike the buddhist and hindu claims so far examined, this would involve no possibility of verification in the memory of the arhat or the *jivanmukta*. It would thus be a purely metaphysical theory – metaphysical in the pejorative sense that its truth or falsity makes no actual or possible experiential difference. When we omit the factor of an actual or latent memory accompanying the lives which are said to be linked in karmic series, we have nothing left which there could be any reason to assert or which could be of any practical interest to anyone. It is only when we add memory – even if this should only become conscious at the end of the series of lives – that we have either the buddhist, the hindu, or the popular conception of reincarnation or rebirth. I shall therefore not pursue further this systematically unverifiable and unfalsifiable conception of packages of 'inner' karma transmigrating without any accompanying consciousness or memory. Our conclusion so far, then, is that the inner karma constituting an individual's basic character either ceases to exist at death (apart, perhaps, from the kind of mental 'husk' referred to above[51]) or continues as the character of that same individual if he lives beyond the grave.

On the other hand, external or circumstantial karma, so far as we can observe it, neither perishes with the individual nor accompanies him into realms beyond this world. It operates within this world, and it usually affects other people at least as much as it affects the agent. For our environment is all the time being changed for better and worse by the actions of others, as we in turn are all the time contributing to the environment in which others live. We have here the notion of collective karma operating both within the history of humanity as a whole and within the various sub-groups which form relatively bounded fields of action – racial, national, cultural and linguistic; and families, classes, castes, etc. Within all these contexts of life we are all the time shaping both the environment which we share with others and also that in which later generations will have to dwell.

Thus we all exist within the common karmic history of humanity, inheriting a world which others have fashioned and fashioning a world in which others must live. Today this common karma of humanity has become more evident than ever before as a field of moral responsibility. This is true both as regards the manifest interdependence of nations and as regards the effects of present policies and life-styles upon the future human environment. The former regional histories have merged in the present century to form a single world history within which events anywhere are liable to have repercussions elsewhere. The earth has become to a great extent a communicational and economic unity in which national decision-makers have a responsibility for the effects of their actions far beyond the borders of their own country. We have all become conscious in recent years, for example, of the effects upon millions of lives of the american 'dominoes theory' in Asia, of European Economic Community policies in relation to developing countries, and of the influence of the oil-producing states upon at least half the world. We have likewise become aware in recent years of the grossly prodigal ways in which we in the west are consuming the earth's limited resources of metals and fuels. And what we are becoming aware of in all these ways is the pressure of world karma.

If, then, reincarnation is not a literal truth, and we do not return in person to bear in later earthly lives the consequences of our present actions, does not the idea nevertheless express mythically the fact that *someone* will have to bear those consequences? And if, following the Buddha (and also the Christ), we transcend the interests of the 'beloved ego', we shall be as concerned for others who must suffer the consequences of our present mistakes as if we were to suffer them ourselves; and we shall be as eager to bring about good consequences for others as for ourselves. The moral meaning of karma is the claim upon us of this non-self-regarding outlook. If the reincarnation doctrine is a religious or ethical myth this, surely, is its positive significance.

Whether, as J. G. Jennings argues, the Buddha himself in effect demythologized the idea of reincarnation and taught the moral reality of collective karma, I do not profess to know. Jennings says,

> The chain of consequence, the individual's moral responsi-bility for every action, word, or thought, the necessity of morality, are throughout assumed in Buddha's teaching. To this extent the force of Karma is assumed by him, as by all his Hindu contemporaries; but the doctrines of lasting personality and of reward and punishment he definitely repudiated. Assuming the common origin and the funda-mental unity of all life and spirit, he assumed the unity of the force of Karma upon the living material of the whole world, and the doctrine of Karma taught by him is collective not individual.[52]

If the post-canonical similes of the flame, the verse and the mango stone, which depict karma as cause and effect without a continuing individual personal life, are true to the Buddha's own thinking, then the concept of collective karma would seem to accord better with his teaching against egoism than does that of purely individual karma. For the latter appeals in the end to self-concern: if you act wrongly now you will yourself reap the consequences in your next or a later life. On the other hand, the idea of collective karma appeals to and perhaps helps to evoke an unselfish love for others, including not only our contemporaries but also their and our descendants. For if we are as concerned about the effects of our actions upon others as upon ourselves we shall no longer need the thought of an individual external karma working through a series of literal rebirths. And if we discount the stories of the supernatural powers of remembering one's former lives and of seeing other people's karmic histories, it is possible that the Buddha's *anatta* ('no soul') doctrine has ethical as well as metaphysical import, and is a call to a selflessness in which the idea of individual karma no longer has any meaning. Perhaps he was teaching both that there is no continuing self to be reborn to bear the consequences of its present actions and also that we must be equally concerned about the consequences of our actions on others within the collective karma of humanity.

This way of demythologizing the doctrine of rebirth and of reinterpreting it in ethical and social terms may well seem – and indeed may well be – a characteristically western way. However, another closely related way, representing a kind of buddhist existentialism, has been suggested by the very original and interesting thai monk, Bikkhu Buddhadasa. He distinguishes between everyday worldly language and religious or Dhamma language, and says:

> In Dhamma language the word ['birth'] refers to the birth of the sense of 'I' and 'me' anytime it arises in the mind. In this sense the ordinary person is born very often, time and time again. A more developed person is born less frequently; a person well advanced in practice is born less frequently still, and ultimately ceases being reborn altogether. Each arising in the mind of the idea of 'I' in one form or another is called a birth. From this point of view birth takes place many times over in a single day. As soon as anyone thinks like an animal, he is born as an animal at that same moment. To think as a human being is to be born a human being. To

think like a celestial being is to be born a celestial being . . .
Thus birth means, in Dhamma language, the arising of the
idea of 'I' and 'me', and not, as in everyday language,
physical birth from the mother's womb.[53]

NOTES

1. O. H. de A. Wijesekera, *The Three Signata*.

2. *Vinaya-Pitaka: Mahavagga*, I, 33 (*The Book of the Discipline*,
vol. IV, p. 19). I have generally quoted from the deliberately rather
literal translations published by the Pali Text Society.

3. I am omitting the diacritical marks from transliterated pali
words.

4. 'Maha-Sudassana Suttanta', *Digha-Nikaya*, II, 198 (*Dialogues of
the Buddha*, part II, pp. 231–2).

5. ibid., p. 232.

6. Sonnet no. 60.

7. *an* is a negative prefix, and *atta* is the pali equivalent of the
sanskrit *atman*.

8. *Visuddhi Magga*, ch. XVI, 90 (*The Path of Purification* by
Buddhaghosa, p. 587).

9. Ashvaghosha, *Acts of the Buddha* (*Buddhacarita*), canto 14,
vv. 2–3, p. 203.

10. *The Buddha's Teaching of Egolessness*, p. 3.

11. V. F. Gunaratna, *Rebirth Explained*, pp. 16–17.

12. *Sanyutta-Nikaya*, III, 104 (*The Book of the Kindred Sayings*,
part III, pp. 87–8).

13. ibid., III, 68 (pp. 59–60; cf. pp. 21, 22–3, 68–9, etc.). Also
Majjhima-Nikaya, I, 138 (*The Middle Length Sayings*, vol. I, pp. 177–
8). On the face of it these sayings assume that there *is* such a true self
or atman, although the orthodox buddhist interpretation denies this.

14. *Critique of Pure Reason*, 'Refutation of Mendelssohn's Proof of
the Permanence of the Soul'.

15. See, e.g., Emil Brunner, *Dogmatics*, vol. III, pp. 383–4, 390–1.

16. The essentially temporal and dynamic character of the physical
world is treated as a comprehensive metaphysical principle in the
explicitly process philosophy of the school of A. N. Whitehead.

17. O. H. de A. Wijesekera, *The Three Signata*, p. 6. So also
Nyanatiloka in *The Buddha's Teaching of Egolessness*.

18. *Sanyutta-Nikaya*, III, 22 (*The Book of the Kindred Sayings*,
part III, p. 21).

19. ibid., III, 67 (p. 59).

20. O. H. de A. Wijesekera, *The Three Signata*, p. 14.

21. *Majjhima-Nikaya*, I, 75 (*The Middle Length Sayings*, vol. I, pp. 100–1).

22. *Sanyutta-Nikaya*, II, 53 (*The Book of the Kindred Sayings*, part II, p. 40).

23. On these two christian traditions, see my *Evil and the God of Love*.

24. *Digha-Nikaya*, II, 157 (*Dialogues of the Buddha*, part II, pp. 175–6).

25. On the history of these terms, see Mrs Rhys Davids, *Indian Religion and Survival*, pp. 66–8.

26. *Milindapanha*, 46 (*Milinda's Questions*, vol. I, p. 63).

27. K. N. Jayatilleke, 'Some Problems of Translation and Interpretation, I', in *University of Ceylon Review*, vol. VII, no. 3 (1949), p. 214.

28. On the striking similarities, as well as the differences, between freudian and buddhist psychology, see Padmasiri de Silva, *Buddhist and Freudian Psychology*.

29. This is stated by the Buddha in the 'Maha-Nidana Suttanta', *Digha-Nikaya*, II, 63 (*Dialogues of the Buddha*, part II, pp. 60–1).

30. Cause in this sense: 'If this is, that comes to be; from the arising of this, that arises; if this is not, that does not come to be; from the stopping of this, that is stopped!' *Majjhima-Nikaya*, II, 32 (*The Middle Length Sayings*, vol. II, p. 230).

31. 'Maha-Nidana Suttanta', *Digha-Nikaya*, II, 55–6 (*Dialogues of the Buddha*, part II, pp. 51–2).

32. Nyanatiloka Mahathera, *Karma and Rebirth*, p. 20.

33. This is stated in the *Anguttara-Nikaya*, I, 34 (*The Book of the Gradual Sayings*, vol. I, p. 31).

34. *Survival and Karma in Buddhist Perspective*, p. 12.

35. e.g., K. N. Jayatilleke, op. cit., ch. 7; V. F. Gunaratna, *Rebirth Explained*, chs. 13, 14.

36. *Anguttara-Nikaya*, I, 36 (*The Book of the Gradual Sayings*, vol. I, p. 33).

37. 'Maha-Sudassana Suttanta', *Digha-Nikaya*, II, 196 (*Dialogues of the Buddha*, part II, p. 229).

38. *Majjhima-Nikaya*, I, 76 (*The Middle Length Sayings*, vol. I, p. 101). The technical term in the pali scriptures for such spontaneous rebecoming, without a birth, is *opapatika* (lit: 'unprocreated'). This mode of rebecoming is referred to, e.g., in the *Sanyutta-Nikaya*, III, 206, 240–1, 246 (*The Book of the Kindred Sayings*, part III, pp. 166, 192–3, 195), and the *Anguttara-Nikaya*, I, 232 (*The Book of the Gradual Sayings*, vol. I, p. 212), V, 343, 345 (*Gradual Sayings*, vol. V, pp. 221–2).

39. Sir Charles Eliot says that 'at the time of the Buddha . . . [reincarnation] was an integral part of popular theology as is the

immortality of the soul in Europe' (*Hinduism and Buddhism*, vol. I, p. 42).

40. The case against the received view is presented by J. G. Jennings in *The Vedantic Buddhism of the Buddha,* particularly pp. xliii–xlv.

41. *Milindapanha,* 71 (*Milinda's Questions,* vol. I, p. 97).

42. *The Dhammapada,* I, 1–2.

43. Galatians 6: 7.

44. William James, *Talks to Teachers on Psychology,* pp. 77–8.

45. *Milindapanha,* 65 (*Milinda's Questions,* vol. I, pp. 89–90).

46. *An Essay concerning Human Understanding,* book II, ch. 27, para. 14. The full passage is quoted on pp. 305–6 above.

47. C. J. Ducasse, *A Critical Examination of the Belief in a Life after Death,* p. 225.

48. See p. 328.

49. *Milindapanha,* 71 (*Milinda's Questions,* vol. I, p. 97).

50. ibid., 77 (p. 106).

51. pp. 140–1.

52. J. G. Jennings, *The Vedantic Buddhism of the Buddha,* pp. xxiv–xxv. See also introductory notes 1–5.

53. Buddhadasa, *Toward the Truth,* p. 68.

CHAPTER 19

Reincarnation – Discriminations and Conclusions

1. A LOGICALLY VIABLE THEORY

We have seen that the notion of reincarnation or rebirth[1] covers a range of meanings from a reasonably straightforwardly factual version, which is in principle verifiable if true, to highly metaphysical versions which seem immune to any kind of verification or falsification. At one end of the scale is the notion that the conscious ego, the remembering, anticipating, choosing, acting self which is now composing these sentences, having died in one body will be reborn in another. However, in this simplest form the belief does not fit certain evident facts. For babies are not born with adult egos, as they would be if they were direct continuations of egos which had died at the end of a normal life-span. The old man in his dotage may return to 'second childishness' but nevertheless his decaying ego, with its slowly crumbling structure of habits and its confused memories, is in a state very different from that of the pliable mental life of a newborn baby. And so we have to open the gate to distinctions which begin by making the idea of reincarnation more credible but threaten to end by emptying it of factual content. We have to say that it is not the conscious ego that is reborn but something else, the soul, lying behind or beneath or above the conscious self. This enduring soul is successively incarnated in many different egos, each of which goes through its own separate life-span, beginning with the unformed mentality of a baby.

What, then, is this eternal or at least very long-lived soul which is said to link together a series of successive ego-histories? According to both the vedantic and the buddhist teachings it is a karmic history consisting in a developing formation of basic character dispositions. These are very general spiritual, moral, intellectual and aesthetic dispositional tendencies capable of being expressed in a wide range of ways in the differing circumstances of successive human lives. Thus presumably a basic religious tendency; or a tendency to be ruthlessly self-seeking; or to be studious and scholarly; or to appreciate music or poetry; or tendencies to gluttony or austerity, to sexual promiscuity or restraint, to quick or even temper, to logical or intuitive thought . . . may be aspects of a soul which incarnates by lodging itself in a fresh embryo and functioning as one of the factors influencing the growth of a new ego.

However, we have seen that if such rather general character traits were all that A had in common with B, it would be virtually meaningless to describe B as A reincarnated. What they have in common could not be specific enough to constitute them as different phases of the same person. They would be different individuals, although individuals whose character profiles overlap to a considerable extent. But such overlapping occurs between very many people. Indeed, as we noted in chapter 16, for every individual in B's generation there must be a large number, doubtless amounting to thousands, of individuals in A's generation whose character profiles overlap as much as A's does with B's; and if these character similarities are all that link earlier and later births of the same soul there would be no more reason to think that B was the reincarnation of A than of A^1, A^2, A^3 . . . And since there would be no more reason to think that B was the reincarnation of one rather than another of many thousands, there could be no good reason on the grounds of character similarity to suppose that he is the reincarnation of any of them. Rather, in a world in which fairly considerable character resemblances occur among the hundreds of millions of human beings in any two generations, B could much more naturally be described simply as a different person from A.

Thus in addition to the transmission of character traits, a link of memory is essential to any theory which identifies individuals as being reincarnations of specific members of an earlier generation, and which thus speaks of a particular series as the successive lives of one and the same soul. It is the link of memory that picks out, say, A^{1843} as the unique individual whose history is continued in the life of B, out of the thousands of others in the same generation whose character profiles qualify them as pre-incarnations of B.

It must not however be insisted that such memory deposits be complete – for we have only fragmentary memories even of the earlier stages of our present life; or that they must be readily available to our consciousness – for we have repressed, and hence unconscious, as well as conscious memories. It is not, on the face of it, unreasonable to suppose that the traumas of death and birth normally deprive the reincarnating self of awareness of its earlier lives. There is a range of possibilities here, from the extreme (which does not however occur) of a memory of previous lives comparable with our normal memory of this life; through intermittent phases of recollection, perhaps occurring between incarnations; to the other extreme, affirmed in hindu and buddhist thought, of no life-to-life memory (except for occasional accidental 'leakages') until the final attainment of enlightenment, when one is able to experience an entire retrospect of all one's innumerable lives. These all seem to constitute possible pictures of the place of human consciousness in the economy of the universe.

There are however important differences – to be discussed in section 6 – in the wider implications of these various possibilities, and in the interests that could be served by the different kinds of reincarnation doctrine to which they give rise. But let us for the moment continue to think of reincarnation in general terms, without specifying more precisely the kind of memory claim which it involves, and consider now its compatibility or otherwise with christian teaching.

2. CHRISTIANITY AND REINCARNATION

Reincarnation is not, and has never been, an orthodox christian belief.[2] But it does not absolutely follow from this that it could never become an orthodox christian belief. The history of Christianity shows a number of instances of important ideas which at one time formed no part of accepted christian teaching but which at a later time have been taught in substantial parts, at least, of Christendom. For example, neither the 'satisfaction' doctrine of the atonement, which has officially prevailed for many centuries within the catholic church, nor the 'penal-substitutionary' atonement doctrine, which generally prevailed until recently in the reformed churches, was known during approximately the first thousand years of christian history: the one was launched by Anselm in the eleventh and the other by Calvin in the sixteenth century. Again, the acceptance by the churches in the late nineteenth and early twentieth centuries of the evolution of the forms of life has brought with it immense changes in christian doctrine which would have seemed impossible to christian thinkers even two centuries ago. Since Darwin's time the pace of theological change has quickened, and he would be a bold prognosticator who claimed to know the limits of change in the next period, which must be characterized by the influence upon one another's developments of the different religions as they meet and interact in the 'one world' created by modern communications.

What specific reasons, however, are advanced for the widely accepted view that the idea of reincarnation is incompatible with christian truth? They are principally four:

1. The first is the negative argument that reincarnation is not taught in the New Testament.

Some have indeed professed to see references to it in certain passages.[3] One is Jesus' implied identification of John the Baptist as Elijah:

> The disciples asked him, 'Then why do the scribes say that first Elijah must come?' He replied, 'Elijah does come, and he is to restore all things; but I tell you that Elijah has already come, and they did not know him, but did to him whatever they pleased. So also the Son of man will suffer at their hands.' Then the disciples understood that he was speaking to them of John the Baptist.[4]

Of this matthean passage, and its marcan parallel,[5] Leslie Weatherhead writes, 'It would be difficult to explain such a passage other than by supposing that they regarded John the Baptist as a reincarnation of Elijah.'[6] However he is here ignoring the Old Testament background of the reference to Elijah. It was believed that Elijah had not died but had been miraculously taken up into heaven in a chariot of fire drawn by horses of fire,[7] and would some day come again to prepare the way for the Messiah.[8] Thus the idea that John the Baptist was

Elijah did not imply reincarnation, in the sense of the soul of Elijah being born again as a baby, but rather a miraculous descent of the prophet from the heavens.[9] An essentially similar explanation applies to the passage in which Jesus asks, 'Who do men say that the Son of Man is?' and his disciples reply, 'Some say John the Baptist, others say Elijah, and others Jeremiah or one of the prophets.'[10] For there was a belief that certain of the prophets had not died but were in heaven assisting the Jews.[11]

The other passage in which some have seen the idea of reincarnation[12] is that in which his disciples asked Jesus concerning a man born blind, ' "Rabbi, who sinned, this man or his parents, that he was born blind?" Jesus answered, "It was not that this man sinned, or his parents, but that the works of God might be made manifest in him." '[13] Whereupon he healed him. The question put to Jesus presupposes either the idea of pre-existent souls (which, according to Bultmann, 'had found its way into syncretistic and Hellenistic Judaism'[14]) which may accordingly have sinned before being born into this world; or the idea that a child may sin in its mother's womb (which is known to have been taught by some of the rabbis from the second and third centuries[15]); or the idea of reincarnation (which however does not appear elsewhere in the biblical or para-biblical[16] literature, but which was certainly known in the graeco-roman world within the broad syncretistic movement of thought known as Gnosticism). Thus our passage may possibly refer to the idea of reincarnation, but may on the other hand refer to either of two other ideas. Or it may, as Bultmann seems to think, be meant to propound two impossible alternatives as a way of rejecting their common presupposition that misfortune is a punishment for sin.[17] However, if the passage does contain a reference to reincarnation, this would not indicate that Jesus believed in reincarnation but would on the contrary show that he rejected it, at least in any form in which it would provide an answer to the problem of apparently undeserved suffering. I therefore conclude concerning the New Testament evidence (a) that it is possible, but not very probable, that there is a reference to the idea of reincarnation in John 9: 2, and (b) that there is no reason at all to think that Jesus or any of the New Testament

writers were sympathetic to the idea; on the contrary, if John
9: 2 is a reference to reincarnation, the following verse is a
repudiation of it.

Just how decisively this should weigh in favour of the conclusion that the concept of reincarnation is radically incompatible with christian truth depends upon one's understanding
of the nature of theology and its relation to the scriptures. I
have already pointed out that there are a number of important
ideas which do not appear in the New Testament but which
have today been accepted into christian thought or which were
accepted in earlier stages of christian history. Thus it is
possible to hold a view of the development of doctrine according to which the absence of the reincarnation theme from the
New Testament is not by itself a decisive reason for judging it
incapable of ever being woven into a context of christian belief.
(On the other hand of course if John 9: 2–3 is held to refer to
reincarnation we have a positive scriptural text against it.)

What, however, of the positive rejection of the idea of
reincarnation by christian writers of the second to fifth centuries, listed in note 2 on pages 392–4 below? Does not this have
weight as evidence of an inherent incompatibility between
Christianity and the reincarnation doctrine? It does; but we
must ask more precisely what the evidence is evidence for,
and how strong it is. It constitutes good historical ground for
holding that the christian theologians of those early centuries
were aware of and rejected the idea of reincarnation. Can we
pass from this to the conclusion that Christians of any period,
including the twentieth and succeeding centuries, should also
reject it? We cannot make this move automatically. For there
are a number of ideas affirmed by those early theologians
which a great many Christians today reject (for example, the
six-day creation of the world, and demonic possession), and
also a number of ideas accepted by Christians today which
would have been incompatible with the thought-world of
thinkers in the second to fifth centuries (for example, biological
evolution, and biblical criticism). Thus we do not, in practice,
adopt their views unquestioningly. We discriminate, taking
account of their reasons for thinking as they did. If those
reasons seem to us cogent, we accept them; and if not, not.
Following this procedure, we shall regard the evidence of the

early apologists as consisting, not simply in the historical fact that they rejected the idea of reincarnation but, more importantly, in their reasons for rejecting it. In so far as these reasons commend themselves to us we shall be led by them to the same conclusion. This procedure is particularly appropriate in view of the fact that the reasons offered by the early christian thinkers are to a great extent rational arguments appealing to the normal canons of logic. They point to the lack of memories of former lives (Tertullian, Irenaeus, Lactantius); to the problem of personal identity (Tertullian); to the fact of population growth (Tertullian); and to the absurdity of the idea of being reborn as an animal or a plant (Tertullian, Lactantius, Gregory of Nyssa). These are all considerations which we have discussed in previous chapters. We found that they have considerable force against the popular conception of reincarnation but very little against the more sophisticated versions found in philosophical Hinduism and Buddhism. Thus although cogent in relation to the targets which these writers had in mind, their arguments are only marginally relevant to the more impressive forms of reincarnation theory, and they cannot be said to provide us with good reasons for rejecting these.

2. A second reason commonly offered is that Christianity attributes an absolute importance to this present life as the period of grace in which our eternal salvation or damnation is to be determined, and that the infinite gravity of the choice facing us would be dissipated if we were able to return to enjoy further spiritual opportunities in further earthly lives.

This argument is at home in the major, augustinian strand of christian tradition developed by the latin Fathers and embodied in the theology of the roman church. But it has no basis in the alternative irenaean type of theology that was originated by the early hellenistic Fathers (prominent among them being Irenaeus in the second century), that languished for many centuries, revived again in the thought of the great nineteenth-century protestant thinker, Friedrich Schleiermacher, and that has become progressively more widespread ever since in both protestant and, recently, catholic theology.[18] From this latter point of view one can fully accept the critique that has been offered by indian writers of the traditional christian conception that men have only one life to live and that their eternal salvation or damnation is determined by their spiritual success or failure in this brief and chancy existence. They often criticize this idea as involving an intolerable unfairness. For example, Sri Aurobindo says that there is 'the difficulty that this soul inherits a past for which it is in no way responsible, or is burdened with mastering propensities imposed on it not by its own act, and is yet responsible for its future which is treated as if it were in no way determined by that often deplorable inheritance, *damnosa hereditas*, or that unfair creation, and were entirely of its own making. We are made helplessly what we are and are yet responsible for what we are, – or at least for what we shall be hereafter, which is inevitably determined to a large extent by what we are originally. And we have only this one chance. Plato and the Hottentot, the fortunate child of saints or Rishis and the born and trained criminal plunged from beginning to end in the lowest fetid corruption of a great modern city have equally to create by the action or belief of this one unequal life all their eternal future. This is a paradox which offends both the soul and the reason, the ethical sense and the spiritual intuition.'[19] In contrast to this the irenaean type of theology sees the divine creation of personal life as taking place through a long and slow process which extends far beyond this present earthly scene. It sees the origin of personal existence in the complexification of matter through the processes of organic evolution, within which at a certain stage man has emerged out of the lower forms of life. It thus differs from traditional hindu thought in that this regards individual human souls as having existed through unlimited time. But so far as their future is concerned there is a considerable area of agreement. For the irenaean type of theology rejects the thought that men are at death distributed to an eternal heaven or hell. It thinks instead in terms of continued responsible life in which the soul-making process continues in other environments beyond this world. Thus it speaks of an intermediate state between this present life and the ultimate heavenly state – the traditional catholic doctrine of purgatory being itself an approach to this idea. Further, in attempting to envisage such an intermediate state, even though necessarily only in very general terms, it postulates many worlds or spheres of existence in addition to this physical world, and envisages the progress of the soul through them towards a final state of perfection in completely fulfilled relationship both to God and to finite beings.

Now in a sense the difference between this picture of man's future and the idea of reincarnation as it was outlined in the previous section is not very great. For they agree concerning the basic principle of continued responsible life in which the individual may still learn and grow by interacting with other human beings in a common environment or environments. They differ only as to *where* this continued life takes place. The christian belief (in the irenaean tradition) has been that it takes place in other worlds beyond this one. The indian belief has been that it takes place by means of repeated returns to this world. But this difference seems relatively slight in comparison with the more fundamental agreement. Indeed, the question whether man's continued life takes the form of progress through other spheres, or progress from incarnation to incarnation within this world, would seem to be a matter of probable judgement rather than of essential christian (of the irenaean type) and hindu or buddhist faith respectively. Apart from the weight of tradition behind us, which is of course very liable to determine what we think, there appears to be no compelling reason why a Christian should not come to believe in reincarnation instead of in continued life in other spheres, or why a Hindu or a Buddhist should not come to believe in continued life in other spheres instead of in reincarnation.[20]

3. It has also been said that 'belief in metempsychosis is fundamentally at variance with the Christian doctrine of the resurrection of the body'.[21] But the word 'fundamentally' here would require a good deal of justifying. The two doctrines – reincarnation and resurrection of the body – are indeed incompatible on the surface. But they agree more deeply in their view of man as a psycho-physical unity, so that life after death must be in a body, and a body which expresses the inner character of the individual. The two doctrines are thus versions of a common view that man lives again as an appropriately embodied being. If he is 'reincarnated' he is thereby

resurrected (brought back) to a new embodied life; if he is 'resurrected' he is thereby reincarnated, i.e. incarnated (enfleshed) again. In its insistence upon man's psycho-physical nature the resurrection doctrine agrees with the reincarnation doctrine as against platonic notions of the immortality of a disembodied soul. Thus considered as pareschatologies, reincarnation and the resurrection of the body are superficially different but more fundamentally in agreement. For the reincarnation doctrine affirms repeated resurrections of a particular kind.

4. A fourth argument often offered for a radical opposition between christian belief and the concept of reincarnation concerns the historical uniqueness of the saving event of Christ's atoning death. This is held to be a sacrifice offered once-for-all for the entire human race, including those who had lived before the incarnation, those who lived contemporaneously with Jesus, and those who have lived or are still to live in the period after his earthly life: Christ does not return again and again to repeat his sacrifice in each new generation. It is sometimes assumed that this element of *Einmaligkeit* in the christian gospel precludes the idea of human reincarnation. But it is not easy to see why it should. For there is no logical connection between the idea that Christ died once only for the sins of the world and the idea that men have only one life in which to accept the benefits of that atoning death. And if with the irenaean and universalist strand of christian thought we reject this latter view, then the uniqueness of God's saving act in Christ, so far from militating against the possibility of a christian doctrine of reincarnation, could be compatible with it. For salvation in Christ might be substituted for the 'enlightenment' or 'liberation' of the indian systems as the goal at which the process of rebirth aims and which brings it to an end. It could be said that the response to God's love made flesh in Christ is the end for the sake of which men are born on earth, and that they go on being reborn until eventually they make that response. In this way the reincarnation doctrine could form part of a christian theology of the irenaean type.

It will be evident from the remainder of this chapter that I am not in fact advocating any such development of christian doctrine – but for reasons other than a supposed basic incompatibility with the christian gospel.

3. SPONTANEOUS MEMORIES OF FORMER LIVES

We have seen that actual or latent memories of one's previous lives are essential to the reincarnation doctrine in any form in which it can be factually true or false. How then should one who does not remember any previous existences estimate the claims of others to have such memories?

We have to consider here both the reports of contemporary and recent individuals who have professed to recall fragments of a previous life, and also the belief that certain spiritually very advanced persons have developed the power to remember a long series of other lives.

I cannot attempt here a detailed examination of the now fairly numerous published cases of supposed memories of an earlier life. It is fortunate however that these have recently been subjected to a scientific scrutiny which has lifted the subject out of the realm of anecdote into that of responsible parapsychological research. Professor Ian Stevenson of the University of Virginia, in *The Evidence for Survival from Claimed Memories of Former Incarnations*[22] and *Twenty Cases Suggestive of Reincarnation*,[23] has examined some of the more important cases of this kind, and in doing so has contributed the most substantial and scientifically responsible treatment of the question so far available. In these cases someone, B (usually a child), has ostensible 'memories' that have apparently not been acquired in the course of his or her present life. They are 'memories' of people, places, circumstances and events that fall outside B's experience. They are however found to fit the life of A, who died before B was born. B is taken to the place where A had lived and is able to recognize A's relatives, perhaps to know his way about the house and the town, and perhaps to recount particulars of A's life of which apparently he (B) could not have known. A number of records of this kind read impressively. Their impressiveness resides however to a great extent in their details and cannot be adequately conveyed by summaries. But there is almost invariably the defect, from the point of view of hard evidence, that no scientifically reliable investigation was made whilst the case was 'raw' and before unconscious hints and clues, as well as errors in observation and almost inevitable exaggerations in the recounting of the tale, could have entered in. Stevenson's enquiries, for example, although they appear to have been as thorough and objective as was feasible in the circumstances, had to be made (in the twenty cases reported at length in his later book[24]) several years after each case first became known, and generally had to be pursued through the intermediary of a local interpreter. These circumstances – and particularly the considerable lapse of time before Stevenson began his enquiries – reduce their evidential value, in my view, below the level at which they can properly be said to *prove* anything. This is not of course to exclude the possibility that stronger cases may be forthcoming in the future. Further, well-authenticated instances (such as Stevenson does not thus far profess to have reported) of birth-marks or congenital deformities exactly reproducing those of the person whose life is 'remembered' might constitute important new evidence.

I should like to draw attention to two particularly puzzling features of these cases suggestive of reincarnation, although unfortunately they point in opposite directions. One is that the people concerned are so often children. Why should it almost always be children who spontaneously 'remember' a previous life, the 'memory' usually fading as they grow up? An obvious answer might be that in childhood they are nearest to that which they are remembering, and forget it as they become more fully absorbed in their present life. Thus the characteristic childhood incidence of these 'memories' tends to support the reincarnationist hypothesis. The other puzzling feature is one upon which a number of writers have remarked – namely, how very many of these cases come from societies in which reincarnation is an accepted belief. An indian investigator, C. T. K. Chari, says, 'It is disconcerting to learn that, out of some 300 alleged cases, over 100 are from India. Can we ignore a cultural predisposition to interpret the facts in accordance with a myth-motif? . . . One casts about for special types of "contagious distribution" which would suggest at once contaminating social and sub-cultural factors. An alleged universal law of rebirth which is so highly conditioned by purely local factors is suspect.'[25] Stevenson's researches also indicate a concentration of apparent previous-life memories in cultures in which reincarnation is a matter of general belief. His international census of cases suggestive of reincarnation, as reported in 1966, contained nearly six hundred cases. About half of these came from the hindu and buddhist cultures of south-east Asia, and many more came from Lebanon and Syria (where the Druses believe strongly in reincarnation), from Brazil (where the belief is widely held), and from Alaska (where the Tlingit Indians are traditional believers).[26] Thus for example Stevenson says, 'Since among most Druses the belief in reincarnation persists strongly without any defensive attitude toward other beliefs, and since parents have little or no objection to the claims made by children to remember a previous life, we find in Lebanon and Syria almost ideal conditions for the development of cases suggestive of reincarnation. . . And we should therefore feel no surprise that the incidence of cases among the Druses is perhaps the highest in the world.'[27] Again, he says that 'the widespread belief in survival (with reincarnation) in Brazil has created a cultural climate favorable to the narration of claimed memories of a previous life. Children who make such assertions have the respect of their parents in unfolding their stories.'[28] He adds at another point that there are also cases suggestive of rebirth in cultures to which the belief is alien: 'For many cases do occur in the West and some in families which have either never heard of reincarnation or never given it any credence.'[29] Nevertheless the broad picture remains one of 'a high correlation between the occurrence of cases suggestive of rebirth and cultural attitudes favoring the telling of "memories" of previous lives'.[30] This fact requires explanation, and explanations readily offer themselves to the effect that the belief induces pseudo-memories in the suggestible minds of the children concerned.

In view of all these ambiguities and uncertainties it seems right at this stage to record an interim verdict of Not Proven: the cases at present available do not oblige us to accept the reincarnation hypothesis. On the other hand they are by no means so weak that we are entitled to ignore them. It thus seems sensible, whilst reserving judgement on these alleged memories of former lives, to ask what would follow if new cases in the future should come to be accepted as evidentially compelling. If we acknowledge that someone is indeed displaying knowledge of a formerly living individual, about whom he could not have known by normal means, and honestly reports this as memory, is any explanation possible other than reincarnation? It may of course be that such cases would not all be susceptible of the same explanation. Stevenson himself discusses several different hypotheses, other than reincarnation, each of which may apply to one or more of his own twenty cases, though he does not think that they can between them convincingly cover all of them. I should like to add one more to the list of possible non-reincarnationist explanations, making use of the psychic factor theory mentioned in chapter 7. This is the theory that after bodily death a mental 'husk' or 'mask' of the deceased person is left behind and is telepathically accessible under certain conditions to living persons. Such a 'husk' may consist of mere fragments of memory, emotion, habit – analogous to isolated pieces of a tape-recording – or of a relatively coherent and cohesive body of such elements and may, I suggested (following C. D. Broad), become linked to the mind of a medium when in trance and be presented under the dramatic guise of a visitor from the spirit world. This hypothesis can be extended to cover the comparatively rare cases of an individual 'remembering' a supposed previous identity and life. It may be that he (or she) is telepathically sensitive in the same sort of way as a medium, and is being influenced by the psychic 'husk' of some deceased person and identifying himself with this.

It is perhaps worth noting, as consistent with this possibility, that in most, or perhaps all, of the more impressive cases of reported memories of former lives – including all of Ian Stevenson's twenty selected cases – the remembered life was the most recent one, with a gap of no more than a few years between its end and the beginning of the reported memories.[31] Likewise the 'spirits' who communicate through mediums have usually only fairly lately died. The recency of the material in each case might be expected if the phenomena have a common origin in persisting psychic traces or 'husks' which presumably gradually fade or decay with the passage of time.

The difference between this and ordinary mediumship

would be that the child (or adult) who 'remembers' a previous identity and life is not in trance but is pursuing an otherwise normal waking life. Whereas a medium deliberately goes into trance intending to be open to the influence of external psychic forces, the normal impingements of mental 'husks' of the dead upon telepathically sensitive persons in dreams and waking impressions must be fleeting and casual and must require the operation of some additional force to bring about the kind of persisting linkage found in the cases we are considering. I would suggest that this additional element is normally supplied by the influence of a culture in which reincarnation is an unquestioned belief. In this way the strong correlation between such cultures and the incidence of previous-life 'memories' can be accorded the importance that it demands.

It is true that Stevenson reports, concerning evidence that the children concerned display ESP capacities outside their 'memories' of a previous life, that 'most show no evidence of such powers, a few show some slight evidence of them, and an even smaller number show behavior quite similar to that of ordinary adult mediums'.[32] But this does not seem to me by any means to settle the matter in the negative. For (a) it does not appear that Stevenson conducted any tests for ESP capacities, and (b) the presence within such a small population of even two or three with full-fledged mediumistic powers may well be significant.

The hypothesis which I am suggesting differs in one important respect from the ESP-plus-personation theory which Stevenson discusses.[33] According to the latter the subject gains information about a deceased individual by retro-cognitive ESP and then misidentifies himself as being that individual reincarnated. As Stevenson points out, such a theory accounts more plausibly, on the face of it, for the child's acquisition of information about a previously living person than for his presentation of that information over a period of years (averaging about seven in the cases which he describes) as a recollection of having been that person. This difficulty is to some extent eased by the hypothesis which I am proposing, in that what is cognized by the subject is not simply a number of items of information about the deceased individual but the actual presence to the subject of fragments – though dead fragments – of that individual's personality. For it is a 'husk' or 'mask' of the deceased person, including some of his memories and dispositional characteristics, that has become attached to the subject's mind. This would perhaps explain his ability to 'recognize' people whom he has not met and places where he has not been before. In these 'recognitions' he is exercising fragments of memory-disposition which are elements of the psychic factor with which he is in contact. The reason why this happens, on the rather rare occasions on which (if we accept some of the reported cases at their face value) it does happen, will be a telepathic sensitivity in some children directed into this particular channel by the influence of the reincarnation belief prevalent in their culture.

With such a theory the idea of reincarnation becomes in effect a matter of degree. There is no rebirth of the full living personality. But there is a kind of reincarnation of parts or aspects of the personality, such attenuated reincarnation being equally compatible with the extinction of the personality as a whole or with its continued life in some other sphere, leaving behind only a mental 'husk' which becomes entangled in the mind of a living child with whom it has perhaps some kind of affinity and through whom its remaining quantum of psychic energy is discharged. This would seem, at any rate in the present state of the scientific investigation of spontaneous 'memories' of former lives, to be one more possible non- or semi-reincarnationist explanation of them.

I shall not discuss here the numerous cases of 'memories' of other lives elicited under hypnosis, because there is no support from professional psychologists for the view that these are other than examples of response to suggestion.

4. YOGIC MEMORIES OF FORMER LIVES

The other reason for believing that memories occur of past lives is the claim that yogis, arhats and other liberated souls have developed the power to remember, not merely their most recent life, but all of their lives back at least through their human stage of existence; and also the power to observe the karmic process at work in the lives and deaths of others. This differs from the fragmentary recollections said to be received by a few ordinary individuals, either spontaneously or under hypnosis, in that a yogi's memory of former lives is under his own control, is as detailed as he wishes it to be, and extends to as many lives as he cares to recall. The most famous account of this in religious literature is that of the Buddha. We read in the pali scriptures:

I, brethren, according as I desire, can remember my divers former lives, that is to say, one birth, or two, or three, or four, or five births, or ten, twenty, thirty, forty, fifty births, or a hundred, a thousand, or even a hundred thousand, or even more than one aeon of involution, or more than one aeon of evolution, or more than one of both involution and evolution: – such an one was I by name, of such a clan, of such a social status, so was I nourished, such happy and painful experiences were mine, so did the span of life end, deceasing thence so did I come to be, there too was I such a name, of such a clan, of such a social station, so was I nourished, such happy and painful experiences were mine, so did the span of life end, deceasing thence so did I come to be here:– I can thus call to mind in circumstances and detail my former lives.

Kassapa, brethren, can do likewise.

I, brethren, according as I desire, [can] behold with purified deva-vision passing that of man, beings as they decease and come to be, mean or excellent, fair or foul; I know them going according to their deeds to weal or woe, thinking:– Lo! these good people whose deeds were evil, whose speech was evil, whose thoughts were evil, abusers of Ariyans, having wrong views and undertaking the acts that (come from) wrong views – they at the separation of the body after death have come to be in the Waste, the Woeful Way, the Downfall, hell. Lo! those good people, whose deeds, whose speech, whose thoughts were good, who abused not Ariyans, of right views and who undertook the acts that [come from] right views – they at the separation of the body after death have come to be in a good destiny, in a bright world. Thus do I behold beings with deva-sight passing that of men, how they decease, and come to be mean or excellent, fair or foul; I know them as going according to their actions to weal or woe.[34]

And it is said that these two powers are ones which all arhats can if they wish (though not all do) develop.

This is a classic passage cited in support of the claim that exalted souls can learn to remember their past lives. But the Buddha Gautama lived two and a half thousand years ago and the stories of his life took literary form several centuries after his death. It is therefore difficult to regard them as hard historical evidence that he enjoyed such a retrospect of thousands of former lives or that other yogis have done so. That the Buddha taught the doctrine of rebirth in some form seems certain, but we are alerted by western biblical criticism to the possibility that the fact that the Buddha taught it may conceivably have led to the development within the buddhist community of the tradition that he remembered his own past lives. It could well be that in the *Jatakas* of the pali canon, in which some 550 of the Buddha's former lives are described, we see this development taking place. For these stories bear unmistakable marks of the legendary. Indeed, for the most part they appear to be traditional folk tales adapted for didactic purposes by the preaching buddhist monks. Mrs Rhys Davids, in her introduction to a volume of selections from the *Jatakas*, says that 'many of the stories, perhaps most, are, as Indian, older than the time when the Sakya, that is, the Buddhist movement, began'.[35] I have already cited one,[36] not from the *Jatakas* but from the 'Maha-Sudassana Suttanta', with its long and detailed description of the wealth and glory of the great king of Kusavati, whom the Buddha declared to have been himself in a former birth; and I have already commented that city walls and palm trees made of gold, silver, beryl, crystal, agate, coral and all kinds of gems[37] belong to the rhetoric of fairy-tale rather than to historical reality. Again, the time-scale of the hundreds of thousands of previous earthly lives referred to in the pali canon reflects an eastern pre-scientific outlook which overestimated the true time-scale of human history as widely as the western pre-scientific outlook underestimated it.

At any rate to the western non-believer in rebirth this story, or possibly legend, of the Buddha must by itself seem an inadequate foundation for so important a doctrine. And yet we do not have in indian religious literature any other similar claims said to have been made by specific historical individuals. In the Bhagavad Gita the Lord Krishna says, 'Many are My lives that are past, and thine also, O Arjuna; all of them I know but thou knowest not';[38] but the incarnate Krishna of the Gita is not an established historical figure. Again, it is often said in general terms that advanced yogis and liberated souls can remember their past lives; but this is not the same as citing particular individuals whose testimony is available to us and concerning whom we have some context of historical knowledge. No such testimony is publicly available apart from that already quoted from the pali scriptures of Buddhism. In western literature there are second-hand references to Pythagoras' recollections of a series of previous lives, and to Ovid's claim to have taken part in the Trojan War, and Julian the Apostate's claim to have been Alexander the Great. And in more modern times Emanuel Swedenborg, and later both of the formidable ladies who successively led the Theosophical Society, Madame H. P. Blavatsky and Mrs Annie Besant, claimed to have developed the capacity to remember former lives. But it is impossible to test these claims or therefore to do more than note that they have been made.[39]

Thus references, such as we often find in the literature of reincarnation, to the authority of yogic experience and the insights of arhats and *jivanmuktas* are in practice of uncertain value. The evidence being offered turns out to be elusive and hard to 'pin down'. There is a pervasive vagueness, a repeated appeal to unproduced witnesses and unidentified authorities. And in short this line of argument is one which is liable to prove much more persuasive to those who already accept the idea of rebirth than to those who are looking for reasons for accepting it.

5. REINCARNATION AND GENETICS

It is, as we have seen, the claim that successive lives are linked together by an actual or latent continuity of memory that makes reincarnation a factual hypothesis, open in principle to confirmation or disconfirmation. We have looked in the last two sections at the evidence offered by claimed memories of former lives and found this inconclusive. Now we ask whether there is evidence in the form of a clash between the reincarnation hypothesis and the process of genetic inheritance as this is being uncovered by modern biological science.

If for the moment we omit the factor of memory, reincarnation asserts that the same basic character dispositions reappear again and again in different individuals. As such, the idea of reincarnation could be seen as a mythological way of referring to the continuity of the genetic material through the ages. For basic characteristics are indeed, like the *linga sharira* of vedantic doctrine, immensely long-lived and do indeed enter successively into the constitution of a series of different individuals in different generations. It is a literal physical fact that genetically based potentialities are continually reincarnated in new individuals and that each of us embodies a living inheritance from the past which constitutes our share in what can be called the genetic karma of the human race. T. H. Huxley, in his Romanes Lecture of 1893, noted this analogy between the physical concept of heredity and the metaphysical concept of karma:

> Everyday experience familiarizes us with the facts which are grouped under the name of heredity. Every one of us bears upon him obvious marks of his parentage, perhaps of remoter relationships. More particularly, the sum of tendencies to act in a certain way, which we call 'character' is often to be traced through a long series of progenitors and collaterals. So we may justly say that this 'character' – this moral and intellectual essence of a man – does veritably pass over from one fleshly tabernacle to another, and does really transmigrate from generation to generation. In the new-born infant, the character of the stock lies latent, and the Ego is little more than a bundle of potentialities. But, very early, these become actualities; from childhood to age they manifest themselves in dullness or brightness, weakness or strength, viciousness or uprightness; and with each feature modified by confluence with another character, if by nothing else, the character passes on to its incarnation in new bodies. The Indian philosophers called character, as thus defined, 'karma'. It is this karma which passed from life to life and linked them in the chain of transmigrations
> . . . [40]

This analogy extends to the process of organic evolution as a whole. Hindu teaching sees the history of a *jiva*, and buddhist teaching sees the processive existence of a karmic bundle, as passing through innumerable incarnations and rising by gradual steps from inorganic matter to very simple forms of organic life, and then through more developed animal forms up to the human; and such a picture corresponds broadly to the process of evolution as depicted by the biological sciences during the last hundred and fifty years.

There are however also very important differences between the stories told respectively by the theories of genetics and evolution on the one hand and karma and rebirth on the other. The most obvious difference is that whereas heredity always goes directly from parents to their offspring, the process of reincarnation never does – children cannot be reincarnations of their own parents. But more importantly, for the question of the compatibility of the doctrine of reincarnation with genetic science, there is a major difference of scale between that which is held by reincarnationists and geneticists respectively to 'reincarnate'. According to the rebirth doctrine, that which passes over from life to life has the scale and complexity of an individual human character – understanding by 'character' the basic structure of dispositions out of which there grows, through interaction with the environment, a self or personality. There is however considerable obscurity in reincarnationist literature concerning the relation between the reincarnating character, or karmic structure, and the series of personalities to which it gives rise. Broadly speaking, the former is thought of as the continuing ground-plan on which different person-alities are successively built. (This ground-plan is of course itself under continuous but slow revision.) But no clear answer is given to the question: What qualities inhere in the reincar-nating entity, and in what degree of specificity? Does one of these reincarnating entities differ from another in, for example, degree of intelligence? In degree of introversion or extrover-sion? In degree of egoism or altruism? In mathematical ability? . . . Or do such qualities inhere in psycho-physical personalities rather than in the much more long-lived karmic structures which produce them? Such questions hang in the air, revealing a disappointing vagueness in a doctrine which has been taught for so many centuries. But it seems clear at least that any continuant from life to life which can be described as the same entity incarnating again and again must constitute an extensive and cohesive system of characteristics. To speak of two psycho-physical individuals as incarnations of the same memory-bearing entity implies a fairly massive continuity underlying the two successive lives. The claim, in particular, that this continuant carries within it a latent memory of all its incarnations requires it to be a substantial unit; for memory, as we experience it, is a function of a whole person.

This reincarnationist picture differs from that presented by the biological sciences. Here that which reappears in life after life is not the macro-unit of a human character but the micro-unit of a gene or a limited group of genes. In the simplest forms of life, reproducing by fission, a new individual is an exact copy of its parent, and therefore it may be said that the same bundle of characteristics is incarnated again and again. However, in the more complex life-forms, where reproduction is based upon a differentiation of sexes, each new individual incarnates a new genetic mixture which has not existed before and will not exist again. It is true that some groups of genes apparently remain linked together over very long periods, giving rise to 'racial' characteristics such as the conjunction of white skin with narrow nose or of black skin with woolly hair. But such stable linkages are common to millions of persons within the same genetic stream. When we come to the individual we find that his detailed genetic make-up is a new and unique combination. We noted earlier[41] that the half of a full human genetic complement carried in each sperm is unique, differing in large or small ways from that carried in each of the three to six hundred million other sperm produced at the same time; and that the half of the full human genetic complement carried in each ovum is likewise unique; so that each embryo is the sole instance of the precise genetic endowment which it embodies. In other words, instead of the same complex combinations of potentialities being handed on intact and born again in another individual, there is a reshuffling of the genes in each conception, always producing a unique new combination. Thus whereas the reincarnationist's picture shows total character structures reincarnating, the biologist's picture shows only small sub-units of character, the genes, reincarnat-ing in ever new combinations and producing new individuals who cannot be said to be continuations of any previous individuals. If we think of the many hundreds of dispositional elements which make up a complete human character as so many threads extending through time, the doctrine of reincar-nation sees these threads as woven together into thick ropes which endure through many centuries, whereas genetic theory sees the threads as continually criss-crossing in new and partially random ways to form fresh combinations in each generation.

Another aspect of this difference is that the idea of reincar-nation involves, whilst modern genetic theory denies, the inheritance of acquired characteristics. The idea of karma requires that the thoughts and actions of the living individual directly affect the developing karmic inheritance which has become incarnate in (or as) himself and which will later become incarnate again in (or as) another individual. In contrast to this, genetic theory has rejected the idea, which seemed possible a hundred years ago, of the inheritance of acquired character-istics. That is to say, it denies that if, for example, a parent learns French his children will inherit a tendency to know French – although of course some of them may well inherit any basic qualities which helped to make the parent a good linguist.

Since the geneticists' and the reincarnationists' pictures are thus so different we must go on to ask whether they are com-patible with one another. Can the two streams of reincarnating characteristics, the one consisting of individual genes combined afresh in every generation, and the other consisting of com-plete human characters being born again and again, coincide? Can each of the thousands of millions of members of each generation be simultaneously a product of both processes?

The question has been surprisingly little considered by advocates of reincarnation. Almost the only serious attempt to deal with it of which I am aware is that of the Cambridge philosopher, J. M. E. McTaggart, in an argument from analogy which has often since been appealed to by others:

In walking through the streets of London, it is extremely

rare to meet a man whose hat shows no sort of adaptation
to his head. Hats in general fit their wearers with far greater
accuracy than they would if each man's hat were assigned
to him by lot. And yet there is very seldom any causal
connexion between the shape of the head and the shape of
the hat. A man's head is never made to fit his hat, and, in
the great majority of cases, his hat is not made to fit his
head. The adaptation comes about by each man selecting,
from hats made without any special reference to his particular head, the hat which will suit his particular head best.
This may help us to see that it would be possible to hold
that a man whose nature had certain characteristics when he
was about to be re-born, would be re-born in a body
descended from ancestors of a similar character. His
character when re-born would, in this case, be decided, as
far as the points in question went, by his character in his
previous life, and not by the character of the ancestors of his
new body. But it would be the character of the ancestors
of the new body, and its similarity to his character, which
determined the fact that he was re-born in that body rather
than another. The shape of the head – to go back to our
analogy – does not determine the shape of the hat, but it
does determine the selection of this particular hat for this
particular head.[42]

Now when McTaggart walked the streets of London, in the
days when nearly all men wore hats, he can have seen only
some half-dozen different types of hat, each in some half-
dozen different sizes. The total number of variations can
hardly have exceeded forty or fifty; for each size and style of
hat was mass-produced and many thousands of different
customers would be wearing different copies of the same hat.
But human bodies come in far more than fifty different
specifications, and the fit between 'soul' and body has to be
far more complex than that between head and hat. As we have
already noted, each genetic constitution is unique, though with
varying degrees of overlap of information with a large number
of others. That being so, we must ask how many different
embryos, each with its own unique set of potentialities, could
provide a suitable body for one particular 'soul'. The answer

might range from one up to many thousands or hundreds of thousands, depending both upon the extent to which human character is determined by the individual's genes and the extent to which, according to reincarnationist theory, specific characteristics are carried over from one incarnation to the next.

As an imaginary extreme, if there were no inherited potentialities guiding and limiting an embryo's development, any embryo would be as suitable as any other to be the vehicle of a particular karmic structure or 'soul'. This extreme case does not of course obtain; for there is undoubtedly a significant degree of genetic influence, although its precise extent has not been determined. We can only say that the greater it is the smaller must be the proportion of embryos which will suit a given 'soul', and the less likely it must be that a large variety of 'souls' seeking to reincarnate at a given time would be able to do so. And from the other end, the more general are the 'soul's' qualities (for instance aesthetically developed rather than specifically musically or specifically poetically talented; or morally evil rather than specifically cruel or specifically lustful) the easier it will be for it to find a suitable embryo, whilst the more specific its qualities the more difficult this matching must be.

But having noted these formal relationships it is not clear that we can take the matter much further. Although the proportionate influences of heredity and environment in the formation of individual personality traits is hard to determine, different geneticists will suggest that the genetic control varies from $\frac{1}{4}$ to $\frac{3}{4}$. There is an even greater range of opinions on the side of reincarnation theory. Hindu and buddhist philosophical treatments generally speak of the life-to-life continuant (*linga sharira* or *vinnana*) as consisting of rather general spiritual and moral dispositions. On the other hand apologists (including the philosophers when functioning as apologists) often point to cases of striking musical or mathematical or other ability in children, and even to such very specific physical phenomena as birthmarks and genetic defects, as evidence for reincarnation.

Thus the reincarnation theory is too fluctuating and vague, and genetic theory too incomplete, for it to be possible to say whether or not the one is finally incompatible with the other. It is clear that genetics offers no positive support to the theory of reincarnation; but the charge that genetics disproves reincarnation must at present receive the open verdict of Not Proven.

6. SOME FINAL CLARIFICATIONS

I find that at the end of this lengthy examination of the doctrine of reincarnation, both in its more popular form and in the versions offered by vedantic and buddhist philosophy, I am not able to come to a clear-cut conclusion either that the doctrine is true or that it cannot be true. For it has emerged that the notion of rebirth is a family of concepts based upon a wide range of different understandings of personal identity, serving several different religious and ethical interests, and open to varying possibilities of confirmation or disconfirmation. All that I can do in conclusion is to try to clarify these various dimensions of the rebirth concept and their relations to one another.

One dimension consists in variations in what we may call the *solidity* of the personal identity that is affirmed from life to life. At one end of the range of possibilities is the notional maximum of full conscious self-identity involving a sufficient degree of memory of past lives to sustain an awareness of continuity spanning hundreds or thousands of years. But this extreme case is not in fact found. Babies are not born with an adult consciousness, as maximally solid self-identity from life to life would require; nor do people normally profess to remember a long series of past lives. At the other extreme is a minimally solid identity in which each incarnation is the existence of a new and distinct person with no memory of any former lives, and connected with other 'incarnations' only through a higher observer (the atman or 'real self') whose vision is to be shared by the last member of the series in a total retrospective awareness.

This range correlates with two others. First, the closer a doctrine of reincarnation stands to the solid-identity end of the scale, the more open it is to the possibility of confirming or disconfirming evidence. For memory claims may be able to be tested; and the fuller and more detailed the identity from life to life the more scope there is for a clash with the findings of modern genetics. However, if, as the discussion in the last three sections has suggested, such tests prove inconclusive, the other variation may be more useful for assessing the acceptability of reincarnation doctrines. This is variation in the extent to which such a doctrine has moral and practical significance – about which more presently.

These three variables – solidity of life-to-life identity, openness to confirmation or disconfirmation, and degree of moral and practical significance – must all be related to the different concerns which a belief in reincarnation may satisfy. There seem to be two main such concerns.

One is the problem of the inequality and inequity of the circumstances of human existence. If this can be attributed to a law of karma working impartially through successive births, evil is thereby rendered both more intelligible and more bearable. For we are not then subject to a regime of cosmic injustice; and any evils under which we may be suffering are, at most, only for this present life and our circumstances may be better in the next. The other concern is for the unity of mankind and indeed of all living beings. To quote a modern buddhist writer, 'Life is One, and in the universal flux of Becoming it is reborn again and again, appearing in ever new forms and rhythmic sequences of birth and death.'[43] We are linked with the past and the future in that we are not atomic individuals, cut off from humanity before and after us, but are continuations of lives lived in the past, whilst other lives in the future will be continuations of ours.

To what extent are doctrines of reincarnation able to meet these two concerns?

The concern for the unity of mankind is not really, I would suggest, well served by the idea of rebirth, and the less so according as we move towards the solid-identity, confirmable, and morally significant end of the scales. The idea that a succession of individuals in the past were all me, and that a further succession of individuals in the future will all be me, does indeed constitute a strong thread of continuity through time. But it is a purely individual thread. The past 'me's' are responsible for the present me, and the present me is responsible for future 'me's'; but I am not thereby rendered responsible either towards my contemporaries (except indirectly in so far as my own karma is benefited by treating them well) or towards persons other than myself in the future. To see human responsibility as running in these individual channels is more likely to diminish than to increase the sense of human unity. The notion of collective karma, which we met in the last chapter, would seem to provide a clearer symbol and a firmer basis for the responsibility of each for all and of all for each, both in the present and through time. For whereas a doctrine of individual karma concentrates the sense of responsibility upon oneself, the thought of the collective karma of humanity, or of all life, turns our responsibility towards others and indeed sets no limit to its scope. And such a notion does not require, but is on the contrary in tension with, the notion of individual reincarnation.

The other concern – to meet the problem of the apparently unjust differences in our human lot – does however seem, at any rate at first sight, to be met by the notion of individual karma working through a succession of births. And for this purpose the more solid the personal identity from life to life the better. For if I am to see the circumstances of my present existence as the consequences of my own actions in previous lives, those previous lives must be *my* lives and the actions done in them must be *my* actions, for which I am and feel responsible. This requires some degree of memory of those lives and a considerable continuity of personal characteristics between one life and the next. It is not enough that some future individual – the perfected 'me' who eventually attains to unity with his 'real self' – will have the experience of 'remembering' a long series of existences, including my present life. *He* may think that he was justly reaping in my present life what he had sown in a yet earlier life. But it is asking too much to expect *me* to think this, on the ground that *he* (not I) will think it in the future. If *I* am to believe that I am myself responsible through my actions in past lives for my present circumstances, then it must be I and not someone else who committed those actions; it is not enough that some 'higher' observer sees my life as one in a series with others. Nor – to speak now in terms of the buddhist philosophy of rebirth – is any lightening of the problem of the inequities of our human lot to be gained from the belief that although there are no continuing souls yet we have each been formed by a developing karmic structure or 'package' which has produced a series of other individuals in the past, is producing 'me' now, and will produce others in the future. For whether an individual has been formed by a karmic 'package' or by inherited genes, he has been produced by forces outside himself and placed within circumstances which he did not choose. Thus the problem created by the inequality of men's birth and circumstances remains. If it is to be met by a doctrine of reincarnation this must involve a fairly solid identity from life to life and must include some degree of memory of former lives.

However I have already argued that even such a theory would not really meet the problem of evil.[44] When we have traced present inequality and inequity back into a previous life it then either exists there as an original and unexplained fact or must be traced back into a yet earlier life. And so long as this regression continues the problem is merely being postponed: it can no more be solved in this way than indebtedness can be abolished by paying a debt with money borrowed from one who must borrow it from another, who must borrow it from another . . . And on the other hand, if we come to a first life from which all the rest have flowed we shall meet the problem in its fullness in the initial inequalities of that first state.

The conclusion which I draw from all these varied considerations is as follows. There are forms of reincarnation doctrine which *may* be broadly true pictures of what actually happens. It may be true, as vedantist teaching claims, that an eternal 'soul' or 'higher self' lies behind a long series of incarnations, and that in the consciousness of that 'real self' all these incarnations are linked together in a way which is not evident to any of the temporary persons who form the series – one of whom I now am. Or it may be true, as buddhist teaching claims, that units or 'packages' of karma (as distinguished from 'higher selves') produce a series of persons, one of whom is me. And in each case it may be true that a future person in the series of which I am now a member may attain to *moksha* or to nirvana and have an experience of seeing the long series of lives, of which mine will have been one, and the karmic linkages between them. But on the other hand, whilst this *may* be a true account of what is happening, such a theory lacks the moral and practical significance of the more popular pictures of reincarnation, according to which *I* – the conscious self now writing these sentences – have lived before and shall live again and am in the course of my present life reaping what I have sown in the past and sowing what I shall reap in the future. This popular conception is what is believed, or vaguely assumed, under the name of reincarnation or rebirth in hindu and buddhist cultures. Such a popular conception has a limited support from the alleged memories of former lives discussed in section 3, but tends to be unconvincing to those outside these cultures, and indeed seems to be slowly losing its hold even within them.[45]

NOTES

1. Also sometimes called metempsychosis, transmigration, metensomatosis, and palingenesis, this last term also being used for the stoic doctrine of the cyclic recurrence of the world.

2. Leslie Weatherhead erroneously and misleadingly asserts that reincarnation 'was accepted by the early church for the first five hundred years of its existence. Only in AD 553 did the second Council of Constantinople reject it and only then by a narrow majority' (*The Christian Agnostic*, pp. 209–10). The fact is that reincarnation was taught within the gnostic movement from which the church early distinguished itself and then treated as a dangerous foe. We have an excellent example of gnostic literature in the coptic *Pistis Sophia*, in which reincarnation is assumed in book I, ch. 7, and book III, ch. 125 (*Pistis Sophia*, pp. 8–10, 262–3). The first christian reference to reincarnation is a passing remark by Justin Martyr, about the middle of the second century, against the idea of human souls passing into the bodies of animals (*Dialogue with Trypho*, 4–5). (Despite this, W. Lutoslawski lists Justin as a believer in reincarnation – *Pre-Existence and Reincarnation*, p. 21.) Irenaeus wrote his extended attack upon the Gnostics, *Against Heresies*, in the last quarter of the second century. In this he criticizes Carpocrates' doctrine of the transmigration of the soul, particularly on the ground that we have no memories of previous lives (book II, ch. 33). About the same time Clement of Alexandria made several brief references to the idea of reincarnation, which he did not accept (*Stromata*, IV, 12; VI, 4). Hyppolytus, early in the third century, mentions again as a heretic the Gnostic, Carpocrates, and his teaching of reincarnation (*The Refutation of All Heresies*,

book VII, ch. 20). The roots of Gnosticism were probably mainly in jewish and eastern rather than greek religio-philosophies; but at some stage the pythagorean and platonic teachings about reincarnation also entered into the debate and we find Tertullian, writing about AD 200, attacking both the platonic doctrine of the soul's pre-existence and the pythagorean doctrine of transmigration (*On the Soul*, chs. 23–4, 28–35). Shortly afterwards Minucius Felix ridiculed the idea of human souls passing into the bodies of animals (*Octavius*, 34); as also did Arnobius towards the end of the century (*Against the Heathen*, II, 16). In the third century the pythagorean doctrine was criticized by Lactantius (*The Divine Institutes*, book III, chs. 18–19). In the fourth century Gregory of Nyssa rejected both the pre-existence of the soul and 'the fabulous doctrines of the heathen which they hold on the subject of successive incorporation' (*On the Making of Man*, ch. 28, 3). And in the fifth century Augustine attacked the notion of reincarnation in the course of controversy with the Platonists (*The City of God*, book X, ch. 30). All this means that the ideas of pre-existence and reincarnation were live issues within the early church; but it does not mean that reincarnation was at any time 'accepted by the early church'.

Again, it has been asserted (for example, by Weatherhead, *The Christian Agnostic*, p. 210) that Origen (*c.* 185–*c.* 254) taught a doctrine of reincarnation. The assertion seems to be based upon a misreading of the texts. Origen affirms the pre-existence of the soul and regards the fortunate and unfortunate circumstances of birth – for example, as healthy or deformed – as rewards and punishments for virtue and sin in the soul's previous existence (*On First Principles*, book II, chs. 9, 6–8). To this extent his teaching is in agreement with the idea of reincarnation. However, this previous existence was not on earth but in the heavens, and did not constitute one of a series of former lives. Origen does not speak of successive incarnations of the soul in different earthly bodies but only of the soul's pre-existence in some higher realm prior to its descent into this world. Indeed, in at least one passage Origen explicitly repudiates a form of reincarnation doctrine. Discussing Celsus' speculation about human souls entering animal bodies, he says, 'Christians, however, will not yield their assent to such opinions: for they have been instructed before now that the human soul was created in the image of God; and they see that it is impossible for a nature fashioned in the divine image to have its [original] features altogether obliterated, and to assume others, formed after I know not what likeness of irrational animals' (*Against Celsus*, book IV, 83). Origen's doctrine of pre-existence, as well as a number of his other teachings, were matters of spasmodic debate in the church during the fourth, fifth and sixth centuries, and Origen or his ideas were condemned by Synods in 400 and 403 (J. F. Bethune-Baker, *An Introduction to the Early History of Christian Doctrine*, p.

153). Either the 'Home Synod' held at Constantinople in 543 or the second Council of Constantinople in 553 – scholars dispute as to which it was – adopted fifteen anathemas against Origen, none of which mentions reincarnation but the first of which reads, 'If anyone asserts the fabulous pre-existence of souls, and shall assert the monstrous restoration (*apocatastasis*) which follows from it: let him be anathema' (*The Nicene and Post-Nicene Fathers*, Series Two, vol. XIV, p. 318).

That Origen did not teach reincarnation is argued by Charles Bigg. *The Christian Platonists of Alexandria*, pp. 198f.; Jean Daniélou, *Origen*, pp. 249–50; and Jaroslav Pelikan, *The Shape of Death*, pp.9 of.

Origen's works were first printed in the fifteenth and sixteenth centuries and influenced the seventeenth-century Cambridge Platonists, and towards the end of that century some minor figures within this movement taught 'metempsychosis'. See D. P. Walker, *The Decline of Hell*, pp. 137–46.

For a survey of the patristic references to reincarnation see Louis Bukowski, SJ, 'Le réincarnation selon les Pères de l'Eglise', in *Gregorianum*, vol. IX (1928), pp. 65–91.

The idea of reincarnation has not been much studied or discussed by modern christian writers. There is a classic early critique, recently reprinted: A. G. Hogg, *Karma and Redemption*. For a well-informed critical treatment by a Christian living within a buddhist culture, see Lynn A. de Silva, *Reincarnation in Buddhist and Christian Thought*. Quincy Howe's *Reincarnation for the Christian* is unfortunately not entirely reliable on the history of christian thought.

3. For example, the passages discussed here are offered (without discussion) as examples of the christian affirmation of reincarnation in *Reincarnation: An East–West Anthology*, ed. Joseph Head and S. L. Cranston.

4. Matthew 17: 10–13.

5. Mark 9: 11–13.

6. Leslie Weatherhead, *The Christian Agnostic*, p. 209. See also Annie Besant, *Reincarnation*, p. 4; W. Y. Evans-Wentz, *The Doctrine of Re-birth*, pp. 17–22; Geoffrey Hodson, *Reincarnation, Fact or Fallacy?*, pp. 20–1.

7. 2 Kings 2.

8. Malachi 4: 5.

9. Tertullian, at the end of the third century, made this point against gnostic teachers of reincarnation: *On the Soul*, 35.

10. Matthew 16: 13–14.

11. 2 Maccabees 15: 14; 2 Esdras 2: 18; and the *Ascension of Isaiah* in the Pseudepigrapha are commonly cited as evidence of such a belief.

12. e.g., Leslie Weatherhead, *The Christian Agnostic*, pp. 208–9; Martin Ebon, *Reincarnation in the Twentieth Century*, pp. 8–9; W. Y. Evans-Wentz, *The Doctrine of Re-birth*, pp. 22–4; Geoffrey Hodson, *Reincarnation*, p. 18.

13. John 9: 2–3.

14. Rudolf Bultmann, *The Gospel of John: A Commentary*, p. 331, n. 8. According to some commentators (e.g., G. H. C. Macgregor, *The Gospel of John*, p. 225), this idea is found in Jeremiah 1: 5, Psalm 139: 16 and Ephesians 1: 4; and the idea of reward and punishment for good and evil in a previous existence in Wisdom 8: 20 ('being good, I entered an undefiled body').

15. Bultmann, op. cit., p. 330, n. 8.

16. It has been said, again by Leslie Weatherhead, that 'one prominent sect, the Essenes, definitely taught it [i.e. reincarnation], and Josephus makes reference to it as if it were commonly accepted' (*The Christian Agnostic*, p. 209). He is referring to Josephus' *Jewish Wars*, book II, ch. 8, para. 14. This reads, '[It is said that] on the one hand all souls are immortal, but on the other hand those of good men only are changed into another body (*metabainein eis heteron soma*) but those of evil men are subject to eternal punishment.' However there is nothing here to indicate that the change into another body is reincarnation, i.e. being born again as a baby on earth. It seems more likely that Josephus had in mind the resurrection of the body, but perhaps (as in the thought of St Paul) in another, 'spiritual' body. Such an idea is found in jewish apocalyptic writings (e.g., 2 Enoch 8: 5; 65: 10; 2 Esdras 2: 39, 45): see D. S. Russell, *The Method and Message of Jewish Apocalyptic*, pp. 376–9.

17. Bultmann, op. cit., p. 331, n. 8.

18. For a comparison between these two strands of christian thought in relation to man's nature and destiny, see my *Evil and the God of Love*.

19. *The Problem of Rebirth*, vol. 16, p. 110.

20. A basic similarity between the ideas of reincarnation and purgatory has been noted by several roman catholic writers. For example, Paul Siwek says, 'But reincarnation reduced to the modest part of "purgatory", remains in perfect conformity with Catholic dogma' (*The Enigma of the Hereafter*, p. 9). A more recent catholic writer who was at one time a Hindu, John Moffitt, says, 'As for the Roman Catholic concept of purgatory, there is what seems to me a real parallel in the concept of *karma* itself. According to this doctrine . . . the soul suffers in a future life on earth (or in a temporary heaven or hell) according to the good and evil desires and deeds it entertained or performed during its earthly life' (*Journey to Gorakhpur*, p. 125).

21. *The Oxford Dictionary of the Christian Church*, ed. F. L. Cross, art. 'Metempsychosis', p. 892.

22. *Journal of the American SPR*, April and July 1960, reprinted as a booklet.

23. *Proceedings of the American SPR*, vol. XXVI, September 1966, reprinted as a separate volume.

24. The cases described in Stevenson's earlier *Evidence for Survival*

are all taken from published records and were not investigated at first hand by Stevenson himself.

25. C. T. K. Chari, 'Some Critical Considerations concerning Karma and Rebirth', in *Indian Philosophical Annual*, 1965, pp. 132–3.

26. *Twenty Cases*, pp. 1–2.

27. ibid., pp. 245–6.

28. ibid., pp. 159–60.

29. ibid., p. 312.

30. ibid., p. 311.

31. On the other hand the alleged group reincarnation described by Arthur Guirdham (*We Are One Another*) involves previous incarnations some seven centuries ago.

32. *Twenty Cases*, pp. 316–17.

33. ibid., ch. 7.

34. *Sanyutta-Nikaya*, II, 213–14 (*The Book of the Kindred Sayings*, part II, pp. 143–4); cf. *Samanna-Phala Suttanta*, 93–4 (*Dialogues of the Buddha*, part I, pp. 90–1).

35. Mrs Rhys Davids, *Stories of the Buddha*, p. xvi.

36. p. 333 above.

37. *Dialogues of the Buddha*, part II, p. 201.

38. IV, 5.

39. For source references and a critical discussion, see Paul Siwek, *The Enigma of the Hereafter*, ch. 5.

40. T. H. Huxley and Julian Huxley, *Evolution and Ethics, 1893–1943*, pp. 69–70.

41. Chapter 2, section 1.

42. J. M. E. McTaggart, *Some Dogmas of Religion*, p. 125. Swami Abhedananda's lecture on 'Heredity and Reincarnation', in *Reincarnation*, was written before the development of modern genetics and contributes nothing.

43. Quoted by Lynn de Silva, *Reincarnation in Buddhist and Christian Thought*, p. 78.

44. Chapter 16, section 3.

45. This is suggested by a survey of the religious beliefs of young indian scientists reported by David Gosling in 'Scientific Perspectives on Rebirth', in *Religion: Journal of Religion and Religions*, vol. IV, spring 1974, pp. 47-58.

Part V

A POSSIBLE
HUMAN DESTINY

CHAPTER 20

A Possible Pareschatology

I. INTRODUCTORY

What is likely to happen to us when we die? If the picture forming through these chapters is at all on the right lines – which, of course, only future experience can reveal, or fail to reveal – the persisting self-conscious ego will continue to exist after bodily death. We shall not however, in most cases, attain immediately to the final 'heavenly' state. Only those whom the religions call saints or buddhas or arhats or *jivan-muktas* have fulfilled the purpose of temporal existence, which is the gradual creation of perfected persons – their perfection consisting, I shall suggest in chapter 22, in a self-transcending state beyond separate ego-existence. But those of us who die without having attained to our perfection continue further in time as distinct egos. What, then, is likely to happen in the next stage of this journey?

On what could we base an answer to such a question? There is a considerable body of material produced by trance medium-ship and automatic writing, which is said to come from persons who have died and to describe at first hand their post-mortem experiences. For reasons discussed in chapter 7 this evidence should be treated with the utmost caution. But nevertheless there is always the possibility that some of it may be authentic in the sense of emanating, though perhaps at several removes, from post-mortem sources. If it agrees in content with other putative evidence, this agreement will at least be worth noting in an area in which we have no certain knowledge and few enough pointers of any kind. A second source may perhaps be found in the traditional wisdom of those religions which affirm an intermediate state or states between this life and the end of our temporal existence. Such a tradition is available to us, above all, in the *Bardo Thödol* or *Tibetan Book of the Dead*, based upon the testimony of yogis who claimed to have direct acquaintance with this intermediate realm. And finally there is the use of reason to criticize these various indications and to speculate on the basis of a general philosophical or theological conception of man's nature and his place in the universe. All these sources together can of course yield no more than a possible pareschatology, concerning which one has to say, as Plato said of his own picture based on the pythagorean traditions and the use of his own reason, 'A man of sense ought not to assert that the description which I have given of the soul and her mansions is exactly true. But I do say that, inasmuch as the soul is shown to be immortal, he may venture to think, not improperly or unworthily, that something of the kind is true.'[1] In search of such a possible picture I propose to look briefly at what is offered in the *Tibetan Book of the Dead* and in western mediumistic communications, and then to consider what may be said by way of reasonable speculation which takes note of these various indications and is consonant with the broad picture of the universe which is assumed in these chapters.

2. THE BARDO WORLD

The *Bardo Thödol*, known in English as the *Tibetan Book of the Dead*,[2] comes from the tantric branch of mahayana Buddhism in Tibet and may well date from about the eighth century AD. It professes to describe the *bardo* (literally *bar*, 'between', *do*, 'two') state between death and rebirth, and was read to the dying person to help him to understand and respond rightly to what was about to happen to him. It outlines the sequence of experiences undergone by the 'soul' or conscious mind during the forty-nine days between death and its return to a new body. (The number forty-nine apparently has symbolic rather than literal significance.) The full map of this intermediate world drawn in the *Book of the Dead* is complex and in describing it here I shall simplify the picture and concentrate upon its main aspects.

During the three and a half or four days required for the *bardo* body to detach itself from the physical body the self is in the first *bardo* state (the *Chikhai Bardo*), in which it is surrounded by an intense and blinding light which is the 'Radiance of the Clear Light of Pure Reality'.[3] It is encountering the ineffable divine Void of mahayana teaching, the Ultimate Reality, and has the opportunity, in principle at least, of immediate entry into nirvana. For if in this bright sea of light in which the self finds itself it is ready utterly to abandon ego-existence and become one with the Light, it attains final salvation and never returns to earth. Accordingly, as a man is approaching death his guru should address him in some such words as these:

> O nobly-born (so and so by name), the time hath now come for thee to seek the Path [in reality]. Thy breathing is about to cease. Thy *guru* hath set thee face to face before with the Clear Light; and now thou art about to experience it in its Reality in the *Bardo* state, wherein all things are like the void and cloudless sky, and the naked, spotless intellect is like unto a transparent vacuum without circumference or centre . . . [4]

For in the transition of death 'the first [glimpsing] of the *Bardo* of the Clear Light of Reality, which is the Infallible Mind of the *Dharma-Kaya*, is experienced by all sentient beings',[5] and there is an opportunity to realize the final nirvanic state of oneness with the Dharma Body or Cosmic Body (*Dharma-Kaya*) of the Buddha.

However, only those who have come close to the complete purification of the self (or, in the language of christian mysticism, to complete self-naughting) can seize this opportunity. The great majority pass through the divine Light without being willing to be absorbed into it. They continue to exist as separate individuals, subject to the power of karma, which now begins to reassert itself. In this second stage of the *bardo* experience (the *Chonyid Bardo*) the self encounters a series of 'karmic illusions'[6] as he becomes aware that he has died. The self is now clothed in a karmic body formed by his own past thoughts and deeds, and he involuntarily fabricates for himself encounters with good and evil powers, the peaceful and wrathful deities. But he is taught in the *Book of the Dead* to recognize these as projections of his own mind:

Alas! when the Uncertain [or illusory] Experiencing of
   Reality is dawning upon me here,
With every thought of fear or terror or awe for all
   [apparitional appearances] set aside,
May I recognize whatever [visions] appear, as the
   reflections of mine own consciousness;
May I know them to be of the nature of apparitions in
   the *Bardo*:
When at this all-important moment [of opportunity] of
   achieving a great end,
May I not fear the bands of Peaceful and Wrathful
   [Deities], mine own thought-forms.[7]

For seven days successive Buddhas and Bodhisattvas appear
in awesome but benign majesty and beauty, shining in their
various distinctive colours; and the soul has the opportunity
of responding to them in trust and entering their paradisal
Buddha-worlds. But because of the intensity of their light and
the overpowering glory of their superabundant life the impure
soul will shrink back to preserve his own pitiful little selfhood.
And so in the following period of seven days it will encounter
again the same blessed Reality, but now seen as wrathful and
terrifying.

O nobly-born, at about that time, the fierce wind of *karma*,
terrific and hard to endure, will drive thee [onwards], from
behind, in dreadful gusts. Fear it not. That is thine own
illusion. Thick awesome darkness will appear in front of
thee continually, from the midst of which there will come
such terror-producing utterances as 'Strike! Slay!' and
similar threats. Fear these not. In other cases, of persons of
much evil *karma*, *karmically*-produced flesh-eating *rakshasas*
[or demons] bearing various weapons will utter, 'Strike!
Slay!' and so on, making a frightful tumult. They will come
upon one as if competing amongst themselves as to which
[of them] should get hold of one. Apparitional illusions, too,
of being pursued by various terrible beasts of prey will
dawn. Snow, rain, darkness, fierce blasts [of wind], and
hallucinations of being pursued by many people likewise
will come; [and] sounds as of mountains crumbling down,
and of angry overflowing seas, and of the roaring of fire, and

the fierce winds springing up. When these sounds come one, being terrified by them, will flee before them in every direction, not caring whither one fleeth. But the way will be obstructed by three awful precipices – white, and black, and red. They will be terror-inspiring and deep, and one will feel as if one were about to fall down them. O nobly-born, they are not really precipices; they are Anger, Lust, and Stupidity.[8]

And there will follow experiences of inexorable judgement before the Lord of the Dead and of ensuing punishments in various hells.

After this, in the third *bardo* (*Lidpa Bardo*) the unliberated soul is drawn increasingly strongly towards its next birth, which shines in its own appropriate colour: 'there will shine upon thee a dull white light from the *Deva*-world, a dull green light from the *Asura*-world, a dull yellow light from the Human-world, a dull blue light from the Brute-world, a dull red light from the *Preta*-world, and a smoke-coloured light from the Hell-world. At that time, by the power of *karma*, thine own body will partake of the colour of the light of the place wherein thou art to be born.'[9] And so the cycle of birth and death rolls round again.

A striking feature of this account of the soul's experiences between physical death and the next phase of its existence is the *Bardo Thödol*'s insistence that the mind creates its own post-mortem world in accordance with its beliefs – in this case as projected by a consciousness formed within the mahayanist faith of Tibet. But as Lama Anagorika Govinda comments, 'The illusory *Bardo* visions vary, in keeping with the religious or cultural tradition in which the percipient has grown up.'[10] For after death, released from the pressures and threats which sustain our self-image in this life, the mind realistically appraises itself in a kind of psychoanalytic experience and the outcome reaches consciousness in the imagery provided by one's religious faith.

If so, what might be the post-mortem experiences of modern secular man? No doubt very varied; but perhaps for some unhappy souls there are hints in the imaginative work of those contemporary novelists and dramatists who have depicted the hellishness of this life in strange, unreal situations of anxiety or terror or self-disgust – as in Sartre's *Huis Clos*, Kafka's *The Trial*, William Golding's *Pincher Martin*, or Samuel Beckett's *The Lost Ones*. Or could it be that for more ordinary people the banal reports provided by the spiritualist movement may be all too probable?

3. THE 'NEXT WORLD' ACCORDING TO WESTERN SPIRITUALISM

Modern western spiritualist literature contains innumerable putative descriptions of the experiences of those who have recently died as related through trance mediumship or automatic writing. We have already seen, in chapter 7, that it remains a puzzling question whether such communications (when not consciously invented by the medium) emanate from persons who have died, or only from the medium's unconscious mind, perhaps telepathically influenced by 'psychic husks' left behind by the dead. However, since we cannot exclude the possibility that some may come from full discarnate personalities, it seems right to take note of their contents. These communications professing to describe the life to come are endlessly repetitive and their themes can be sufficiently illustrated from a few representative sources.[11]

According to this literature there is a psychic double of the body, an astral or etheric body, which detaches itself at death from the physical corpse until the connecting links between them are broken.[12] The astral body then either sleeps or is in a confused half-conscious state, sometimes called 'hades' in the spiritualist literature. This state may last for a longer or shorter time, said to average three or four days. The soul or astral being then wakes up into the next phase, which is a dreamworld or sphere of illusion, reflecting the individual's own expectations and desires. For many people it may be so like earth that they do not at first realize that they have died. Thus, in one of these communications we read:

> I have been very busy helping new arrivals. You would be surprised how few people have any idea that they have left a body behind them. You see you don't feel any different except that you haven't any pain or feeling of weakness and

those who come over through an air disaster or other
accident are the most difficult to deal with. One has to be
very patient with them for they just can't believe that they
are what the world calls 'dead'.[13]

Another 'communicator', having realized that he has died,
says 'my body's very similar to the one I had before. I pinch
myself sometimes to see if it's real, and it is, but it doesn't
seem to hurt as much as when I pinched the flesh body.'[14]
In the spiritualist literature this realm is often called Summer-
land, or the Memory-world, or the plane of illusion. For some
it can be an experience of delightful wish-fulfilment, as
described in this script produced by automatic writing:

> The scenery is just marvellous, more beautiful than anything
> I have seen on Earth and as you know I have travelled to
> many lovely places in the world. I have never seen anything
> so wonderful as the flowers, there is nothing to spoil them;
> no frosts, or bad storms, or blight. The perfume they emit
> is glorious and their colour unbelievable. I find great joy in
> my garden, which is so like my lovely Seahaven, and I am
> full of gratitude to God for having given me this lovely
> replica.[15]

In this happy state illnesses are shed and bodily deformities
disappear; and 'if we are getting on in years we can return to
that period in life known as the prime and there we can stay'.[16]
But for others it may be a purgatorial experience, as indicated
in one of the communications professing to come from the
famous early psychical researcher, F. W. H. Myers, after his
death, through the medium Geraldine Cummins:

> The cold selfish man in Illusion-land may dwell in darkness,
> for it is not within the power of his ego to throw itself
> outwards, to express itself in the fantasy of fulfilled desires.
> He is thrown more than ever inwards by the shock of death.
> He believes that he has lost everything. He loses contact
> with all except the sense of his own thinking substance. A
> nightmare of darkness prevails for a time, prevails as long
> as he lives within his morbid sense of loss, within his desire,
> which is merely to gratify himself without any regard for

others. There may be only night in Illusion-land for the abnormally selfish man.[17]

In this same series of 'communications' the following broader picture is painted: 'When they shuffle off the heavy body, when in a finer shape they take flight from it, they frequently do not realise the fundamental unreality of earth. They hunger for the dream that was home to them. Then these souls knock and the door is opened, they enter into a dream that, in its main particulars, resembles the earth. But now this dream is memory and, for a time, they live within it. All those activities that made up their previous life are re-enacted, that is, if such is their will. They can, at any time, if they choose, escape from the coil of earth memories, from what I might call the "swaddling clothes" of the life after death . . . Of course the hour comes when his spiritual perceptions awaken, when he seeks to escape from the memory-dream, when, in short, he realises his own increased intellectual powers, and, above all, his capacity for living on a finer plane of being. Then he passes from the State of Illusion and enters upon an existence which few communicating intelligences have ever attempted to describe to man.'[18]

As these last sentences indicate, the plane of illusion represents only a phase in what is intended to be the upward movement of the soul. As one 'communicator' reports, 'You know there are many different spheres in this world, many of them far higher than the one I and those of my family and yours are now living on. These spheres are all much more beautiful than even this one and those who live there are all more highly evolved spiritually than we who have only recently come to this world.'[19] There are said to be seven planes, the lowest being that of physical matter; the next, the plane of 'hades', described as a confused borderland between earthly life and the next world; then the plane of illusion, in which most souls spend a considerable time; and then beyond this a plane of 'colour', a plane of 'flame', and plane of 'light', and finally a plane beyond time in which souls become one with God. Of these last two states we read in the 'Myers' communications:

The purpose of the Sixth plane of being might be described as 'The assimilation of the many-in-one,' the unifying of all those mind-units I have called souls, within the spirit. When this aim has been achieved, the spirit which contains this strange individualised life passes out Yonder and enters into the Mystery, thereby fulfilling the final purpose, the evolution of the Supreme Mind.[20]

There is an analogy between this conception and the picture towards which, I shall suggest in chapter 22, the official eschatologies of the major world religions convergingly point.

To return to what some of the spiritualists call the plane of illusion, this represents only a stage – though it may be a lengthy stage – in the soul's pilgrimage, and when the individual has come to greater self-knowledge and is ready to move beyond this temporary haven, his next 'death' or transition occurs. In the 'Myers' scripts we read, 'For a short while after his entry into that state the soul is at peace, warring desires are quiescent; but they wake again at the time the dream is beginning to break . . . After a while this life of pleasure ceases to amuse and content him. Then he begins to think and long for the unknown, long for a new life. He is at last prepared to make the leap in evolution and this cloudy dream vanishes.'[21]

So much, then, for the spiritualist evidence. It is in very broad agreement, as regards the *bardo* state, with the *Tibetan Book of the Dead* and, as regards the many 'planes of existence', with the writings of Swedenborg.[22] Such sources will repel many orthodox Christians, to whom the kind of picture which they indicate will seem extremely fanciful and unlikely. But is it really more fanciful or unlikely than the heaven, hell and purgatory of traditional christian belief?

4. CRITIQUE OF THE IDEA OF THE IMMORTAL EGO

The broad picture of man and his place in the universe on which the present speculation is based is teleological, presenting our life in time as a movement towards a goal. The *telos* to which our existence is directed can be formally described as human perfection, man's full humanization, the total realization of the potentialities of finite personal life or, in the daring language of eastern orthodox Christianity, man's divinization.

We can only experience the nature of this human fulfilment as we come to participate in it; but we have anticipatory glimpses of aspects of it, under the special conditions of this world, in the lives of the great saints of the various religious traditions. Life, then, is a soul-making or person-making process. We exist in order to grow through our free inter-actions with a challenging environment towards a human perfection which lies far beyond our present state.

It is evident that such a completion is very seldom (if ever) achieved in the course of this present life. Generally the varied experiences of life bring some growth in understanding of oneself, in acceptance of others, in willingness for sacrifice, and some expansion of the capacity to love and be loved. Very often, in these ways men and women take in the course of their lives a smaller or larger step towards their full human-ization. But too often people are so treated by life that they never have the opportunity, or sufficient opportunity, to develop their properly human potential, and end their lives as hard, selfish, embittered personalities who have turned their backs upon the possibilities of human fellowship. Or worse, men become possessed by evil and perhaps live and die violently as enemies of mankind. Thus in this life a few men and women advance a great deal and may come to be recog-nized as saints; most perhaps advance a certain amount; whilst yet others fail to advance at all, or even degenerate towards a sub-human condition. Accordingly, it seems clear (as I have argued in chapter 8) that if we do indeed exist under the aegis of a cosmic person-making purpose, that purpose must hold us in being beyond this present earthly life.

Assuming, then, on the basis of this conception of the meaning of human existence, that our lives are not confined to the present earthly scene but continue in some form after death, how should we suppose our total career to be divided? Is bodily death the only break in it, so that it consists of two phases – this short earthly life, followed by an unending post-mortem life? Or is our present life the first of a series of limited phases of existence, each bounded by its own 'death'?

It seems to me that the various relevant considerations, although far from unanimous or decisive, point on balance to the latter possibility. On the one hand the endlessly prolonged life cf finite egos seems to be theoretically possible; but on the other hand it is debatable whether this would be a prolonged *human* life and whether therefore it could serve the purpose of the gradual creation of perfect humanity.

It has been questioned whether personal identity can be conceived as holding over unlimited time. For whilst such identity is very difficult to define satisfactorily, it certainly seems to involve memory. But could human memory stretch out to infinity? Austin Duncan-Jones argued that it could not. He claimed that if we define personal identity partly in terms of memory then, whilst our possible life-span could no doubt greatly exceed our normal earthly threescore years and ten, it could nevertheless not be prolonged for ever:

> In ordinary life as we know it, only a limited number of acts of memory, with a limited content, can take place in a limited time. As time passes, the number of happenings available to be remembered increases. It follows that if all that is memorable gets remembered equally often, any given memorable event must be remembered more and more rarely as time passes. Thus, if I were alive a million years hence, I should need to be able to recall, not only the events of my life up to now, but the events of over 20,000 other periods of equal length. Let us suppose that each of these 20,000 periods has an equal claim on my memory a million years hence. It seems to follow that every event must be remembered more and more readily as time passes. We have then a gradual fading of connections between one part of a person's life and another. In that case it would seem to follow that every person would progressively become more and more unlike a person as we know persons now. Connections would become looser and looser. If we imagine someone in his millionth year, or whatever high number we choose to take, his connections with the earlier parts of his life will be unimaginably scattered and thin compared with what we are used to.[23]

I think that Duncan-Jones is making an important point here, though not one which constitutes a 'knock down' refutation of the idea of the immortal ego. No doubt an endlessly living finite individual could continue indefinitely to have contact with an increasingly long past, although it would necessarily be a more and more tenuous and 'gappy' contact. For example, if one had spot-memories in a logarithmic progression so that, for example, each earlier recalled event was separated from the last by an interval equivalent to that separating the latter from the present day,[24] one could then retain an ever fainter connection with an ever-lengthening past. But as well as memory we have to take account of the unceasing change through time without which we should no longer be living persons. If we conceive of people as continuing to develop during an endless future, as we each have throughout our past, we encounter a limit to the individual's capacity to identify himself with earlier states in which he was very different.

Indeed, we begin to notice these limits even within the span of an earthly life. When I read the diary which I wrote when I was fifteen years old I know that it is *my* diary, and with its aid I remember some of the events recorded in it; but nevertheless I look back upon that fifteen-year-old as someone whose career I follow with interest and sympathy but whom I do not *feel* to be myself. What then would it be like – assuming further continued change – for me to read that same diary in fifty million years' time? What we can call our span of self-apprehension (on analogy with the span of apprehension of which the psychologists write) seems to be limited, so that I should not think of the person who was in some sense me fifty million years ago, or even five hundred years ago, as *me* in any personally significant or morally momentous sense.

These considerations indicate that it is possible to think of personal identity in different ways for different purposes. There is a distinction between what can be called objective, or physical, or indeed metaphysical identity, from the point of view of a hypothetical external observer; and subjective identity, from the point of view of the consciousness in question. In terms of the former, we can conceive of a person living for ever as a resurrected being who retains the same body, or the same bodily form, or even (if there is such a thing) the same spiritual substance, throughout eternity. On the other hand, if we are concerned about identity from one's own point of view, and as a matter of moral and 'existential' significance, the situation is very different. When I imagine myself thinking of one who was alive a million years ago, though objectively continuous with myself now, I find that the increasing attenuation of memory combined with the increasing inner distance, produced by continuous personal change, from an individual who lived so very long ago, amount to a real discontinuity. Personal identity has clear and unproblematic boundaries only when assimilated to physical identity. Subjective identity, on the other hand, has a variable and misty temporal horizon. When we consider the self-apprehension of the moral being as extending back into the past we find that whilst its span is indefinite it is not unlimited. For parts of us are dying and parts are being born all the time.[25] One cannot say how long an individual could remain morally the same person, for there are no sharp boundaries or cut-off points; but one can say that whereas I (JH[1975]) am substantially the same person as JH[1965], any JH of a million years hence will not be substantially the same person and will not include, or will only include notionally, within his span of self-apprehension the JH who is now writing this book.

These considerations do not absolutely require the picture of many lives in many worlds in preference to that of a single endlessly prolonged post-mortem existence. For there could be an unending life in which one's self-apprehension extends back over a certain period and then gradually fades, the stretch of time which it covers changing continuously as the self advances into the future. But on the other hand we have found no positive advantage in the notion of the immortal ego as compared with that of a series of lives, each with its own beginning and end. We can now go on to ask if there is any positive attraction in this latter picture. And I think that there is when we take account of the historically and culturally conditioned nature of the human self. For we have been formed as empirical egos within a particular culture and a particular epoch of history. The language in which we think and speak, the structure of society through which we are related to our neighbours, the traditions and *mores* which we inherit, the state of public knowledge, the unconscious framework of presuppositions through which we perceive the world, the contingencies of political history . . . have all helped to make us what we are. I am a twentieth-century middle-class Englishman, and it is in substantial part in virtue of this that I am the particular person that I am; strip all these culturally conditioned characteristics away and I should be someone else – or perhaps no one! Thus my existence is as an inhabitant of this earth in the twentieth century AD, with England as part of it; and it is hard to see how I, as a twentieth-century Englishman, could still be in any real sense the same person in a radically different environment, whether on this earth or elsewhere, ten million years hence. As historical men and women we are part of a particular phase of a particular world: we are not the angelic beings who can be imagined as a-historical denizens of eternity. For, as the ethnologists and sociologists have so abundantly shown, 'the ways of becoming and being human are as numerous as man's cultures. Humanness is socio-culturally variable.'[26]

Another aspect of our embeddedness within a particular cultural and historical milieu is the dependence of our purposes upon the circumstances of that milieu. In existentialist language, I have, or am, a project or a complex of projects; and this provides the basis of my identity through time as experienced by myself. So long as threads of conscious intention, hope, fear, ambition, etc., connect the consecutive states, I identify the earlier person as being myself. But human projects are related to the possibilities and opportunities of the world in which we live. Indeed, perhaps the only kind of project that we can have which is not defined in terms of the particular character of our world is the religious project of liberation from sin and illusion into a perfect relationship with or within Ultimate Reality.

From this point of view the human being fits rather well the vedantic conception of him as a basic spiritual project being incarnated in a series of different empirical egos, each formed by and living within its own historico-cultural setting. I do not claim that the alternative notion of a moral development which proceeds continuously through infinite time – as envisaged, for example, by Kant[27] – is logically impossible. No doubt within an eternal existence there could be relatively distinct phases in which particular purposes, and hence personal growth, are possible. But what is thus vaguely adumbrated is made more concrete and emphatic in the picture of a series of limited existences each lived out within its own world (or, in the vedantic and buddhist versions, within different stages of the history of this world). The considerations which have led us to postulate growth through purposive life – which, as we have seen, occurs in finite situations within which concrete purposes are possible – seem to be more easily accommodated by the theory of many lives in many worlds than by the idea of the immortal ego.

Further, not only does the notion of human purposes and their success and failure, and of one's life as a complex of projects, seem to cohere best with our mortal condition, but many other aspects of human existence as we know it are likewise bound up with the fact of death – courage, which is ultimately courage in face of the threat of death; fear, which is ultimately fear of annihilation; love and tenderness, which ultimately involve the possibility of mortal sacrifice for another; tragedy, which assumes the finitude of life and a terminus to hope; and the relationships between the generations, between parent and child, between young and old, between one historical epoch and another, and the passing on of tasks, achievements and problems from one generation to the next. I do not say that we cannot conceive of loves and hates and purposes enduring through unending time; but I doubt whether they would be *human* loves and hates and purposes. It seems that if the boundary of death were removed, and we were faced with a limitlessly open future stretching to infinity, what we now know as human nature would be transformed out of existence. There would no longer be a basis for the familiar emotional stuff of human life, with its parameters of love and hate, hope and fear, self-sacrifice, achievement and failure, tragedy and nobility; and the distinctions between older and younger, between generation and generation, between epoch and epoch would disappear in a universal endless longevity. Thus when we try to contemplate the contradictory notion of immortalized mortals our thoughts turn away from what we know as human existence to something for which we are more inclined to invoke the notion of the angels.

These considerations suggest the likelihood that if the human ego is immortal, or if it persists for a period which multiplies very many times the length of an earthly life, its post-mortem existence occurs in successive sections rather than as one continuous unit. Thus it may be that periodic death (like periodic sleep[28]) divides up an existence which, as finite creatures, we can only live in limited phases. Its recognition of this is, as we have seen, a virtue of the indian conception of reincarnation. The basic idea does not however have to take the form of repeated rebirths in this world. There is also the possibility of repeated 'rebecomings' in other spheres beyond this world. Instead of a horizontal line, the image is then that of a line moving upwards in what we can call vertical rather than horizontal reincarnation. This, at any rate, is the possibility to be developed in the next section.

5. MANY LIVES IN MANY WORLDS

Let us suppose (in accordance with the teaching of the *Bardo Thödol*) that in the moment of death, when the ego ceases to be organically related to this world, its final self-transcending perfection is possible and it may, if it is ready, enter the ultimate state whose nature we must attempt to consider in chapter 22.[29] But in the great majority of cases we are not able to face Ultimate Reality, or even to be conscious that it confronts us, and so we continue our individual ego-existences. In that case we regain consciousness in a post-mortem state which, according to the indications both of the *Bardo Thödol* and of western mediumistic communications, is subjective or dream-like. As such it is an experience through which the individual encounters aspects of his own total self, including its unconscious depths, of which he was not directly aware in his waking life on earth. This is an experience of self-discovery and of the realization of what one has become through the good and bad choices, the brave facings of difficulties and the cowardly turnings away from them, the self-givings and refusals to give, the generosities and selfishnesses, the impulsive acts of creation and of destruction, and all the varied cumulative thoughts, emotions, intentions, hopes and fears and dreams – beautiful and ugly, healthy and vicious, splendid and contemptible, humane and fiendish – which have been continuously modifying our conscious and unconscious nature between birth and death. This gradually formed psychic structure is, in eastern terms, our karma. It is what we have become in the course of what we have done. And in the first phase of existence after death, as the ego is freed from the constraints of the physical world, this karma (according to our hypothesis) makes itself known to us in experiences both of wish-fulfilment and of self-judgement. Price's theory, discussed in chapter 14, is perhaps a picture of this. The 'realistic dreams' in which it consists may take many different forms, depending largely upon the beliefs and the consequent anticipations of different individuals. We should accordingly expect any echoes from the next world, received by some kind of extra-sensory awareness, to vary considerably from culture to culture. The *Bardo Thödol* describes the post-mortem experiences of a devout tibetan Buddhist, in which, having shrunk from the Clear Light of Ultimate Reality, he encounters a series of benevolent deities who offer him salvation in their various realms of bliss. But if the good within him, which would respond to these invitations, is not sufficiently powerful to carry him into these worlds, then he goes on to encounter wrathful deities who represent the evil within him. As the *Bardo Thödol* makes clear, these beneficent and wrathful deities are all projections of his own mind. His experience of encounter with them leads to the realization that he must live again, and to the selection of an appropriate next birth. On the other hand a devout Christian, before the modern erosion of traditional belief by the influence of our modern scientific culture, would have had a quite different post-mortem experience. His coming to self-awareness would have taken the form of a divine judgement formed largely out of materials provided by the New Testament – a great assize in the presence of throngs of angels, saints and martyrs, presided over either by the towering figure of God the Father seated on a great white throne and shining in unapproachable light, or alternatively by Christ, the Lamb of God, seated on a throne and surrounded by his apostles. There might be angels reading from the Book of Life. And from this divine judgement he would proceed towards something which he would anticipate under the imagery of heaven or purgatory or hell. His expectations might then create for him a period of blissful or painful experiences according to the pattern of his beliefs. Perhaps some present-day Christians might encounter the gracious and tender Christ-figure of liberal Christianity, as in this passage produced by automatic writing: 'He is wonderful to look on. His hair shone as though the sun lit it up. It was of a colour hard to describe. His face was beautiful in its expression of infinite love and compassion. He wore a white garment like you see in the pictures and it was so white that it too shone as though light radiated from it. He truly is the Light of the World.'[30] These would be christian equivalents of the maha-yana buddhist experiences described in the *Bardo Thödol*. But a unitive christian culture, strong enough to impose its distinctive form upon men's after-death experiences, is now a thing of the past, at any rate in most nominally christian countries. An inhabitant of our present secularized culture would – we may surmise – be more likely, in the absence of any vivid and compelling religious or other expectations, to find that his next world is in many ways very like our present world. Since he would not know what else to expect, his subjective post-mortem environment would have to be based upon his memories of this world. Accordingly, he might not at first even realize that he had died. He would probably find himself in the kind of duplicate earth – with houses, streets, food, trees, etc. – described in so many of the mediumistic communications. Whether the other people referred to in these communications are real persons, independent centres of consciousness and will, or only parts of the content of an elaborate subjective experience, is problematic. The *Bardo Thödol*, supported by some of the spiritualist evidence, suggests that this intermediate moment between one state of human existence and the next is solipsistic and that the mind's experiences in it are purely subjective. I shall therefore, in developing a possible pareschatology, assume that the immediately post-mortem phase is subjective and dream-like, and that it can take either a sharply defined form, reflecting an imagination effectively conditioned by a powerful religious culture, or be experienced as a kind of continuation of earthly life.

But even within this latter there will, if we are right in thinking of it as a transitional phase, be factors which sooner or later give rise to a felt need for something different. These might take the form either of positive intimations of higher realms and better possibilities of existence, felt in moments of enlightenment; or of a negative reaction against the boredom and emptiness of the current existence. The 'dead' who profess to speak through mediums often refer to higher spheres to which people sooner or later gravitate. And in agreement with this picture their communications cease after a while: the messages nearly always profess to come from the fairly recently departed. Nevertheless even the possibly few years of the post-christian westerner in 'illusion land' are longer than the *bardo* experience described in the *Tibetan Book of the Dead*, whose symbolic 'forty-nine days' is presumably a matter of weeks rather than years. Could it perhaps be that a powerful religious mythology of judgement has the function of speeding the transition of those who whole-heartedly accept it; but that for those with no dramatic imagery to focus and intensify their coming to self-awareness the process tends to be more prolonged?

When the *bardo* experience is over for an individual, what happens next? Here we are beyond the range of any supposed reports and can only speculate in the broadest possible terms on the basis of the assumptions from which we have been working. What we are thereby led to postulate is a transition, sooner or later, from the *bardo* world of illusion to a further embodiment in another world in another space.[31] Will this re-embodiment be, as in our present world, a birth as an immature creature which has to grow into its new existence, or an arrival as an already fully formed individual within the new environment? This question is connected with two further very obscure issues. One is the question whether our present life is our first or whether, as Hinduism and Buddhism teach, we have lived many times before. I have discussed this in chapter 19, tentatively concluding against the idea of previous lives. If that conclusion is correct, the formation of an earthly human self in the way described in chapter 2 is an initial formation, and there need be no presumption that subsequent re-becomings in other worlds will repeat the same pattern. The other question concerns the place of sex and reproduction in these other worlds.[32] Are we in future lives male and female, with our sexual nature playing the same pervasive role as in this life, and do we mate and reproduce? In support of this possibility it may be said that if we are each to remain, to self-apprehension, the same person from life to life we must continue to be sexual beings, with an appropriate bodily structure designed for the reproduction of the species. In that case, presumably children are born into the next world, those children – or their 'souls' – having previously lived on this earth. We then have essentially the hindu or buddhist picture of reincarnation, but from one world to another instead of within the same world. Or, alternatively, is it the case that 'when they rise from the dead, they neither marry nor are given in marriage, but are like angels in heaven'?[33] In that case there seems no reason to think of the transition to the next world as involving the end of the present conscious self and the formation of a new self through the gradual process of growth from baby to adult. The same self would continue, though translated into a new environment and with perhaps only fading memories of a previous life in another world. Our sexuality would presumably have some analogue in the new environment, but one which is somehow an end in itself rather than a means to reproduction.

But these are questions which must remain unanswered in our present life. As to whether embodiment in the next world takes a form very like or somewhat like or totally unlike our earthly shape; and what the concrete business of that world will be – these are questions about which we can scarcely even speculate. We cannot say anything about the next world beyond the *bardo* state except that it will be a real spatio-temporal environment, functioning in accordance with its own laws, within which there will be real personal life – a world with its own concrete character, its own history, its own absorbing and urgent concerns, its own crises, perils, achievements, sacrifices, and its own terminus giving shape and meaning to existence within it. For moral and spiritual growth, as we know it, depends upon interaction with other people within a common environment. Science-fiction writers today freely create pictures of life on other planets, often in the remote future, including worlds inhabited by rational and moral creatures, sometimes far more advanced than ourselves, who bear no physical resemblance to earthly human beings;

and this kind of exercise of the imagination could equally well be regarded as creating pareschatological myths of other worlds in other spaces.

And then in due course, whether after a longer or a shorter period than our present earthly life, we shall presumably again 'die' and undergo another transition, via another *bardo*-type experience, into yet another life in yet another world. We cannot know how many such worlds or series of worlds there are; and indeed the number and nature of the individual's successive embodiments will presumably depend upon what is needed for him to reach the point at which he transcends ego-hood and attains the ultimate unitive state, or nirvana, to be discussed in chapter 22. The hindu and buddhist pictures of the universe suggest an immense time-scale of salvation, with each strand of karmic history being incarnated millions or even a beginningless infinity of times. But if we think, in a more western mould, of the divine creative process as moving towards a goal, then the number of embodiments will be finite. When we look at the best human lives, we can conceive of humanity reaching its perfection in them within one more life, and in others within a very few more. But when we look at the worst human lives we are more inclined to think in terms of tens or hundreds of lives . . . At any rate it certainly seems that some will require a smaller and others a greater number of embodiments. But since we know nothing of the specific conditions of these postulated other existences we cannot develop our picture beyond the thought of a plurality of lives in a plurality of worlds; adding that each stage will have the relative autonomy which makes it a 'real life', with its own exigencies and tasks and its own possibilities of success and failure.

To what extent may memory be carried over from life to life? If what was said earlier in this chapter about the limits of our human span of self-apprehension and of effective personal memory is correct, much will depend upon whether the lives are many or few. If they are very few they may all be remembered. But if they are numerous we should not expect them to be at all clearly or fully recalled. There would be some memory of the immediately past life, perhaps tending to fade as one becomes more absorbingly engaged in the new existence which has succeeded it. There might be some awareness of the fact of many previous lives, perhaps identified in memory by some general characteristic of each embodiment, somewhat as an old man who moved house frequently in childhood might remember the different houses but recall very little detail of his life in each of them. But if we try to do more than note these possibilities, drawn by analogy from our present experience, we shall only be building speculations upon speculations.

Let us instead ask what basis there is, within this picture, for our present concern with the ultimate future product of the creative process. Let us suppose, optimistically and for the sake of argument, that to reach the point of final ego-transcendence is going to take me nineteen or twenty further embodiments; and let us suppose that my lives have each about the same span, thus perhaps adding up to some fourteen or fifteen hundred years. It would follow from the picture which I have suggested that the 20th JH, whilst he will remember the 19th, and will have some general recollection of there having been others before that, will probably have virtually no recollection of the life of the present JH, and would in any case have far greater difficulty in identifying himself with me than the difficulty which I have acknowledged in identifying myself with the writer of my own diary at the age of fifteen. But if he (the 20th JH, some fifteen centuries hence) will not include me within his span of self-apprehension, why should I include him in mine? Why should I be in any way concerned about such a being of the distant future, or do anything to bring him into existence?

The answer, I think, is that our relationship to our future perfected selves is in fact a fairly remote one; that it is appropriate that we should only think occasionally about so distant a prospect; that in acting rightly within our immediate situation we forward our own development towards that perfection without having specifically to calculate with it in view; but that there is here a sufficient basis for such occasional thoughts as we properly entertain of our future selves at the end of the temporal journey. For although the human span of self-apprehension does not seem capable of extending to anything like fifteen hundred years, yet the moving area of consciousness will have changed continuously from one which includes me, the 1st JH, to one which includes the 20th JH at the other end of the same personal history. Each link in the chain will be consciously connected with the one next before it, although it may well be that none of them will be directly conscious, in either perception or memory,[34] of the chain as a whole. But this is only an extension on to a larger scale of the relationship to time with which we are already familiar. We live in the moving present with a memory which, in general, illuminates the more recent past more vividly than the remoter past, and with this brightly illuminated band of time moving continuously forward and thus changing in content.

It is true that we find it much easier to identify ourselves retrospectively with our remembered past than prospectively with our yet to be experienced future; and this is natural enough in view of the fact that the past exists, or has existed, whereas the future has not. Our detachment from it is roughly proportional to the degree of change to be expected in ourselves and our circumstances. The youth of, say, sixteen can barely imagine himself at the age of seventy. And I can barely imagine myself nineteen or so embodiments hence in a state fit to participate in the Vision of God. In each case we concentrate upon the situations in which we are involved, with at most very occasional thoughts about the remote future. For the motivations for living arise in the present and relate to relatively close rather than very distant consequences. And this, surely, is as it ought to be. What we do should be worth doing for its own sake, as intrinsically right or intrinsically enjoyable. But in the kind and degree of continuity that obtains between the fifteen-year-old and the seventy-year-old, and again between the 1st and the 20th JH, there is sufficient basis for such thoughts about our ultimate future as come to us from time to time.

In conclusion, let us return to the broad picture of the human person progressing through ever higher spheres of existence towards a final state which may, I shall suggest in the next chapter, transcend individual ego-hood. Such a thought is consonant with one suggested interpretation of the 'many mansions' of which the Jesus of the Fourth Gospel spoke. For the *monai* ('mansions' or, better, 'resting-places') are, said William Temple, 'wayside caravanserais – shelters at stages along the road where travellers may rest on their journey'.[35] The broad theme is a very ancient one in both east and west, the following being a christian expression of it in the writings of the fourth-century theologian, Gregory of Nyssa:

> Thus though the new grace we may obtain is greater than what we had before, it does not put a limit on our final goal; rather, for those who are rising in perfection, the limit of the good that is attained becomes the beginning of the discovery of higher goods. Thus they never stop rising, moving from one new beginning to the next, and the beginning of ever greater graces is never limited of itself. For the desire of those who thus rise never rests in what they can already understand; but by an ever greater and greater desire, the soul keeps rising constantly to another which lies ahead, and thus it makes its way through ever higher regions towards the Transcendent.[36]

NOTES

1. *Phaedo*, 114d.
2. *The Tibetan Book of the Dead or the After-Death Experiences on the Bardo Plane, according to Lama Kazi Dawa-Samdup's English Rendering*, ed. W. Y. Evans-Wentz.
3. op. cit., p. 95.
4. ibid., p. 91.
5. ibid., p. 92.
6. ibid., p. 101.
7. ibid., p. 103.
8. ibid., pp. 161–2.
9. ibid., pp. 173–4.
10. 'Introductory Foreword', ibid., p. lxii.
11. Robert Crookall offers a useful analysis of the contents of a wide range of such sources in *The Supreme Adventure: Analyses of Psychic Communications*.
12. The idea that co-extensive with the physical body there is an ethereal double, in which our consciousness is centred, and which detaches itself at death, is very ancient and is indeed 'one of the most persistent beliefs of mankind' (Benjamin Walker, *Beyond the Body*,

p. 49). It is also claimed that the astral body sometimes floats loose from the physical body and that some people can deliberately practise 'astral projection', observing in their astral body events at a great distance from their sleeping physical body. Such cases are described in, e.g., Sylvan Muldoon and Hereward Carrington, *The Phenomena of Astral Projection*; Robert A. Monroe, *Journeys out of the Body*; and J. H. M. Whiteman, *The Mystical Life*. There seems to be no good reason to deny that these descriptions generally correspond to experiences undergone by those reporting them. But their interpretation remains highly problematic. A minimal interpretation would attribute the information gained about distant events to clairvoyance and telepathy, presented to consciousness in the dramatic form of the experience of astral travel. But whether this minimal interpretation is sufficient I do not profess to know.

13. Grace Rosher, *Beyond the Horizon*, p. 10.

14. Sir Oliver Lodge, *Raymond Revised*, p. 112.

15. *Beyond the Horizon*, pp. 22–3.

16. ibid., p. 25.

17. Geraldine Cummins, *The Road to Immortality*, pp. 48–9.

18. ibid., pp. 36–7.

19. *Beyond the Horizon*, p. 28.

20. *The Road to Immortality*, p. 71.

21. ibid., pp. 39, 49.

22. Emanuel Swedenborg, *Heaven and Its Wonders and Hell*.

23. A. Duncan-Jones, 'Man's Mortality', in *Analysis*, vol. 28, no. 3 (January 1968), p. 68.

24. As was suggested by Bernard Mayo in a paper given to the Birmingham University Philosophical Society in 1968.

25. See an interesting relevant article by Derek Parfit: 'Personal Identity', in *Philosophical Review*, January 1971.

26. Berger and Luckmann, *The Social Construction of Reality*, pp. 66–7.

27. Immanuel Kant, *Critique of Practical Reason*, part I, book II, ch. 2, sect. 4.

28. An analogy which I have developed in 'Towards a Christian Theology of Death', in *Dying, Death and Disposal*, ed. Gilbert Cope, pp. 23–4.

29. Perhaps this possibility of final self-transcendence in the moment of death corresponds to the idea of the 'final decision' in roman catholic theology. Thus Ladislaus Boros speaks of a 'total awareness and presence of being' in this moment of truth (*The Moment of Truth*, p. 7).

30. Grace Rosher, *Beyond the Horizon*, p. 35.

31. I have argued in chapter 15, section 2, that the idea of resurrection or reconstitution requires the notion of spaces in the plural.

32. See Ludwig Feuerbach's perceptive stress on this question in

The Essence of Christianity, part I, ch. 18.

33. Mark 12: 25.

34. Unless of course the hindu and buddhist doctrine is true of a total recall at the end of the *samsaric* process.

35. William Temple, *Readings in St John's Gospel*, vol. II, p. 226.

36. *From Glory to Glory: Texts from Gregory of Nyssa's Mystical Writings*, from sermon 8, pp. 212–13.

CHAPTER 21

Moksha, Nirvana and the Unitive State

1. EASTERN AND WESTERN VIEWS OF MAN

We now approach the final but at the same time the most speculative and tentative phase of the enquiry. We have seen reasons for declining to share the materialist rejection of any hope (or fear) of life after bodily death. We then looked at the various conceptions of the life to come in the religious teachings of both west and east. Several different pictures of post-mortem existence in terms of resurrection, reincarnation, and disembodied consciousness seem possible, and one or other of these may well be not far from the truth. But these pictures all constitute what I have called pareschatologies, referring to the next stage of human existence. They apply to a future in which the individual is still moving towards the perfection, or perhaps the transcendence of individual perfection, which is the goal of temporal existence. But they do not apply to that ultimate state itself. For we have seen that eastern theories of reincarnation point explicitly, and that western theories of the immortal ego, by their inability to match the thought of unending time, point implicitly to an eternity which is not merely a further prolongation of the temporal process.

In attempting to think about this final human destiny, can we still usefully listen to both west and east? Or have we come to a final parting of the ways between the oriental and occidental paths of thought? This might well appear to be so. For the characteristic western and eastern conceptions of man's final goal seem to stand in sharp contrast and indeed irreconcilable contradiction. In western – or rather semitic – religious thought ultimate reality has predominantly been conceived as the personal creator God and man as a finite personal being made in the divine image for fellowship with his Maker. This is the basis of the idea of the unlimited value of the individual human person or soul. Religiously, the high point in the expression of this idea occurred in Jesus' teaching about God as our loving heavenly Father, who knows each of his human children so that the very hairs of our heads are numbered. He cares for each like a shepherd seeking a lost sheep, or a needy widow searching for a lost coin, and he lavishes his love upon each like a father welcoming back a long-lost son.[1] Philosophically, the high points are Plato's *Phaedo*, affirming the immortality of the rational and ethical soul; Descartes's *cogito ergo sum*, taking the existence of individual self-consciousness as the necessary starting-point for thought; and Kant's founding of ethics upon the free autonomous person seen as an end in himself. In politics the idea of the inherent value of the individual human being has worked itself out in the decay of feudalism, the eventual abandonment of slavery, the gradual growth of democracy, and in the advance of women towards full social equality with men. The common theme is that of each human person as a child of God.

This starting-point leads to doctrines of immortality which include the preservation and enhancement of individual existence beyond the grave, such doctrines being either social or mystical. The former centre upon the idea of the Kingdom of God as a society of completed persons dwelling together in ideal harmony in the divine presence. In this picture the individual human personality retains his individuality, but in a perfected form. The latter, more mystical understandings of eternal life involve the notion of the beatific vision of God. Here the soul is so absolutely centred upon God that other human beings seem irrelevant. Indeed, much of the traditional language of the mystical union is modelled on that of the sexual union of two lovers, completely absorbed in one another. Thus in these different ways the semitic emphasis has been firmly upon the value of the individual human soul, as an object of God's love, and upon the perfecting of finite personality and its eternal preservation in the divine presence.

In contrast to this the characteristic emphasis of the religions of indian origin has been upon the ultimate unimportance and indeed unreality of individual personality. According to the hindu philosophy of advaita Vedanta, the Ultimate Reality, Brahman, is beyond all human categories. Ignorance (*avidya*) of this reality gives rise to an illusory world (*maya*) of apparent individuals and things. The illusion of individual personal life, one may say, is real as long as it lasts. It persists until the 'individual' realizes his identity with the real self, Atman, which is at the same time Brahman. He then ceases to exist as a separate finite person and resumes existence as the eternal Atman/Brahman. This self-realization is the individual's salvation (*moksha*) – his deliverance from the otherwise endless round of rebirths in the anxiety-fraught illusion of this world. Freedom from evil, or attainment of the ultimate good, is thus not through the enhancement and perpetuation of human individuality, but through its abolition in the merging of finite ego-consciousness into the infinite consciousness.

Again, in Buddhism, in both the theravada and mahayana traditions, the individual personality is seen as merely a temporary bundling together of transitory elements. So far from the human ego being of permanent significance, the technique of salvation consists in a dismantling of this bundle by negating the craving for existence which holds it together. Thus in Buddhism as well as in Hinduism there is a radically negative attitude to that which in the semitic faiths is said to endure for ever as the object of God's eternal love. And in cultures dominated by this valuation of individual personality the life of the present world has seemed less important and there has been less stress upon social justice and technological progress than in the west.

I shall however try to show that this at first sight stark opposition between the insights of east and west holds only on the surface. I shall argue that the eschatologies developed within Christianity, Hinduism and Buddhism are each essentially open-ended. They are pointers beyond the known which do not profess to delimit the boundaries or describe the contents of that towards which they point. And if we presume that the teachings of these great religious traditions have arisen out of permanently significant experiences at the interface between the human and the divine we shall be open to the possibility that their eschatologies offer convergent indications, each pointing beyond our present human experience and yet each pointing in the same direction.

I believe that this is what in fact we find. In seeking to

substantiate this I shall not be offering a synthesis of the insights of east and west, nor some third position to which each can be regarded as approximating. I shall be suggesting, rather, that in the major forms of religious life of both west and east we find men looking towards an ultimate human destiny which is beyond their sight, and which can only be conceived in the most general terms; and that we observe these lookings to be oriented in the same direction. I shall be content to display the pointing fingers within each tradition, believing that in their convergence they offer us the best clue that we have to the ultimate destiny of man.

2. HINDU UNDERSTANDINGS OF MOKSHA

Within Hinduism, advaita Vedanta – the non-dualist inter- pretation of the Vedanta – of the school of Shankara (*c.* 788– *c.* 820 AD) stands at a logical extreme by reference to which all other indian religious systems can be located. That is to say, monistic philosophy cannot be taken further than Shan- kara takes it. In his thought the relation of the human individual to the Absolute, Brahman, is one of unqualified identity; and the illusion of finite individuality, in terms of which there are 'I's' unaware of their ultimate non-existence as separate entities, and of their real identity with the Absolute, is caused by the inexplicable fact of *avidya* (ignorance of reality) and the inexplicable enclosure of 'fragments' or 'moments' of the universal consciousness in enveloping veils of *maya*. (This seems to be the place where the *advaitist* philosophy makes the appeal, which all systems of religious thought have to make at some point, to incomprehensible facts in order to account for the existing situation.)

The goal of the illusory phenomenon of plural human existence is thus a discarding of the illusion of individuality. In a characteristic *advaitic* simile, individual *jivas* are like jars enclosing space. Once the jars are broken the space which they had enclosed remains as sheer space.[2] Accordingly, in the final state of release (*moksha*) human individuality has been totally left behind: 'Just as . . . the bees prepare honey by collecting the juices of different trees and reducing them into one essence, and as these juices possess no discrimination, so that they might say, "I am the essence of this tree, I am the essence of that tree", even so . . . all these creatures though they reach Being do not know that they have reached the Being.'[3] Again,

> As rivers flow and disappear at last
> In ocean's waters, name and form renouncing,
> So too the sage, released from name and form,
> Is merged in the divine and ultimate existence.[4]

Thus souls finally merge into the Infinite without individual consciousness, memory, or boundaries of any kind.

But although advaita Vedanta is probably the best known of the indian philosophical systems in the west, it constitutes the religion of comparatively few spiritually and intellectually elite individuals; and it would be quite unrealistic to regard it as the central religious tradition of India. As Santosh Sengupta says in his discussion of the western misunderstandings of Hinduism, 'There are schools of Vedanta that are opposed to the pure monism of Shankara-Vedanta. It is therefore wrong to treat the latter as if it were *the* Vedanta. Theistic Vedanta and Vaisnava theism are more representative of the practising faith of the Hindus than is Shankara-Vedanta. Indeed contemporary Hinduism is characterized by an opposition to Shankara-Vedanta.'[5] For the actual religious life of India has long been in practice theistic, and its most influential scripture has long been the post-vedic Bhagavad Gita. The greatest of the non-monist vedantic thinkers was Ramanuja (11th century AD – possibly 1017–1137). In distinction from, and indeed in opposition to, Shankara's monistic philosophy Ramanuja taught a *vishishtadvaita* (modified non-dualism) in which Brahman and finite human selves are in one sense the same and in another sense distinct. For Ramanuja, Brahman is not the impersonal Absolute but the personal Lord. He is the Supreme Person (*Purusottama*) or Supreme Self (*Paramatma*), and the right human relationship to him is one of love and devotion. Ramanuja uses many similes to indicate the sense in which God and his creatures are the same: 'Sometimes he calls the soul a part of God, sometimes the body of God, sometimes a mode of God, sometimes an attribute or qualification of God and sometimes as absolutely dependent on, and controlled, supported and utilized by God.'[6] Of these, the most fundamental simile is of God as the soul of the world, with the world (including human persons) as his cosmic body. But Ramanuja did not mean by a body simply and literally what the word connotes in western literature. He defined 'body' as follows: 'Any substance that an intelligent being is able completely to control and support for his own purposes, and the essential nature of which is entirely subservient to that intelligent self, is his body.'[7] Thus if Brahman sustains and controls the universe, it can be called his body; and conversely, as creator, preserver and ruler of the universe, Brahman can be called its soul. For Ramanuja the soul-body relationship expresses absolute lordship, ownership and control, so that he can even say, 'Brahman who, because He is the Inner Controller of finite selves, has these selves, along with their bodies, as His modes.'[8] That God is the supreme self ensouling the cosmos means that 'in the heart of all beings who constitute My body, I am seated as their Self (*atma*), for to be the "Self" means that I am entirely their support, controller, and owner'.[9]

Thus finite souls are identical with God in the sense that they have no being independently of him and are totally his creatures, existing through his creative will, instruments of his purpose, his possessions, wholly at his disposal – and thus, by Ramanuja's definition, part of his cosmic body. But in another sense they each have their own distinct though derivative existence. For they are objects of the divine love and are called to be lovers of God. Ramanuja speaks of God as 'overwhelmed by His love for His sinful creatures who have come to Him for refuge';[10] and interprets the Lord Krishna, in the Bhagavad Gita, as saying of the devotees' offering of fruit and flowers, 'Even though I am the Lord of all and My desires are ever fulfilled . . . I consume such an offering as if I had received something unimaginably dear.'[11]

Consistently with this doctrine of the divine love Ramanuja holds that the finite *jivatmans* persist as individuals even in the final state of *moksha* (release):

> To maintain that the consciousness of the 'I' does not persist in the state of final release is again altogether inappropriate. It in fact amounts to the doctrine . . . that final

release is the annihilation of the Self . . . Moreover, a man who suffering pain, mental or of other kind, . . . puts himself in relation to pain – 'I am suffering pain' – naturally begins to reflect how he may once for all free himself from all these manifold afflictions and enjoy a state of untroubled ease; the desire of final release thus having arisen in him he at once sets to work to accomplish it. If, on the other hand, he were to realise that the effect of such activity would be the loss of personal existence, he surely would turn away as soon as somebody began to tell him about 'release' . . . Nor must you maintain against this that even in the state of release there persists pure consciousness . . . No sensible person exerts himself under the influence of the idea that after he himself has perished there will remain some entity termed 'pure light'! – What constitutes the 'inward' Self thus is the 'I', the knowing subject.[12]

Indeed, a large part of indian thought has opposed the *advaitist* theory that there is ultimately only one self. As B. N. K. Sharma says, 'The Advaita philosophy of Samkara unhesitatingly rejects the doctrine of plurality of selves. But almost all other systems of Indian philosophy such as Jainism, Purva-Mimamsa, Nyaya-Vaiseshika, Samkhya-Yoga and the theistic schools of Vedanta of Ramanuja, Madhva, Nimbarka, Vallabha and Caitanya hold that plurality of selves is not *merely* an empirical fact.'[13] For most of these schools, the *jivas* (souls) are still in some way plural within the ultimate state of *moksha* (liberation) and enjoy some kind of individuality. For example, Madhva said that '*Moksha* would not be worth having, if the atman [or *jiva*] does not survive as a self-luminous entity therein'.[14] Thus whilst the range of hindu understandings of man's final state includes the thought of total absorption into the Infinite Consciousness, the larger stream of thought, carried within the *bhakti* faith of the ordinary devotee, has affirmed a continuing identity in which the soul is both somehow part of the life of God and yet somehow still exists in a personal relationship of love to God.

3. NIRVANA IN THERAVADA BUDDHISM

The buddhist conception of man's final goal as nirvana (pali: nibbana) has been and is understood as variously as the christian concept of eternal life. It is not my purpose (nor is it within my competence) to make assertions about what the Buddha really taught; indeed the evidence is so conflicting, or at best ambiguous, that it may well never give rise to full agreement.[15] The prevailing popular view in the west, promulgated by some of the early european students of Buddhism,[16] has been that nirvana signifies nothingness or extinction and accordingly that to attain it is to cease to exist. The basis for this view is that the pali 'nibbana' means literally 'blowing out' (as in the blowing out of a candle) or 'going out' (as in the going out of a fire through lack of fuel). This has led many Christians to conclude that to achieve nirvana means to escape from earthly suffering by ceasing to be. In its crudest form this annihilationist conception of nirvana is quite certainly mistaken; for the attainment of nirvana is held to be possible in this life. Thus the Buddha himself did not cease to exist when he attained nirvana, but lived and taught on earth for some forty-five years; and the buddhist scriptures refer to hundreds of other then living arhats (or arahants),[17] i.e. men and women who had attained nirvana. And indeed, according to the pali canon the Buddha explicitly repudiated the annihilationist interpretation of his teaching: 'There are some recluses and brahmans who misrepresent me untruly, vainly, falsely, not in accordance with fact, saying: "The recluse Gotama is a nihilist, he lays down the cutting off, the destruction, the disappearance of the existent entity." But as this, monks, is just what I am not, as this is just what I do not say, therefore these worthy recluses and brahmans misrepresent me untruly, vainly, falsely.'[18] We should therefore have no difficulty in accepting the following statement by the well-known contemporary Theravadin, Nyanaponika Mahathera:

> In Buddhist countries of the East . . . there is now, as far as is known to the writer, not a single Buddhist school or sect that favours a nihilistic interpretation of Nibbana. Contrary to erroneous opinions, voiced mainly by uninformed or

prejudiced Western authors, Theravada, i.e. the tradition prevalent in Burma, Ceylon, Thailand, etc., is definitely averse to a view that regards Nibbana as mere extinction.[19]

Nirvana does undoubtedly involve annihilation, but it is the annihilation of evil in the individual: 'The destruction of lust, the destruction of hatred, the destruction of illusion, friend, is called Nibbana.'[20] Indeed, more fundamentally, that which has been annihilated is ego-consciousness: 'Thinking on there being no self, he wins to the state wherein the conceit "I am" has been uprooted, to the cool [i.e. to Nibbana], even in this life';[21] 'He who doth crush the great "I am" conceit – this, even this, is happiness supreme.'[22] Nirvana is thus a psychological state in which the self-positing ego has been abolished and in which there is accordingly freedom from the cravings which make human life a self-perpetuating cycle of anxious self-concern. It was in this condition of inner freedom that the Buddha dwelt after his Enlightenment:

> Nibbana have I realised, and gazed into the mirror
> of the Dhamma, the Noble Truth,
> I am healed of my wound;
> Down is my burden laid; My task is done;
> My heart is utterly set free.[23]

In this state the living person, whilst remaining physically and psychologically a separate individual, with his own past and subject to the effects of his own past, is no longer dominated by the desires and aversions, hopes and fears, joys and alarms which arise from experiencing the world in the perspective of an ego concerned for its own survival and pleasure.[24] This absolute inner freedom is not experienced as an affective numbness but as a state of tranquil joy:

> When such conditions are fulfilled, then there will be joy, and happiness, and peace, and in continual mindfulness and self-mastery, one will dwell at ease.[25]

It must however immediately be added that whilst such statements are to be taken seriously they are not intended as literal descriptions of nirvana. In its fullness the state of nirvana is not describable but only experienceable – and that only by the few who have attained to it through immense efforts of self-discipline extending, according to buddhist belief, over a long series of lives.

The Buddha's Eightfold Path to arhatship – involving right understanding, right thought, right speech, right action, right livelihood, right effort, right mindfulness and right concentration – is largely a training in ethical attitudes. Accordingly morality provides at least a negative criterion of arhatship: if someone is morally imperfect he or she cannot have attained to nirvana. Thus it is recorded in the pali canon that a king, seeing various ascetics pass by, asked the Buddha whether any of them were arhats, and received the reply:

> Hard is it, sire, for you who are a layman, holding worldly possessions, dwelling amidst the encumbrances of children, accustomed to Benares sandalwood, arrayed in garments and perfumed unguents, using gold and silver, to know whether those are Arahants, or are in the Path of Arahant-ship. It is by life in common with a person, sire, that we learn his moral character; and then only after a long interval if we pay good heed and are not heedless, if we have insight and are not unintelligent. It is by converse with another, sire, that we learn whether he is pure-minded . . . It is in time of trouble, sire, that we learn to know a man's fortitude . . . It is by intercourse, sire, that we learn to know a man's wisdom . . . [26]

A parallel is perhaps worth noting between the extinction of all motivations of personal desire and aversion in the arhat and the transcendence (but not extinction) of individual desires and aversions in Kant's man of duty who acts on the basis of pure rationality.[27] Because reason is objective and impartial, such a man acts on universally valid principles for which the agent is neither more nor less important than anyone else. He has not attained to nirvana because, although he is ruled by objective reason rather than by the needs and desires of an individual ego, yet there can still be conflicts within him between these two sources of motivation. The universality of reason has not totally replaced the particularities of an individual history. On the other hand, what Kant calls the holy will, in which there is no such conflict and which always spontaneously wills in accordance with the universal and impartial principles of pure rationality, might be described as a moral arhat. This last phrase would however be misleading if it were taken to imply that arhatship is a state of ethical achievement; for it lies beyond moral goodness.[28] Nevertheless, the kantian parallel may be a useful stepping-stone to the more positive and mysterious things that are said about nirvana in the pali canon. For just as Kant's holy will is not only free from the domination of individual desires and aversions, but grounded in something positive, namely pure reason, so also – according to many of the texts – the arhat is not only free from the four bonds of sense desire (*kama*), craving for existence (*bhava*), (false) views (*ditthi*), and ignorance (*avijja*), but is grounded in a positive transcendent reality. These positive texts are far too numerous and impressive to be ignored, and yet there is no consensus among pali scholars, whether buddhist or non-buddhist, as to their interpretation. For example, nirvana is 'the unborn . . . unageing . . . undecaying . . . undying . . . unsorrowing . . . stainless';[29] it is 'deathless';[30] again, 'Nibbana, bliss supreme'[31] and 'Above, beyond Nibbana's bliss, is naught.'[32] In the *Sanyutta-Nikaya* a series of forty-three terms is applied to nibbana, including 'the further shore', 'the unfading', 'the stable', 'the undecaying', 'the invisible', 'the taintless', 'the peace', 'the deathless', 'the excellent', 'the blissful', 'the security', 'the wonderful', 'the marvellous', 'the free from ill', 'the island', 'the cave of shelter', 'the stronghold', 'the refuge' and 'the goal'.[33] But perhaps the most important of the positive texts is the much discussed page 80 of the *Udana*:

> Monks, there exists that condition wherein is neither earth or water nor fire nor air: wherein is neither the sphere of infinite space nor of infinite consciousness nor of nothingness nor of neither-consciousness-nor-unconsciousness; where there is neither this world nor a world beyond nor both together nor moon-and-sun. Thence, monks, I declare is no coming to birth; thither is no going (from life); therein is no duration; thence is no falling; there is no arising. It is not something fixed, it moves not on, it is not based on anything. That indeed is the end of Ill.

Again:

> Monks, there is a not-born, a not-become, a not-made, a not-compounded. Monks, if that unborn, not-become, not-made, not-compounded were not, there would be apparent no escape from this here that is born, become, made, compounded.[34]

Do these positive characteristics imply any answer to the question, What becomes of the arhat, the one who has attained to nirvana, after his bodily death? There are two main schools of thought on this issue among contemporary theravada Buddhists. One holds that whilst nirvana as such is not annihilation, but a positive state of egolessness enjoyed by the arhat so long as he lives (whether in this or a heavenly world), yet when his life ends there remains no individual personality with its craving for existence to lead to further rebecoming. At this point he simply passes out of existence. He has escaped from the round of *samsara* and is no more:

> The old craving exhausted, no fresh craving rises,
> Freed from thought of future becoming
> They like barren seeds do not spring again,
> But are blown out just like a lamp.[35]

This view, which I shall call the minimal theravada interpretation of nirvana, fully grants its positive character, as against the conception of it as nothingness, whilst however denying that it is more than a psychological state. Thus when the experiencing consciousness ceases at the arhat's death, nirvana ceases for him – or he ceases for nirvana. For nirvana exists or occurs only as a state of a living arhat. This minimal theravada interpretation agrees with western Humanism and Marxism in their affirmation of final extinction. It is however incompatible with the materialistic conception of man on which these philosophies rest, for the innumerable rebirths, the many-levelled spirit worlds and the devas would be regarded as products of fantasy from a western materialist point of view. Nevertheless its partial agreement with materialism prompts a basic criticism of the minimal theravada eschatology. In contrast to western materialism it depicts the universe as being enormously complicated and yet, in spite of all the complications, no less ultimately pointless than is the materialist's universe. For western science-oriented Humanism, the world and man are simply the natural phenomena that they seem to be. Man is a product of biological evolution, and individuals perish absolutely at death as in all other animal species. Human life has no transcendent meaning or destiny. The strength of this view lies in its economy; it does not 'multiply entities beyond necessity'. In contrast, the minimal theravada picture of the universe involves a riotous multiplication of entities – and yet without mitigating in the least its ultimate pointlessness. The human enterprise moves towards the final non-existence which materialism teaches, although according to minimal Theravada the path to non-entity is enormously more prolonged. But this prolongation does not give it value; on the contrary the long road of *samsara* is thought of as something to be endured rather than enjoyed, a process whose end is the great object of hope. And yet this end is only extinction. One could accordingly imagine a 'minimal Theravadin' wishing that western materialism were true! He might well complain (had there been a creator to complain to) that if he must exist only to be exterminated, at least let him be exterminated cleanly and quickly, instead of being continually brought back for further torment. I argued in chapter 8 that the humanist and materialist vision is profoundly pessimistic and tragic. If there is any philosophy which is even more pessimistic, it is the minimal and ultimately annihilationist version of theravada Buddhism. It does not of course follow that such compound pessimism is false; but we may devoutly hope that it is!

However, the more orthodox theravada interpretation denies that nirvana is simply a psychological state and sees it as an ineffable transcendent spiritual reality – 'the permanent, immortal, supramundane state which cannot be expressed by mundane terms'[36] – and teaches that in some fashion which we cannot describe the arhat whose individual career has ended is one with this infinite transcendent reality. For the Buddha distinguished between two states of nirvana which in the following text are ascribed respectively to this life and beyond it:

One state is that in this same life possessed
With base remaining, tho' becoming's stream
Be cut off. While the state without a base
Belongeth to the future, wherein all
Becomings utterly do come to cease.[37]

This duality has solidified in buddhist thought into the distinction between nirvana, as a state of the still living psychophysical individual, and parinirvana ('nirvana without qualification'), which lies beyond and outside the process of rebecoming.

Some commentators understand parinirvana as the final and complete ending of individual selfhood in the infinite and eternal Reality. The arhat has already negated in himself all egoity or sense of self so that, with the final breaking up of the *nama-rupa* (the psycho-physical individual) that was 'him', 'he' becomes fully one with the Infinite. Thus Dr Vajiranana says, 'The fabric of the world and the "self" break up, leaving only the infinite, the element uncreated and unformed. This is the state of Nibbana that the finite mind cannot grasp.'[38] This is not in any sense the immortality of the earthly individual, for all that made up his individuality has been abolished. Parinirvana is on this view an undifferentiated unity into which purified consciousness merges as 'the dewdrop slips into the shining sea'.[39] Thus beyond death the arhat both is and yet is not. He no longer exists as a separate individual; but on the other hand the only aspect of him that was ever ultimately real remains eternally real as or in the Infinite Reality from which it has been temporarily separated by ignorance and illusion. Such a paradoxical 'is' and 'is not' matches the Buddha's deliberately mysterious reply to the question whether he would exist after death: he reminded Anuruddha that in this present life a Tathagata (i.e. a Buddha) is essentially mysterious, so that one should not presume to speculate about his state after death.[40] On another occasion the Buddha said that after death Tathagata is free from everything called form and is 'deep, immeasurable, unfathomable as is the great ocean'.[41]

This might be interpreted along *advaitic* lines as saying that in parinirvana he is no longer distinguishable from the great ocean of Spirit of which he was formerly an individual drop. Others, however, hold that according to the Buddha death makes no significant difference to an Enlightened One, and that beyond the process of rebirth he eternally *is* in some way that is at present unimaginable by us. Thus Rune Johansson, in the course of his survey of every use of 'nibbana' and its cognates in the pali *Nikayas*, discusses the 'deep, immeasurable ocean' analogy and says that it 'proves that the Tathagata (i.e. the Buddha) was thought to continue existing in some form after death, as the ocean certainly exists'.[42] He further cites one of the passages in which the Buddha declares that no one can hope to know what the Buddha's state is after death, for 'I say that a Tathagata cannot be known even in this life',[43] and comments that this 'proves that there is no essential difference between a living Tathagata and a dead Tathagata'.[44] His conclusion concerning the post-mortem state of one who has attained nirvana is that it is 'perhaps a diluted, undifferentiated, "resting" existence, more or less impersonal but still recognizable'.[45] This, or even more than this, seems to be consonant with another significant passage, in which nirvana is referred to as an abode of bliss:

> But, friends, inasmuch as having fostered righteous states and dwelling therein, in this very life one would live pleasantly. Unharassed, free from life's fret and fever, and, when body dissolves, after death one may look for the abode of bliss, therefore does the Exalted One approve of the accomplishing of righteous states.[46]

As I have already insisted, I am neither concerned nor am I competent to try to adjudicate between these rival interpretations of the pali canon. The Buddha's recorded sayings are mysterious and lend themselves to differing understandings. But the major interpretations constitute significant eschatological hypotheses which we ought not to lose sight of.

4. NIRVANA IN MAHAYANA BUDDHISM

When we turn from the Theravada to the Mahayana we find that Buddhism has developed in this wider form into a metaphysical system which is much less agnostic and humanistic than the theravada teaching – which latter may, however, well have remained closer to the mind of the historical Gautama. A central mahayanist development occurs in the doctrine of the Three Bodies (*trikaya*) of the Buddha, the physical body, the body of bliss, and the cosmic body. There have been many incarnate Buddhas, Gautama being the most recent, and there will be more in the future. The Buddha's *Nirmanakaya*, or physical body, is the earthly body of one of these enlightened ones. The *Sambhogakaya* ('Body of Bliss') consists of a transcendent Buddha, intermediate between an historical Buddha and the Infinite and Absolute Reality, which is the *Dharmakaya* (the 'Dharma Body' or cosmic body) of the Buddha, which is 'the Buddha seen as the Absolute'.[47] Thus the Dharma Body of the Buddha is the Ultimate Reality, beyond our human understanding, also known as the Void or Emptiness (*sunyata*), Suchness, the One, and as nirvana. The Dharma Body is unitary, but is manifested in a multiplicity of transcendent Buddhas, who are divine beings forming the Body of Bliss. These are thought of in popular mahayana faith as personal divinities with power to lead their worshippers to rebirth in their heavenly realms of blessedness. (The most widely worshipped is Amitabha, or Amida, Lord of the Pure Land paradise.) In mahayanist, and particularly tantric, philosophy however they are often thought of as powerful mental images of aspects of Absolute Reality, and thus as symbols or myths expressing our finite human awareness of the ultimate. There is implied here the thought that the God whom men worship may be a projected image expressing our best (but still inadequate) conception of a reality which in its fullness altogether transcends the reach of the human mind.

Thus in the Mahayana 'the Buddha' no longer signifies an individual arhat who lived long ago. Gautama was merely one of the physical bodies of the eternal Buddha who is Dharma or Truth; he was the Dharma made flesh.[48] Thus far the structural parallel with the christian idea of the incarnation of the eternal Logos is evident,[49] though whereas there is only one Second Person of the Trinity there are innumerable Buddhas – although, again, ultimately all the Buddhas are one. And in catholic or mahayana Buddhism the Buddha came to draw men into his Dharma Body as, in mahayana or catholic

christianity, the Christ came to draw men into his Mystical
Body.

This cosmic or Dharma Body of the Buddha is also nirvana.
And again, as in the Fourth Gospel eternal life is to be known
and enjoyed now, in the midst of this earthly life, so also
nirvana may be attained and experienced now. The world is
then transformed in the arhat's experience and he discovers
that *samsara*, the process of transitory, imperfect and suffering
existence, is none other than nirvana; for from the ultimate
standpoint which he has now achieved all reality is one. In the
words of Nagarjuna, the great mahayanist systematizer,

> There is no difference at all
> Between Nirvana and Samsara.[50]

And in the words of the tantric *Saraha*,

> As is Nirvana, so is Samsara.
> Do not think there is any distinction.[51]

In the unity of the Absolute, which is nirvana, there are no
longer separate individuals, for all have become Buddha,
nirvana, the Absolute. As Conze puts it, 'What is it that
separates me from the Absolute? Only the act of appropriating
a part of the universe to myself. Where that act is surrendered,
no barrier is left.'[52] Individual selfhood has been transcended.
To quote Saraha again:

> In this state of highest bliss
> There is neither self nor other.
> 'This is myself and this is another.'
> Be free of this bond which encompasses you about,
> And your own self is thereby released.
> Do not err in this matter of self and other.
> Everything is Buddha without exception.[53]

And yet it seems that there is still some kind of individual
consciousness in nirvana even though the boundaries of the
different consciousnesses have become, so to speak, mutually
transparent. Thus another great mahayana thinker, Asanga,
says, 'On the pure level there is neither unity nor plurality of
Buddhas, (not plurality) for like space they have no bodies,
(and not unity) for formerly they had bodies.'[54] Conze says of

those who attain to enlightenment, 'They are then swallowed up in the Absolute and lose their distinctive personalities. Nevertheless, and it is almost impossible to explain this, they do not all become the same, but retain some separate and distinctive features.'[55]

5. THE UNITIVE STATE IN CHRISTIAN MYSTICISM

If it were true that the eastern religions aim at the abolition of selfhood and Christianity at its preservation, they would indeed be pointing in opposite directions. But this is not in fact the case. We have seen that Buddhism and Hinduism seek the total renunciation of the human 'me' and 'mine' so that the arhat or the *jivanmukta* becomes one with the Infinite, whether this is conceived non-personally, as Dharma/nirvana or Brahman, or personally as the divine Thou of the Bhagavad Gita. But we have also seen that the sense in which the human individual is believed to become 'one with the Infinite' ranges from absorption 'without trace', to a hard-to-define state of both unity and diversity in which there is a merging into one, and yet the many remain somehow many even when they have become one. And on the christian side there has also been a range of emphases, in that the stress upon the absolute value of the individual person has always been accompanied by an equal stress upon self-giving, loving the neighbour as much as oneself, the abandonment of self-will, the losing of the self, the surrender of the beloved I. Thus Zaehner says that 'Christianity agrees with Hinduism in that it insists that the immortal self can only be found if the empirical self, the "I" dies'.[56] This aspect of Christianity has been developed, in relation to God, in the mystical tradition of the unitive life, in which a human will becomes one with the divine will; and in relation to man, in the tradition of self-giving love and in the modern rediscovery of personality as essentially interpersonal. These are both directly concerned with the present life; but in showing us the christian equivalent of nirvana they may also point towards the christian equivalent of parinirvana as the ultimate state of perfected creaturely existence.

There are various kinds of mysticism, one common classification being into nature-mysticism, concerned with our one-

ness with nature as a whole; soul-mysticism, seeking knowledge
of the self in isolation from all else; and religious mysticism,
or God-mysticism, seeking oneness with the divine source and
ground of our being.[57] We are concerned here with the God-
mysticism which has always been a strand within the christian
tradition. Here the mystic's ultimate goal is the unitive life, or
unitive state, which is also the beatific vision of God. 'The
last stage of the journey, in which the soul presses towards the
mark, and gains the prize of its high calling', says W. R. Inge,
'is the unitive or contemplative life, in which man beholds
God face to face, and is joined to Him.'[58] In this state 'the
death of selfhood is complete, an utter transformation of
personality has taken place, so that a new creature is born, a
new and permanent change of consciousness has been brought
about. The soul is fully united with That which beyond all
appearances is; it is "oned" with God.'[59]

The movement of christian mysticism towards its goal in
the unitive life has been classically described by Evelyn
Underhill in her monumental study, *Mysticism*, from which I
shall illustrate the central feature which particularly concerns
us here. This is the paradox that, in the perfect relationship
between the human and the divine, human individuality
remains and yet is totally emptied of selfhood. It has become,
in buddhist terminology, *anatta*, selfless. As Delacroix expressed it, 'At its term, it [the mystical life] has, as it were,
suppressed the ordinary self, and . . . has established a new
personality, with a new method of feeling and of action. Its
growth results in the transformation of personality: it abolishes
the primitive consciousness of selfhood, and substitutes for it
a wider consciousness: the total disappearance of selfhood in
the divine, the substitution of a Divine Self for the primitive
self.'[60] This complete openness of the human to the divine is not,
or not mainly, a matter of mystical ecstasies and trances but
of the everyday consciousness of the person who has attained
to the level of the unitive life. It was perfectly expressed by
St Paul: 'It is no longer I who live, but Christ who lives in
me.'[61] For as the mystic completes the cycle which led him to
withdraw from the world into contemplation, and then to
return to the world as a servant of God, he becomes a transformed agent of the divine will. As Ruysbroeck said, 'he dwells

in God; and yet he goes out towards created things, in a spirit of love towards all things, in the virtues and in works of righteousness. And this is the supreme summit of the inner life.'[62]

Evelyn Underhill characterizes the highest reaches of the contemplative life as follows:

The chief, in fact the one essential, preliminary is that pure surrender of selfhood, or 'self-naughting', which the trials of the Dark Night tended to produce. Only the thoroughly detached, 'naughted soul' is 'free', says the *Mirror of Simple Souls*, and the Unitive State is essentially a state of free and filial participation in Eternal Life. The chief marks of the state itself are (1) a complete absorption in the interests of the Infinite, under whatever mode It happens to be apprehended by the self, (2) a consciousness of sharing Its strength, acting by Its authority, which results in a complete sense of freedom, an invulnerable serenity, and usually urges the self to some form of heroic effort or creative activity: (3) the establishment of the self as a 'power for life', a centre of energy, an actual parent of spiritual vitality in other men.[63]

For the great christian mystics have experienced the paradox that when a human being has totally surrendered his existence to God, so that his life has been taken up into the divine life, true selfhood is at last realized, a self which is entirely transparent to and controlled by the presence and love of God. Thus Boehme, for example, wrote:

I give you an earthly similitude of this. Behold a bright flaming piece of iron, which of itself is dark and black, and the fire so penetrateth and shineth through the iron, that it giveth light. Now, the iron doth not cease to be; it is iron still: and the source (or property) of the fire retaineth its own propriety: it doth not take the iron into it, but it penetrateth (and shineth) through the iron; and it is iron then as well as before, free in itself: and so also is the source or property of the fire. In such a manner is the soul set in the Deity; the Deity penetrateth through the soul, and dwelleth in the soul, yet the soul doth not comprehend the

Deity, but the Deity comprehendeth the soul, but doth not
alter it (from being a soul) but only giveth it the divine
source (or property) of the Majesty.[64]

Or as Irenaeus had earlier put it, 'those who see God are in
God, and receive of His splendour'.[65] Is there a pointer here
to man's ultimate relationship to God? According to the
mystics, there is. Suso projected this experience into man's
final existence in the direct presence of God, and in this
passage we see again the theme of an absorption in which the
ego is negated without personality being obliterated:

> 'Lord, tell me', says the Servitor, 'what remains to a blessed
> soul which has wholly renounced itself?'
> Truth says, 'When the good and faithful servant enters
> into the joy of his Lord, he is inebriated by the riches of the
> house of God; for he feels, in an ineffable degree, that which
> is felt by an inebriated man. He forgets himself, he is no
> longer conscious of his selfhood; he disappears and loses
> himself in God, and becomes one spirit with Him, as a drop
> of water which is drowned in a great quantity of wine. For
> even as such a drop disappears, taking the colour and the
> taste of wine, so it is with those who are in full possession
> of blessedness. All human desires are taken from them in an
> indescribable manner, they are rapt from themselves, and
> are immersed in the Divine Will. If it were otherwise, if
> there remained in the man some human thing that was not
> absorbed, those words of Scripture which say that God must
> be all in all would be false. His being remains, but in another
> form, in another glory, and in another power. And all this
> is the result of entire and complete renunciation.'[66]

Summarizing her discussion of this central feature of
christian mysticism, Evelyn Underhill says: 'All the mystics
agree that the stripping off of personal initiative, the I, the
Me, the Mine, utter renouncement, or "self-naughting" –
self-abandonment to the direction of a larger Will – is an
imperative condition of the attainment of the unitive life.
The temporary denudation of the mind, whereby the contemplative made space for the vision of God, must now be
applied to the whole life. Here, they say, there is a final

swallowing up of that wilful I-hood which we ordinarily recognize as ourselves. It goes for ever, and something new is established in its room. The self is made part of the mystical Body of God; and, humbly taking its place in the corporate life of Reality, would "fain be to the Eternal Goodness what his own hand is to a man".'[67] If I may offer just one further illustrative quotation from the mystics themselves, the author of the *Theologia Germanica* asks what true obedience to God is:

> I answer, that a man should so stand free, being quit of himself, that is, of his I, and Me, and Self, and Mine, and the life, that in all things, he should no more seek or regard himself, than if he did not exist, and should take as little account of himself as if he were not, and another had done all his works. Likewise he should count all the creatures for nothing. What is there then, which is, and which we may count for somewhat? I answer nothing but that which we may call God.[68]

Thus in christian mysticism there is something analogous to the widespread eastern conviction that our approach to Ultimate Reality involves the transcending of ego-hood. We are to become so transparent to the divine life that we no longer live as separate self-enclosed individuals.

To what do these very significant converging indications point?

NOTES

1. Luke 15: 1–24.
2. 'As on the destruction of the jar, etc., the ether enclosed in the jar, etc., merges in the *Akasha* (the vast expanse of ether), even so the individuals merge in the Universal Spirit' (Gaudapada, *Karika*, III, 4).
3. *Chandogya* Upanishad, VI, 9, 1–2 (*The Principal Upanishads*, p. 459).
4. *Mundaka* Upanishad, III, 2, 8.
5. Santosh Chandra Sengupta, 'The Misunderstanding of Hinduism', in *Truth and Dialogue*, ed. John Hick, p. 100.
6. Chandradhar Sharma, *A Critical Survey of Indian Philosophy*, p. 354.

7. *Sribhasya*, 2.1.9, trans. John B. Carman in *The Theology of Ramanuja*, p. 127.

8. *Vedarthasamgraha*, para. 20, trans. Carman, op. cit., p. 124.

9. *Gitabhasya*, 10.20, trans. Carman, op. cit., p. 128.

10. ibid., introduction (Carman, op. cit., p. 197).

11. ibid., 9.26 (Carman, op. cit., p. 193).

12. *The Vedanta-Sutras with the Commentary of Ramanuja*, I.1.1, part III, trans. George Thibaut (*Sacred Books of the East*, vol. XLVIII, pp. 69–70).

13. B. N. K. Sharma, *Madhva's Teachings*, p. 77.

14. Quoted by Sharma, op. cit., p. 144.

15. Thus Edward Conze begins a chapter of his *Buddhist Thought in India*: 'A history of Buddhist thought might be expected to begin with an account of the teachings of the Buddha himself . . . The nature of our literary documents makes such an attempt fruitless and impossible' (p. 31).

16. See G. R. Welbon, *The Buddhist Nirvana and Its Western Interpreters*, ch. 2.

17. *Arhat* is the sanscrit and *arahant* the pali word.

18. *Majjhima-Nikaya*, I, 140 (*The Middle Length Sayings*, vol. I, p. 180).

19. Nyanaponika Mahathera, *Anatta and Nibbana*, p. 5.

20. *Sanyutta-Nikaya*, IV, 250 (*The Book of the Kindred Sayings*, part IV, p. 170).

21. *Anguttara-Nikaya*, IV, 353 (*The Book of the Gradual Sayings*, vol. IV, p. 233; Hare normally translates *nibbana* as 'the cool').

22. *Udana*, II, 1 (*The Minor Anthologies of the Pali Canon*, p. 13).

23. *Theragatha*, canto X ('Kisa-gotami'), trans. P. Vajiranana, *The Buddhist Doctrine of Nibbana*, p. 18.

24. Cf. *The Dhammapada*, ch. 26, 3 (verse 385).

25. *Digha-Nikaya*, I, 196 (*Dialogues of the Buddha*, part I, p. 261).

26. *Sanyutta-Nikaya*, I, 77–8 (*The Book of the Kindred Sayings*, part I, p. 105).

27. *Fundamental Principles of the Metaphysics of Morals*, ch. 1.

28. The arhat 'has transcended both good and evil' (*The Dhammapada*, v. 39; cf. 267 and 412, and *Sutta-Nipata*, 520, 636, 790).

29. *Majjhima-Nikaya*, I, 163 (*The Middle Length Sayings*, vol. I, pp. 206–7).

30. ibid., I, 172 (p. 215).

31. *The Dhammapada*, v. 203, p. 176.

32. *Therigatha*, 476 (*Psalms of the Early Buddhists*, vol. I, p. 169).

33. *Sanyutta-Nikaya*, IV, 369–71 (*The Book of the Kindred Sayings*, part IV, pp. 261–3).

34. *Udana*, 80 (*The Minor Anthologies of the Pali Canon*, part II, pp. 97–8).

35. *Sutta-Nipata*, v. 235, trans. P. Vajiranana, *The Buddhist*

Doctrine of Nibbana, p. 28.

36. Narada Thera, *The Dhammapada*, pp. 24–5, in commentary on v. 21.

37. *Itivuttaka*, 38–9 (*The Minor Anthologies of the Pali Canon*, p. 144).

38. P. Vajiranana and Francis Story, *The Buddhist Doctrine of Nibbana*, p. 29.

39. Sir Edwin Arnold, *The Light of Asia*, last line.

40. *Majjhima-Nikaya*, I, 140 (*The Middle Length Sayings*, vol. I, p. 179).

41. ibid., I, 487 (*The Middle Length Sayings*, vol. II, p. 166).

42. Rune Johansson, *The Psychology of Nirvana*, p. 61.

43. *Majjhima-Nikaya*, I, 140.

44. op. cit., p. 61.

45. ibid., p. 64.

46. *Sanyutta-Nikaya*, III, 9 (*The Book of the Kindred Sayings*, part III, p. 10).

47. Edward Conze, *Thirty Years of Buddhist Studies*, p. 71. 'Dharma' is a word of many and rich meanings, centring on the ideas of 'reality' and 'truth'.

48. In the burmese New Testament the Gospel of St John begins (in Burmese), 'In the beginning was the *Dhamma* . . . ' (Trevor Ling, *A History of Religion East and West*, p. 87).

49. 'The advent of a Buddha in the world is not an accident, the lucky chance of a human being happening to attain enlightenment. It is a deliberate descent of the Divinity, incarnating Itself as human being' (T. R. V. Murti, *The Central Philosophy of Buddhism*, p. 286) – though in the Madhyamika system, with which Murti was principally concerned in his book, a distinctly docetic and non-historical view was taken of Gautama's life.

50. *Treatise on Relativity*, ch. 25, v. 19, trans. T. Stcherbatsky, *The Conception of Buddhist Nirvana*, p. 77.

51. *Saraha's Treasury of Songs*, v. 102 (*Buddhist Texts*, p. 238).

52. *Buddhist Thought in India*, p. 227.

53. *Saraha's Treasury of Songs*, vv. 27, 105, 106 (*Buddhist Texts*, pp. 228–38).

54. *Mahayana-Sutralankara*, ch. IX, v. 26, p. 76.

55. Conze, *Buddhist Thought in India*, p. 166.

56. R. C. Zaehner, *Evolution in Religion*, p. 97.

57. R. C. Zaehner, *Mysticism, Sacred and Profane*, p. 168; F. C. Happold, *Mysticism*, pp. 53–5.

58. W. R. Inge, *Christian Mysticism*, p. 12.

59. F. C. Happold, *Mysticism*, p. 94.

60. H. Delacroix, *Etudes sur le Mysticisme*, p. 197, quoted by Underhill, op. cit., p. 498.

61. Galatians 2: 20.

62. *L'Ornement des Noces Spirituelles*, book II, ch. lxxiii, quoted by Underhill, op. cit., p. 522.

63. *Mysticism*, pp. 497–8.

64. *The Threefold Life of Man*, ch. VI, 88, quoted by Underhill, op. cit., p. 504. Cf. p. 206 above.

65. *Against Heresies*, book IV, ch. 20, para. 5.

66. Suso, *Buchlein von der Wahrheit*, ch. 4, quoted by Underhill, op. cit., p. 507.

67. *Mysticism*, p. 508.

68. *Theologia Germanica*, ch. XV, pp. 48–9.

CHAPTER 22

A Possible Eschatology

I. THISWORLDLINESS AND OTHERWORLDLINESS

What conclusions suggest themselves – however tentatively – out of this study of the pareschatologies and eschatologies of west and east?

Having seen reasons against accepting a materialist account of man,[1] the simplest and least speculative analysis of human nature would rely upon a twofold distinction between body and mind, the various other terms which we meet – such as soul, spirit, ego, self, person, jiva, atman – being regarded either as synonyms for mind or as names for the mind-body complex. However, we have been led beyond this to a threefold analysis which in its western version is body-soul-spirit and in its eastern version body-mind-atman. Each body is an individual physical organism occupying a separate volume of space. The mind or soul is closely related to the body, being known to us as embodied mind, an aspect of a psycho-physical individual. But mind is also related to spirit or atman, which is supra-individual, the presently unconscious unity of humanity or perhaps even of created life as a whole. Accordingly the set of basic terms which seems most suited to the vocabulary of a global theology will include body, mind and atman.

We also have a use for two further families of words – 'ego, egoity, and egoism', referring to the embodied mind as a self-enclosed individual over against others and seeking its own preservation and enhancement; and 'person, personality, personal', referring to the embodied mind in its relationship to other embodied minds and interacting with them in a society of persons.[2]

The religions of indian origin have focused upon the negative character of human egoity and have identified man's true good as liberation from it. They see the atman as imprisoned and its universality obscured in the individuality of the flesh; and consequently they see the egoity of individual consciousness as resisting the self-realization of the atman, the universal self. Their path to salvation is accordingly the way of individual self-negation, the renouncing of egoity and the consequent realization by the individual of his deeper identity as atman. This saving work has to be done separately in and by each individual. Thus the main eastern emphasis has been upon the transformation of the individual, the purifying of the solitary self in its 'flight of the alone to the Alone'. This is expressed in the age-old indian tradition of a man at some stage leaving his family and his possessions and living in solitary poverty in order to turn from the illusions of the material world to the realities of the spirit. 'Lead me', he prays, 'from the unreal to the real! Lead me from darkness to light! Lead me from death to immortality!'[3] Seen in this perspective the world is a snare and a delusion; and no call is heard to change it, no commitment to make human society a realm of justice and righteousness, no attempt to realize a kingdom of heaven on earth.

It should not however be thought that either the individualistic or the world-renouncing aspect of this tradition is peculiar to the east. A like individualistic strain occurs, although less centrally, in the semitic religions in the lives of the hermits and in the solitary stages of the contemplative life: it was after all a western thinker who spoke of the flight of the alone to the Alone.[4] And in medieval Europe the celibate religious life was felt to be closer to God than life amid the disorders, tensions and violence of the secular world. The cloistered life of the monastery and nunnery was the 'gate of Paradise',[5] and those who dwelt there were regarded as vicariously holding open the door of salvation for the worldly majority. Such ideas involved a rejection of the bodily and secular as a hindrance to the spiritual life, comparable with the traditional indian attitude to the world as *maya*, ultimately unreal and therefore ultimately unimportant.

However, as a result of the immense cultural changes which from about the beginning of the sixteenth century have formed the modern world, the western outlook has radically changed and now centres more upon the tension between egoity and personality, with the way from ego to atman lying through personal life, i.e. through the individual's relationships to others. Even in the early and medieval periods such symbols as the messianic banquet, the heavenly city, the Kingdom of Heaven, the communion of saints, and the mystical Body of Christ had witnessed to this corporate aspect of salvation; and today the social gospel, political theology, black theology, liberation theology and the theology of revolution are emphasizing it afresh. However, once again we must not think of the basic theme of mutual concern as confined to one culture or period. After the Buddha attained to his enlightenment, two and a half thousand years ago, he spent the rest of his long life travelling through India to teach and enlighten others, taking great pains to adapt his message to the individual needs of his hearers. Indeed, he described himself in this way: 'Monks, there is one person whose birth into the world is for the welfare of many folk, for the happiness of many folk: who is born out of compassion for the world, for the profit, welfare and happiness of devas and mankind.'[6] This is not the expression of a religious impetus which seeks and terminates in one's own private salvation. Indeed, any missionary faith, such as Buddhism, is by definition concerned for humanity at large. And in mahayana Buddhism one of the supreme expressions of universal love has been developed in the powerful myth of the Bodhisattva, the enlightened and compassionate being who delays his own final liberation until he has shown all his human brethren the way to their own salvation.

Thus instead of a stark and unrelieved contrast between the notions of corporate salvation through service to the neighbour, in the semitic faiths, and individual salvation by rising above the world in the faiths of indian origin, the picture is varied, complex and developing. Indeed, the growth of a christian social conscience in the west in relation to such evils as slavery and economic exploitation, and the rise of the social gospel, may be largely due to other more humanistic factors stemming from the Renaissance of the fifteenth and sixteenth centuries, the Enlightenment of the eighteenth century, and the secular revolutionary movements of the nineteenth century, rather than coming spontaneously out of the christian faith under the inner pressure of its own inherent logic; for otherwise why was Christianity not concerned with social justice from the beginning? And it may be that as the hindu and buddhist cultures of the east (as also the semitic cultures of the islamic near east) go through analogous transitions and upheavals, as indeed they are now doing, they too will discover a religious basis and motive for social concern. If so, they will of course be influenced by the western development – as Gandhi, for example, was influenced by Christianity. But it may still be the case that a religious commitment to attain human justice and social righteousness, latent as a possibility in all the world faiths and explicit long ago in some of the ancient hebrew prophets, has only become a major force within human civilization through the interaction of religion with humanistic values and impulses which have arisen as religion has declined, and which have also produced the quasi-religion of Marxism.

Whether the path of salvation is seen as going straight from ego to atman, or from egoity through the personal to the atman, the basic human situation of deep need or unsatisfactoriness is recognized by all the great traditions. In all of them a distinction is drawn, with differing degrees of sharpness, between on the one hand what is variously termed God, Brahman, Ultimate Reality, the Unconditioned, the Absolute, the Eternal, and on the other hand the created, produced or emanated realm, including man. Further, in all these traditions Ultimate Reality is thought of in both personal and non-personal terms, though with greater stress on the personal in the semitic and on the non-personal in the indian religions. The hindu distinction between Brahman *nirguna* ('without attributes') and Brahman *saguna* ('with attributes') is an explicit statement of this duality which could well be adopted universally; for the discourse of every major religious tradition acknowledges both these aspects of the Ultimate. *Saguna* God (to vary the phrase) is God in relation to man, God known and worshipped as personal, powerful, loving and good. He is the *Bhagavan*, the personal Lord of the Bhagavad Gita, of the Bible, of the Koran, of the Torah and of the bhakti hymns of India. *Nirguna* God is God in Himself or in Itself, in His or Its eternal and absolute being, beyond the scope of all human categories including 'Him' and 'It'. This is the pure Being, Being-itself, the Ground of Being, the Abyss of Being, the Godhead, the *Ungrund* of Christianity's thomist and mystical theology.

And in all these traditions the religious problem or task is man's transition from a wrong to a right relation to this Ultimate Reality. They all recognize, in terms of their own mythologies, that man is at present in a state of separation or alienation, in the overcoming of which lies his final good. He is wrapped in veils of *avidya* (ignorance) which hide reality from him; or he is a 'fallen' creature, set at an epistemic distance from his maker. Further, these traditions agree that the root of man's fallenness or of his separation from Ultimate Reality lies in his ego-ism, his worshipping of self rather than God, his false belief in the independent reality of the 'I', his *cor curvatus in se*, the heart turned in upon itself. In experiencing the separated self as supremely real and important he is living in illusion, cut off from the divine life and from his own more abundant life within it. And of course the self-love which sunders us from Ultimate Reality divides us at the same time from one another; for our proper relationship to God is corporate, in the interpersonal atmanic life.

We have already noted that the religious traditions speak of two ways of transcending the self-positing ego which separates us from one another and from the divine. One is an inner or mystical way whereby the contemplative opens his spirit progressively to the presence of God and is drawn by grace into the divine life, or whereby the meditator comes to realize his oneness with Brahman or passes through egolessness to nirvana. The other is the outer way of love for one's fellow creatures, expressed in selfless service to one's suffering human brethren. In earlier days, before the rise of democracy and when the ordinary individual had virtually no power over the political and economic circumstances of his life, this typically took the form of the acts of mercy of a St Francis to needy individuals. More recently it has also taken the form of the revolutionary political leadership (often but not always non-violent) of a Gandhi or a Martin Luther King or a Camilo Torres.

In the very few in whom the human has been so fully united with the divine that men and women have come to worship them as Lord and to weave around their memories myths of the incarnation of Ultimate Reality in human form, the internal and external ways have been combined and an intense inner life of prayer or meditation has been indissolubly united with an outer activity of self-giving service to the world. Thus Jesus, the Christ, having realized a perfect human relationship to God as son to father, could spend whole nights communing with his Heavenly Father whilst spending his days in active teaching and healing. Thus Gautama, the Buddha, having realized a perfect human relationship to another aspect of Ultimate Reality, spent long hours in meditation and long days in tireless teaching. The lesser spirits who pray or meditate but do not act in the world, or who act but do not meditate or pray, thereby show that however high they may tower above the rest of us they yet lack the perfect balance and wholeness of the supreme leaders of humanity.

2. THE PARESCHATON

Although in the end the individual cannot be saved in isolation from the society of which he is ultimately a part, yet still society is composed of individuals and it is individual people who are to be saved. For the development of civilization has involved the breakdown of the closely knit tribal group whose members thought of themselves more as parts of a larger whole than as autonomous individuals. According to our hypothesis, the ultimate development of human life is to come full circle, though on a higher level, culminating in a new corporateness in which egoity has been transcended. But in the present age it is the now existing individuals who must freely transcend their own egoity.

The main weight of the christian tradition has insisted that this earthly life is the only environment in which the individual can either come of his own volition, or be brought by divine grace, to the 'saved' relationship with God; and thereafter his individual existence is to be perpetuated in heaven (perhaps via purgatory) or in hell. I have argued that this scheme is unrealistic both as regards what is to happen before death and as regards what is to happen after death. If salvation in its fullness involves the actual transformation of human character, it is an observable fact that this does not usually take place in the course of our present earthly life. There must, then, be further time beyond death in which the process of perfecting can continue. The traditional scheme is equally unsatisfactory on its post-mortem side. I have argued that the doctrine of hell is morally intolerable;[7] and that in any case the notion of the immortal ego, the finite person continuing endlessly through time, involves profound conceptual difficulties.[8]

There is nevertheless an important insight behind the traditional christian insistence that the time of grace, in which we may respond to God, is limited by the boundary of death. For it is the prospect of its termination that gives urgency and meaning to our life in time. This fact does not however necessitate the doctrine of one short life followed by an eternity in heaven or hell. The same fact is taken up into the alternative schemes of eastern thought in the idea of reincarnation, with many successive lives, each ended by its own death. Here the spiritual urgency of life is in one sense relaxed, in that our present existence is not regarded as the only one; and a welcome consequence of this has been that the religions of indian origin have never felt a need to convert anyone by force to their beliefs – for people will come to the truth when they are ready for it, if not in this life then in another. But these faiths have insisted, in agreement here with the christian tradition, that it is only in incarnate lives on this earth, and not in the many heavens and hells beyond it, that karma can be worked out and progress made towards final liberation. However, I have argued for yet a third possibility, other than eternal-heaven-or-hell or repeated earthly reincarnations, namely that of a series of lives, each bounded by something analogous to birth and death, lived in other worlds in spaces other than that in which we now are.[9] This hypothesis accepts both the insistence upon the need for life to be lived within temporal limits and the conviction that the soul can only make progress in the incarnate state towards its final goal. But it differs from the western tradition in postulating many lives instead of only one, and from the eastern tradition in postulating many spheres of incarnate existence instead of only one. The hypothesis has been presented more fully – though still necessarily only as a possibility glimpsed in outline – in chapter 20.

But if we are to live many lives in the future, may we not have lived many lives in the past? I have already acknowledged that there are forms of the reincarnation doctrine – according to which we have indeed lived many times before – that cannot be disproved.[10] But the broad conception of many successive lives can be held in different forms; it may affirm a first life or it may assume a beginningless infinity of existences. Both theories have their advantages and disadvantages. According to hindu belief the reincarnating *jiva* is eternal. The universe forms, develops, dissolves and then forms again in a cyclical movement which has no beginning or end. The *jivas* or souls are part of this eternal process and thus have no beginning. Within such a picture the future immortality of the soul presents no problems. There is however the very different problem of meaninglessness. The cosmic process, infinite into both past and future, serves no purpose and moves toward no fulfilment. For even when the *jivas* have at last become one in the eternal consciousness of Brahman the process begins again in an endless breathing out and breathing in of the realm of emanated being. If, on the other hand, we affirm a divine creation, then the human individual has a beginning and it is entirely possible that the present life is in fact – as it appears to be – his first life. But then it is his immortality that becomes problematic. If he began at birth, why should he not end at death? As Santayana said, 'the fact of having been born is a bad augury for immortality'.[11] But although a bad augury, it may nevertheless not be a fatal one. And in favour of this being each person's first life there is both the positive fact that the individual does *seem* to be formed *ab initio* in the womb from which he is born to this present life, and the negative fact that human beings do not normally remember any previous existence. Admittedly neither of these arguments is decisive. But we have seen that the more popular conception of reincarnation, according to which the *same* person or self lives again and again, readily becomes diffused into the conception of a continuity of spiritual life being expressed in a series of different empirical selves – an idea which is far removed from the notion that *I* have lived many times before and shall live many times again. On the other hand something like the more 'solid' conception of reincarnation can apply to the idea, outlined in chapter 20, of future lives in other worlds. This theory thus has the advantage of allowing for the moral and spiritual growth of one and the same self through many lives towards its final self-transcending perfection. It is mainly for this reason that it seems to me the more acceptable form of many-lives doctrine.

But if we do not postulate previous lives, how do we account for the glaring inequities and inequalities of human birth? I have already pointed out that this problem cannot be met by tracing it back into a regression of previous existences.[12] If there is any 'solution' to the problem of evil, it must be one which looks to the future rather than to the past; and I have suggested above,[13] and have tried to develop more fully elsewhere,[14] a theodicy based upon the final creation of infinite good out of the ambiguities and contradictions of life as we know it.

3. THE ESCHATON

The major traditions of religious experience and thought, whilst each offering its own firmly drawn pareschatology delineating man's condition as a still separate ego beyond this life, all speak with appropriate reticence about the unknown final state in which – according to a spectrum of views – men are drawn individually into the divine kingdom, and God is 'all in all'; or in which finite selves, having shed their egoity, live within the divine life in some form of which we can barely conceive, contributing the results of their past histories to a larger whole in which however they are no longer separate and autonomous units; or in which the ever changing states which constitute human existence in time are abolished and the eternal state of nirvana realized; or in which there is a total absorption of the finite within an undifferentiated unity, leaving no connection with past individuality. At one extreme of this range of speculations is the western conception of the immortal ego, perfected within the divine kingdom; and at the other extreme is the *advaitist* conception of the ultimate non-existence of the finite individual. But the idea of the immortal ego involves serious difficulties, as we have seen,[15] and is modified within the western tradition in the thought of a life in God which is still pluralistic but in which nevertheless egoity has been transcended.[16] And the opposite idea of total absorption – the raindrop merging into the sea – empties the temporal existence leading to it of all significance and value

except the negative value of a barrier to be broken through or
an evil to be escaped from. This extreme view is modified in
eastern thought by the *bhakti* sense (developed philosophically
by the Vishishtadvaitins) of a continuing relationship between
finite selves and the Infinite Lord. Can we spell out any
further this point towards which the more eastern aspects of
traditional western thought seem to converge with the more
western aspects of traditional eastern thought?

Modern insights into the nature of personality may be
helpful here. The medieval christian conception of personality
was classically formulated by Boethius in his definition of a
person as an individual rational substance (*persona est naturae
rationabilis individua substantia*[17]). Here the person was seen
as a discrete spiritual atom who could in principle exist alone
as the sole created spirit, standing in relationship only to his
Creator. This individualistic conception operated as an
assumption within european thought down to about the end
of the nineteenth century, and the epistemological problems
to which it gave rise provided the agenda for a great deal of
western philosophy from Descartes onwards. But more
recently there has been a rediscovery, led by the jewish thinker
Martin Buber and others, of the essentially interpersonal
nature of personality. 'I' exist over against 'thou', so that it
takes at least two persons for there to be one person! The individual is a product of the community. Not only does he
physically require two parents in order to be born, but
psychologically he requires relationships with other human
beings to develop his own latent personal humanity. Human
affection and human training make him a social being, and
human language inducts him into one or other of the cultural
forms in which distinctively human life occurs. A permanently
solitary person is thus logically impossible, for we are persons
only through our relationship with other persons: personal
existence is essentially interpersonal.

Can we extend this insight to the conclusion that the perfecting of personal individuality is a transcending of it? Could
it be that as the separate human ego-selves attain to their
several human perfections the boundaries between them become
transparent and human existence becomes more corporate
than individual? The distinction between the self as ego and

the self as person[18] suggests that as the human individual becomes perfected he becomes more and more a person and less and less an ego. Since personality is essentially outward-looking, as a relationship to other persons, whilst the ego forms a boundary limiting true personal life, the perfected individual will have become a personality without egoity, a living consciousness which is transparent to the other consciousnesses in relation to which it lives in a full community of love. Thus we have the picture of a plurality of personal centres without separate peripheries. They will have ceased to be mutually exclusive and will have become mutually inclusive and open to one another in a richly complex shared consciousness. The barrier between their common unconscious life and their individual consciousnesses will have disappeared, so that they experience an intimacy of personal community which we can at present barely imagine.

In the triune conception of God as three persons in one and one in three christian thought offers an important model for a community so intimate and harmonious as to constitute a single corporate person. This conception has a long history within christian thought and has been developed at different times and in different schools of theology in widely different ways. The history of the doctrine reveals a tension between its two sources. One source is the biblical material to which the doctrine appeals, in which two of the three members of the Trinity, the Father and the Son, are presented as individual persons each of whom speaks as 'I' and is addressed as 'Thou', and who indeed address one another in this way.[19] The other source consists in the vehicles of philosophical terminology and the paths of philosophical reasoning through which the doctrine was developed. This was not originally concerned with three persons in our modern sense of three centres of consciousness, but with three *hypostases* constituting one *ousia* – three distinguishables constituting one reality. *Hypostasis* was latinized as *persona*, which originally signified a role, being derived from the masks worn by actors on the roman stage to indicate the parts being played – a meaning expressed in the more modal conceptions of the Trinity. *Persona* was then turned into english as 'person', acquiring the modern meaning of an individual centre of consciousness and will – a change of sense which thus comes back full circle to the personal divine individuals of the biblical narratives.[20] This modern notion of person is used in the 'social' conception of the Trinity as consisting of three distinct but intimately related personal centres. Thus Leonard Hodgson has said that 'according to the revelation of Himself which God has given to us men in history there are three elements perfectly unified in the Divine life, and each of these elements is itself a Person . . . the Divine unity is a dynamic unity actively unifying in the one Divine life the lives of the three Divine persons'.[21] But such a doctrine is not intended to be taken to the point of tritheism. In the terminology already adopted in this book, we can say that the three divine selves or consciousnesses are not self-enclosed egos, existing over against each other, but mutually constitutive personal centres whose relationships with one another form a rich and complex unity.

Let us now apply this trinitarian conception of the one-in-many and many-in-one to the eschatological community of perfected human persons. For, as John Burnaby has written, 'God has made men apt to find their completion in communion, because such communion is a likeness of the mutual love in which and through which Three Persons are One God'.[22] Their corporate unity as a single personal life will be as real as the internal complexities of that life. There will be many persons, in the sense of many centres of personal relationship, not however existing over against one another as separate atomic individuals but rather within one another in the mutual coinherence or interpermeation (*perichoresis, circuminsessio*) which has been predicated of the Persons of the Trinity. The many persons will accordingly no longer be separate in the sense of having boundaries closed to one another. They will on the contrary be wholly open to one another. There will be a plurality of centres of consciousness, and yet these will not be private but will each include the others in a full mutual sharing constituting the atman, the complex collective consciousness of humanity. We can hardly hope to specify such a speculation more precisely; for it refers to a possible state far beyond our present experience. It seems nevertheless to be a permissible projection from this to the ultimate fulfilment of the potentialities of human community, involving both the extension of our present individual histories into the eschaton and at the same time their increasingly interpersonal character – even to the point of being no longer self-enclosed egos but members of a perfect community of mutually open centres of consciousness.[23]

In what sense will the members of such a 'perfect community of mutually open centres of consciousness' still form a plurality of individual selves? In the model of the divine Trinity, understood as three centres of consciousness, we have to say of the different persons that they just *are* three different persons in some ultimate metaphysical sense. We can then add that being three they nevertheless exist in a totally harmonious relationship to one another so as to constitute a complex personal unity. Likewise we must say of the perfect human selves that they just *are* so many different selves, each with its own unique character and history, but that in the ultimate state they are so harmoniously interrelated as to form the immensely complex personal unity of mankind, a human unity which perhaps requires all these different unique contributions. I have used the name atman for this deeper or higher consciousness or self, of which human individuals are constituent aspects -- separated now by egoity but finally to be united in a perfect community of personal relationships – because the idea of the ultimate oneness of mankind, although not confined to the religions of indian origin, has been most explicitly affirmed by them. But there is a christian basis for the idea of the corporate unity of mankind in the myth of the common descent of the human family from Adam and Eve; and for the idea of a corporate relationship to God in the Old Testament doctrine of the covenant between Israel and Jahweh. Israel was of course only a fragment of mankind; but in the New Testament the New Israel, the church, is potentially and in principle universal; and Christ, whose 'body' the church is, is referred to as the second Adam in whom the whole human race is to receive a new and higher life. Thus in the mystical Body of Christ humanity is to become one in many and many in one. John Donne expresses this thought in a striking analogy:

> All mankind is of one author, and is one volume; when one man dies, one chapter is not torn out of the book, but

translated into a better language; and every chapter must be so translated: God employs several translators; some pieces are translated by age, some by sickness, some by war, some by justice; but God's hand is in every translation, and his hand shall bind up all our scattered leaves again, for that library where every book shall lie open to one another.[24]

Is this ultimate state to be thought of as being in time; and as an embodied state? The two questions are linked although not identical. Time is the dimension in which change occurs; for it is only in the flow of time that the same finite entity can have different and incompatible characteristics.[25] Whilst there can be change without body, namely mental change, the change in which we are involved is that of embodied minds in space-time. And if we have been right in holding that the development of human character towards its self-transcending perfection involves interaction between a plurality of people in a common environment, then it seems to presuppose such individual embodiment in time.[26]

But when this development is completed it may be that embodiment is no longer necessary. And again, it may be that time, as the dimension of change, is likewise no longer necessary. Thus it is possible that the ultimate state, in which human selves have found their unity in the atman, is beyond both matter and time, or at least time as we know it. That is to say, objective or clock time is an aspect or dimension of the physical universe; and for the human consciousness to cease to be related to the one is presumably for it to cease to be related to the other. On the other hand subjective or inner time is an aspect of consciousness, and is as such capable of immense variations:[27] time can 'go slowly' or 'go fast' and can in certain 'timeless moments' even approach the classical christian conception of eternity as 'the simultaneous and complete possession of infinite life' (*interminabilis vitae tota simul at perfecta possessio*).[28]

It may, then, be that in progressively 'higher' worlds (i.e. worlds which are the environments of ever more morally and spiritually perfect modes of existence) the interpersonality of mutual love becomes the universal principle of life, whilst self-protective egoity withers away, so that the individual's series

of lives culminates eventually in a last life beyond which
there is no further embodiment but instead entry into the
common Vision of God, or nirvana, or the eternal consciousness of the atman in its relation to Ultimate Reality.

This last phrase implicitly rejects the *advaitist* view that
Atman *is* Brahman, the collective human self being ultimately
identical with God, in favour of the more complex *vishishtadvaitist* interpretation of the Upanishads, which is in turn
substantially in agreement with the christian conception of
God as personal Lord, distinct from his creation.[29] But to
argue for this would take us beyond the limits of this book.
Our eschatological speculation terminates in the idea of the
unity of mankind in a state in which the ego-aspect of individual consciousness has been left behind and the relational
aspect has developed into a total community which is one-in-
many and many-in-one, existing in a state which is probably
not embodied and probably not in time. In the midst of this
present 'fallen' or illusion-bound existence, in which the
human fragments look at each other through the slits of
separate ego-masks, the sense of our ultimate belonging together
in total community is the unselfish love which the New Testament calls *agape*. Christians see this awareness of human unity
expressed above all in the life and teaching of Jesus. As perfect
man he was love incarnate, living in ideal relationship to
Ultimate Reality so far as this is possible for a single individual
prior to the perfecting of humanity as a whole. What Christians
call the Mystical Body of Christ within the life of God, and
Hindus the universal Atman which we all are, and mahayana
Buddhists the self-transcending unity in the Dharma Body of
the Buddha, consists of the wholeness of ultimately perfected
humanity beyond the existence of separate egos.

NOTES

1. Chapter 6.
2. Cf. chapter 2, section 5 above.
3. *Brihadaranyaka* Upanishad, I, 3, 28.
4. Presumably these famous words are a version of the final phrase

of Plotinus' *Enneads* (*fuge monou pros monon*) which is translated by Stephen MacKenna (*The Enneads*, p. 625) as 'the passing of solitary to solitary'. About the same time one of the desert Fathers of the christian church used the phrase 'alone to the alone (*solus ad solum*)' (Helen Waddell, *The Desert Fathers*, p. 18).

5. Cf. F. Heer, *The Medieval World*, p. 40.

6. *Anguttara-Nikaya*, I, 20 (*The Book of the Gradual Sayings*, vol. I, p. 14).

7. Chapter 10, section 2.

8. Chapter 20, section 4.

9. Chapter 20, section 5.

10. Chapter 17, section 6; chapter 19, section 1.

11. George Santayana, *Reason in Religion*, p. 240.

12. pp. 308–9.

13. Chapter 8, section 3.

14. *Evil and the God of Love*, part IV.

15. Chapter 20, section 4.

16. Chapter 21, section 5.

17. *Contra Entzychen et Nestorium*, ch. 3.

18. See chapter 2, section 5. Buber uses the alternative terminology of 'person' and 'individuality' – *I and Thou*, pp. 64–5.

19. e.g. Mark 1: 11; John 17: 1f., etc.

20. The history of the notion of personality has been told by C. C. J. Webb in *God and Personality*.

21. L. Hodgson, *The Doctrine of the Trinity*, p. 95.

22. Quoted by M. C. D'Arcy, *The Mind and Heart of Love*, p. 113.

23. There is interesting support for such an idea in Lynn de Silva's concept of *anatta-pneuma* or non-egocentric mutuality in *The Problem of the Self in Buddhism and Christianity*. Teilhard de Chardin also looked forward, within the future evolution of man, to the development of 'an organic super-aggregation of souls', a 'harmonised collectivity of consciousnesses equivalent to a sort of super-consciousness' (*The Phenomenon of Man*, pp. 248, 251). His conception differs from that outlined here in that the Omega point of which he spoke is to be experienced in this world, and whilst those then alive will participate in it, it is not clear what is to happen to the many generations of human beings who will already have lived and died.

24. John Donne, *Devotions*, Meditation 17, p. 108.

25. Kant said that 'only in time can two contradictorily opposed predicates meet in one and the same object, namely, *one after the other*' (*Critique of Pure Reason*, 'Transcendental Aesthetic', sect. 2, p. 76); and Schopenhauer defined time as 'the possibility of opposite states in one and the same thing' (*The Fourfold Root of the Principle of Sufficient Reason*, p. 32).

26. This principle is independent of the metaphysical question, raised for example by H. H. Price's discussion of 'the next world'

(see above pp. 274–5), whether or not matter is, as Berkeley argued, ultimately mind-dependent.

27. See, e.g., John Cohen, 'Subjective Time', in *The Voices of Time*, ed. J. T. Fraser; and Robert J. Maxwell, 'Anthropological Perspectives', and Victor Gioscia, 'On Social Time', in *The Future of Time*, ed. H. Yaker, H. Osmond and F. Cheek.

28. Boethius, *The Consolation of Philosophy*, book V, ch. 6. I have quoted F. H. Brabant's translation of this famous phrase in *Time and Eternity in Christian Thought*, p. 64.

29. For an advocacy of the form of theism that is substantially common to Christianity and hindu Vishishtadvaita, see Ninian Smart, *The Yogi and the Devotee*.

Bibliography of Works Cited

*Books are generally listed under author or editor where known,
otherwise under title.*

Abhedananda, Swami, *Reincarnation*, 1899, 10th ed. (Ramakrishna Vedanta Math, Calcutta, 1973).

Aldwinckle, Russell, *Death in the Secular City* (Allen & Unwin, London, 1972).

Alger, W. R., *A Critical History of the Doctrine of a Future Life* (Widdleton, New York, 1869).

Alphonso-Karkala, J. B., *An Anthology of Indian Literature* (Penguin, Harmondsworth, 1971).

Althaus, Paul, *Die Letzten Dinge* (Bertelsmann, Gütersloh, 1933).

Analysis (Oxford).

Annual Abstract of Statistics, no. 108 (H.M. Stationery Office, London, 1971).

Anthony, Sylvia, *The Discovery of Death in Childhood and After* (Allen Lane, London, 1971, and Basic Books, New York, 1972).

Arendzen, J. P., 'Heaven', in *The Teaching of the Catholic Church*, vol. II (Macmillan, New York, 1956).

Ariès, Philippe, *Centuries of Childhood* (Jonathan Cape, London, and Alfred Knopf, New York, 1962).

   Western Attitudes toward Death (John Hopkins University Press, Baltimore and London, 1974).

Armstrong, D. M., *A Materialist Theory of Mind* (Routledge & Kegan Paul, London, and Humanities Press, New York, 1968).

Arnold, Sir Edwin, *The Light of Asia*, 1879 (Theosophical Publishing House, Wheaton, Ill., 1969, and Routledge & Kegan Paul, London, 1971).

Ashvaghosha, *Acts of the Buddha (Buddhacarita)*, trans. E. H. Johnston (Baptist Mission Press, Calcutta, 1936).

Augustine, St, *The City of God*, trans. M. Dods (T. & T. Clark, Edinburgh, 1871, and Random House, New York, 1950).

Aurobindo, Sri, *The Problem of Rebirth* , 1952 (Birth Centenary Edition vol. 16 Sri Aurobindo Ashram, Pondicherry, 1972).

Ayer, A. J. (ed.), *The Humanist Outlook* (Pemberton, London, 1968).

Baillie, John, *And the Life Everlasting* (Charles Scribner's Sons, New York, 1933, and Oxford University Press, London, 1934).

Barth, Karl, *Church Dogmatics* (T. & T. Clark, Edinburgh, and Charles Scribner's Sons, New York), vol. II, part 2 (1957), vol. III, part 2 (1960), vol. IV, part 3 (1961).

   The Humanity of God, 1956 (John Knox Press, Richmond, Va, 1960, and Collins, London, 1961).

Berger, Peter, and Thomas Luckmann, *The Social Construction of Reality*, 1966 (Doubleday, Garden City, N.Y., 1967, and Penguin, Harmondsworth, 1971).

Besant, Annie, *Death – and After?* (Theosophical Publishing Society, London, and The Path, New York, 1893).

    Reincarnation, 8th ed. (Theosophical Publishing House, Adyar and Wheaton, Ill., 1963).

Bethune-Baker, J. F., *An Introduction to the Early History of Christian Doctrine*, 9th ed. (Methuen, London, 1951).

Bhagavadgita, The, trans. S. Radhakrishnan, 2nd ed. (Allen & Unwin, London, 1949, and Harper & Row, New York, n.d.).

Bhagavad-Gita, The, trans. R. C. Zaehner (Clarendon Press, Oxford, 1969).

Bigg, Charles, *The Christian Platonists of Alexandria* (Clarendon Press, Oxford, 1886, and AMS Press, New York, 1970).

Bleeker, C. J., and Geo Widengren (eds.), *Historia Religionum* (E. J. Brill, Leiden, 1969).

Blueprint for Survival, A (Penguin, Harmondsworth, and Houghton Mifflin, New York, 1972).

Boase, T. S. R., *Death in the Middle Ages* (Thames & Hudson, London, and McGraw-Hill, New York, 1972).

Book of the Dead, The (Egyptian) (British Museum, London, 1933).

Book of the Discipline, The, trans. I. B. Horner, vol. IV (Luzac, London, 1951).

Book of the Gradual Sayings, The (Luzac, London), vol. I, trans. F. L. Woodward (1951), vol. IV, trans. E. M. Hare (1965), vol. V, trans. F. L. Woodward (1972).

Book of the Kindred Sayings, The (Luzac, London), parts I (1950) and II (1952), trans. C. A. F. Rhys Davids, parts III (1954) and IV (1956), trans. F. L. Woodward.

Bornkamm, Gunther, *Jesus of Nazareth*, 1956 (Hodder & Stoughton, London, and Harper, New York, 1960).

Boros, Ladislaus, *The Moment of Truth: Mysterium Mortis*, 1962 (Burns & Oates, London, 1965), published in the USA as *The Mystery of Death* (Seabury Press, New York).

Borst, C. V. (ed.), *The Mind-Brain Identity Theory* (Macmillan, London, and St Martin's Press, New York, 1970).

Brabant, F. H., *Time and Eternity in Christian Thought* (Longmans, Green, London and New York, 1937).

Brandon, S. G. F., *The Judgment of the Dead* (Weidenfeld & Nicolson, London, 1967, and Charles Scribner's Sons, New York, 1969).

Brim, Orville G., Jr, Howard E. Freeman, Sol Levine and Norman A. Scotch (eds.), *The Dying Patient* (Russell Sage Foundation, New York, 1970).

Broad, C. D., *Lectures on Psychical Research* (Routledge & Kegan Paul, London, and Humanities Press, New York, 1962).

    The Mind and Its Place in Nature (Kegan Paul, Trench, Trubner, London, and Harcourt, Brace, New York, 1925).

Brooke, Rupert, *The Poetical Works of Rupert Brooke* (Faber & Faber, London, 1946).
Brunner, Emil, *Dogmatics*, vol. III, 1960 (Lutterworth, London, and Westminster Press, Philadelphia, 1962).
Buber, Martin, *I and Thou*, 2nd ed. (Charles Scribner's Sons, New York, 1958, and T. & T. Clark, Edinburgh, 1959).
Buddhadasa, *Toward the Truth*, ed. Donald K. Swearer (Westminster Press, Philadelphia. 1972).
Buddhaghosa, *The Path of Purification*, trans. Nyanamoli (R. Semage, Colombo, 1956).
Buddhist Scriptures, trans. Edward Conze (Penguin, Harmondsworth, 1959).
Buddhist Texts, ed. Edward Conze (Bruno Cassirer, Oxford, 1954, and Harper & Row, New York, n.d.).
Bultmann, Rudolf, *The Gospel of John: A Commentary* (Basil Blackwell, Oxford, and Westminster Press, Philadelphia, 1971).
Burns, Norman T., *Christian Mortalism from Tyndale to Milton* (Harvard University Press, Cambridge, Mass., 1972).
Burton, J. H., *The Life and Correspondence of David Hume* (William Tait, Edinburgh, 1846, and B. Franklin, New York, 1967).
Caird, George B., *The Gospel of St Luke* (A. & C. Black, London, and Seabury Press, New York, 1968).
Caird, George B., *et al.*, *The Christian Hope* (SPCK, London, and Allenson, Naperville, Ill., 1970).
Campbell, Keith, *Body and Mind* (Macmillan, London, and Doubleday, Garden City, N.Y., 1970).
Caponigri, A. Robert (ed.), *Modern Catholic Thinkers: An Anthology* (Burns & Oates, London, 1960, and Books for Libraries, Freeport, N.Y., 1970).
Carington, Whately, *Telepathy*, 2nd ed. (Methuen, London, 1945).
Carman, John B., *The Theology of Ramanuja* (Yale University Press, New Haven, Conn., 1974).
Charles, R. H., *Eschatology*, 2nd ed., 1913 (Bailey Brothers, London, and Schocken Books, New York, 1963).
Choron, Jacques, *Death and Western Thought* (Collier-Macmillan, London, and Collier, New York, 1963).
Church Teaches, The (B. Herder, St Louis and London, 1955).
Concilium (Search Press, London, and McGraw-Hill, Ontario).
Conze, Edward, *Buddhist Thought in India* (Allen & Unwin, London, 1962, and University of Michigan Press, Ann Arbor, 1967).
    Thirty Years of Buddhist Studies (Bruno Cassirer, Oxford, 1967, and University of South Carolina Press, Columbia, 1968).
Cope, Gilbert (ed.), *Dying, Death and Disposal* (SPCK, London, 1970).
Cornford, F. M., *From Religion to Philosophy* (Edwin Arnold, London, and Longmans, Green, New York, 1912).
Crookall, Robert, *The Supreme Adventure: Analyses of Psychic Communications* (James Clarke, London, and Fernhill, Atlantic Highlands, N.J., 1961).

Cross, F. L. (ed.), *The Oxford Dictionary of the Christian Church* (Oxford University Press, London and New York, 1958).

Cullmann, Oscar, *Immortality of the Soul or Resurrection of the Dead?* (Epworth Press, London, 1958).

Cummins, Geraldine, *The Road to Immortality* (Ivor Nicholson & Watson, London, 1932).

Dahl, M. E., *The Resurrection of the Body* (SCM Press, London, 1962).

Daniélou, Jean, *Origen* (Sheed & Ward, London and New York, 1955).

Dante Alighieri, *The Divine Comedy*, trans. Dorothy L. Sayers (Penguin, Harmondsworth), vol. I (1949), vol. II (1955), vol. III (1962).

D'Arcy, M. C., *The Mind and Heart of Love* (Faber & Faber, London, 1945, and H. Holt, New York, 1947).

Darlington, C. D., *Genetics and Man* (Allen & Unwin, London, and Macmillan, New York, 1964).

Davids, C. A. F. Rhys, *Indian Religion and Survival* (Allen & Unwin, London, 1934).

   Stories of the Buddha (Chapman & Hall, London, and Frederick A. Stokes, New York, 1929).

Denzinger, H., *Enchiridion Symbolorum Definitionum et Declarationum de Rebus Fidei et Morum*, 24th ed. (Herder & Herder, Barcelona, 1946).

Dhammapada, The, trans. Narada Thera, 2nd ed. (Vajirarama, Colombo, 1972).

Dialogues of the Buddha, trans. T. W. and C. A. F. Rhys Davids (Luzac, London), part I, 1899 (1956), part II, 1910 (1952).

Donne, John, *Devotions*, 1624 (Abbey Classics, Simpkin, Marshall, London, and Small, Maynard, Boston, 1926).

Dostoyevsky, Fyodor, *The Brothers Karamazov*, trans. Constance Garnett (Heinemann, London, 1912, and The Modern Library, New York, 1950).

Dublin, Louis I, *Factbook on Man – from Birth to Death*, 2nd ed. (Collier-Macmillan, London, and Macmillan, New York, 1965).

Ducasse, C. J., *A Critical Examination of the Belief in a Life after Death* (Charles C. Thomas, Springfield, Ill., 1961).

Dunne, John S., *The City of the Gods: A Study in Myth and Mortality* (Macmillan, New York, 1965, and Sheldon Press, London, 1974).

Durkheim, Emile, *The Elementary Forms of the Religious Life*, 1912 (Allen & Unwin, London, and Macmillan, New York, 1915).

Ebon, Martin, *Reincarnation in the Twentieth Century* (New American Library, New York, 1969, and Signet Books, London, 1970).

Ecologist, The (London).

Edwards, David, *The Last Things Now* (SCM Press, London, 1969, and Judson Press, Valley Forge, Pa, 1970).

Eliot, Sir Charles, *Hinduism and Buddhism*, 3 vols. (Edward Arnold, London, 1921, and Barnes & Noble, New York, 1954).

Elliot, Gil, *Twentieth-Century Book of the Dead* (Charles Scribner's

Sons, New York, 1972, and Penguin, Harmondsworth, 1973).

Encyclopædia of Religion and Ethics, 12 vols. (T. & T. Clark, Edinburgh, and Charles Scribner's Sons, New York, 1908-21).

Evans-Pritchard, E. E., *Nuer Religion* (Oxford University Press, London, 1956).

Evans-Wentz, W. Y., *The Doctrine of Re-birth* (Maha-Bodhi Press, Colombo, 1921).

　(ed.) *The Tibetan Book of the Dead or the After-Death Experiences on the Bardo Plane, according to Lama Kazi Dawa-Samdup's English Rendering*, 1927, 3rd ed. (Oxford University Press, London and New York, 1957).

Eysenck, H. J., *Crime and Personality* (Paladin Books, London, 1970).

Feifel, Herman (ed.), *The Meaning of Death* (McGraw-Hill, New York, 1959).

Ford, Arthur, *The Life beyond Death* (G. P. Putnam's Sons, New York, 1971, and Sphere Books, London, 1974).

Fordham, Frieda, *An Introduction to Jung's Psychology* (Penguin, Harmondsworth and Baltimore, 1953).

Fraser, J. T. (ed.), *The Voices of Time* (George Braziller, New York, 1966, and Allen Lane, London, 1968).

Frazer, J. G., *The Belief in Immortality and the Worship of the Dead*, 3 vols. (Macmillan, London, 1913-24, and Barnes & Noble, New York, 1968).

Freud, Sigmund, *Collected Papers* (Hogarth Press, London, 1925).

Fuller, R. H., *The Formation of the Resurrection Narratives* (Macmillan, New York, 1971, and SPCK, London, 1972).

Galloway, Allan D., *Wolfhart Pannenberg* (Allen & Unwin, London, 1973).

Gaudapada, *Karika*, in *The Mandukyopanishad with Gaudapada's Karika*, trans. Swami Nikhilananda (Sri Ramakrishna Ashrama, Mysore, 1936).

Get Off Their Backs (Third World First, Oxford, 1972).

Glaser, Barney G., and Anselm L. Strauss, *Awareness of Dying* (Aldine, Chicago, 1965, and Weidenfeld & Nicolson, London, 1966).

Glasson, T. F., *The Second Advent*, 2nd ed. (Epworth Press, London, 1947).

Gorer, Geoffrey, *Death, Grief, and Mourning* (Cresset Press, London, 1965, and Doubleday, Garden City, N.Y., 1967).

Gregorianum (Pontificia Universitas Gregoriana, Rome).

Gregory of Nyssa, St, *From Glory to Glory: Texts from Gregory of Nyssa's Mystical Writings*, ed. Jean Daniélou and Herbert Musurillo (Charles Scribner's Sons, New York, 1961, and John Murray, London, 1962).

Grieve, A. J., *Peake's Commentary on the Bible* (Nelson, London, 1919).

Guardian, The (London).

Guirdham, Arthur, *We Are One Another* (Neville Spearman, Jersey, 1974).

Gunaratna, V. F., *Rebirth Explained* (Buddhist Publication Society, Kandy, 1971).

Gurney, E., F. W. H. Myers and F. Podmore, *Phantasms of the Living* (Trübner, London, 1886, and Scholars' Facsimiles and Reprints, Gainesville, Fla, 1970).

Guthrie, W. K. C., *The Greeks and Their Gods* (Methuen, London, 1950, and Beacon Press, Boston, 1951).

Guy, H. A., *The New Testament Doctrine of the 'Last Things'* (Oxford University Press, London and New York, 1948).

Hamilton, Peter, *The Living God and the Modern World* (Hodder & Stoughton, London, 1967, and United Church Press, Philadelphia, 1968).

Happold, F. C., *Mysticism* (Pelican, Harmondsworth and Baltimore, 1970).

Harman, G., and D. Davidson (eds.), *Semantics of Natural Language* (Reidel, Dordrecht, 1972).

Harrington, Alan, *The Immortalist: An Approach to the Engineering of Man's Divinity* (Random House, New York, 1969, and Panther Books, Frogmore, 1973).

Hartshorne, Charles, *The Logic of Perfection* (Open Court, Lasalle, Ill., 1962).

Haynes, E. S. P., *The Belief in Personal Immortality* (Watts, London, and G. P. Putnam's Sons, New York, 1913).

Head, Joseph, and S. L. Cranston (eds.), *Reincarnation: An East-West Anthology* (Theosophical Publishing House, Wheaton, Ill., 1968).

Heer, F., *The Medieval World* (Weidenfeld & Nicolson, London, 1962, and New American Library, New York, 1964).

Heidegger, Martin, *Being and Time* (SCM Press, London, and Harper, New York, 1962), trans. from 7th ed. of *Sein und Zeit*.

Heidel, Alexander, *The Gilgamesh Epic and Old Testament Parallels*, 2nd ed. (Chicago University Press, Chicago, 1949).

Hibbert Journal (London).

Hick, John (ed.), *Classical and Contemporary Readings in the Philosophy of Religion*, 2nd. ed. (Prentice-Hall, Englewood Cliffs, N.J., and London, 1970).

  Evil and the God of Love (Macmillan, London, and Harper & Row, New York, 1966, and Fontana, London, 1968).

  Faith and Knowledge, 2nd ed. (Macmillan, London, and Cornell University Press, Ithaca, N.Y., 1966, and Fontana, London, 1974).

  God and the Universe of Faiths (Macmillan, London, and St Martin's Press, New York, 1973).

  (ed.) *Truth and Dialogue* (Sheldon Press, London, and Westminster Press, Philadelphia, 1974).

Hinton, John, *Dying* (Penguin, Harmondsworth and Baltimore, 1967).

Hodgson, L., *The Doctrine of the Trinity* (Nisbet, London, 1943, and Charles Scribner's Sons, New York, 1944).

Hodson, Geoffrey, *Reincarnation, Fact or Fallacy?*, 5th ed. (Theosophical Publishing House, Adyar and Wheaton, Ill., 1966).

Hogg, A. G., *Karma and Redemption*, 1909 (The Christian Literature

Society, Madras, 1970).
Homer, *Iliad*, trans. Lang, Leaf and Myers, rev. ed. (Macmillan, London, 1919, and St Martin's Press, New York, 1961).
    Odyssey, trans. Butcher and Lang (Macmillan, London, 1949, and Collier, New York, 1961).
Houghton, Walter E., *The Victorian Frame of Mind, 1830-1870* (Yale University Press, New Haven, Conn., 1957).
Howe, Quincy, *Reincarnation for the Christian* (Westminster Press, Philadelphia, 1974).
Hügel, F. von, *Eternal Life* (T. & T. Clark, Edinburgh, 1912).
Huizinga, J., *The Waning of the Middle Ages* (Edward Arnold, London, 1924, and Longmans, Green, New York, 1949).
Hume, David, *Dialogues concerning Natural Religion*, 1779 (Clarendon Press, Oxford, 1935, and Bobbs-Merrill, Indianapolis, 1947).
Huxley, T. H. and Julian, *Evolution and Ethics 1893-1943* (Pilot Press, London, 1947), published in the USA as *Touchstone for Ethics 1893-1943* (Harper, New York, 1947).
Indian Philosophical Annual, 1965 (University of Madras, Madras, 1967).
Inge, W. R., *Christian Mysticism* (Methuen, London, and Charles Scribner's Sons, New York, 1899).
Irenaeus, *Against Heresies*, Ante-Nicene Fathers, vol. I, ed. A. Roberts and J. Donaldson (Eerdmans, Grand Rapids, Mich., 1956).
Jaeger, Werner, *The Theology of the Early Greek Philosophers* (Clarendon Press, Oxford, 1947).
James, E. O., *The Beginnings of Religion* (Hutchinson, London and New York, 1948).
James, William, *Talks to Teachers on Psychology* (Longmans, Green, London and New York, 1899).
Jaspers, Karl, *The Origin and Goal of History*, 1949 (Routledge & Kegan Paul, London, and Yale University Press, New Haven, Conn., 1953).
Jayatilleke, K. N., *Survival and Karma in Buddhist Perspective* (Buddhist Publication Society, Kandy, 1969).
Jennings, H. S., *The Biological Basis of Human Nature* (Faber & Faber, London, and W. W. Norton, New York, 1930).
Jennings, J. G., *The Vedantic Buddhism of the Buddha* (Oxford University Press, London, 1947).
Johansson, Rune, *The Psychology of Nirvana* (Allen & Unwin, London, 1969, and Anchor Books, Garden City, N.Y., 1970).
Journal of the American Society for Psychical Research (New York).
Journal of Philosophy, The (Columbia University, New York).
Journal of the Society for Psychical Research (London).
Journal of Theological Studies (Clarendon Press, Oxford).
Julian of Norwich, *The Revelations of Divine Love*, trans. James Walsh (Burns & Oates, London, 1961).
Jung, C. G., *Collected Works*, ed. Herbert Read, Michael Fordham and Gerhard Adler, 2nd ed. (Princeton University Press, Princeton, and Routledge & Kegan Paul, London), vol. 7, *Two Essays on*

Analytical Psychology (1966), vol. 8, *The Structure and Dynamics of the Psyche* (1969, 1970), vol. 9, part 1, *The Archetypes and the Collective Unconscious* (1968, 1969), vol. 9, part 2, *Aion: Researches into the Phenomenology of the Self* (1968).

Jüngel, Eberhard, *Death*, 1971 (St Andrew Press, Edinburgh, and Westminster Press, Philadelphia, 1975).

Kant, Immanuel, *Critique of Pure Reason*, trans. N. Kemp Smith (Macmillan, London, and St Martin's Press, New York, 1958).

The Moral Law (Hutchinson, London, 1948, and Barnes & Noble, New York, 1956), trans. H. J. Paton from 2nd ed. of *Grundlegung zur Metaphysik der Sitten* (Riga, 1786).

Kastenbaum, Robert, and Ruth Aisenberg, *The Psychology of Death* (Springer, New York, 1972, and Duckworth, London, 1974).

Kaufman, Gordon D., *Systematic Theology: A Historicist Perspective* (Charles Scribner's Sons, New York, 1968).

Kaufmann, Walter (ed.), *Existentialism from Dostoevsky to Sartre* (Meridian Books, New York, 1956, and Thames & Hudson, London, 1957).

Kavanaugh, Robert E., *Facing Death* (Nash Publishing, Los Angeles, 1972).

Keck, Leander E., *Perspectives on Death* (Abingdon Press, Nashville, Tenn., 1969).

Kirk, K. E., *The Vision of God* (Longmans, Green, London and New York, 1931).

Kübler-Ross, Elisabeth, *On Death and Dying* (Macmillan, New York, 1969, and Tavistock Publications, London, 1970).

Lamont, Corliss, *The Illusion of Immortality*, 3rd ed. (Philosophical Library, New York, 1959, and Elek Books, London, 1962).

Leadbeater, C. W., *The Soul's Growth through Reincarnation*, ed. C. Jinarajadasa (Theosophical Publishing House, Madras), vol. I, 2nd ed. (1949), vol. II (1948), vol. III (1950).

Leibniz, G. W., *Philosophischen Schriften*, ed. C. I. Gerhardt, vol. IV (Weidmannsche Buchhandlung, Berlin, 1880).

Leibrecht, Walter (ed.), *Religion and Culture* (SCM Press, London, 1958, and Harper, New York, 1959).

Lévy-Brühl, Lucien, *Primitive Mentality*, 1922 (Allen & Unwin, London, and Macmillan, New York, 1923).

Lewis, H. D., *The Elusive Mind* (Allen & Unwin, London, and Humanities Press, New York, 1969).

The Self and Immortality (Macmillan, London, and Seabury Press, New York, 1973).

Lifton, Robert Jay, and Eric Olson, *Living and Dying* (Wildwood House, London, and Praeger, New York, 1974).

Ling, Trevor, *A History of Religion East and West* (Macmillan, London, and St Martin's Press, New York, 1968).

Lodge, Sir Oliver, *Raymond or Life and Death* (Methuen, London, and George H. Doran, New York, 1916).

Raymond Revised (Methuen, London, 1922).

Lucas, John, *The Freedom of the Will* (Clarendon Press, Oxford, and

Oxford University Press, New York, 1970).

Lutoslawski, W., *Pre-Existence and Reincarnation* (Allen & Unwin, London, 1928).

McCabe, Joseph, *Spiritualism: A Popular History from 1847* (T. Fisher Unwin, London, and Dodd, Mead, New York, 1920).

McGatch, Milton C., *Death: Meaning and Mortality in Christian Thought and Contemporary Culture* (Seabury Press, New York, 1969).

Macgregor, G. H. C., *The Gospel of John* (Hodder & Stoughton, London, 1928, and Doubleday, Doran, Garden City, N.Y., 1929).

Macmurray, John, *Interpreting the Universe* (Faber & Faber, London, 1933).

McTaggart, J. M. E., *Some Dogmas of Religion* (Edward Arnold, London, 1906, and Greenwood Press, New York, 1968).

Mahayana-Sutralankara, ed. Sylvain Levi (Librairie Honoré Champion, Paris, 1907).

Malcolm, Norman, *Problems of Mind* (Harper & Row, New York, 1971, and Allen & Unwin, London, 1972).

Marchant, James (ed.), *Immortality* (G. P. Putnam's Sons, London and New York, 1924).

Marxsen, Willi, *The Resurrection of Jesus of Nazareth*, 1968 (SCM Press, London, and Fortress Press, Philadelphia, 1970).

Maslow, A. H. (ed.), *New Knowledge in Human Values* (Harper, New York and London, 1959).

Maugham, Somerset, *Of Human Bondage*, introd. Richard A. Cordell (Heinemann, London, 1952, and Random House, New York, 1956).

Middle Length Sayings, The, trans. I. B. Horner (Luzac, London), vol. I (1954), vol. II (1957).

Migne, J. P. (ed.), *Patrologia Latina* (Paris, 1844-64).

Milinda's Questions, trans. I. B. Horner, vol. I (Luzac, London, 1969).

Mills, Liston O. (ed.), *Perspectives on Death* (Abingdon Press, Nashville, 1969).

Mind (Basil Blackwell, Oxford).

Minor Anthologies of the Pali Canon, The, trans. F. L. Woodward, part II (Oxford University Press, London, 1948).

Mitchell, M. E., *The Child's Attitude to Death* (Barrie & Rockliff, London, 1966, and Schocken Books, New York, 1967).

Moffitt, John, *Journey to Gorakhpur* (Holt, Rinehart & Winston, New York, 1972, and Sheldon Press, London, 1973).

Moltmann, Jürgen, *Theology of Hope*, 1964 (SCM Press, London, and Harper & Row, New York, 1967).

Monroe, Robert A., *Journeys out of the Body* (Souvenir Press, London, and Doubleday, Garden City, N.Y., 1972).

Muldoon, Sylvan, and Hereward Carrington, *The Phenomena of Astral Projection* (Rider, London and New York, 1951).

Murdock, G., *Our Primitive Contemporaries* (Macmillan, New York, 1934).

Murti, T. R. V., *The Central Philosophy of Buddhism*, 2nd ed. (Allen & Unwin, London, and Humanities Press, New York, 1960).

Muston, C. R., *Recognition in the World to Come, or Christian Friendship on Earth Perpetuated in Heaven*, 2nd ed. (London, 1831).

Myers, F. W. H., *Human Personality and Its Survival of Bodily Death* (Longmans, London, 1903, and New York, 1904).

Nayak, G. C., *Evil, Karma and Reincarnation* (Visva-Bharati University, Santiniketan, 1973).

New Society (London).

Nicene and Post-Nicene Fathers, The, Series Two, vol. XIV (Eerdmans, Grand Rapids, Mich., 1956).

Nickelsburg, George W. E., Jr, *Resurrection, Immortality, and Eternal Life in Intertestamental Judaism* (Harvard University Press, Cambridge, Mass., 1972, and London, 1973).

Nietzsche, Friedrich, *Thus Spake Zarathustra*, part I, 1883, trans. A. Tille, revised M. M. Bozman (J. M. Dent, London, and E. P. Dutton, New York, 1933).

Nikhilananda, Swami, *Man in Search of Immortality* (Allen & Unwin, London, and Ramakrishna-Vivekananda Center, New York, 1968).

Nineham, D. E., *The Gospel of St Mark* (Penguin, Harmondsworth, 1963, and Baltimore, 1964).

Nyanaponika Mahathera, *Anatta and Nibbana*, 2nd ed. (Buddhist Publication Society, Kandy, 1971).

Nyanatiloka Mahathera, *The Buddha's Teaching of Egolessness* (Word of the Buddha Publishing Committee, Colombo, 1957).

  Karma and Rebirth (Buddhist Publication Society, Kandy, 1959).

Oesterley, W. O. E., *Immortality and the Unseen World: A Study in Old Testament Religion* (SPCK, London, and Macmillan, New York, 1921).

Osty, Eugène, *Supernormal Faculties in Man*, 1922 (Methuen, London, 1923).

Pache, René, *The Future Life* (Moody, Chicago, 1962, and Marshall, Morgan & Scott, London, 1972).

Pannenberg, W., *The Apostles' Creed*, 1972 (SCM Press, London, and Westminster Press, Philadelphia, 1972).

  Jesus – God and Man, 1964 (Westminster Press, Philadelphia, 1967, and SCM Press, London, 1968).

  Theology and the Kingdom of God, 1967 (Westminster Press, Philadelphia, 1969).

  What Is Man?, 1962 (Fortress Press, Philadelphia, 1970).

Parrinder, E. Geoffrey, *The Indestructible Soul* (Allen & Unwin, London, and Barnes & Noble, New York, 1973).

Pascal, Blaise, *Pensées*, trans. W. F. Trotter (J. M. Dent, London, and E. P. Dutton, New York, 1932).

Peace at the Last: A Survey of Terminal Care in the United Kingdom (Calouste Gulbenkian Foundation, London, 1960).

Peake, A. S. (ed.), *The People and the Book* (Oxford University Press, London, 1925).

Pelikan, Jaroslav, *The Shape of Death* (Abingdon Press, Nashville,

Tenn., 1961, and Macmillan, London, 1962).

Penelhum, Terence, *Survival and Disembodied Existence* (Routledge & Kegan Paul, London, and Humanities Press, New York, 1970).

Phillips, D. Z., *Death and Immortality* (Macmillan, London, and St Martin's Press, New York, 1970).

Philosophical Review (Cornell University, Ithaca, N.Y.).

Philosophy (Cambridge University Press, London).

Piaget, Jean, *The Language and Thought of the Child*, 3rd ed. (Routledge & Kegan Paul, London, and Humanities Press, New York, 1959).

Pieper, Josef, *Death and Immortality*, 1968 (Burns & Oates, London, and Herder & Herder, New York, 1969).

Pistis Sophia, trans. G. R. S. Mead (John M. Watkins, London, 1947, and University Books, Secaucus, N.J., 1974).

Pittenger, W. Norman, *'The Last Things' in a Process Perspective* (Epworth Press, London, 1970).

   Process Thought and Christian Faith (Nisbet, London, and Macmillan, New York, 1968).

Plato, *The Last Days of Socrates*, trans. Hugh Tredennick (Penguin, Harmondsworth and Baltimore, 1954).

   Phaedo, trans. B. Jowett, 4th ed. (Clarendon Press, Oxford, 1953).

Plotinus, *The Enneads*, trans. Stephen MacKenna, 3rd ed. (Faber & Faber, London, 1962).

Prince, Morton, *The Dissociation of a Personality*, 1905 (Longmans, Green, London and New York, 1919).

Principal Upanishads, The, trans. S. Radhakrishnan (Allen & Unwin, London, 1953, and Humanities Press, New York, 1969).

Pringle-Pattison, A. S., *The Idea of Immortality* (Clarendon Press, Oxford, 1922, and Kraus Reprint, New York, 1971).

Proceedings of the Aristotelian Society (London).

Proceedings of the Society for Psychical Research (London).

Psalms of the Early Buddhists, trans. C. A. F. Rhys Davids (Luzac, London, 1964).

Psychology Today (CRM, Del Mar, Calif.).

Puzzled People (Victor Gollancz, London, 1947).

Radhakrishnan, S., and C. A. Moore, *A Sourcebook in Indian Philosophy* (Princeton University Press, Princeton, and Oxford University Press, Bombay, 1957).

Radin, Paul, *Primitive Religion* (Dover Publications, New York, 1937, and Hamish Hamilton, London, 1938).

Rahner, Karl, *On the Theology of Death*, 1961 (Burns & Oates, London, and Herder & Herder, New York, 1965).

   Sacramentum Mundi, vol. II (Burns & Oates, London, and Herder & Herder, New York, 1968).

   Theological Investigations, vol. XIII (Darton, Longman & Todd, London, and Seabury Press, New York, 1975).

Religion in Geschichte und Gegenwart, Die (Mohr, Tübingen, 1957-65).

Religion: Journal of Religion and Religions (Routledge & Kegan Paul,

London and Boston).

Religion and Society (Bangalore).

Religious Studies (Cambridge University Press, London).

Renou, Louis, *Religions of Ancient India* (Athlone Press, London, 1953, and Schocken Books, New York, 1968).

Review of Metaphysics, The (Catholic University of America, Washington, D.C.).

Rhine, J. B., *Extrasensory Perception* (Faber & Faber, London, and Society for Psychical Research, Boston, 1935).

   New Frontiers of the Mind (Farrar & Rhinehart, New York, 1937, and Faber & Faber, London, 1938).

Ringgren, Helmer, *Israelite Religion* (SPCK, London, 1966).

   Religions of the Ancient Near East (SPCK, London, and Westminster Press, Philadelphia, 1973).

Robinson, H. Wheeler, *The Religious Ideas of the Old Testament* (Duckworth, London, 1913, and Allenson, Naperville, Ill., 1956).

Robinson, J. A. T., *The Body* (SCM Press, London, and Allenson, Naperville, Ill., 1952).

   In the End, God, 1950 (Fontana, London, and Harper & Row, New York, 1968).

Rohde, Erwin, *Psyche: The Cult of Souls and Belief in Immortality among the Greeks*, 1894 (Kegan Paul, Trench, Trubner, London, 1925, and Books for Libraries, Freeport, N.Y., 1972).

Rosher, Grace, *Beyond the Horizon* (James Clarke, London, and Attic Press, Greenwood, S.C., 1961).

Rousseau, Jean Jacques, *Emile*, 1762, trans. Foxley, 1911 (Everyman Library, Dent, London, 1950, and E. P. Dutton, New York, 1966).

Rowell, Geoffrey, *Hell and the Victorians* (Clarendon Press, Oxford, and Oxford University Press, New York, 1974).

Russell, Bertrand, *The Autobiography of Bertrand Russell*, vol. III (Allen & Unwin, London, and Simon & Schuster, New York, 1969).

   Mysticism and Logic (Longmans, Green, London, 1918).

Russell, D. S., *The Method and Message of Jewish Apocalyptic* (SCM Press, London, and Westminster Press, Philadelphia, 1964).

Sacred Books of the East, vol. XLVIII (Motilal Banarsidass, Delhi, 1971).

Santayana, George, *Reason in Religion* (Constable, London, and Charles Scribner's Sons, New York, 1905).

Sartre, J.-P., *Being and Nothingness* (Philosophical Library, New York, 1956, and Methuen, London, 1957).

Schofield, J. N., *The Religious Background of the Bible* (Thomas Nelson, London, 1944).

Schopenhauer, Arthur, *The Fourfold Root of the Principle of Sufficient Reason*, trans. K. Hillerbrand (George Bell, London, 1889).

Schweizer, Eduard, *The Good News according to Mark*, 1967 (John Knox Press, Richmond, Va, 1970, and SPCK, London, 1971).

Scott, Nathan A., Jr., *The Modern Vision of Death* (John Knox Press,

Richmond, Va, 1967).

Scottish Journal of Theology (Scottish Academic Press, Edinburgh).

Shankara, *Vakyavritti*, trans. Swami Jagadananda (Sri Ramakrishna Math, Madras, 1967).

Sharma, B. N. K., *Madhva's Teachings* (Bharatiya Vidya Bhavan, Bombay, 1970).

Sharma, Chandradhar, *A Critical Study of Indian Philosophy* (Motilal Banarsidass, Delhi, and Lawrence Verry, Mystic, Conn., 1964).

Shneidman, Edwin S., *Deaths of Man* (Quadrangle, New York, 1973, and Millington, London, 1975).

Silva, Lynn A. de, *Reincarnation in Buddhist and Christian Thought* (Christian Literature Society of Ceylon, Colombo, 1968).

  The Problem of the Self in Buddhism and Christianity (Study Centre for Religion and Society, Colombo, 1975).

Silva, Padmasiri de, *Buddhist and Freudian Psychology* (Lake House Press, Colombo, 1973).

Simon, Ulrich, *Heaven in the Christian Tradition* (Rockliff, London, and Harper, New York, 1958).

Siwek, Paul, *The Enigma of the Hereafter* (Philosophical Library, New York, 1952).

Smart, Ninian, *Doctrine and Argument in Indian Philosophy* (Allen & Unwin, London, and Humanities Press, New York, 1964).

  The Yogi and the Devotee (Allen & Unwin, London, and Humanities Press, New York, 1968).

Smythies, J. R. (ed.), *Brain and Mind* (Routledge & Kegan Paul, London, and Humanities Press, New York, 1965).

  (ed.) *Science and ESP* (Routledge & Kegan Paul, London, and Humanities Press, New York, 1967).

Soal, S. G., *The Experimental Situation in Psychical Research* (Society for Psychical Research, London, 1947).

Soal, S. G., and F. Bateman, *Modern Experiments in Telepathy* (Faber & Faber, London, and Yale University Press, New Haven, Conn., 1954).

Solzhenitsyn, Alexander, *Cancer Ward*, trans. Nicholas Bethell and David Burg (Penguin, Harmondsworth, 1971, and Farrar, Strauss & Giroux, New York, 1974).

Sophia (Melbourne University, Melbourne).

Spencer, Theodore, *Death and Elizabethan Tragedy* (Pageant Books, New York, 1960).

Staal, J. F., *Advaita and Neoplatonism* (University of Madras, Madras, 1961).

Stcherbatsky, T., *The Conception of Buddhist Nirvana* (Academy of Sciences of the USSR, Leningrad, 1927).

Stendahl, Krister (ed.), *Immortality and Resurrection* (Macmillan, New York, 1965).

Stevenson, Ian, *The Evidence for Survival from Claimed Memories of Former Incarnations* (M. C. Peto, Tadworth, 1961).

  Twenty Cases Suggestive of Reincarnation (American Society for Psychical Research, New York, 1966).

Strawson, William, *Jesus and the Future Life*, 2nd ed. (Epworth Press, London, 1970).

Streeter, B. H., *Immortality* (Macmillan, London and New York, 1917).

Swedenborg, Emanuel, *Heaven and Its Wonders and Hell*, 1758 (Swedenborg Foundation, New York, 1956, and the Swedenborg Society, London, 1958).

Taylor, John V., *The Primal Vision* (Allenson, Naperville, Ill., 1963, and SCM Press, London, 1965).

Teilhard de Chardin, Pierre, *The Phenomenon of Man* (Collins, London, and Harper, New York, 1959).

Television and Religion (University of London Press, London, 1964).

Temple, William, *Readings in St John's Gospel*, vol. II (Macmillan, London, and St Martin's Press, New York, 1942).

Theologia Germanica, trans. Susanna Winkworth (Macmillan, London, 1937).

Theology Today (Princeton, N.J.).

Thomas Aquinas, St, *On the Truth of the Catholic Faith*, trans. Vernon J. Bourke (Image Books, New York, 1956).

Thomas, John F., *Beyond Normal Cognition* (Boston Society for Psychical Research, Boston, 1937).

Thorpe, W. H., *Animal Nature and Human Nature* (Methuen, London, and Doubleday, Garden City, N.Y., 1974).

Thouless, Robert H., *From Anecdote to Experiment in Psychical Research* (Routledge & Kegan Paul, London and Boston, 1972).

Tillich, Paul, *Systematic Theology*, vol. III (University of Chicago Press, Chicago, 1963, and Nisbet, London, 1964).

Times, The (London).

Toksvig, Signe, *Emanuel Swedenborg: Scientist and Mystic* (Faber & Faber, London, 1949, and Books for Libraries, Plainview, N.Y., 1972).

Toynbee, Arnold, *et al.*, *Man's Concern with Death* (Hodder & Stoughton, London, 1968, and McGraw-Hill, St Louis, 1969).

Tripathi, R. K., *Problems of Philosophy and Religion* (Banaras Hindu University, Varanasi, 1971).

Tupper, E. Frank, *The Theology of Wolfhart Pannenberg* (Westminster Press, Philadelphia, 1973, and SCM Press, London, 1974).

Tylor, E. B., *Primitive Culture*, 1871 (John Murray, London, 1903, and P. Smith, Gloucester, Mass., 1970).

Tyrrell, G. N. M., *Apparitions*, rev. ed. (Gerald Duckworth, London, 1953, and Macmillan, New York, 1970).

     Science and Psychical Phenomena (Methuen, London, 1938).

Unamuno, Miguel de, *The Tragic Sense of Life*, 1913, trans. J. E. C. Flitch (Dover, New York, 1954, and Fontana, London, 1962).

Underhill, Evelyn, *Mysticism*, 1911 (Methuen, London, 1914, and E. P. Dutton, New York, 1961).

University of Ceylon Review (Colombo).

Vajiranana, P., and Francis Story, *The Buddhist Doctrine of Nibbana* (Buddhist Publication Society, Kandy, 1971).

Vasiliev, L. L., *Experiments in Mental Suggestion*, 1962 (Institute for the Study of Mental Images, Church Crookham, 1963).

Vivekachudamani, trans. Swami Madhavananda, 8th ed. (Advaita Ashrama, Calcutta, 1970).

Waddell, Helen, *The Desert Fathers* (Constable, London, 1936, and Barnes & Noble, New York, 1974).

Walker, Benjamin, *Beyond the Body* (Routledge & Kegan Paul, London and Boston, 1974).

Walker, D. P., *The Decline of Hell* (Routledge & Kegan Paul, London, and University of Chicago Press, Chicago, 1964).

Wallis, H. W., *The Cosmology of the Rigveda* (Williams & Norgate, London, 1887).

Ward, Barbara, and René Dubos, *Only One Earth* (Penguin, Harmondsworth, and Norton, New York, 1972).

Weatherhead, Leslie, *The Case for Re-Incarnation* (City Temple, London, 1957).

 The Christian Agnostic (Hodder & Stoughton, London, 1965, and Abingdon Press, Nashville, Tenn., 1972).

Webb, C. C. J., *God and Personality* (Allen & Unwin, London, and Macmillan, New York, 1918).

Weil, Simone, *Waiting on God*, 1950 (Routledge & Kegan Paul, London, 1951, and Harper & Row, New York, 1973).

Welbon, G. R., *The Buddhist Nirvana and Its Western Interpreters* (University of Chicago Press, Chicago and London, 1968).

Whiteley, D. E. H., *The Theology of St Paul* (Basil Blackwell, Oxford, 1964).

Whiteman, J. H. M., *The Mystical Life* (Faber & Faber, London, 1961).

Wiener, Norbert, *The Human Use of Human Beings*, 1950 (Avon Books, New York, 1967, and Sphere Books, London, 1968).

Wijesekera, O. H. de A., *The Three Signata* (Buddhist Publication Society, Kandy, 1970).

Williams, Bernard, *Problems of the Self* (Cambridge University Press, Cambridge and New York, 1973).

Wilson, Michael, *The Hospital – A Place of Truth: A Study of the Role of the Hospital Chaplain* (Institute for the Study of Worship and Religious Architecture, Birmingham, 1971).

Wittgenstein, Ludwig, *Tractatus Logico-Philosophicus*, trans. D. F. Pears and B. F. McGuinness (Routledge & Kegan Paul, London, 1972, and Humanities Press, Atlantic Highlands, N.J., 1974).

Yaker, H., H. Osmond and F. Cheek (eds.), *The Future of Time* (Doubleday, Garden City, N.Y., 1971, and Hogarth Press, London, 1972).

Zaehner, R. C., *Evolution in Religion* (Clarendon Press, Oxford, and Oxford University Press, New York, 1971).

 Mysticism, Sacred and Profane (Oxford University Press, London and New York, 1957).

Acknowledgements

The author and publishers would like to acknowledge their gratitude
for permission to quote from the following books; the Revised Standard
Version of the Bible, copyrighted 1946, 1952, © 1971, 1973 by
Division of Christian Education of the National Council of the
Churches of Christ in the USA; *The Problem of Rebirth* by Sri
Aurobindo in the Birth Centenary Edition, published by Sri Auro-
bindo Ashram, Pondicherry; *The Tibetan Book of the Dead or the
After-Death Experiences on the Bardo Plane, according to Lama Kazi
Dawa-Samdup's English Rendering*, edited by W. Y. Evans-Wentz,
and reprinted by permission of the Oxford University Press, Oxford
and New York; *The Logic of Perfection* by Charles Hartshorne,
reprinted by permission of the Open Court Publishing Company, La
Salle, Illinois, © 1962 by the Open Court Publishing Company;
Being and Time by Martin Heidegger, published by SCM Press,
London, and Harper & Row, New York and reprinted by permission
of Basil Blackwell, Oxford; *Milinda's Questions*, translated by I. B.
Horner, published by Luzac, London, and reprinted by permission
of the Pali Text Society, London; *Indian Philosophical Annual*, 1965,
published by the University of Madras, Madras; some paragraphs
of chapters 16 and 17 are reprinted, with permission, from 'The
Idea of Rebirth – a Western Approach', in the *Indian Philosophical
Annual*, vol. VI, 1971, published by the University of Madras,
Madras, and from 'Reincarnation: a Critical Examination of One
Form of Reincarnation Theory', in *The Journal of Religious Studies*,
vol. III, no. 1, 1971, published by Punjabi University, Patiala; *Some
Dogmas of Religion* by J. M. E. McTaggart, published by Edward
Arnold, London, and Greenwood Press, New York; *Of Human
Bondage* by Somerset Maugham, published by Heinemann, London,
and Random House, New York, and reprinted by permission of the
Estate of W. Somerset Maugham, William Heinemann Ltd, and
Doubleday & Co. Inc., New York; 'Resurrection Bodies and Resur-
rection Worlds' by A. Olding, in *Mind*, October 1970, published by
Basil Blackwell, Oxford; *What Is Man?* by Wolfhart Pannenberg,
published by Fortress Press, Philadelphia; *Death and Immortality*
by D. Z. Phillips, published by Macmillan & Co. Ltd, London, and
St Martin's Press, Inc., New York, reprinted by permission of
Macmillan, London and Basingstoke; *On the Theology of Death* by
Karl Rahner, © 1961, 1976 Herder KG Freiburg im Breisgau &
Burns & Oates, London, published by Burns & Oates, London, and
Herder & Herder, New York, used by permission of The Seabury
Press, Inc.; *Beyond the Horizon* by Grace Rosher, published by
James Clarke & Co. Ltd, London, and Attic Press, Greenwood, S.C.;

Being and Nothingness by Jean-Paul Sartre, copyright 1943 Jean-Paul Sartre, first published 1943 under the title *L'être et le néant* by Gallimard, and this translation published by Methuen & Co. Ltd, London, and Philosophical Library, New York; *The Modern Vision of Death* by Nathan A. Scott, Jr, © 1967 by M. E. Bratcher, used by permission of John Knox Press, Atlanta; 'You and Death' by Edwin S. Shneidman, in *Psychology Today*, June 1971, copyright © 1971 Ziff-Davis Publishing Company, reprinted by Permission of *Psychology Today* Magazine; *Systematic Theology*, vol. III, by Paul Tillich, © The University of Chicago, published by Nisbet, London, and University of Chicago Press, Chicago; *Mysticism* by Evelyn Underhill, published by Methuen & Co. Ltd, London, and E. P. Dutton, New York; *The Book of the Kindred Sayings*, translated by F. L. Woodward, published by Luzac, London, and reprinted by permission of the Pali Text Society, London.

Index

LaVergne, TN USA
09 January 2011
211729LV00003B/1/A